The Political Humanism
of Hannah Arendt

The Political Humanism of Hannah Arendt

Michael H. McCarthy

LEXINGTON BOOKS
Lanham • Boulder • New York • Toronto • Plymouth, UK

Published by Lexington Books
A wholly owned subsidiary of Rowman & Littlefield
4501 Forbes Boulevard, Suite 200, Lanham, Maryland 20706
www.rowman.com

10 Thornbury Road, Plymouth PL6 7PP, United Kingdom

Copyright © 2012 by Lexington Books
First paperback edition 2014

All rights reserved. No part of this book may be reproduced in any form or by any electronic or mechanical means, including information storage and retrieval systems, without written permission from the publisher, except by a reviewer who may quote passages in a review.

British Library Cataloguing in Publication Information Available

Library of Congress Cataloging-in-Publication Data

The hardback edition of this book was previously cataloged by the Library of Congress as follows:

McCarthy, Michael H., 1942-
The political humanism of Hannah Arendt / Michael McCarthy.
p. cm.
Includes bibliographical references and index.
Political and social views. 2. Humanism. I. Title.
JC251.A74M394 2012
230.5—dc23
2012021598

ISBN 978-0-7391-7719-8 (cloth : alk. paper)
ISBN 978-0-7391-9287-0 (pbk. : alk. paper)
ISBN 978-0-7391-7720-4 (electronic)

∞™ The paper used in this publication meets the minimum requirements of American National Standard for Information Sciences—Permanence of Paper for Printed Library Materials, ANSI/NISO Z39.48-1992.

Printed in the United States of America

Contents

Preface	vii
Introduction: the Political Humanism of Hannah Arendt	1
Notes	

1 THE CITY IN RUINS   25
   Totalitarianism as a Limit Situation
   The Burden of Our Time
   The Sources of Our Political Crisis
   Notes

2 LOOK TO THE GREAT AND COMMON WORLD   63
   The Spirit of Arendtian Politics
   The Cultural Convictions of Modernity
   The Victory of the *Animal Laborans*
   Notes

3 OUR TRADITION OF POLITICAL THOUGHT   111
   Overcoming Tradition
   Greek Political Philosophy
   The Platonic Inheritance
   Aristotle's Practical Philosophy
   Poiesis and *Praxis*
   Ruling and Being Ruled
   The Best Way to Live
   Notes

4 THE MARXIST REVERSALS OF TRADITION   179
   Progress and Disillusion
   Dialectical Materialism

The Critique of Capitalism
The Arendtian Critique of Marx
The Glorification of Labor and the Naturalization of Man
Violence as the Essence of Politics
The Science of Historical Necessity
Marxism As Ideology: An Arendtian Critique
The Merits and Limitations of Marxism
Notes

5   THE DISCONTENTS OF LIBERAL DEMOCRACY and THE CONTINUING RELEVANCE OF ARENDTIAN THOUGHT   237
PART I
The Critical Appropriation of Tradition
The Old and the New
The Discontents of Liberal Democracy
A Crisis of Legitimacy
The Promise and Perils of Globalization
American Democracy Revisited
Toward a New Progressive Agenda
E Pluribus Unum: The Challenge of Contemporary Pluralism
PART II
The Critique of Liberalism
Public Liberty
Participation and Representation
The Primacy of Politics Over Economics
The Social Question Revisited: Distributive Justice and Political Equality
The Renewal of Civil Society
The Common World and the Common Good
Healing the Rift Between Thought and Action: The Importance of Practical Wisdom
Is There A Way To Get There From Here?
Notes

Selected Bibliography   301

Index   305

Preface

Hannah Arendt was one of the most important political thinkers of the twentieth century. A European by birth, culture and education, she reached maturity during what Eric Hobsbawm has called the age of catastrophe. Between 1914 and 1945 the stabilizing structures of modern Europe collapsed. While the parliamentary democracies of England and France remained impotent, fascist regimes consolidated their power in Italy and Spain, and popularly supported totalitarian governments emerged in Hitler's Germany and Stalin's Soviet Union. Totalitarianism was an unprecedented form of human domination, based on ideology and terror, which slaughtered millions of innocent people in the name of utopian ideals. Although Nazi Germany was defeated eventually, the two world wars had transformed Europe from the center of world civilization to a demoralized continent in ruins. From Arendt's critical perspective, the political and economic collapse of Europe extended to its intellectual, moral and cultural traditions as well. The vital human connection between the past and present had been severed; conscientious citizens were now forced "to think without banisters" (*denken ohne Geländer*).

At the end of the Second World War when the horror of the Holocaust became known, Hannah Arendt committed herself to a work of remembrance and reflection. Intellectual integrity demanded that we comprehend and articulate the genesis of totalitarian terror. What earlier spiritual and moral collapse had made totalitarianism possible? What was the basis of its evident mass appeal? To what cultural resources and political institutions could we turn to prevent its recurrence? After long years of study, Arendt concluded that the deepest crisis of the modern world was political, and that the continuing appeal of totalitarian mass movements demonstrated how profound that crisis had become.

The crisis she identified could be discerned on four distinct but interconnected levels: cultural, theoretical, institutional, and normative. The world-alienation of modernity had promoted a mass culture antithetical to republican self-government and especially prone to ideological manipulation. Our theoretical capacity to critique this culture and the ideologies it spawns is compromised because our inherited traditions have systematically misrepresented the nature of political experience. By substituting making (*poiesis*) for action (*praxis*), command and coercion for persuasion and agreement, and technical mastery for political excellence and judgment our traditional theorists have darkened the common perception of politics and reduced it to a servant of economic needs and concerns. The striking rise of economics to its present cultural supremacy has transformed the public realm into a sphere of necessity rather than freedom, while the enduring attractions of freedom have been confined to the individual pursuit of private happiness. As a result, the demoralized individuals who live within mass societies lack the informed commitment to public liberty that is needed to sustain the republican spirit. And without that spirit, the lost spirit of the great democratic revolutions, modern citizens no longer know what to require of themselves and their political leaders, now how to judge responsibly their public conduct and speech.

For Arendt, the modern political crisis is also a crisis of humanism. The radical totalitarian experiment was rooted in two fundamentally distorted images of the human being. The agents of terror believed in the limitless power generated by collective organization, a power wielded and justified by appeal to historical necessity. The victims of terror, by contrast, were systematically dehumanized by the ruling ideology, and then brutally deprived of their legal rights and their moral and existential dignity. Hannah Arendt's political humanism explicitly challenges both of these distorting images, the first because it dangerously inflates human power, the second because it subverts human freedom and agency. Human beings living together on the earth, in a humanly constructed world and within a web of fragile human connections are neither sovereign masters nor superfluous animals. Rather, they are singular and unique persons capable of distinguishing themselves through action and speech, and requiring both a public realm of freedom and excellence and a private realm of security and intimacy to protect and enhance their dignity.

In the tradition of civic republican thinkers that stretches from Aristotle to Charles Taylor and Michael Sandel, Arendt made the concepts of political liberty, civic virtue and public happiness essential to her understanding of genuine citizenship. Equipped with these normative principles, she directly challenged the reductive modern anthropologies that had reduced human beings to calculating economic animals. The ideological reduction of the human person had not only been used to justify totalitarian terror; it had also contributed to the political alienation of democratic citizens in contemporary liberal societies. If we are to recover a more authentic understanding of the human being, we will need a much richer and deeper conception of citizenship than conservatism, liberalism or Marxism provides.

Hannah Arendt's political humanism develops over several decades. It begins with her examination and appraisal of *The Origins of Totalitarianism* (chapter 1). It expands with her critical retrieval of the *vita activa* in *The Human Condition* (chapter 2). These two early works provide the intellectual horizon for her genealogical critique of "our tradition of political thought." In developing that critique, she amplifies her civic republican vision of citizenship by contrasting it with the dominant political visions that have shaped the western tradition (*Between Past and Future, On Revolution, Eichmann in Jerusalem, Lectures on Kant's Political Philosophy*).

Chapters 3 and 4 present Arendt's critique of the tradition in its most salient and formative aspects. Many commentators on Arendt cite the importance of her genealogical criticism; very few seek to develop, understand and appraise it. I found that in providing this evaluative contrast, the merits and limitations of her thought became considerably clearer and more focused.

In the last decade of Arendt's life, she applied her civic republican insights to *The Crises of the Republic* and augmented her earlier study of the *vita activa* with a complementary account of The *Life of the Mind (Thinking and Willing)*. Arendt's political thought is repeatedly criticized for its limited relevance to contemporary politics; she is said to be nostalgic for ancient republics irretrievably lost. In the final chapter, I address this important criticism by correlating Arendt's insights and oversights with the realities of contemporary liberal democracy. Thus the textual strategy and expository order of this book are closely connected to the complex process of Arendt's intellectual and political development.

Introduction: the Political Humanism of Hannah Arendt

Je n'ai pas de traditions, je n'ai pas de parti, je n'ai point de cause, si ce n'est celle de la liberte et de la dignite humaine.
Alexis de Tocqueville
Souvenirs – 144

I should have loved freedom at all times, but in the time in which we live, I am ready to worship it.
Democracy in America, Vol II, 340

The dignity of the human person has been the central concern of modern humanism. From Pico Della Mirandola to Hannah Arendt, humanists have celebrated the creative capacities of men and women and have encouraged their desire to transform nature and history. They have also risen in defense of human dignity when it has been systematically threatened or violated. In ascribing dignity to human existence, they have been asserting the intrinsic worth of every person without regard for their specific place in a social or cultural hierarchy. Human beings are ends in themselves worthy of unconditional respect; they are not simply means or instruments subordinated to some higher purpose. In the moral categories of Immanuel Kant, means have exchange value or price, while ends have dignity and worth.

Kant located the source of human dignity in the autonomy of pure practical reason. For Kant, human beings are worthy of respect because they are the legislators of the universal moral law. Kant's enlightenment humanism was distinctively modern because it grounded human dignity in active freedom or responsible agency. The modern conceptions of human existence are inseparable from theories of freedom and the deeper and truer their understanding of freedom the more compelling their account of human worth.

In classical antiquity, freedom was predicated of *bioi*, complex forms of life centered on a specific human activity. For a form of life to be liberal or free, it had to be independent of biological necessity and human coercion. It had to be an intrinsically desirable way of living, allowing human beings to actualize what is divine or godlike in their natures. Both Plato and Aristotle agreed that the philosophical life, the life in search of wisdom, enjoyed the greatest freedom and dignity. Thought and contemplation, the central activities in the philosophical *bios,* are both instances of solitary freedom. In thought, the philosopher engages in an internal dialogue with himself; in contemplation he becomes silent before the revealed presence of God or eternal truth. The characteristic freedom of the *bios theoretikos* draws the lover of wisdom away from the human circle and from the cooperative ventures the presence of others makes possible.

The most influential modern conception of freedom is based on production rather than contemplation. Modernity rejects the ancient preference for the theoretical life and coordinates freedom directly with constructive agency. According to the moderns, we are most free when making or creating rather than when thinking or knowing. In the course of making or building, we exercise technical mastery over nature and control natural materials and energies for our own purposes and ends. The isolated artisan in his studio provides a good model for the modern picture of freedom. Through the exercise of craftsmanship, the artisan brings the raw materials of nature into accord with his individual intentions and aims.

Both the ancient and the modern paradigms of liberty are based on activities performed when alone. Despite their evident dissimilarities, solitary thought and sovereign craftsmanship are equally independent of human association. In grounding human dignity on freedom and then modeling freedom on making or thinking, it is easy to ignore the striking fact of human plurality. It is not man in the singular but human beings in the plural who inhabit the earth. Although the human creature may be made in the image and likeness of the Biblical God, the Creator's singularity stands in direct contrast to the creature's multiplicity. In the memorable words of Genesis 1:27, "male and female created He them." (though the Christian God is explicitly conceived as a community of persons).

If plurality is an essential feature of the human condition, then it should enjoy a central place in the understanding of human dignity and freedom. To think freedom under the condition of plurality is to discover the limits of sovereignty and individual autonomy as ideals of liberty. Despite their insights, neither Pico, nor Kant, nor modern technological humanism provides an adequate conception of cooperative agency. Each of these thinkers and traditions fails to situate freedom securely in the web of human association; each fails to acknowledge the dependence of our limited autonomy on the prior condition of communal belonging. Only by belonging to a common world of meaning do we become capable of solitary reflection; only by apprenticeship in a community of craftsmen do we learn how to make what is durable and lasting. But communal belonging is not merely an enabling condition of individual initiative. There are distinctive modes of freedom that require the presence of others; there are important forms of activity that depend on collaboration; there is an essential connection between secure human dignity and active citizenship in a free society.

To emphasize the public aspect of liberty is not to deny freedom of thought or production. But it is to set limits on images of freedom based on these solitary experiences. When liberty is connected with plurality, it is reasonable to ask what forms of community offer the strongest support for human freedom and the greatest protection for human dignity. It is a sign of our complexity that we need to belong to many different communities in order to become fully human. The ancient Greeks believed that the *polis*, the distinctively political form of association, offered the greatest potential for freedom. Although the internal connection between liberty and citizenship is no longer self-evident, there are two great western political traditions that still insist on their interdependence. The tradition of civic humanism, which draws inspiration from the ancient republics of Greece and Rome, continues to uphold the ideal of public liberty. The modern revolutionary tradition, whose origins are traceable to Machiavelli, has also made political liberty a good worth fighting to establish. Despite intense debates between civic republicans and Jacobin revolutionaries, they share the conviction that active political citizenship is an essential part of a good human life.

Hannah Arendt, a contemporary political humanist, openly embraced these classical republican convictions. Because she was ardent in defending human dignity, she became a friend of public liberty, articulating the civic republican vision with remarkable passion and depth. The key to her thought, I believe, was her attention to human plurality and her insistence that the deep political implications of plurality have never been fully acknowledged. Her thought is often strikingly original, not because she concentrated on arcane subjects, but because she examined familiar phenomena from an unfamiliar perspective. A case in point is her reflection on human existence from the perspective of natality or birth.

A philosophical anthropology centered on human mortality, on the fact that human beings die alone, and, in dying, withdraw from the company of others, naturally emphasizes human solitude. There is a striking analogy between our permanent disappearance from the world in death and the provisional withdrawal from human affairs that occurs whenever we think. Theories of human existence keyed to the fact of mortality, typically highlight thought rather than action, solitary withdrawal rather than engagement in the human circle, and the private rather than the public dimension of freedom. But Arendt shows clearly how these priorities are reversed when birth rather than death becomes the focus of reflective attention. At birth, new human beings insert themselves into an old world, rather than receding from its ranks. Children renew the world by their appearance within it, providing a basis for worldly hope; in this respect, birth is the contrary of death, which constantly threatens the world with despair. Birth reminds us vividly of our situated existence and of our profound dependence on other persons. We do not choose to be born but are given the gift of existence by our parents. With this fundamental gift, we receive several others: the earth, our natural home, the world, our humanly created dwelling place, the different communities within which we develop and exercise our humanity.

Concentrating on the reality of birth dispels the illusions of human autonomy and sovereignty. We are situated inescapably in a complex web of human relationships; within that web we are educated, we acquire language, we master the arts and virtues required for adult existence, we become citizens and assume our share of worldly responsibility. Speech and action, the specifically political faculties, allow human beings to actualize the potential inherent in their birth. Speech permits new human beings to share with their elders their distinctive perceptions of the common world. The bonds of civic community are created through this public conversation that humanizes the world and those who belong to it. The capacity to act, to begin or initiate unpredictable processes, is directly analogous to the nature of birth. Every human birth is a new beginning in an old world; and each child is born with the capacity to begin, the capacity for freedom. But human speech and action require the presence of others for their intelligibility. Speech would be meaningless if other persons could not understand what was said and respond to its claims and appeals appropriately; and action would be futile without peers to witness and remember what was done, or cooperative partners to carry through what the individual agent began.

Hannah Arendt's spirited defense of public liberty did not occur in an historical vacuum. Her *apologia* for freedom was neither an academic exercise nor a piece of disinterested scholarship. For her, the most dangerous threats to human dignity in this century were caused by extreme political alienation. It was the alienation of the European masses from parliamentary democracy that led to the rise of totalitarian governments. Even in the liberal democracies, like England and the United States, where civic alienation is less advanced, there has been a marked decline in political legitimacy. Evidence of this decline can be found in the loss of governmental authority, a diminished sense of civic obligation, low levels of electoral participation, and a growing contempt for traditional political parties and their leaders. On Arendt's thoughtful analysis, these are not transient historical phenomena

Introduction: the Political Humanism of Hannah Arendt

easily corrected with the passage of time. They are structural features of the modern world directly connected to the modern understanding of human existence and freedom.

Hannah Arendt chose to serve the cause of liberty in four inter-related ways: as a thinker, teacher, storyteller and judge. Although she carefully distinguished thought from action, she treated them as functional complements rather than contraries. Action and speech require thought to clarify their meaning and importance; human words and deeds will be forgotten unless recollective thinking transforms them into episodes in a memorable story. Arendt was convinced that the great western thinkers and storytellers had neglected the public dimension of liberty. Because of this neglect, a major part of our republican political inheritance had been left to us without a testament.[1] Deep and original thinking is needed to remedy this failure, but in contemporary life such thinking has become exceedingly difficult. There are numerous sources of thoughtlessness to contend with: a reliance on clichés and slogans as a substitute for independent reflection; an habitual inattention to what we are actually doing and saying; a dependence on shopworn ideologies whose automatic thought patterns serve as a buffer against the revelatory power of experience; the loss of candor and courage under the levelling pressure of mass society; the appeal to traditions of political thought that no longer address the vital concerns of our age.

Although thinking is a solitary activity, it greatly depends on the framework of categories and principles the thinking person inherits. We assimilate those categories in acquiring language and rely on them to understand and appraise what we do. Most of us are content to think within an existing tradition, trusting in the linguistic resources it offers for making sense of existence. But Hannah Arendt believed that the dominant western traditions had distorted or misrepresented political experience rather than rendering it intelligible. Her revisionary criticisms of both ancient and modern political theory closely resemble Heidegger's challenge to western metaphysics and Nietzsche's genealogical critique of morals. These deliberately subversive thinkers wanted to transform the inherited languages in which we think and speak about being and the good. According to Arendt, western political theories were chiefly created by philosophers, theologians or scientists rather than citizens or statesmen. Perhaps this explains the common flaw marring their credibility and relevance. Their categories of analysis and appraisal are not based on political events or on experiences rooted in human plurality but on solitary activities like thinking and making. Moreover, their emphasis on ruling as the essential political activity obscures the dependence of genuinely political relations on human equality. Rather than helping us understand and appreciate the actual contours of political experience, the dominant traditions have disparaged the importance of plurality, largely ignored public liberty, blurred important distinctions within the active life, and converted the history of republican freedom into a narrative of dialectical necessity. Because of these powerful prejudices, we cannot rely on the great traditions, ancient or modern, to guide our understanding and judgment of political events.

If Arendt's critical suspicions are justified, the contemporary political thinker is faced with a formidable challenge. The deep political alienation of our century threatens human dignity and freedom, but "our tradition of political thought" lacks the resources to address this threat effectively. The prevailing cultural climate encourages thoughtlessness rather than authentic reflection, but our need to think, to examine the insistent realities of personal and public life, is inseparable from our need for meaning. Thinking is the sustained human effort to understand or make sense of experience. In political thinking we attempt to clarify the fundamentals of politics and to articulate the criteria by which they should be judged. When our inherited traditions can no longer be trusted, the need for free and independent thinkers becomes urgent. Hannah Arendt aspired to be such a thinker and modeled her *"selbst denken"* on the philosophers she most admired: Socrates, Augustine, Scotus, Lessing, Kant and Heidegger. She respected these thinkers because of their intellectual courage and freedom; they had remained independent of tradition's authority and were willing, as she said, "to think without banisters."[2]

Independent thinking of the sort Arendt attempted is not systematic and progressive but foundational and critical. Faced with a crisis in politics, we need to rethink the basic principles of human association. Faced with a systemic assault on human dignity, we need to rethink its foundation in the nature of the human person. Faced with an erosion of public liberty, we need to reestablish the interdependence of plurality and freedom. These foundational tasks are obligatory for the critical thinker who challenges the answers of the tradition but does not dismiss them, who seeks to recover the past and not to forget it.[3]

But where are the resources for independent foundational thinking to be found? Hannah Arendt sought them in observable phenomena, in the concrete experiences of political life; in natural languages, in the original linguistic expressions created to name and describe new political realities; in historical events and in the memorable stories that attempted to disclose their meaning and importance; in a return to the questions with which the tradition began rather than to its carefully codified answers; in appropriating the retrievable past rather than in ideological speculations on the future. To think in this exploratory way is to do for our time what Socrates had attempted to do for his. Not to produce secure epistemic results, but to liberate citizens from prejudice, to pry open unexamined opinions, to cast new light on familiar realities, to prepare human beings to judge for themselves when the ancestral rules of conduct no longer apply.[4]

If the political thinker withdraws from the human circle to think for herself, the engaged citizen returns to the public realm to share her thinking with others. The sharing of insights is the work of a teacher, and it was as teacher and storyteller that Hannah Arendt partly fulfilled her civic obligations. She believed that the genuine teacher is inspired by a dual love, love for the old and common world that needs to be conserved and protected by its adult inhabitants, and love for the young, the energetic newcomers, who need to be welcomed into that world and taught to become at home in it. The voice of the teacher is that of an older citizen transmitting a common culture and language to younger peers about to accept responsibility for the commonweal. Through this successful transmission of meaning and memory, the young learn to know and care for the world and to identify themselves with its future. Arendt believed that civic education should deliberately cultivate the *humanitas* of its students. It should free them from self-centered concern with economic necessity and utility, and awaken within them the spirit of liberality, a love of the world and its culture that transcends their natural egoism.

Arendt was a student, of course, before she became a teacher, and her teaching depended greatly on her personal educational history. Who were the teachers that had cultivated her *humanitas*? She openly acknowledged her reliance on the Greek and German poets, who, as she said, keep watch over the storehouse of memory and create the words by which human beings live.[5] She had a complex relation to the culture of the ancient world, openly criticizing Greek political philosophy while making constant appeals to Greek and Roman political experience and language. She looked with disdain on the anti-political culture of early Christianity, but admired the life and teaching of Jesus himself. Her only acknowledged political mentors were republican and revolutionary thinkers: Pericles, Machiavelli, Montesquieu, Jefferson and de Tocqueville. Philosophically, she belonged to the German tradition of Lessing, Kant, Hegel, Nietzsche, Husserl, Jaspers and Heidegger. Her debt to Heidegger was immense and profoundly complicated. Her understanding of human action as self-revelation, her conception of public discourse as disclosure and concealment, her emphasis on temporality as the horizon of human existence, her radical critique of the western intellectual tradition, all these important aspects of her thought bear the stamp of Heidegger's influence. Although she greatly admired Heidegger as a thinker and teacher, she was deeply critical of his political stance and what she saw as his one-sided analysis of human existence.[6]

Perhaps Arendt's greatest strength as a teacher was her ability to resist the modern propensity for half-truths. She is difficult to classify in conventional political categories because she combined and connected what modern ideologies have fiercely opposed. She deeply distrusted the sterile oppositions between left and right, progressive and conservative, communitarian and individualist. "Nothing compromises the understanding of political issues and their meaningful debate more seriously than the automatic thought reactions conditioned by the beaten path of ideologies born in the wake and aftermath of the French Revolution."[7] Since the early nineteenth century conservatives and liberals, progressives and radicals have tended to treat complementary principles as mutually exclusive polarities. But it is only against the background of a common world of meaning that individual differences can truly reveal themselves. And it is only in the midst of a community of peers that personal distinction and excellence can be appreciated. A credible political philosophy needs to connect what the ideologists of both left and right have consistently separated: an old world with young citizens; the spirit of conservation with a commitment to civic initiative; worldly permanence with the eruption of miraculous novelty; the security of law with institutions of republican freedom. To overcome the dichotomies governing modern political thought we need a theory of situated freedom that respects human dignity and individual rights and reveals their dependence on the protection of personal privacy and the imperative of political engagement.

The story telling of poets, historians, citizens and teachers is a primary form of civic education. Although Arendt rejected the authority of tradition, she deeply feared the loss of the past. She understood tradition as our inherited account of the past, but she regularly distinguished the interpretive stories from the actual events to which they referred. A break with tradition did not mean an end to recollective story telling, but the creation of new stories that looked at the past with fresh eyes. The actions and passions, the words and deeds that constitute human affairs are doomed to futility unless memory and narrative save them from oblivion. In a political community composed of mortal citizens, birth and death are regularly changing the roster of active participants. The constant threat of civic disintegration is offset by remembrance and story telling which rescue the dead from forgetfulness and orient the newcomers in the civilizing ways of the world. Enduring political communities are associations of memory that express their collective identity through the stories they tell of their common past. As sources of civic education, these stories reveal the unfolding history of a particular people, but they're not limited to recording its landmark events. At the core of political teaching is the larger human story that preserves both the best and the worst that human beings have done. Political cooperation is the primary source of collective power and it radically extends the human capacity for good and evil. The history (*Geschichte*) of politics is the ambiguous record of what human beings have done with their precious public freedom.[8]

Stories contribute as nothing else can to the understanding of human existence, for the storyteller gathers the events of the past into an intelligible pattern that illumines the world of the present. Hannah Arendt often cited the cautionary maxim of her political mentor de Tocqueville, "When the past ceases to cast its light on the future, the mind of man wanders in obscurity."[9] The exercise of the mind is subject to two inescapable constraints. The mind needs to reflect on what it has witnessed or heard to satisfy its natural hunger for meaning; but it cannot retain or preserve in memory what it proves unable to connect. Remembrance and story telling meet these constraints by creating a factual record of the past and by distilling from that record a humanly comprehensible meaning. Paul Ricoeur has said that memory and narrative are the primary sources of authentic hope; by preserving the meaning of what lies behind us, they provide reasons for believing there is meaning before us.[10] The political narratives of Hannah Arendt are a source of both hope and warning, for they serve to disclose the *perils* of politics as well as its great possibility.

It is instructive to remember that her earliest stories portrayed political life at its worst. The totalitarian death camps of Nazi Germany and Stalinist Russia, on which she originally concentrated, are a constant reminder of the grotesque potential of cooperative action. In three of her books, *The Origins of Totalitarianism, Men in Dark Times* and *Eichmann in Jerusalem*, she recounts the complex pattern of events that culminated in this systematic assault on human dignity and freedom. Politically inspired anti-Semitism, racially motivated imperialism, the devastating violence of the great wars and the catastrophic effects of global depression, created the setting for the emergence of totalitarian governments in the heart of Europe. Drawing on Montesquieu's political taxonomy that distinguishes the traditional forms of government based on their spirit (*espirit*) or energizing principle, Arendt concluded that the totalitarian regimes of twentieth century Europe were historically unprecedented. Following Aristotle, Montesquieu had criticized despotism, whose animating principle is fear of the tyrant, as the worst kind of government. But Arendt argued that traditional despotism, though it denied human beings political liberty, did not deprive them of the freedom to think and speak in their private homes. By contrast, the totalitarian assault on freedom was meant to be unlimited. According to Arendt, the defining principles of totalitarian politics are ideology and terror; ideology seeks to abolish the free exercise of thought, while terror is aimed at eliminating freedom of action and speech. Their intended effect is the total control of human activity, with terror compelling human behavior from without and ideology compelling the human mind from within. In its representative institution, the extermination camp, totalitarianism deliberately dehumanized its victims, first destroying their capacity to think and act, then leveling their individual differences and distinct personalities until they became in their mute submission almost indistinguishable from the brutes.

A terrible irony pervades the totalitarian experiment in complete domination. When human beings aspire to absolute freedom, to be the uncontested masters of nature and history, they inevitably become agents of terror rather than liberty, turning themselves into executioners and their victims into corpses and skeletons. In seeking to become more than human, the agents of terror end by effacing their own humanity as well as that of the innocent people they terrorized.

Hannah Arendt never forgot the example of the European death camps. For her, they served as a warning against many things: the threatening potential of political mass movements, the inherent dangers in an atomized and fragmented society, the profound instability of the European moral inheritance in our secular age. But they also provided an inverted model of what political action should really be striving for. If the death camps were holes of oblivion and anonymity, then an authentic *polis* should be a community of remembrance and personal distinction. If the camps had eliminated spontaneity and driven human beings into brutelike silence, then the public realm should be a space of freedom where human beings reveal their uniqueness in word and deed. If the camps systematically destroyed human dignity through ideology and terror, then a true republic must render dignity secure by guaranteeing each citizen's civil and political rights and by ensuring that all persons will be publicly judged based on opinions they freely express and actions they really perform. If the camps turned human beings into naked and submissive animals, then genuine politics should create a world where they can live like free men and women.

Hannah Arendt's account of western political history was strikingly antiprogressive. She had open contempt for the liberal theory of progress, an ideology based on the achievements of modern science and technology rather than on the extension and protection of human liberty. For her, the grim events of the twentieth century had dispelled the innocence of liberalism and forced us to reexamine the meaning of human progress and decline. Because of her civic republican convictions, she made the establishment of political freedom and the protection of human rights the touchstone of collective wellbeing. But the history of republican liberty is not marked by a uniform pattern of advance or decline. In the Arendtian story, public liberty enjoys brief periods of glory and greatness, long centuries of neglect and disparagement and intermittent episodes of retrieval and restoration. The strongest political commitment to public liberty occurred in the ancient republics of Greece and Rome. "Never before or since have human beings thought so highly of political activity and bestowed so much dignity on the political realm."[11] There was a rebirth of this ancient republican ideal in the northern Italian cities of the Renaissance, inspired by the civic humanism of Machiavelli and Guiccardini. In the democratic revolutions of the eighteenth century, the celebrated example of the Roman republic was deliberately appropriated with uneven results. The drafters of the American constitution found in republican Rome a model for dividing governmental power, but in France the commitment to public liberty faltered under the pressure of "the social question" and the Jacobin reliance on terror. The political history of nineteenth and twentieth century Europe was marked by several experiments with the council system, a federated union of local republics in which political power is generated through popular initiative. This alternative model of republican governance, however, failed to displace the class-based party system of the continental nation-states that it actively opposed. But Arendt believed that mounting distrust of political parties, national governments, and nineteenth century ideologies has led thoughtful citizens throughout the world to yearn for a civic republican alternative to the status quo.

Arendt conceived her idealized republic of liberty as the complete antithesis of the totalitarian death camp. An organization of human beings founded on terror was to be replaced by a political community animated by freedom. As Arendt understood the spirit of freedom, it has both negative and positive aspects.[12] It requires that citizens be free from the demands of biological necessity and practical utility, so that they might assemble as peers in the spirit of liberality. Genuinely free citizens are united by their knowledge, love, and shared responsibility for the common world. Because they are legally and politically equal, their civic transactions are marked by debate and persuasion, rather than coercion or command. The traditional assumption that rule is the basic political relationship is explicitly rejected. Although the republic of liberty is governed by laws, its primary purpose is not ruling and being ruled, but the revelation of personal identity in public speech and action and voluntary cooperation for the sake of collective greatness and glory. Arendt's model of the free republic is clearly based on Pericles' funeral oration to the citizens of Athens and on Machiavelli's portrait of humanistic *virtù* in the *Discourses on Livy*. In the public realm of the Arendtian city, epiphanic personal initiatives, spontaneous communal action, and memorable historic events are expected to become commonplace. The uninspired prose of public administration and governance gives way to the heroic poetry of the ancient republic.[13]

At one level it is clear that Hannah Arendt continued the historic fascination of German philosophers with the classical *polis*. In this respect, she reenacted a pattern that Hegel, Nietzsche and Heidegger had already established. What is less clear is the purpose for which she invoked her idealized model of the classical city. Was it intended as a trans-historical norm by which all political communities should be measured? Was it a model to be imitated by modern citizens and statesmen who live under radically different social conditions from the ancient Greeks? Was it a narrative reminder intended to inspire contemporary civic republicans in their quest for a community of freedom, or a citation of the neglected past, in the spirit of Walter Benjamin, meant to shatter the mindless complacency of the present age? In different narrative contexts, Arendt's portrait of the free republic appeared to serve all of these critical functions, but it is difficult to say with assurance which goal was her primary concern. In the following chapters, we shall examine Arendt's republic of liberty with critical care. But at this point, I simply want to raise some exploratory questions that later chapters will probe in detail. 1) Is public freedom rather than justice, the primary purpose of republican politics? 2) How are the stipulated political ends of individual greatness and collective glory related to the traditional *telos* of the common good? 3) On what forms of personal and civic virtue does Arendtian liberty rely, and what virtues does it seek to encourage and foster among republican citizens? 4) On what socioeconomic arrangements does the republic of liberty depend for its popular acceptance and enduring stability? And within the global economy, to what range of citizens is the Arendtian model of politics really available? 5) How idealized is her portrait of Periclean democracy, how selective her espousal of Machiavelli's republican vision and how candid her recounting of the ambiguous history of republican patriotism? 6) Does her sweeping political narrative obscure the contrast between ancient and modern republicanism, particularly in its account of the spirit animating the American Revolution? Finally, is her allegiance to the council system as a model for political reform open to the criticism Benjamin Constant levelled at the revolutionary Jacobins, namely, that they refused the French people the kind of liberty they actually wanted and imposed on them a model of liberty they no longer desired? Is Arendt in danger of encouraging despotism in the hope of promoting liberty?

There are two critical periods in the Arendtian story of public freedom; the first coincides with the political splendor of the ancient Greek and Roman republics, the second with the emergence of the modern revolutionary tradition. For Arendt, the American, French and Russian revolutions were the most important political events in the modern age. But the historical narratives through which those events are remembered seriously distorted their political meaning and importance. The revolutionary wars of liberation have been consistently overemphasized; the true purpose of revolution, the constitution of an enduring realm of freedom, has been regularly neglected. As a result, revolution has come to symbolize a violent struggle for public power rather than a concerted attempt to establish lasting institutions of liberty.[14] The true meaning of the revolutionary spirit, the shared commitment of a people to republican self-government has never been fully articulated. This spirit, which Arendt describes as "the nameless treasure" of the revolutions, has been obscured by several factors:[15] the traditional prejudice that political activity is a public burden only accepted under duress; the lack of an articulate theorist to clarify the true meaning of the American Revolution, the only one of the great revolutions actually to establish freedom; the powerful influence of Hegel and Marx, whose memorable narratives of the French Revolution emphasized dialectical necessity rather than public liberty as their central explanatory category. From Arendt's perspective, the American Revolution was an ambiguous political success. The new constitution contained many elements of which she approved: a structure of national unity based on the principle of political federation, the articulate division of numerous governmental powers, the protection of individual liberties and civil rights. But by failing to incorporate the colonial townships into the federal system of differentiated power, the constitution left the ordinary citizen without a space of public liberty in which to act. The American Revolution gave freedom to the people, but did not provide them with public forums where they could regularly exercise and enjoy it. It gave them the right to political representation but failed to grant them elementary republics for their civic education and political development. The sad result was that for the vast majority of citizens, the revolutionary spirit of republican liberty, of direct engagement and participation in public affairs, eventually withered away.

Profound conceptual confusions attended this loss of civic vitality. Political liberty, the right to participate in republican self-government, became confused with the civil liberties that preserve our security and individual rights. Public happiness, the active collaboration with our peers in securing the common good of the body politic, was reduced to the utilitarian formula of the greatest private happiness of the greatest number. And public spirit, the creation through debate and argument of a responsible conception of the public good, was degraded into the despotism of public opinion as measured by the polling techniques of a consumer society. Thus, the constitutional failure to secure elementary spaces of liberty for individual citizens was compounded by a theoretical failure to clarify for posterity what the true purpose of the revolution had been.

For Arendt, the history of the great modern revolutions is redolent with irony. The partially successful American Revolution lacked a competent theorist to articulate its deepest meaning and achievement; the radically unsuccessful French revolution, whose original quest for freedom was thwarted by violence and terror, had brilliant interpreters whose theoretical narratives transformed a momentous political event into a benchmark of historical inevitability.

As a result, historical necessity rather than freedom became the basic category of revolutionary thought and the critical contributions of political liberty were attributed to vast impersonal forces beyond the influence of human deliberation and choice. Hannah Arendt's retelling of the revolutionary story as a central part of her political narrative has the revisionary intention of restoring human action and freedom rather than lawful necessity to the thematic center of revolutionary thought.

Arendt wanted to understand the past so that she might eventually pass judgment upon it. She was a fearless and independent judge of human beings, of their actions and failures to act, of the communities and institutions they created or allowed to decay. Her political narratives of liberty and terror are filled with controversial judgments that often aroused the ire of her readers and critics.[16] Perhaps these passionate controversies goaded her to reflect on the activity of judging, for she gradually developed a complex analysis of what she called "our most political mental faculty."[17] In her philosophical analysis of thinking, she relied heavily on the example of Socrates; in her treatment of memory and will she drew liberally from the work of Augustine. But for the understanding of practical judgment, she turned primarily to Kant, especially to his third critique. Following Kant, she characterized judging as a public activity of reflective appraisal, an activity in which we praise or censure the object, event, person or institution that we presume to judge.

Judging is an essentially political act, an exercise of public freedom conducted among equals, that seeks to achieve through debate and argument an evaluative consensus. By exchanging persuasive arguments with our peers, by wooing them to share our reflective assessment of human affairs, we gain their respect and friendship and make ourselves at home in the world. Judging, according to Arendt, is a retrospective activity that emerges from reflection on earlier sensible appearances. In this respect, willing and judging are temporal opposites, for willing always deals with the future, the not yet, and judging with the past, the no longer. The bulk of the human past disappears from consciousness as soon as it has occurred; but we remember and preserve that portion of the past that we particularly care about, and in remembering our past, we gradually prepare it for understanding and judgment. The act of judging completes the recurrent cycle of action, remembrance, reflection and articulation by incorporating the past into a meaningful story and rendering our verdict upon it.

For Arendt, the appropriate objects of human judgment are historical particulars, individual persons, unique events, concrete situations, political communities, each with its independent dignity and character. She deeply resisted the subsumption of these historical particulars into the universal categories of philosophy and science. Individual persons are to be judged on the basis of their own words and deeds, not as type specimens of a biological species, representative members of an ethnic group or social class, or anonymous participants in an irresistible mass movement. Historical events have their own integrity and intelligibility; they should not be reduced to instances of a pervasive historical trend or to illustrations of a causally determined natural process. The reflective judgments of historians should be like those of judges in a court of law who are asked to appraise this particular person or event as a unique being or occurrence and not to subsume what is judged under the rubric of an explanatory universal.

But who is entitled to judge, and what are the virtues that belong to the person who judges wisely and well. Because Arendtian judgments are retrospective rather than deliberative, they are the responsibility of the spectator rather than the actor, of the historian and poet rather than the hero, of those who observe rather than those who compete in the festival of life. According to Arendt, the good judge must be like Homer who looked with an impartial eye on the heroism of Argives and Trojans, or like Herodotus, who openly praised the greatness of both Greeks and Persians.[18] Once again, it is *humanitas*, a knowledgeable attachment to the common world superseding narrow partisanship, which is required of a trustworthy judge. The man or woman with *humanitas* is the intended fruit of a liberal civic culture: he or she is informed, disinterested, courageous, the bearer of an "enlarged mentality" which transcends self-interest and partisan allegiance. The good judge is intensely thoughtful, for sustained independent thinking is the best preparation for judgment, and the habitual failure to think makes us unfit for it.[19] In truth, we can find in the spirit of Arendtian judgment the humanistic spirit of Arendtian politics as a whole. That spirit is liberal, aristocratic, deeply committed to debate and persuasion, and inspired by an active concern for the common world. The political humanism of Hannah Arendt summons human beings to a secular form of self-transcendence in which private interest is replaced by devotion to the public world, and our limited individual perspective on that world is enlarged by appropriating the alternative standpoints and considered opinions of others. While thinking and contemplation are solitary activities, teaching, storytelling, and judging are inherently communal and political. The reasons that we offer in support of our judgments are intended to persuade a community of peers whose differing opinions we consider *sine ira et studio* , without anger and partisan zeal.[20]

If judging is an exercise of shared rationality, what are the relevant criteria for appraising the *res publicae*, for assessing the action and speech that occur in the public realm? It is easier to identify the criteria Arendt rejects than to be certain of those she considers appropriate. She insists that political judgments are not religious, nor are they subject to the religious criteria of goodness and sanctity. In politics, we do not judge the souls of other persons nor consign them to everlasting reward or punishment. If there are final judgments to be made of human beings, they belong exclusively to God who alone can read the human soul, and not to their civic peers who lack this divine capacity. This is the partial but important truth expressed in the biblical imperative: "Judge not so that you shall not be judged."[21] Arendt enters more contested territory when she argues that moral criteria are of limited relevance in appraising political phenomena. She bases this questionable claim on several disputable grounds. First, that moral reflection essentially concerns the integrity of the individual self, whereas political judgment concerns the web of relations within a community of citizens bound together by their shared responsibility for the world.[22] In Arendt's graphic spatial imagery, religious faith connects the solitary human being to a transcendent and invisible God; morality engages a man or woman in intercourse with him or herself, while politics leads citizens to converse with one another through the medium of a common world. There is a critical difference between the authoritative commands of conscience that tell the particular self what to do and avoid and the persuasive arguments we address to our fellow citizens in seeking their agreement and support. To use Arendt's deliberately contrastive idiom, morality issues commands on behalf of the self's integrity, but politics persuades for the sake of a common world.[23]

Arendt believes that the dominant moral traditions of the West shed little light on the nature of political judgments. Utilitarian criteria are not applicable to politics, for action and speech are not means to ends and should not be judged on the strength of their cumulative outcomes. But Kantian moral criteria have equally limited relevance. The maxims and motives that provide the spur to free actions are not the appropriate basis for their political assessment. Nor are political realities to be judged by subsuming them under the natural law, by comparing them to established customs, by deducing them from moral first principles, nor extracting them dialectically from a theory of human nature and society. Finally, they are not to be judged by the pragmatic criteria of worldly success, a vulgar temptation Arendt liked to rebut by quoting an aphorism of Cato, the renowned Roman statesman: "The cause of the victors pleased the gods but the cause of the vanquished pleased Cato."[24] As her praise of the Paris commune of 1871, the Russian soviets brutally destroyed by Bolshevik despotism, and the short lived Hungarian revolution of 1956, should make clear, her political judgments more often sided with the ostensible losers in history rather than the victors.

But her articulation of positive criteria for political appraisal is often incomplete or obscure. She insists that the criteria should be secular not sacred, commonly accepted not idiosyncratic, inherently liberal, like action and speech themselves, and not based on concern for survival or utility. There is a strong emphasis on public excellence, but a lack of clarity about the nature of excellence in politics. There is a repeated stress on historical greatness and a Nietzsche-like assertion that greatness transcends the strictures of existing law, but the cited examples are deeply problematic and difficult to reconcile with the requirements of justice.[25] Arendt develops an important but controversial analogy between aesthetic and political judgments; both of these forms of appraisal focus on worldly appearances, on what the public world should contain and how it should look. But if beauty is the appropriate measure in the aesthetic domain, what is its legitimate political counterpart; and if beauty is discerned through the disinterested pleasure it offers the spectator, is there an analogous pleasure that accompanies the perception of political excellence? Does Arendt's analogy of sensible beauty aestheticize politics; does the emphasis on Periclean or Machiavellian greatness de-moralize it? What are the proper connections between politics and justice, between republican liberty and the moral and intellectual virtues, between historical greatness and the enduring requirements of the commonweal? Arendt insists that the responsible appraisal of temporal particulars is not governed by precedent, principle or rule. But judges and juries who exercise judgment are properly subject to those very constraints. Although Arendt's understanding of judgment, like her correlative conception of action, is clearly important and provocative, in both cases she raises more questions than she is able to answer persuasively.

One of the critical questions concerns the objectivity of political judgments: For whom are they valid and why? Arendt brusquely rejects two familiar responses as mistaken. Because good judgments are supported by reasons, they are not arbitrary expressions of preference, limited in their validity to the selective taste of the judger. Arendt takes sharp exception to the ancient maxim, "*De gustibus non est disputandum*," because judgments of taste are public concerns, matters of intense debate, in which reasons and arguments are given to secure the agreement of peers. But these supporting reasons are persuasive not demonstrative in nature. They cannot compel or coerce universal assent as matters of fact or truths of reason are alleged to do.[26] Arendt explicitly contrasts the universal validity of scientific cognition with the restricted validity of evaluative judgments. Political and aesthetic judgments can secure intersubjective agreement, but the scope of their persuasive power is limited to men and women of good taste. For those who lack the impartiality, disinterestedness and reflective intensity of the good judge, even the most rational arguments may not suffice.[27] Specific virtues are required then not only to reach sound judgments on one's own but to be persuaded by the discerning judgments of others. While there is considerable merit to Arendt's analysis of evaluative objectivity, it still leaves two important matters unresolved. She fails to clarify the type of reasons it is appropriate to offer in support of political judgments (the question of suitable *criteria* again) and she deeply oversimplifies the objectivity of epistemic judgments that also rely heavily on the virtues of cognitional subjects.[28]

Many of the problems with Arendt's theory of judgment can be traced to an over-reliance on the Kantian model. In Kant's epistemology, both theoretical and practical reason are credited with universal and exceptionless judgments. Both the laws of nature and the laws of freedom are alleged to be invariant and necessary. Pure practical reason, the autonomous source of the categorical moral imperatives, is explicitly distinguished from technical reason whose directives are limited to imperatives of skill or counsels of prudence. The hypothetical imperatives of technical reason have restricted validity for the rational will because they are conditioned by self-interest and personal desire. In his third critique, Kant discovered a form of practical reasoning which is impartial and disinterested, like the autonomous moral will, but whose judgments are of limited personal validity, like those of technical reason (though not, of course, for the same reasons). Arendt modeled her analysis of political judgment on the Kantian theory of aesthetic appraisal. There were several reasons to support this selective appropriation of Kant. Aesthetic judgments privilege the role of the disinterested spectator; they take phenomenal particulars, sensible objects and events, as their intentional objects; they presuppose a community of judging peers whose freedom of judgment is respected in the lively exchange of evaluative debate and argument. Each of these constitutive features is assigned an important place in Arendt's account of political judgments. But as already noted, there are clear limits to the comparison between sensible beauty and political excellence, between the disinterested pleasure elicited by aesthetic appearances and the appropriate grounds for judging political agents, actions, institutions, and cultures.

To heighten this contrast, let us very briefly examine an alternative approach to practical reason that avoids some of the Arendtian difficulties. The alternative is offered by Aristotle, to whose political theory Arendt was greatly indebted, in his salient account of *phronesis*, the distinctive virtue of the statesman.[29] Focusing on the statesman reorients the analysis of judgment from the spectator to the political agent, from retrospective remembrance to prospective deliberation. The statesman's attention is also concentrated on particulars, on highly concrete human situations of choice; and Aristotle recognizes the insufficiency of universal principles to determine the right course of action within these particular contexts. Aristotle also believes that most ethical and political judgments are persuasive rather than demonstrative in character; their objective validity is restricted to the concrete circumstances in which they arise and to which they are specifically applicable.[30] It is only the *phronimos*, the practically wise leader or citizen, who can discern the right course of action in difficult cases and then explain why it is right to his peers in the political community.

To be practically wise a statesman must also be morally virtuous; *phronesis* cannot exist apart from the full range of moral virtues. The essential dependence of good judgment on moral virtue and wisdom indicates that Aristotle does not separate ethics from politics as Arendt tends to do. The *phronesis* of the statesman manifests itself in sound deliberation, culminating in political judgments that specify how the good of the whole community can best be advanced by this course of action. Sound judgment is dependent on practical wisdom, and wisdom, in turn, on a judge who is morally good and who knows how to actualize the communal good here and now.

Aristotle's insertion of the moral virtues and the common good into the center of political reflection, counter balances the Arendtian emphasis on beauty just as his stress on practical wisdom challenges the Arendtian focus on taste. When politics is directed to the common good rather than to epiphanic public appearances, it can preserve the Arendtian emphasis on public liberty while placing liberty itself in the service of justice and communal well being. Arendt seemed to fear that an Aristotelian approach to the *telos* of politics would subvert the dignity of action and speech, converting political conduct into an instrument for achieving extra-political ends. But a nuanced understanding of Aristotle's internal teleology should allay this questionable fear.[31] Political goods are inseparable from the virtuous civic activities through which they are realized, and, as Arendt rightly insists, public liberty is an essential condition of their just and responsible attainment.

By embracing the cause of liberty and dignity in an age where they were gravely endangered, Arendt was following the example of Alexis de Tocqueville, the great nineteenth century French liberal thinker. Like Arendt, Tocqueville was born into a dying world as a new one struggled to be born. His birth coincided with the collapse of the *Ancien Regime*, the aristocratic French feudal order and his life overlapped with the great democratic revolutions of Europe and North America. The central theme of Tocqueville's thought was the uncertain fate of human liberty in these new democratic societies. While Tocqueville accepted the emerging democratic order as more just than its aristocratic predecessor, he was troubled by the dangers democracy posed to liberty and to an elevated conception of the human being.[32]

What are the dangers to liberty in the irreversible movement of modern history towards democratic equality? According to Tocqueville, liberty is threatened by the following constellation of forces: a dramatic growth in the power of the central government which becomes increasingly remote, bureaucratic, impersonal and paternalistic; the loss of intermediate political associations which moderate the relations between democratic citizens and the central political authority; a retreat by uprooted individuals into the narrow confines of their private lives with a corresponding disengagement from public affairs. (Tocqueville describes this political phenomenon as "democratic individualism.")[33] When these factors coalesce the probable result is a new form of political despotism, the despotism of the democratic majority, in which the isolated and atomized individual is left powerless before the bureaucratic state and the tyranny of majority opinion.

In brilliant and memorable prose, Tocqueville explains why democratic despotism is especially to be dreaded by the friends of liberty. It makes the life and property of human beings insecure; it weakens their civil and individual rights, like the rights to free speech and freedom of worship; and as despotism has traditionally done, it abolishes meaningful political liberty, the effective participation by ordinary citizens in the practice of self-government. As citizens become more dependent on the state and less confident of their own capacities, their opinions and conduct become increasingly uniform. As the power of majority opinion expands, the individual's willingness to challenge and oppose it contracts. As human beings become ever more similar, nearly all signs of personal greatness, nearly all forms of nobility and heroism, disappear. This level egalitarian plain of atomized uniformity and blandness is Tocqueville's nightmare image of democratic despotism.[34]

Based on his experiences and conversations in America, Tocqueville concluded that the despotism of the democratic majority was a permanent threat not an historical inevitability. After observing public life in the New England townships, he argued that preserving local political liberty was the strongest protection against the majoritarian tyranny he feared. Adopting Montesquieu's concept of republican government, he modified its requirements to fit the circumstances of continental republics in a democratic age. In this way, he outlined a new science of republican liberty based on the following principles: the decentralizing of public administration; the distribution of political power towards local units of authority (the principle of subidiarity); the reliance on voluntary associations to mediate the transactions between citizens and their government; the enlightened self-interest of a democratic people firmly committed to the rule of law, respect for individual rights, a free and independent judiciary and press, and an educated readiness to participate regularly in public life. For Tocqueville, an active, informed, responsible citizenry was the best, perhaps the only, antidote to the poison of democratic individualism. "Feelings and opinions are recruited, the heart is enlarged and the mind developed by the reciprocal influence of human beings on one another."[35]

Hannah Arendt was born a century later than Tocqueville, but his deepest concerns pervade her political thought. Both of them were aristocratically minded thinkers devoted to the liberty and dignity of the human person; both of them feared that the dangers to liberty in their age were unprecedented; both sought to lessen these dangers by strengthening political liberty and renewing the ideal of republican self-government. However, Arendt believed that the political crisis of the twentieth century was far more severe than the one Tocqueville had faced. As she saw it, the bourgeois liberalism of the nineteenth century, which celebrated the pursuit of private interest both institutionally and culturally, had devalued the meaning of citizenship; the political authority of the European nation states had eroded, and the class structure of Europe had disintegrated into a mass society that radicalized the atomization and loneliness Tocqueville had forecast. Shaken by global war and depression, Europe had been overwhelmed by ideological mass movements that culminated in the criminal regimes of Nazi Germany and Stalinist Russia. Under totalitarian rule Tocqueville's worst fears had been grotesquely exceeded. The zero point of human liberty and dignity became the daily reality of the death camps as the bright dreams of European humanism perished in the ashes of Treblinka and Auschwitz.

At the close of the Second World War when the reality of the holocaust became known, Hannah Arendt committed herself to a work of remembrance and reflection. Was it possible to comprehend and articulate the genesis of totalitarian terror? What earlier spiritual and cultural collapse had made it possible? To what resources and institutions could we now turn to prevent its recurrence? After years of intensive and passionate study, Hannah Arendt concluded that the deepest crisis of the modern world was political, and that the emergence of popularly supported totalitarian movements in the heart of Europe demonstrated how profound that crisis had become. The crisis to which she referred could be discerned on four distinct but interconnected levels: cultural, theoretical, institutional and normative. The world alienation of modernity has created a mass culture antithetical to republican self-government and especially prone to ideological manipulation. Our theoretical capacity to critique this culture and the seductive ideologies it spawns is limited because our inherited traditions have systematically misrepresented the nature of political experience. By substituting making for action, command and coercion for persuasion and debate, and technological mastery for political excellence and wisdom our political theorists have darkened the common perception of politics and reduced it to a servant of economic concerns. The rise of economics to its modern supremacy has transformed the public realm into a sphere of necessity, rather than freedom, while human freedom, with its irresistible force and attraction, has withdrawn into the diverse pursuits of private happiness. As a result, the political institutions of mass society lack the traditions and practices of public liberty that are needed to cultivate and sustain the republican spirit. And without that spirit, the lost spirit of the revolution, modern citizens no longer know what to require of themselves and their political leaders nor how to judge responsibly what they do and say.

In its most compressed and unsparing form, this is Hannah Arendt's analysis of our political situation today. Though her judgment is harsh, it is not fatalistic. Historical inevitability does not govern the conduct of human affairs. Each of the elements in our political crisis is subject to challenge and redress, and, as her own life has shown, the individual person is not condemned to impotence and despair. The critical thinker can challenge the oversights and distortions of traditional political theory, the dedicated teacher can oppose the culture of *humanitas* to the complacent egoism of our consumer society, the gifted storyteller can remind us of both the greatness and wretchedness of our common past, and the individual citizen can speak and act, cooperating with others in the unending work of protecting human dignity and renewing human liberty. "*Omnia praeclara tam difficilia quam rara sunt.*" "All truly excellent things are as difficult as they are rare."[36]

NOTES

1. Hannah Arendt, *Between Past and Future* (1961; New York: Viking Press) pp. 3-15.
2. See Melvyn Hill, *Hannah Arendt: The Recovery of the Public World* (1979; New York: St. Martin's Press) p. 314; p. 336.
3. " The disappearance of prejudices simply means that we have lost the answers on which we ordinarily rely without even realizing they were originally answers to questions. A crisis forces us back to the questions themselves and requires from us either new or old answers, but in any case direct judgments." Arendt, *Between Past and Future*, p. 174.
4. See Arendt, "Thinking and Moral Considerations: A Lecture," *Social Research*, (Fall 1971) pp. 417-446.
5. See Arendt, *The Human Condition* (1958; Chicago: University of Chicago Press) pp. 167-174 and Arendt, *Men in Dark Times* (1983; New York; Harcourt Brace) p. 249. Arendt often acknowledged her profound gratitude for the blessings of poetry.
6. For Arendt's complex relation to Heidegger's thought, see Dana Villa, *Arendt and Heidegger: The Fate of the Political* (1996; Princeton: Princeton University Press); Elizabeth Young Bruehl, *Hannah Arendt: For Love of the World* (1982; New Haven: Yale University Press); L. P. Hinchman and S. K. Hinchman, "In Heidegger's Shadow: Hannah Arendt's Phenomenological Humanism," Review of Politics (1984).
7. Hannah Arendt, *On Revolution* (1963; New York: Viking Press), p. 225.
8. See Arendt, "The Concept of History" and "What is Freedom?" *Between Past and Future*, pp. 41-90 and 143-171.
9. Alexis de Tocqueville, *Democracy in America*, Vol. II (1945; New York: Vintage Books), p. 349.
10. See Paul Ricoeur, *Time and Narrative*, (1984; Chicago: University of Chicago Press).
11. Hannah Arendt, *Between Past and Future*, p. 154.
12. See Arendt, "What is Freedom?" *Between Past and Future*, and *The Human Condition*, pp. 28-37.
13. Arendt relies heavily on the contrast between the political and the social as a way of distinguishing public administration (a social function) from heroic action (the *raison d'être* of politics). This contested dichotomy runs through all of her writing but it is most fully developed in "The Public and the Private Realm," *The Human Condition*, pp. 22-73.
14. See the important contrast between liberation from tyranny and the constitution of freedom in *On Revolution*, p. 140.
15. See "The Revolutionary Tradition and Its Lost Treasure," *On Revolution*, pp. 217-285.
16. The most hostile response was evoked by her analysis and appraisal of the Eichmann trial. See *Eichmann in Jerusalem: A Report on the Banality of Evil*, (1963; New York: Viking Press). For the most bitter and relentless criticism see Jacob Robinson, *And the Crooked Shall Be Made Straight*, (1965; New York: Macmillan). For the larger context of the protracted dispute, see Ron Feldman, *The Jew as Pariah*, (1978; New York: Grove Press).
17. See Arendt, "The Crisis in Culture," *Between Past and Future*, pp. 218-226 and Arendt, *Lectures on Kant's Political Philosophy*, (1982; Chicago: University of Chicago Press).
18. See Arendt, *Between Past and Future*, pp. 262-263.
19. Hannah Arendt returned repeatedly to the close connection between thoughtfulness and the capacity for sound judgment. See *Eichmann in Jerusalem*, pp. 294-298; *The Life of the Mind*: Vol. I. *Thinking* (1978; New York: Harcourt Brace) pp. 3-16 and "Thinking and Moral Considerations: A Lecture," *Social Research*, (Fall 1971).
20. See Arendt, "Truth and Politics" *Between Past and Future*, pp. 227-264 and "The Crisis in Culture" for the dependence of valid judgments on disinterestedness and impartiality.
21. The Gospel of St. Matthew, 7:1.
22. See Arendt, "Civil Disobedience," *Crises of the Republic* (1972; New York: Harcourt Brace) pp. 58-68.
23. See Arendt, *Between Past and Future*, pp. 218-223 and *Crises of the Republic*, pp. 62-68.

24. See Arendt, *The Life of the Mind: Thinking*, pp. 216. *"Victrix causa deis placuit, sed victa Catoni."*

25. This concern applies to her praise of Periclean Athens, Republican Rome and Machiavellian *virtù*. Arendt's sharp separation between political and moral criteria is particularly questionable.

26. See Arendt, "The Crisis in Culture" and "Truth in Politics," *Between Past and Future*, pp. 218-223 and pp. 241-264.

27. See Arendt, *Between Past and Future*, pp. 221-224.

28. Arendt's epistemological reflections are always interesting, but they tend to be advanced as personal *apercus and obiter dicta* rather than as part of a comprehensive analysis of objectivity, knowledge and truth.

29. For the similarities between *phronesis* and taste, see Arendt, *Between Past and Future*, p. 221. For Aristotle's concise description of *phronesis*, see Nicomachean Ethics, Book VI, where he compares and contrasts the different intellectual virtues.

30. See Aristotle's strictures on practical inquiry in the *Nicomachean Ethics*, Book 1, chapter 3 and Book VI, chapters 4 and 5.

31. See Alasdair MacIntyre, *After Virtue*, (1981; Notre Dame: Notre Dame University Press) pp. 188-189, and Bernard Lonergan, *Third Collection* (1985; Mahwah: Paulist Press) p. 24.

32. See Tocqueville, *Democracy in America*, vol II, pp. 349-352. "A state of equality is perhaps less elevated, but it is more just: and its justice constitutes its greatness and its beauty."

33. Tocqueville, Democracy, II, pp. 104-113.

34. Tocqueville, *Democracy*, II, pp. 334-348.

35. Tocqueville, *Democracy*, II, p. 117.

36. Spinoza, *Ethics*, Part V, Proposition XLII.

Chapter One

THE CITY IN RUINS

The great object in our time is to raise the faculties of men, not to complete their prostration.[1]

TOTALITARIANISM AS A LIMIT SITUATION

The ablest Greek philosophers agreed that the origin of philosophy is in wonder. Socrates, in the *Theaetetus*, praised wonder (*thauma*) as the source of philosophical reflection; Aristotle, in the *Metaphysics*, clearly identified it as the historical beginning of the theoretical life. "For it is owing to their wonder that men both now begin and at first began to philosophize."[2] Aristotle maintained that the primordial object of wonder was the physical universe. His claim is supported by the history of pre-Socratic thought that initially focused human inquiry on the origin and order of the natural world. In the beginning philosophy and cosmology were one.

What struck the first philosophers was the beauty and harmony of nature, in particular the lawful motions of the heavenly bodies. For them, nature was a *kosmos*, a well-ordered whole in which cosmic justice, the temporal equilibrium of the elemental opposites, was scrupulously observed. This perpetual cosmic order served as a model against which the human quest for order and justice was eventually measured. Yet if cosmic justice was assured in the realm of nature, it was at all times a *telos*, an end to be aimed for, in human affairs. In their constantly changing relations with one another, human beings did not naturally enjoy the ordered harmony so visibly present in the evening sky. However intently citizens might aim at justice in the life of the city, they invariably fell short of the mark. The earthly *polis* never became a *kosmos*; its imperfect and partial order never secured the silent admiration of the philosophical few. When the city finally gained the close attention of the Greek philosophers, it was discord rather than harmony, disorder rather than justice that dominated their field of vision.

Western political philosophy has its origin in the crisis of the ancient city, in the disintegration of the civic whole rather than in its achievement of fullness and power. It was only after Athens, the greatest of the Greek cities, had suffered defeat in the war with Sparta, that Plato gave the *polis* a central place in philosophical thought. He made Athens, Socrates' native city, the dramatic center of his dialogues, and he made the *polis* itself a fundamental theme of Socratic discourse.[3] In both cases, however, it was not wonder at the city's ordered beauty, but distress and unease at its tragic decline that required philosophers to think about it. If Socrates redirected the attention of philosophy from the *kosmos* to the *polis*, he did so because stressful perplexity (*aporia*) had become as important as silent wonder in initiating philosophic activity.

The Socratic Platonic origin of political philosophy leaves its mark on the ensuing tradition. Although the pathos of decline is less striking in Aristotle's *Politics* than in Plato's *Republic*, still, Aristotle, in his portrait of the ancient city, is describing a pattern of political life that has already lost its historic vitality. His influential descriptions of the independent Greek *polis* commemorate an ideal that no longer exists rather than an observable pattern flourishing before his eyes. In St. Augustine's *The City of God*, the sombre Platonic inheritance is even more pronounced. Augustine is moved to sustained political reflection by the Vandals' sacking of Rome and by his deepening awareness that the days of the Empire are numbered. Like Plato, he responds to the ruin of the temporal city by evoking the image of an eternal republic. True citizenship is to be found neither in Athens nor in Rome but in the ideal republic or the city of God. Both Augustine and Plato refuse to abandon the language of citizenship and the metaphor of political community, but they transfer their application from decaying historical cities to an ahistorical or transhistorical commonwealth. They seem jointly to believe that only a just and eternal city is actually worthy of the name.

When we turn from the classical tradition to the modern, we find the importance of political crisis remaining constant. Angered by the repeated invasions that beset the Italian city-states and bitter at the Church's disruptive role in political affairs, Machiavelli appeals for a united Italy cleansed of both clerical and foreign influence. Once again it is the fact of political decline that occasions intense theoretical reflection. But Machiavelli is a modern as well as a traditional thinker. He looks neither to heaven nor to an ideal republic for political salvation, but to an as yet unrealized commonwealth. It is love for an actual country, a state, yearned for but not yet realized, rather than love of God or love of truth, that shall restore meaning to devalued citizenship.[4] The emergence of the secular nation-state, which Machiavelli dreamed of but never directly experienced, marks the transition between medieval and modern political history. As Athens had exemplified the *polis* of classical antiquity, and Rome had provided the historic model for world-empire, so in modern Europe, France represented the nation-state *par excellence*. Yet in the French nation of the eighteenth century, modern political forms were combined with a legal and social order rooted in medieval feudalism. The French revolution was precipitated not by a crisis of the nation-state but by the eroded legitimacy of the aristocratic social order to which it was historically joined. As de Tocqueville's investigations convincingly demonstrated, the centralized political institutions developed by the French monarchy survived the collapse of the *Ancien Regime*.[5] In fact, the Napoleonic phase of the revolution carried to its limit the process of political centralization deliberately undertaken by the Bourbon kings. According to de Tocqueville, the central question raised by the tumultuous French experience was whether the modern nation-state could combine a democratic social revolution with the institutions, practices and customs of political liberty. Like Tocqueville, nearly all of the great nineteenth century political theorists found their point of departure in the history of the French revolution. The political philosophies of Kant, Burke, Hegel and Marx are as closely tied to that cataclysmic event as Plato's and Augustine's were to the earlier crises of Athens and Rome. A deep and comprehensive knowledge of European history provides the best guide to western political philosophy, because each great theoretical initiative was a sustained attempt to understand the meaning and importance of some central political event. Through all of the nineteenth and for the early twentieth century, the critical event around which political reflection turned was the unfinished revolution in France.

Is there a parallel benchmark for political reflection in our time? Is there a central event of the twentieth century that commands the attention and study of our ablest political thinkers? Hannah Arendt, one of the most original political philosophers of the postwar era, claimed that there was. She identified this event with the totalitarian terror that dominated eastern and central Europe during the nineteen-thirties and forties. In a century scarred by political horror she chose to take her bearings from, perhaps, the darkest horror in recorded time, the totalitarian reality as it reached its developed form in Hitler's Germany and Stalin's Russia.[6] She believed that this political reference point was fundamentally different from its historical antecedents. Totalitarianism represented more than a crisis in existing political order. It constituted an ultimate or limit situation, without historical precedent or analogue, a transformative event that posed an unparalleled threat to human dignity. Because the reality of this overwhelming event was so extreme, she suspected that the human mind would recoil from the task of confronting it. Against this understandable reaction of collective avoidance and denial, she insisted that we, her worldly peers, acknowledge the depth of what happened, that we try to comprehend the factual reality and meaning of totalitarianism, without lessening the burden of comprehension by appeals to precedent or resort to analogy. Behind this passionate insistence rooted in her intellectual courage and personal history, lay a general belief in the revelatory power of limit situations. According to Arendt, exceptional events, whether glorious or terrible, are more deeply revealing of human possibility than the ordinary patterns of behavior that serve as their background and contrast. She took the classic Aristotelean principle that *telos* reveals *eidos*, that the essence of a thing is fully disclosed in its perfected state, and gave it an extended and unusual application. For her, historical events serve a complex educational function. As the Athenian *polis* in its Periclean splendor disclosed the potential greatness of the political realm, so the death factories of totalitarian terror reveal the depth of indignity to which human beings may be reduced through systematic planning and effort. A comprehensive political philosophy must take full account of both types of event. We need both the monitory and exemplary lessons of history to understand the full dependence of secure human dignity on the soundness and legitimacy of the political realm.

Arendt emerged from her postwar study of totalitarianism with three enduring convictions: that totalitarianism was a radically new phenomenon, entirely without precedent in world history; that our inherited political and moral categories were inadequate to describe or appraise it; and that it revealed, by their complete abolition, the fundamental conditions on which the existence of human dignity depends.[7] The political phenomenon of tyranny or despotism was deeply familiar to both ancient and modern theorists. They knew from experience the reality of arbitrary rule and the exclusive usurpation of political power by the tyrant. They were familiar with coercion in public affairs and the restriction of freedom to the circumscribed space of the private household. Almost without exception, they dreaded despotism and assigned it a place of dishonor in their elaborate political taxonomies.[8] But neither ancient nor modern political communities had any experience of the totalitarian attempt at total domination over the human person. The total domination attempted by the Nazis and Stalinist Russia is radically different from arbitrary despotic rule. In its most revealing institutional form, the extermination camp, it deliberately creates conditions under which people no longer wish to live. Totalitarianism recognizes no boundary between public and private freedom, and deprives its victims of liberty in every humanly recognizable form. While conditions in the camps could not destroy the native capacities of men and women, they did effectively destroy the possibility of their meaningful use. The assault on the requirements of freedom was twofold. Totalitarian ideology, with its pretense to limitless temporal knowledge, actively destroys the truth of the past and the unpredictability of the future, and seeks to eliminate from historical memory the lives of those it has condemned to death. Totalitarian terror, the animating principle of the death camps, destroys the public and private spaces human beings need for their free movement and interaction.[9] It drives its victims together like herds of animals until they become indistinguishable from one another in their mute suffering. The extermination camp effectively isolates its victims from every aspect of reality except pain, death and unrelieved humiliation. It confines them to life within a humanly constructed world whose only intelligible purpose is the mass production of corpses.[10]

Both the Hebraic Torah and the Christian Decalogue clearly command "thou shalt not kill." But the totalitarian regimes in Germany and Russia introduced modes of systemic evil of which our moral traditions had taken no account. Here, human thought is confronted with a radical evil so improbable that the criminals who commit it are more credible in their denials of wrongdoing than are their victims in their pleas for redress.[11] Totalitarian evil is radical in two respects: the motives of those who plan and execute it are utterly disproportionate to the reality of what they actually do. Hard headed common sense, which demands a reasonable balance between ends and means in its assessment of action, is tempted to deny the full reality of the death camps because the canons of utility it implicitly assumes are not observed there. Human beings commit crimes against one another, far worse than murder, but there are no discoverable motives or practical aims to render their deeds intelligible. There is the undeniable fact of terror, but no plausible explanation adequate to its occurrence and magnitude.

What is the fate worse than murder to which the victims of totalitarianism were subjected? It is the systematic deprivation of their juridical, moral and existential identity. The process of total domination progressively strips its victims of every dimension of their personal dignity until they are left naked, like animals, with nothing more than their sheer numerical individuality to distinguish them from one another.[12] The initial assault was on the legal or juridical standing of the human person. Insofar as human beings are citizens, members of an established political body, they enjoy certain legal rights and protections. Through the device of denationalization, however, human beings may be stripped of their citizenship and placed beyond the pale of enforceable law. By placing the concentration camps outside the normal penal system that connects punishment directly to crime, the totalitarian rulers expose their victims to an arbitrary and relentless violence against which they have no recourse or appeal. Since the residents of the camps have committed no statutory offense, there is no longer a discernible connection between imprisonment and crime, between punishment and legally established guilt. Yet, deprived of citizenship and the enforceable legal rights it guarantees, to whom can they appeal to secure the natural rights that ostensibly belong to them as human? The first lesson driven home to Europe's stateless persons during the nineteen-thirties and forties was that the deprivation of citizenship effectively deprived them of enforceable rights of every kind. To be stateless essentially meant to be rightless; to lose one's political and legal identity meant complete vulnerability to arbitrary violence and torture.[13]

The loss of political identity and security immediately placed the moral dignity of the human being in jeopardy. Part of that dignity clearly resides in the freedom of the individual conscience to choose between good and evil. In the limit case, it means the capacity voluntarily to sacrifice one's life rather than to participate in wrongdoing. The efficacy of conscience implicitly presupposes that the moral agent has a meaningful choice between right and wrong, between noble and base, between just and unjust, however difficult it may be in particular cases to distinguish between them. This basic moral presupposition was undermined by the actual conditions in the extermination camps. When those in authority require a mother to choose between the death of her son or her daughter, when inmates are ordered to play the role of executioner with their fellow prisoners, then the decisions of conscience have become entirely equivocal. The moral agent is reduced to despair before such grotesque alternatives.

There remains, one might think, the possibility of heroic resistance against systematic terror. As long as one lived outside the iron grip of the camps, meaningful resistance remained conceivable.[14] But within the institutional structure of the camps themselves, this otherwise plausible assumption lost its validity. From Hannah Arendt's perspective, human resistance continues to be meaningful, even when it cannot succeed in preventing injustice, as long as there are witnesses who can testify to its occurrence.[15] But the deliberate purpose of the death factories was to render death anonymous, to deprive its victims of all hope for remembrance and to condemn the only living witnesses of their suffering to an identical fate. When it seems no longer to make a difference whether one lives or dies, human beings often go to their doom like sheep. After all forms of practical reflection, choice, and action have been rendered futile, little remains of the vaunted moral dignity of the person.[16]

The foundation of our existential dignity is the fact of human plurality. By plurality, Arendt means that each human being is unique, unexchangeable with any other, a singular person, a particular subject with a life story peculiarly his own. "Man's dignity demands that he is seen, every single one in his particularity, reflecting as such, but without any comparison and independent of time, mankind in general."[17] As animals, human beings are individual members of a finite biological species, but as distinctively human they are existential subjects capable of independent thought and spontaneous and unpredictable action. The confirmation of a person's unique identity occurs in his appearance before other persons, in the discourse they exchange and in the deeds they perform together. Since the solitary subject cannot actualize his singular identity alone, he requires the enabling presence of peers. He requires a common space of appearance where he can reveal himself to his equals and receive their recognition, acknowledgment and response. But Arendt concluded that the ultimate purpose of totalitarian rule was to destroy the uniqueness of the individual personality, to eliminate the conditions of human spontaneity and to reduce all human conduct to the level of conditioned behavior. "Total domination strives to organize the infinite plurality and differentiation of human beings as if all of humanity were just one individual."[18] By depriving the individual person of political and legal rights, by creating extreme conditions that subvert the autonomy of conscience, by confining human existence to the company of the dead and the dying, and by robbing human beings of every meaningful opportunity to exercise their freedom and uniqueness, it is possible to diminish the reality of the person until the most striking difference still apparent among the victims of terror was the fact of their distinct bodily forms. By the time they were finally murdered, the victims of the death camps had often come to resemble the naked and impotent animals their executioners had asserted they were.[19]

Totalitarian rule carries to its limit a systematic process of human deprivation. By depriving human beings of the goods and rights essential to their humanity, it indirectly reveals what the full actualization of human dignity requires. Radical evil is deeply instructive because it forces us to acknowledge realities that we normally take for granted. It is a profound reminder of how much human beings lose when they are denied a private place of their own in the world and a public realm where their political, moral and existential identity is confirmed. Totalitarianism deprived its victims of two essential conditions human beings need in order to be at home on the earth. First, it took away their private homes, their personal places of refuge and shelter; then, it withdrew their citizenship, their legal standing, their right to governmental protection and due process, their exercise of civic and political liberty. The fundamental importance of having a secure legal and political identity was never more evident than at the very moment it was deliberately destroyed. "We became aware of the existence of a right to have rights, to live under a framework where one is judged by one's actions and opinions, and a right to belong to some kind of organized community, only when millions of people emerged who had lost and could not regain these rights."[20]

What is the responsibility of a reflective human being faced with an historical reality of this magnitude? Hannah Arendt believed that human thought and speech would lose their integrity if they refused to come to terms with what had happened. She could not return to the familiar life of the mind until she understood how totalitarianism in Europe had been possible. The only way survivors of the holocaust could bear these limitless sorrows was to put them into an intelligible story that disclosed their deeper meaning and significance.[21] Such was the existential intention of *The Origins of Totalitarianism*. This extraordinary text, published six years after the war's conclusion, was not intended as a work of historical scholarship. It is, rather, a deeply reflective personal account of the century of European decline that climaxed in the occurrence of totalitarianism. It is a story constructed with the aid of a single controlling image, that of radical dissolution and subsequent crystallization. This heuristic image provides the framework for the central question to which the book provides a partial answer. What were the hidden dynamics that dissolved the institutional and moral structures of European civilization, thereby releasing the fragmentary elements later to crystallize in Nazism and Stalinism? *The Origins of Totalitarianism* is a many-leveled story, drawing on history, literature, philosophy and political theory, but refusing to stay within the limits of any scholarly discipline. It is the work of a thoughtful and compassionate humanist, profoundly sensitive to an unprecedented assault on human dignity and driven to political reflection by events so grave that they shattered the moral horizon within which we normally think and act. "The worst had lost all of their fear and the best had lost hope of ultimate judgment and grace."[22]

THE BURDEN OF OUR TIME[23]

Hannah Arendt was born in Königsberg, Prussia in 1906. She spent her youth in Weimar Germany, a land scarred by the Great War and its aftermath of revolution and persistent economic and political instability. She was a brilliant student, blessed with the gift of an exceptional education, and marked from the very beginning of her life by the sense of being an outsider.[24] Over time she acquired familiarity with and command of the greatest texts of Western thought, but she remained fiercely independent of their authors. Her deepest intellectual roots lay in the German poetic and philosophical tradition, the tradition of Goethe, Heine, Lessing, Rilke, Kant and Nietzsche. During her extended university career, she studied with some of the most important German thinkers of this century, Edmund Husserl, Martin Heidegger and Karl Jaspers. She received from them a rare sensitivity to the revelatory power of language and a philosophical style based on the description and conceptualization of the structures of appearance.[25] Her earliest theoretical interests, that were theological rather than political, are reflected in her doctoral dissertation completed under Jaspers on St. Augustine's understanding of love.[26]

A secular Jew, sensitive since childhood to the cruelty of anti-Semitism, she emigrated from Germany in 1933 after Hitler's ascent to political power. This disruptive emigration began an eighteen-year period of continuous statelessness; she knew from immediate experience the plight of the displaced person seeking refuge and protection in an alien land. After leaving

Germany, she lived and worked in Paris until 1940. These were the depression years and Jewish refugees were often unwelcome in France. Native French unemployment had already become a sensitive domestic issue, and the large numbers of Jews fleeing to France from the East complicated an already difficult economic and political situation. During her years of exile in France, Hannah Arendt deliberately refrained from traditional philosophical activity. Apparently, the academic practice of philosophy seemed indecent to her while darkness descended steadily over Europe. When Paris capitulated to Hitler's armies in the spring of 1940, she was sent with other Jewish refugees to a detention camp in southern France. In the interval of uncertainty between the collapse of the French army and the consolidation of the Vichy government, she left the detention camp and was able to reunite with her husband Heinrich Blücher. Together with Hannah Arendt's mother, Martha, the Blüchers fled from Europe in 1941 to seek exile in the United States.[27]

During the remaining years of the war she worked in New York for various Jewish relief organizations. When the war ended, she attempted to understand how the civilized Europe into which she was born had been effectively destroyed. She came to believe that the collapse of European civilization had its origins in the nineteenth century, that the process of disintegration was accelerated by the slaughter of the World War I, and that the final dissolution occurred during the dark decades between the two wars. On her account, the moral, political, and social order of Europe had already crumbled before the death camps began their terrible work. Those who had survived that historic collapse now lived in a city in ruins. No inherited form of human security could still be relied upon uncritically. The structure of the political universe, the integrity of the moral order, the shared spiritual and cultural convictions that allow human beings to live together in peace, each of these human foundations had to be reconstructed anew.

There could be no return to the past, nor advance into the future, until the people of the West confronted the abyss that had opened in their midst. Hannah Arendt never abandoned these unsettling convictions, rooted in the experience of profound sorrow and loss. They explain the constant foundational character of her political thought. She deeply believed that western civilization had been uprooted in the twentieth century and that the institutional structures left standing by the cataclysm had been secretly damaged when the whole world had shaken to its depths.

Aristotle's maxim that the beginning is more than half of the whole is profoundly true in the case of Hannah Arendt. For her, the life of the mind resumed in earnest after the war, but her thought remained focused on the dark times that had preceded it. Although she did her most important intellectual work in America, she was at heart a European permanently marked by her experience in Europe between the wars. When she wrote of *Men in Dark*

Times it was to the darkness of twentieth century Europe that she chiefly referred.[28] It was in Europe that her intelligence and sensibility were formed and her memory stocked with lasting literary and historical allusions. She believed, with Augustine, that the seat of the mind is in memory, and though her most important thoughts and judgments were framed on the western shore of the Atlantic, they were essentially directed to European events. It is important for an American reader of her work to remember this fact, because many insights and convictions that seemed evident to her on the strength of personal experience are only accessible through argument or inference by those whom history has treated less harshly.

Arendt once wrote of Machiavelli that he "represented the culture that is born of humanism, becoming aware of political problems because they are at a crisis."[29] There is ample evidence that she understood her eventual absorption with politics in similar terms. She was by nature and education a humanist, not a political philosopher. But personal experience and sustained historical reflection convinced her that the most urgent crisis of the modern world is political.[30] Since no one can flee from a crisis and retain self-respect, she taught herself to look at human affairs from a distinctively political perspective. In adopting this standpoint, she considered herself an outsider, for she was primarily a thinker and teacher rather than a political agent. Perhaps she benefitted from the intellectual distance the outsider enjoys, for she discovered a dignity and importance in political life that nearly all her contemporaries failed to discern.

Although she never absolutized the political perspective, never forgot that it is but one legitimate standpoint among many, she chose to think and write from it exclusively until almost the end of her life.[31] This fact helps to account for both the originality and the consistency of her thought. As a critical humanist, she focused her attention on human existence and the human condition, but as a political humanist she approached her subject from an unfamiliar direction. Hers was not the theological perspective that viewed the human being as a child of God; nor the naturalistic perspective that conceived of humans as a higher species of biological animal; nor the traditional philosophic perspective that emphasized their intellectual and cognitive capacities. She never denied the partial validity of these alternative standpoints, but she seemed to believe that they could not provide the transforming insight and guidance that our century most required. The City, the classical symbol of political existence, was in ruins; it was the dignity of the human being as citizen of the city that must first be retrieved and reclaimed.

With her emphasis on human beings as citizens, Hannah Arendt took deliberate exception to both bourgeois and romantic individualism, the dominant nineteenth-century images of the human person. Considered historically, Romanticism was a revolt against bourgeois society, opposing the integrity of the heart and the interior life to the personal corruption engendered by economic and social ambition.[32] Because the romantic individualist saw the public realm under the aspect of competitive social struggle, he believed that public life inherently threatened the integrity of human existence. This controlling belief drove him to seek authenticity in the region of the heart apart from the corrupting presence and influence of others. Romanticism identified the authentic self with this inward realm of personality shielded from public light and attention and segregated from the turmoil of political action. To be truly human, a person must refrain from competition with his peers, either enjoying immediate communion with nature or absorbed in heroic interior struggle. The romantics saw correctly the threat bourgeois society posed to genuine intimacy, but they were unable to conceive of a credible politics founded on active and responsible citizenship. The Romantic conception of human existence opposed the spirit of compassion and wonder to the spirit of acquisitiveness. It rejected the naturalistic reduction of humans to selfish calculating animals driven by material desires and the urge for conspicuous display. Its portrait of the authentic life emphasized generosity against selfishness, the riches of hidden feeling versus the emblems of visible wealth, and deliberately chosen solitude against the quest for social recognition. Despite its relentless critique of bourgeois existence, romanticism shared the bourgeois prejudice that political life is an acquisitive struggle for scarce resources and that genuine human fulfillment is properly a private affair.

Some form of Marxism or socialism has been the expected rejoinder to these opposing strains of nineteenth century individualism. Marxism celebrates socialized humanity and the solidarity of the human species against the acquisitive bourgeois and the ineffectual romantic. It accepts the bourgeois emphasis on productive labor, while envisaging a socialized economy based on cooperation rather than competition. It endorses the romantic commitment to human compassion, but insists that it be institutionalized in a utopian economic and political order to be practically effective. Ostensibly, Marxism is committed to the dignity of political life. It conceives of history as a group or class struggle that will eventually culminate in the elimination of classes and the attainment of universal solidarity. But the Marxists are closer to the bourgeois vision of public life than they often acknowledge. Both Marxists and classical liberals agree that the public realm is dominated by the struggle for economic power; they disagree in their account of the primary agents in the struggle and in their views of its eventual resolution. Marxists oppose social classes to private individuals, the anarchy of the market to the benign effects of the invisible hand, and the radical end of history to unlimited progress through unregulated economic competition. When the focus of attention is restricted to economic contrasts, these familiar differences appear fundamental. But from the perspective of a genuinely autonomous politics not subordinated to economic imperatives, the similarity between these fierce modern rivals is far more striking. They share a common vision of the human being as an economic animal, preoccupied with life and the goods that sustain it, and concerned with public affairs only as they serve the economic interests of the individual, the class, or the species. Even under the most desirable conditions, they believe that politics exists to serve economic ends; that the city and the citizen have no independent dignity or purpose of their own. To use the idiom of Hannah Arendt, in both classical liberalism and Marxism, the human laborer, the *animal laborans*, has assumed complete priority over the human citizen, the *zoon politikon*.[33]

According to Hannah Arendt, none of the dominant modern theories of human existence provide an adequate conception of politics and citizenship. Their systemic failure forces the serious theorist to revisit the pre-modern traditions in which *praxis* and *lexis*, distinctively political capacities, are recognized as the specifically human *ergon* or function.[34] Hannah Arendt's absorption with Greek and Roman political thinking was not based on nostalgia for the remote past.[35] She turned to the Greeks because they had founded the original cities in which the recognition of human dignity and liberty was inseparable from one's actual political standing. We can learn therefore from ancient practice what modern theory can no longer teach us, namely, what it once meant to call human beings political animals. Arendt's selective appropriation of ancient political culture should be seen for what it was, the conscious effort by a political humanist to recover the original meaning of political language whose revelatory power had been lost in the modern age.

For the ancient Greeks, what did it mean to say that politics is the specifically human activity? It presupposed an ontological placement of humanity between the gods and the brutes. When human beings engage in productive labor, in the activities required for the maintenance of life, they are comparable to animals in their biological needs and concerns; when they withdraw from the exigencies of public affairs in order to contemplate the truth in solitude, they become similar to gods. It is only when they participate with their fellow citizens in political life, in the reciprocal exchange of words and deeds that they exist and act purely as men. Political existence is the properly human form of life to which neither the beasts nor the gods have access.[36] To say that man is a political animal is to claim that only in the life of the *polis*, in the company of his civic peers, in the revelation of his personal uniqueness and excellence before others, does a man attain to properly human stature. Our biological or species identity is given to us at birth, but only in the active life of the *polis*, the *bios politikos*, do we become distinctively human. Three interdependent strands of thought are united in this classical matrix which modern anthropology seems unable to combine: an emphasis on the unique individual person, the singular citizen, the irreplaceable *who*; the dependence of a significant and actualized personal identity on the constitutive presence of a plurality of peers; the acknowledgement of a properly public activity, action or speech, in which each person may aspire to excellence through cooperative interaction with political equals. In authentic political experience, the dignity of the individual person is sensibly manifest, publicly recognized and legally protected. With the loss of an independent political realm, human beings lose the clearest visible evidence and the most secure collective guarantee of their singular worth and potential.

This brief schematic contrast of Greek political culture with modern anthropology is not intended as a solution to the contemporary political crisis. Its purpose is rather to show how obscure and opaque traditional political language has become for our contemporaries.[37] Our operative notions of politics have lost contact with their linguistic and experiential roots to such a degree that the essential connection between human dignity and meaningful political participation is no longer evident.[38] Thus, we are inevitably sceptical or perplexed when told that the primary threat to human existence in our time is political.

The concept of a political crisis raises problems of a different kind. The danger here is one of overreliance on an important evaluative category. A useful word intended to mark a significant division in historical time or the turning point in a threatening illness, a time in which institutional or individual life is at stake, is now regularly used whenever human beings find themselves in a jam, no matter how temporary. Overuse of the word 'crisis' has cost the term its intended gravity. This semantic change is unfortunate because we still need a common expression to designate those periods in history when inherited forms of order have lost their authority, when "the past has ceased to cast its light on the future and the mind of man wanders in obscurity."[39] Tocqueville's image of historical discontinuity is helpful because it recognizes how sharply time is divided when a source of light on which human beings have depended suddenly goes out. It seems that we only discover our reliance on the light shed by the past when it no longer shines. Since it is not light that we perceive but the world light makes visible, we become most aware of light's presence by its unexpected withdrawal.

Hannah Arendt uses a discursive rather than a visual metaphor to express this condition of deep, unanticipated perplexity. In a crisis we lose confidence in the answers on which we ordinarily rely without ever having realized they were originally answers to questions.[40] The occurrence of crisis should drive thought back to the questions themselves and to the experiences that first elicited them. The initial perception of loss may be converted to gain, for crises have the power to obliterate complacency and bias. By depriving us of unexamined certainties, they can pry us open to whatever fresh experience has disclosed of the matter at hand. For Hannah Arendt, the political crisis of the twentieth century calls us to rethink, without the prejudices or assumptions of tradition, the basic problems of human living together.[41]

More than the fact of political crisis, Arendt's greatest fear was our unreadiness to face it with courage and honesty. As though the horrors of global war, systematic terror, and cultural and institutional collapse were not sufficient cause for sorrow, they had occurred in a culture unwilling or unable to think about them. After the war, what human beings required was the healing reconciliation with existence that only authentic understanding can bring.[42] What they received, instead, were counterfeit substitutes for thought: ideologies, claiming to unravel the tangle of history, although they had lost touch with real events and the nature of historical time, common sense explanations for what clearly outraged common sense, and appeals to tradition when the authority of tradition itself had been cast into question. Perhaps there was no deeper sign of our theoretical and practical burden than our shared incapacity to bear it like adults.

THE SOURCES OF OUR POLITICAL CRISIS

Arendt often drew a sharp distinction between theoretical and political crises. In the seventeenth century, the new science of nature created profound difficulties for philosophy because it challenged the traditional concepts of knowledge and truth. Yet in its immediate impact modern physics directly affected only those who had made the practice of inquiry the effective center of their lives. A political crisis, by contrast, affects us all, because it results from a breakdown in our established forms of living and acting together. Although the continuing crisis of our time has an important connection with the advent of modern science, it is primarily political, rather than scientific, in character. What disintegrated after World War I was not our traditional cosmology, but the cultural, political and social fabric of Europe.[43] Given Europe's central place in the history of the West, this fact by itself was sufficiently grave.

But Arendt believed that something still more fundamental was at stake. Even those countries spared the totalitarian experience were threatened by the moral and intellectual decay that had preceded it. Intellectually and culturally, though not institutionally, America and England were in a similar situation to that of eastern and central Europe. If this controversial claim is true, it is because the crisis to which Arendt referred existed at many different levels. At the most immediate level, the political and social orders deriving from the French revolution had lost their incorporative power. Politically speaking, this meant a decline in the legitimacy of the nation-state; socially, it meant the transformation of an industrial class system into mass-society.[44] According to Arendt, it was the conjunction of these two related events that made totalitarian mass movements possible. A second level of disorder, its moral and spiritual dimension, corresponds to the modern rejection of what Arendt calls the *Roman Trinity*: religion, tradition and authority.[45] These interdependent foundations of a stable political realm go back to the origins of the Roman republic. As long as they were culturally and institutionally secure, western political and moral life was assured of essential continuity. However, Hannah Arendt believed that all western countries, no matter how stable their political institutions may appear, have lost the security that the Roman Trinity had historically provided. In this respect, both shores of the Atlantic now share a common fate and a common state of danger.

Increasing economic instability revealed the fragility of the class structure supporting the modern nation-state. The quest for new reliable foundations disclosed the inadequacy of our inherited political categories and principles. The combination of these two events points to a third and distinct source of political crisis. We are unprepared theoretically to address and resolve the fundamental questions of politics. When we turn for help to "our tradition of political thought," we find it lacking in the foundational resources we need.[46] Neither the conservative desire to restore our political tradition, nor the modern eagerness to abandon it, strikes Arendt as the correct response to our plight. We must learn instead, to think our way forward against the tradition, to question its categories, assumptions and paradigms, if we are to recover a genuine sense of political experience and language and a critical appreciation of the merits and limitations of political life.

There is an historical progression linking these different sources of political crisis. The theoretical failure can be traced back to the origin of political philosophy in the Socratic Platonic dialogues. The weakening of the Roman Trinity began at the onset of modernity with the historic convergence of the Protestant Reformation and the Copernican revolution. The decisive events that made Europe politically and socially vulnerable to totalitarianism were preceded by a century of institutional decline. There is no single causal chain linking these different levels of crisis to specific historical events. It is simply not true that the nation-state declined because the Roman Trinity lost its stabilizing power, or because philosophers have traditionally held the practice of politics in low esteem. Arendt did not believe there were strict causal chains in human history as there are in the natural order. Significant historical events become intelligible when we place them in the proper narrative context, but the memorable incidents in that story are not the causes of those events in any nomological sense.[47] The metaphor of critical sources of decline does not imply a sequential pattern of causal dependence; rather it points to distinct strata of intelligibility that must be understood in conjunction before we can comprehend where we are and have been politically speaking.

The *Origins of Totalitarianism and Men in Dark Times* contain Hannah Arendt's most detailed account of our present political disorder. Taken together these books present a dramatic and powerful story of institutional decline: the weakening of the nation-state, the collapse of the nineteenth-century class system, and the destruction of the European international order. Her story is told with the help of three contrasting intellectual constructs. Each of these constructs represents a dominant political mentality, a representative way of thinking and acting characteristic of a particular historical period and culture.[48] These representative characters are modeled on Plato's famous political typology from books eight and nine of the *Republic*.[49] Following Plato's example, Arendt introduces them within a narrative of precipitous political decline. Following Hegel's controversial practice in the *Phenomenology of Spirit*, Arendt identifies each of these representative characters with the governing mentality of a particular epoch in European history.

Hannah Arendt's explanatory narrative begins with the revolutionary spirit of the eighteenth century. In its civic republican form, this was the spirit of the patriotic citizen, the independent individual drawn from the ranks of the people as a whole who accepted personal responsibility for the conduct of public affairs. The animating motive of the republican citizen was his strong love of country; he enjoyed genuine solidarity with the people of his nation and a broader solidarity with those contemporaries who shared his concern for the world.[50] In Arendt's judgment, the French Revolution, originally inspired by civic republican ideals, ended in disaster because it failed to found its new political order on the principles of authentic citizenship. The clash of competing class interests shattered the solidarity of the French people and fractured the community of citizens into antagonistic social groups. The French nation-state emerged intact from the wreck of the revolution, though it was no longer based on the ideal of a united political community. The competitive struggle between the nobility, the bourgeoisie and the urban proletariat prevented the mutual cooperation among citizens that the republican ideal required.[51]

Divided by severe class conflict, the nineteenth-century nation-state faced a continual problem of political unity. It attempted to solve this problem by basing political and legal rights on the possession of a homogenous national identity that transcended differences in social class. The nation state was unified insofar as its citizens shared a common language, territory and ethnic history. This unity became apparent in moments of inter-national conflict, when the struggle between rival nations overrode their internal divisions. But the *union sacré* created by foreign threats to territory or security was always precarious. Powerful class divisions simultaneously separated the citizen-soldiers united in combat against a common national enemy. In periods of national emergency, one spoke and acted as a patriotic citizen, but at all other times as a member of one's limited class or party.[52]

The political institutions of the nation-state reflected this pervasive polarity. In those European countries that enjoyed representative government, politics was organized around the party system. The different parties were not formed to represent the comprehensive national good but the class interests of their particular constituents. In their parliamentary activities and policies, they conducted themselves in an openly partisan manner; thus the deeply entwined class and party system prevented the formation of an active citizenry prepared to act responsibility for the people as a whole. It was an axiom of European class politics that neither individual citizens nor the party to which they belonged was responsible for the national interest. National responsibility was assigned exclusively to the executive organs of the state that were expected to transcend the partisanship of classes and parties and to represent the nation as a whole.[53] The state was the only symbol of collective unity in a political context where partial and limited interests were dominant. In the nineteenth century, the state's greatest achievement, the equal extension of national law to all of its citizens, reflected this narrowly universal intent.

Hannah Arendt contended that the fate of the European nation-state and of the international comity of nations was directly connected with the history of the Jews. In the midst of a divided class society, the Jews represented a trans-national body of persons whose primary loyalties were European rather than national. The Jews did not constitute a distinct social class, nor did they have an organized political party to represent them. Their political power and influence depended entirely on the financial support they provided to the different national governments and from their ability to guarantee direct lines of communication across national boundaries. The Jews were the quintessential good Europeans, who symbolized a common European interest that neither national rivalry nor partisan struggle had completely destroyed. As long as national governments remained strong and independent of particular class interests, and as long as nationalist loyalties did not preclude an active sense of European identity, the political position of the Jews was relatively secure. However, both of these important conditions ceased to obtain during the final quarter of the nineteenth century. In Arendt's judgment, the primary factor accounting for their removal was the rise of European imperialism.[54]

Because Arendt's analysis of the dynamics of imperialism is exceptionally complicated, we will limit ourselves here to a brief outline of her argument. During much of the nineteenth century the bourgeoisie had been indifferent to the financial projects of the various European state governments. They had been content to leave the Jews in the influential position of inter-European bankers. But a surplus of capital resources and a lack of attractive European investment opportunities increasingly tempted European capital into the remote continents of Asia and Africa. From a purely economic standpoint, the expansion of private business interests into foreign lands was attractive. It promised unparalleled rates of profit and new opportunities for the employment of European nationals without work; as Arendt ironically remarks, the enterprise of imperialism provided an ostensible refuge for superfluous men and superfluous money.[55] But bourgeois indifference to state governments and their financial activities abruptly halted with these major new commitments of capital abroad. Those who had invested heavily in foreign enterprises had a clear interest in protecting their financial investments. They therefore demanded that the nation-state provide financial and military security for their speculative holdings. They claimed that their own economic interests and the larger interests of the nation as a whole had become identical. On Arendt's critical analysis, the capitalist bourgeoisie succeeded in convincing the state administration that the economic interests of a particular class now coincided with the national good. As the bourgeoisie became increasingly engaged in imperial politics, they preempted the traditional banking functions of the Jews. This realignment was critical because it meant that an inter-European source of state finance had been replaced by a narrowly class-bound and nationalist source. By this route, the competitive spirit of nineteenth century capitalism was directly injected into the European state system.[56]

If the public spirit of the independent citizen represents the political ideal of eighteenth century republicanism, then the political stance of the capitalist bourgeoisie represents the outlook of nineteenth century liberalism. In her compelling account of European political decline, Hannah Arendt regularly opposes these two contrasting character types: the republican citizen whose love of country and concern for the world transcend self-interest; and the bourgeois capitalist prepared to sacrifice both country and world in the pursuit of private advantage. The opposition between these two political mentalities is fundamental. The citizen steadfastly refuses to allow private interest to interfere with public duty, the bourgeois capitalist demands that public institutions serve private interests and needs. Hannah Arendt portrays the emergence of European imperialism in the last quarter of the nineteenth century as an unqualified victory for the spirit of bourgeois capitalism.

Arendt's sustained critique of economic liberalism is partly based on its alliance with imperialism and on her conviction that imperialism severely damaged the foundations of the nation-state. The political legitimacy of the nation had rested on two basic principles: the right of a people with a common culture and language to their own political institutions, the equal application of law within a national state to all its citizens. The imperialist adventure required the nation-state to violate both of its legitimating principles, for it denied political autonomy and the impartiality of law to the territories it conquered and subjugated. The spirit of European nationalism as it penetrated the continents of Africa and Asia was quickly transformed into racism. Only the appeal to European racial superiority could explain why principles

that were valid for Europeans were invalid for the peopl
From the beginning of the imperialist project, the colon
European states were inconsistent with their own source
macy.⁵⁷

New methods of administration had to be devised
nized peoples since they were not to be governed like the citiz
home country. As the indigenous peoples of Asia and Africa did not want the Europeans on their land, their resistance had to be suppressed by military force. The dominant role of the army in the colonial territories helps to explain the emergence of an imperial bureaucracy as an explicit substitute for national government. According to Arendt, the modern reliance on bureaucracy as a method of political administration has its origin in military practice. In place of a political relationship between equal citizens, who are expected to observe the rule of law in their common transactions and to give each another a respectful account of their conduct, it substitutes rule by decree and secret administration. The colonial governors are no longer accountable to the colonized people they govern, nor are they constrained in their actions by a stable framework of law. A political chasm opens up between the unaccountable few who are licensed to command and the subjugated many who are required by force to obey their dictates and decrees. During the imperial era, a constant tension existed between the national governments in Europe and the bureaucratic administrators appointed to rule in the conquered territories. The former were accustomed to the constraints of constitutional government and the rule of law, the latter to the secretive habits of despotism and tyranny. There was, however, this important asymmetry between the two cases. The extension to the colonies of constitutional law and conduct would have meant the effective end of imperialism, while applying the methods of colonial bureaucracy to the home country would have abolished its political liberty.

Imperialism inserted the capitalist economic principles of relentless expansion and competition into an international political system already weakened by national rivalries and partisan conflict. The imperial ideal of unlimited empire violated the important territorial boundaries of the nation and it threatened the stability of national law. Imperial governance, as we have remarked, was inconsistent with the nationalist principle of a limited homogenous population sharing legal and political equality. The competitive spirit of capitalism was equally damaging to the international relations among European states. They now became engaged in an unlimited struggle for wealth and territory outside of Europe. During the nineteenth century this imperial rivalry did not destroy their willingness to compromise national differences, however intense. The inter-European spirit, although clearly weakened by imperial competition had not yet been extinguished. The terrible slaughter of the First World War shattered the remaining bonds of ropean unity. In fact, the Great War seemed to set in motion a chain reaction of catastrophes from which Europe has not fully recovered.[58] At the war's end, the victors largely redrew the political map of Europe to satisfy the principle of national independence, but the immediate instability of the ensuing peace pointed to the inherent limits in the nationalist principle. In the early nineteen twenties, uncontrolled inflation devastated a whole class of small property owners in Germany; in the thirties, the disaster of global depression struck and the European states appeared unable to control the resulting economic and social disarray. During both decades, revolutionary unrest and civil war caused the constant migration of unwelcome refugees across national boundaries. The cumulative result of these disruptive events was politically and spiritually devastating. "Homelessness on an unprecedented scale, rootlessness to an unprecedented depth."[59]

During the nineteenth century the stability of the nation-state had coincided with that of the European class system. Social classes were still able to unite private individuals on the basis of their common economic interests. This bond of mutual interest and activity could survive because the individual members of the class still shared a limited concern for the common world.[60] But partisan and competitive national politics organized around narrow class interests was singularly unsuited to the requirements of Europe after the war. During the nineteen twenties and thirties, the European class system broke down under the weight of growing masses of people who had become declassed and uprooted by economic and political events outside their control. As the traditional classes and parties declined and as the state proved increasingly ineffective in dealing with the mounting problems, hatred and cynicism began to play a central role in public affairs. In Europe during the depression, there emerged a common anxiety that a major catastrophe was coming, but the existing political powers seemed unable to prevent it. The mounting unease was heightened by a failure of political will in both economic and foreign policy. The shared perception of governmental impotence heightened contempt for representative institutions; the party system, parliamentary democracy, the national state itself lost the trust and support of the people. The severe decline in public authority coincided with the rise of mass movements that openly claimed to stand above the party, the state and the law. The mass appeal of extra-legal solutions was based on the widespread conviction that they could master the political and economic crises, as Europe's democratic institutions could not. This proved, of course, to be a counsel of despair for it permitted an unprecedented criminality to invade the political realm almost without popular challenge. The earliest victims of political criminality were the European Jews who had symbolized the authority of the state and the spirit of international cooperation that were now in full retreat. It was this functional and symbolic connection between the Jews and the declining European state system that partly explains why they became the chosen political targets of the new mass movements. In attacking the Jews, popular demagogues were activating a more complex and deep-rooted pattern of hatred and contempt. According to Arendt, it was neither eternal Anti-Semitism nor mere historical contingency that explains why European Jewry and the structure of the European nation-state rose and fell together.[61]

Under the intensifying pressure of war, inflation, mass unemployment and forced emigration, the social and political stratification of the nation-state collapsed. This meant the end of a social and economic structure based on stable and clearly defined classes.[62] Since the effectiveness of the traditional party system depended on class stability, the rapid erosion of that stability left the political realm in chaos. The process of social atomization, which first began when belonging to a class replaced independent republican citizenship in the nation, dramatically intensified. From Arendt's civic republican perspective, independent citizens are properly united to one another by their shared love of country and by their mutual concern for the world. The members of a particular social class, by contrast, are joined by the much weaker bond of overlapping economic interests. To the degree that these interests are still grounded in objective reality, they continue to preserve a limited portion of the world as a tenuous connection among individual citizens. Though a politics based on competing class interests is no substitute for the free interaction of republican citizens, it does take account of the limited worldly realities to which the different classes remain sensitive. Though the world of class politics is a severely truncated world, it still retains a foundation in empirically confirmable fact. But this can no longer be said of the mass society that emerges from the breakdown of the class system or of the mass movements that supplanted the traditional political parties. "The masses grew out of the fragments of a highly atomized society whose competitive structure and concomitant loneliness had been held in check only through membership in a class."[63]

When the economic and political structures in Europe lost their integrity between the wars, the classes cracked open releasing their members into a threatening social void. It was out of these declassed human beings that the new social mass was created. According to Arendt, human beings constitute a mass society when they no longer have their membership in the common world to draw them together and keep them apart. If the active independent citizen is the political ideal of civic republicanism and the self-interested bourgeois capitalist the prototype of nineteenth century liberalism, then the socially and politically atomized individual is the breeding ground of the twentieth century's mass movements. The chief characteristic of mass man, Arendt's third political character type, is his political isolation and social loneliness, his lack of the normal interpersonal relations that are mediated through participation in a public world.[64] Republican citizens are reciprocally connected through their cooperative membership in the same body politic; the members of a social class are united through their mutual economic interests and concerns; the isolated individuals who coexist in a mass society are the victims of radical worldlessness. In their worldless condition, they symbolize the frailty of human interconnection that economic disaster, political impotence and spiritual decline can effectively destroy.[65]

The mentality of mass society reflects the historical conditions that brought it into being. It emerges from the collapse of the European class system and the increasing impotence of partisan politics based on class rivalry. Its individual members are united not by their love of world or country but by their hatred of the status quo.[66] Dislocated and frightened by historical forces beyond their control, they see themselves as superfluous beings whose lives are deprived of personal meaning and importance. While their counterparts in a traditional social class are still moved by appeals to self-interest and personal gain, they no longer experience the public world as open to their individual desires and intentions. Excluded from a meaningful relation to the world and their fellow citizens, they become strangely selfless, believing that history has made them individually expendable. This growing loss of interest in their own wellbeing is not an expression of civic or moral generosity, but a psychological escape from the intolerable burden of personal and public responsibility.[67]

It is very important to distinguish the sociological concept of an aggregative mass from the republican notion of a politically unified people. The mass is that portion of the people who "because of sheer numbers and indifference or a combination of both cannot be integrated into any political organization based on common interest."[68] For Arendt, a unified people prepared for action in history is a free association of independent citizens with their own perceptions and judgments of the world to connect them together. Lonely individuals who feel abandoned by everything and everybody constitute the mass. Their loneliness should not be confused with physical isolation from other persons, because unlike voluntary solitude, it cannot be put to meaningful human use. The artist in the isolation of his studio, or the thinker in a room of her own, is not really lonely. They have withdrawn from the world voluntarily to do in private what they cannot do well in the presence of others. But they remain bound to the reality of the world through the works of art they create or through the memories and experiences that initiate their personal reflection. Loneliness, in contrast to solitude, is the experience of being abandoned or cut off when one stands in the presence of others; it is the limit position in the modern process of social alienation and atomization, a desperate way of being and feeling that is exceedingly hard to endure. "The deprivation of objective worldly relations to others and of the reality guaranteed through them has become the mass phenomenon of loneliness."[69]

Radical loneliness, the painful sense of exclusion from the work of the world and from the intercourse of human fellowship, helps to explain the broad appeal of twentieth-century mass movements. According to Arendt, these dangerous movements are the social and political substitutes for nineteenth-century classes and the political parties that were organized to represent them. They provide an artificial sense of belonging together to human beings made homeless and worldless by history.[70] Desperately oversimplified ideologies play the integrative role in these mass movements that the public and objective world plays in genuine politics. Ideologies substitute a logically consistent fantasy world for the intractable historical facts that the dispossessed find increasingly intolerable. On Arendt's distinctive use of the term, an ideology is the logical elaboration of a single explanatory idea, such as race or class.[71] An ideology systematically develops the implications of that idea through a process of strict logical inference, and then claims for these conceptually generated implications the central role in the explanation of history. Ideologies are desperate attempts to make history intelligible by means of a fixed idea, *an idée fixe*, alleged to possess universal explanatory import. They direct their seductive appeal to that growing number of lonely people who cannot accept the complex intelligibility of human existence. Since ideologies are logically constructed fictions, how can they be sustained against the challenge of verifiable fact? Hannah Arendt accounts for their unusual tenacity in two ways: the dislocated masses bear such resentment against the actual world that they refuse to accept its reality. Moreover, the fantasy world created by ideology has a linear logic and unyielding consistency that historical reality never possesses. When human beings are no longer capable of thinking authentically about reality, the logical rigor of a shared ideology serves as an appealing replacement.

Human beings have a permanent need to think, to make sense of their existence in one way or another.[72] If genuinely open, exploratory thinking proves too difficult or too painful, demagogic ideologies are now readily available as alternative sources of meaning and coherence. The second reason for their plausibility is an intellectual consequence of loneliness. In the world of the lonely, no one is reliable and nothing familiar can be safely relied upon. Deprived of communal relationships with other persons and things, relationships that confirm our shared sense of reality, the lonely individual is cut off from common sense and thrown back on himself and his fears. But the isolated self he encounters in private reflection no longer has confidence in reality as it appears to the senses. The lonely man is therefore confined within the circle of his growing suspicion; he does not trust himself as a reliable partner in the internal dialogue of thought, nor does he trust his perceptual experience as a way of understanding the world.[73] Without the collaborative agreements of common sense or the internal concurrence with oneself that reflective thinking provisionally achieves, logical reasoning remains his only secure intellectual resource. The competing ideologies of our time offer different explanatory premises for logical deduction to work with; thus, we have the idea of a master race, or a messianic class, or a redemptive technology, or a global Jewish or capitalist conspiracy. It is the desperation of loneliness that makes the ideological pattern compelling. A lonely man "always deduces one thing from the other and thinks everything for the worst."[74]

It was political and social homelessness that prepared disoriented human beings to join the mass movements of the twentieth century. It was their alienated loneliness, which had become an intolerable experience for the homeless masses that prepared them to submit to totalitarian domination. Organized loneliness, bound together by ideology and made possible by radical world alienation, is the greatest political danger of our time. The ancient Biblical warning from *Genesis* has retained its cautionary force. "It is not good that man should be alone."[75]

It may be objected that this radical breakdown in social and political order was confined to the European continent and that Hannah Arendt exaggerates when she insists on a general political crisis in the West. She readily acknowledged that England and North America had emerged from the war with their basic political institutions intact. But she held that the cultural and theoretical dimensions of the crisis applied to them with equal validity. These subtler aspects of the modern crisis, although more difficult to discern and articulate, have left all western nations politically vulnerable. They concern the deepest intellectual and moral foundations on which western political institutions and communities rest.

The republican citizens whose free association constitutes the life of the well-ordered city are mortal beings with a limited life span. Through their natality they enter a world that anteceded their birth and which is intended to survive their death. These human beings are partly children of nature, residents of the earth, biological creatures like the other terrestrial animals. But they also belong to human history, to the common world of the city, to a political vocation that summons them to transcend their animality and to become fully human. This second dimension of their existence depends, of course, upon the vitality and strength of the first. Human beings must satisfy the requirements of life before they can begin to live well. The ancient Greeks originally founded the *polis* so that human mortals might do something great and memorable before they died. As Pericles described its purpose in his celebrated funeral oration, the *polis* was the site for enacting historical deeds and the commemorative center of their lasting remembrance. To mortal men haunted by the fear of futility, of leaving no trace of their brief stay on the earth, the *polis* was treasured as a protection against oblivion.[76] But to serve this commemorative function it must endure through historical time, providing a narrative bridge between the generations keeping the memory of the dead alive. In the critical eyes of their Roman conquerors, the splendor of Greek civic culture was sadly of short duration. Torn by incessant internal strife and weakened by protracted and devastating wars, the Hellenic cities lost their political independence to the Macedonian hegemony in the fourth century. Despite the undisputed political greatness of the Greeks, they failed to achieve the "miracle of permanence" they actively longed for.[77]

Arendt believes we must look to the Romans, our other great classical political ancestors, to discover how historical splendor can be combined with temporal stability. Despite numerous challenges, the public realm created by the Romans survived for more than seven hundred years. Even when the Empire eventually decayed, the Romans transmitted its founding principles to the Roman Catholic Church. Arendt calls these principles that have held together the great temporal and spiritual institutions of the West the "Roman Trinity."[78] All three principles bear Latin names; in this respect they differ from the majority of classical political terms whose linguistic origins are Greek. The three elements in the Roman Trinity are: religion, from *re-ligare*, to bind back; tradition, from *traducere*, to lead across; authority, from *auctor*, founder or father and *augere* to augment or increase. These principles find their common origin in the Roman experience of the sacredness of foundation. The Romans believed that the founding of their city was a sacred and unique event to which the rest of human history was inseparably bound. This founding experience was narrated in Virgil's great epic poem, the *Aeneid*. As the poem memorably reveals, Aeneas escaped from the ruins of Troy, bearing the gods of his household, in order to recreate his native city in the western Mediterranean. This poetic re-creation is meant to reverse the tragic fate of the Trojans at the conquering hands of the Greeks. Aeneas is the *auctor* or founder who establishes the new city to which all future Roman citizens will belong. His act of foundation provides the constant reference point for the Romans' subsequent political life. Unlike the classical Greeks, who considered the creating of cities and the establishing of colonies an important but frequent occurrence, the Romans treated their founding as an event without sequel.[79] The stated purpose of their political life was to augment the act of foundation by preserving and extending the power of the original city. The heroic military and political deeds that maintained and extended Roman rule had an explicitly religious significance, for they were consciously bound back to their great antecedents and ultimately to the experience of foundation itself. Roman tradition preserved the public memory of these deeds and transmitted their compelling story across the generations. To become a Roman citizen, to belong to this noble and heroic tradition, was to bear the gravity of the past on one's shoulders. Those who could carry its historical weight in their public lives enjoyed authority for they alone proved worthy of augmenting the original actions of the founder. The three elements in the Roman Trinity, therefore, constitute a unified political and cultural whole. All presently existing authority is bound back to the foundational act from which it springs and is carried forward by tradition that preserves the required continuity between the past and the future.[80]

The Roman Trinity could survive the demise of the Empire because its spiritual principles were ultimately embodied in the self-understanding of the Catholic Church.[81] Within the Roman Catholic conception of Christianity, Jesus of Nazareth assumed the role of the community's founder, the historical community of Christians took the place of the Roman Republic and the apostles and their successors became the Christian equivalents of leaders whose authority rested on unbroken connection with the founding events. The Christian tradition continues to carry forward all that is judged to be memorable in the community's past: the life, death, and resurrection of Jesus, the good news of the kingdom of God, the acts of the Apostles, the lives of the saints, and the doctrinal teaching and practice of the Church. The stabilizing power of these originally Roman principles and cultural practices should be evident, for the Catholic Church, founded by a Palestinian Jew and periodically persecuted by Rome and its imperial successors, has achieved an unparalleled institutional permanence across the earth.

Within the framework of the Roman Trinity, the community's preservation of the memorable past is of primary importance. The present and the future retain their authentic meaning only if they preserve their vital connection to the founding events. The rituals and narratives of tradition transmit to successive generations the greatness of those original events, providing a perpetual model for posterity. The young members of the community learn from these stories how to become worthy of their common ancestors. Traditional stories also provide the foundation of the community's ethical practice; they teach what must be done and avoided if the authentic spirit of the beginning is to survive. Authority clearly rests with those who are older, closer to the ancestral origin, and united to that sacred beginning by rites of ordination and transmission. The spiritual and intellectual culture of the community has its deepest roots in memory, the faculty of depth, which insures the gravity of an otherwise weightless present. Were the community's leaders to be divorced from the past by a failure of memory, or separated from the origin by a break in the ancestral connection, then their claim to authority would lose its legitimating ground. Without religion and tradition to support it, the Roman model of authority cannot survive. As a political relationship, authority depends on the voluntary acceptance by those who obey of the institutional legitimacy of those who command. Whenever the Roman Trinity has sustained an enduring political community, a common religion and tradition have been its primary sources of legitimacy.[82]

A second source of the modern political crisis has been the erosion of authority, not only in politics, but in western religion and morality as well. The decline of ancestral authority was neither sudden nor unexpected; the central events in modern history have all been at variance with the Roman cultural mentality. We shall mention only the most significant moments in a cumulative process that took several centuries to complete:[83] the emancipation of secular power from ecclesiastical authority during the Italian Renaissance; the rupture of Christian unity in the Reformation with the concomitant decline in the Church's mediating role between human beings and God; the pathos of novelty that animated the scientific revolution whose leading interpreters revolted against tradition and what they saw as the dead weight of the inherited past; the radical critique of religious belief during the Enlightenment that deprived western culture of a common theological inheritance; the nineteenth-century break with classical humanism that carried the scientific revolt of the seventeenth century into the new human sciences; the industrial revolution that effaced the traditional distinction between the public and the private realms of human life; the political and economic upheavals of the twentieth century that left millions of homeless people displaced and uprooted. In the seventeenth century the West lost a securely anchored philosophical tradition as its guide to the past. In the eighteenth and nineteenth centuries we lost our common belief in the unifying dogmas of Christianity and in the metaphysical and theological foundations of the moral order. Although ethical and political conduct did not immediately decline as a result of these cultural changes, moral imperatives and obligations gradually deteriorated into unreflective habits that nobody quite understood but which the majority continued to obey because they remained familiar.[84] Social conformity became an almost sacred requirement of stability because compliance with the beliefs and behavior of the dominant culture was the only guarantee of moral security. Western political communities, now held together by the bonds of unexamined custom and habit, were no longer able to give a persuasive account of their moral and spiritual foundations. As the unsettling dynamics of modernity accelerated, increasing numbers of people ceased to feel at home politically; they no longer believed in the laws under which they lived, nor respected the authority of those entrusted with command. Long before the tragic events of the twentieth century took their remorseless toll, Europe had become politically fragile and morally unstable.[85]

It is a defining mark of modernity that it looks to the future rather than the past as its inspiration for action; and it grants intellectual authority not to poets, statesmen and priests, the representatives of an enduring tradition, but to scientists and engineers, those who claim to predict and control what is yet to occur. The cultural spirit of modernity is basically antithetical to the Roman Trinity. It is, therefore, not surprising that traditional authority gradually lost its meaning for modern men and women and an acceptable place in their institutional lives. According to Arendt, the political implications of this cultural loss are extremely grave. It is not clear that political communities can achieve the permanence and stability they require without some reliance on a principle of authority. But the perceived need for authority in the political realm is not sufficient to restore a cultural legacy that was lost over several centuries of change. As Hannah Arendt emphasized, genuine authority rests on a common legitimating tradition that establishes clear relations of command and obedience among the members of a community. But this shared tradition, in either its secular or religious form, is precisely what the acids of modernity have destroyed. So far we have no credible idea of what to put in its place. "We are confronted anew without the religious trust in a sacred beginning and without the protection of traditional and therefore self-evident standards of behavior with the elementary problem of human living together."[86]

With our economic and political institutions shaken by global depression and war and their moral foundations weakened by the modern spirit of suspicion and distrust, political thinking is driven back to its original ground. Historically, this has meant a return to the Greek thinkers and statesmen who formulated our basic categories of political discourse; theoretically, it has meant an attempt to recover through articulate reflection the underlying principles and norms of political activity. Arendt believed that political philosophy should seek to align our inherited categories and principles with the basic experiences and events they are intended to articulate. It should seek to reconstruct our shared understanding of political life from its origin in the concrete experiences of citizens and statesmen. The tacit presupposition of this reflective task is that political experience and theoretical understanding are in harmony, that the ideas conceived and expressed by the mind actually illumine the concrete patterns of experience to which they refer.

But what if this basic assumption is unwarranted and the concepts and principles we have inherited from Greek philosophy were in fact based on experiences drawn from outside the political realm? In that case, our common intellectual inheritance would handicap political reflection, and the genuinely political experiences would be left without adequate expression or recognition. If this critical conjecture were true, it would mean that "our tradition of political thought" is fundamentally flawed, and that, as a consequence, we now approach political reality ill prepared to understand and to judge it. Hannah Arendt's revisionary critique of the western tradition is based on just this contentious assertion. She repeatedly insisted that Plato created Western political philosophy on a fundamentally discordant note, and that the distorted beginning he bequeathed us has proven to be more than half of the whole.[87] In Arendt's counter narrative, Plato's depiction of the *polis* was dominated by the Athenian execution of Socrates and by his own political failures in Sicily. Responding to these grave disappointments, Plato concluded that ordinary political life was incompatible with philosophy and with the constitutive virtues of the true philosopher. He articulated this basic opposition in a memorable parable, the *Republican* myth of the cave, deliberately intended to reverse the classical understanding and appraisal of politics. Ever since the Ionian milkmaid first laughed at Thales for having his feet on the earth but his mind on the heavens, ordinary humans had chided philosophers for their eccentric withdrawal from the world of reality. Plato chose to answer this recurrent criticism by standing it completely on its head.

His vivid philosophical poetry depicted the political realm as a shadowy cave, an insubstantial world based on deceptive illusion. The shadows that appear to the residents of the cave are only a fleeting semblance of what is truly real. The unreflective citizens who dwell in this darkness are obsessed with flickering images about which they offer ungrounded and contradictory opinions. They struggle intensely for political honors and offices but the whole affair is, in truth, much ado about nothing. The bright, substantial world of true being, the realm of the invisible Platonic forms, lies entirely above the space of sensible appearances, above the illusions and unstable opinions that dominate the discourse of the cave. In contrast to the unreflective cave dwellers, the very few authentic philosophers gradually discover that neither being nor truth exists in the *polis*. They voluntarily withdraw from the city's shadowy darkness in order to ascend to the sunlit sky of ideas. There, beneath the light and warmth giving sun, the visible symbol of the Good, they are able to contemplate what is permanently and totally beautiful. Absorbed in their contemplative delight, they have no desire to return to the shadow land from which they escaped. But for the sake of the city and its desperate need for wisdom, they are compelled to abandon their philosophical home and to resume life among their confused fellow citizens. Their return to the cave is marked by severe disorientation, for the genuine philosopher, now filled with true knowledge of being, is again surrounded by opinionated cave dwellers for whom shadowy becoming is the only reality. These men are hostile to the truth with which the philosopher returns; they band together to kill him rather than accepting his insight and counsel. Even if the philosopher's reluctant sojourn in the cave does not end in death, he still perceives public life as an unwelcome burden, a necessary duty that keeps him from the true life of thought and contemplation.[88]

Four powerful objections to politics can be extracted from Plato's mythical criticism. The first is theological or transcendent. Even at its best, politics is entirely human, all too human. It circumscribes human consciousness within an ontological horizon whose dominant figure is the human being. But this horizon effectively conceals all that transcends human beings in dignity and beauty. To attain eternal rather than perishable beauty, humans must intellectually abandon the *polis* in which ordinary men but not gods are at home. Only in the company of authentic divinity can the spirit of the philosopher find rest. The second criticism is metaphysical. Human events and political affairs are constantly in flux. Individual citizens come into being and pass away; cities rise and fall; reputations are made and broken; nothing that is permanent and unchanging ever appears or endures. It is only outside the temporal flux of the political realm that true invariant being can be discovered. On one reading of Platonic metaphysics, all that is genuinely real is eternal and immutable, unaltered by time and mortality. If human beings are to share in this experience of eternity, they must detach themselves from the cares of the *polis* to pursue the theoretical life in solitude. The epistemological criticism of politics is the natural complement of these metaphysical objections. Political discourse, since it always refers to a world in disorderly flux, can never rise above the level of opinion (*doxa*), can never achieve or express genuine knowledge (*episteme*). Partisan rhetoric is regularly exchanged to defend and rebut inconstant opinions, but it is confined to the appearances or semblances of things rather than their true being. There is an unbridgeable epistemic divide between knowledge and opinion that parallels the ontological separation of being and becoming. Plato appeals to these hierarchical divisions to separate the theoretical life of the philosopher from the active life of the dedicated citizen. When the true philosopher returns to the world of the cave, he is forced to use rhetoric, to convey by means of opinion and uncertain persuasion what he inwardly possesses as knowledge. While citizens in the *polis* live together through the medium of language, their celebrated speeches and arguments are typically empty of truth. The supreme form of knowledge, the knowledge of the Good, cannot be put into words and its solitary bearer keeps silent about what is closest to his heart.

Plato's final criticism of politics is ethical and existential in nature. It reflects his ambivalent attitude, one perhaps endemic to philosophers, towards human life as it is actually given to us on this earth.[89] The deepest loyalty of the true philosopher belongs to the ideal republic, the city in speech, rather than to his native city. As a seeker of truth, he cannot assent to the deceptive opinions and conventional laws on which all existing cities are founded. He is, inevitably, a stranger among his fellow citizens, since he does not share their deepest convictions and attachments. When he joins his peers in political activity, he must compromise his standards of excellence to theirs. On returning to the cave, the true philosopher is confined to unhappy choices: to withhold from the city the liberating truth that might save and transform it, or to obscure and corrupt that truth by making it political, thus converting genuine knowledge into another unstable opinion.[90]

Despite profoundly different interpretations of its meaning and purpose, Plato's *Republic* is unquestionably the most influential text in the history of political theory.[91] The Myth of the Cave occupies a central position in the *Republic* and in the tradition of political thought that it initiated. Even those successors of Plato who rejected the ontological *chorismos* (separation) between cave and sky, accepted his critical contrast between politics and philosophy. Hannah Arendt believed that the philosophers who began "our tradition of political thought" chose to defend and protect their new way of life (*bios*) by explicitly opposing it to the *bios politikos*. The first theoretical accounts of political life were offered by men suspicious of politics and openly opposed to its claims of importance. Although Aristotle directly criticized Plato's *Republic* and generally treated the *bios politikos* with honor, in the concluding book of the *Nicomachean Ethics* he portrays the contemplative and political lives as historical rivals. In defending the supremacy of theoretical activity, he emphasizes the numerous ways in which *praxis* is inferior to *theoria*.[92] While Aristotle's intention is not to denigrate politics but to elevate philosophy, the rhetorical contrast leads him to depict political activity in an unfavorable light. Since Aristotle knew the classical Greeks' supreme regard for politics, he deliberately emphasized its limitations in order to make the strongest case for the ethical supremacy of the *bios theoretikos*.

The *Republic* of Plato and the *Politics* of Aristotle lay the groundwork for the classical tradition of political thought. But, if Arendt is correct, they leave the pre-Socratic political heritage of the Greeks without adequate articulation and expression. The analytical categories that have dominated the western understanding of politics are essentially Greek, but, on Arendt's revisionary account, they fail to articulate specifically Greek political experiences.[93] They are based instead on elaborate metaphors drawn from the non-political realm. Let us briefly examine two important examples on which her revisionary criticism rests. The essential condition of politics is plurality, the fact that human beings in the plural, not man in the singular, inhabit the earth. Politics presupposes the interaction of unique and equal persons capable of mutual communication and criticism and sustained engagement in cooperative action. Yet Plato's images of political activity are modeled on the experiences of man in the singular. The philosopher-ruler is compared to an architectural craftsman who builds the republican city with the help of compliant apprentices. It is the philosophical architect alone who knows how the city should be built; his fellow citizens who voluntarily execute his directives and commands are comparable to construction workers following the finished designs of a master architect. In this deliberately authoritative image, a place is reserved for human plurality only in the giving and receiving of orders between rulers and ruled, between masters and subordinates. But the political ruler determines the correct course of action in isolation from the ruled, as the builder conceives his plans in the solitude of the studio. The isolated ruler's solitary vision of the forms (*eide*) beyond the cave and his authoritative use of eidetic knowledge to govern the *polis* become the guiding image of traditional political theory. When the political role of other citizens is recognized, they appear in the image of obedient subordinates who benefit from the ruler's singular wisdom but take no active part in shaping it. Since the philosophical ruler consents to rule only reluctantly, under the constraint of necessity and coercion, we end with a theoretical and symbolic account of politics deprived of its splendor and dignity.[94]

Arendt's second example is drawn from Aristotle's *Politics*. Unlike Plato, Aristotle explicitly refuses to reduce *praxis*, political action, to *poiesis* or fabrication.[95] From her critical perspective, Aristotle remains more faithful to Greek practice and culture than his teacher, but he still remains under the powerful spell of the *Republic*. In particular, he follows Plato by making the assignment of rule the central concern of political theory. The taxonomy of political institutions is based on the distribution of governing authority. Each city has a distinctive *politeia*, or constitution, a way of determining the appropriate power relations between the governors and the governed. The basic political regimes Aristotle recognizes are differentiated by criteria pertaining to the allocation of rule. There is the rule of one, few or many; rule founded on virtue, wealth, or numbers; rule with or without adherence to law; rule for the sake of the rulers or the ruled. Aristotle modifies the *Republic's* typology of regimes, but reinforces its emphasis on rule as the primary political relationship.[96] Plurality is restored to a central place in political life, but the relations among citizens, since they are founded on governance, presuppose an underlying inequality among them. According to Arendt, Aristotle is torn between two conflicting conceptions of the *polis*, which he never effectively reconciles. Under one description, the *polis* is a community of equals joined in voluntary association for the sake of living well;[97] under the other, it is a community of inequality organized around the practices and requirements of effective political authority.

Arendt insisted that both Plato and Aristotle based their political theories on essentially pre-political experiences. The ruler-ruled relation between human beings did occupy a central position in Greek life, but it belonged to the domestic rather than the political realm of activity.[98] Within the household, masters ruled over their slaves and parents jointly governed their children; within the sphere of education, teachers exercised authority over their pupils and master craftsmen over their apprentices. In all of these relations of rule or authority, structural inequality is clearly presupposed. Whether the purpose of rule is to serve the stronger or the weaker party, the former in the case of slavery, the latter in education and parenting, it is the evident inequality between rulers and ruled that makes rule either possible or necessary. Aristotle uses the contrast between slavery and education to distinguish between despotic and royal rule, and he supports the claim of the virtuous to political authority by citing the relevant inequalities of intellect and character. The category of rule, therefore, is never a wooden or a rigid instrument in his hands. Nevertheless, the combined theoretical influence of Plato and Aristotle was so formidable that the framework of rule and authority came to dominate the subsequent history of political theory. As a result, the political realm was conceived as a domain of structural inequality, even though this contradicted the origin of the *polis* as a voluntary association of equals committed to the quest for immortalizing excellence.[99] The philosophical portrait of the city thus concealed and obscured those fundamental experiences that depend on the political equality of citizens. "It is only after one ceases to reduce public affairs to the business of dominion that the original data of human affairs will reappear in their authentic diversity."[100]

This is not the moment to explore that authentic and important diversity. Our present intention is to acknowledge a theoretical dimension of politics that needs to be carefully examined. Although thought and action are significantly different activities, they are, Arendt argued, mutually complementary. Action needs thought to guide, assess and complete it, while thought needs action to preserve its relevance, integrity and gravity. Arendt deeply believed that "our tradition of political thought" had failed in both its narrative and conceptual functions. It failed to provide the West with a compelling story of political events that made the greatness of politics a part of our common memory and education; it also failed to articulate a set of categories and principles adequate to the nature and dignity of political experience. It endowed us instead with a complex of concepts, metaphors and images that have historically biased our perception of politics and disposed us to think about political reality in alien terms. Despite her clear admiration for Plato's philosophical brilliance, Hannah Arendt vigorously criticized his theoretical legacy because it deprived the *bios politikos* of its genuine splendor and dignity.

But the radical evil of the concentration camps, the unprecedented nature of totalitarian terror, the advent of an atomized mass society, and the declining legitimacy of the nation state have combined to weaken the authority of our inherited tradition. These momentous events have also revealed our common unreadiness to comprehend and judge the most pressing modern realities. By disclosing the limits of tradition as a guide to understanding the present, they have forced us to reexamine the most fundamental political questions and issues. This is the task Hannah Arendt chose for herself as a political humanist. Although she no longer bowed to the tradition's authority, she was profoundly unwilling to abandon its study. She believed that the obligation of responsible thinkers in our time was to discover a new way of understanding the past and the present, a way no longer confined within the parameters of our inherited political theories. She called this critical revisionary activity learning "to think without bannisters," and she made it the central enterprise of the last half of her life.[101] Our goal in the following chapters will be to think along with her as she beats a track across this largely uncharted sea.[102]

NOTES

1. Alexis de Tocqueville, *Democracy in America* (1840; New York: Vintage Books, 1960), vol. II, p. 93.
2. Aristotle, *Metaphysics*, Bk. 1,982b12. Aristotle's language clearly reflects the Platonic passage in the *Theaetetus*, though the two accounts of wonder are importantly different.
3. The *Republic, the Statesman and the Laws* are generally considered Plato's "political dialogues" for each of them focuses on right order in the *polis*. But the political significance of philosophy and the political context of Socrates' life are dramatically evident throughout Plato's work. To appreciate Plato's understanding of politics all the dialogues should be taken into account.
4. See especially chapter 26 of *The Prince*, An Exhortation to Liberate Italy from the Barbarians, where Machiavelli employs biblical imagery in support of his revolutionary project.
5. Alexis de Tocqueville, *The Ancien Regime and the French Revolution* (1856; Franklin Square: Harper and Brothers), pp. 50-60.
6. The degree of similarity between Nazi Germany and the Soviet Union is intensely disputed. See Margaret Canovan, *Hannah Arendt: A Reinterpretation of Her Political Thought* (Cambridge: Cambridge University Press, 1992) pp. 17-23. Also Bernard Crick, "On Rereading *The Origins of Totalitarianism*" in M. A. Hill (ed), Hannah Arendt: *The Recovery of the Public World* (New York: St. Martin's Press, 1979) p. 29.
7. I agree with Canovan that the best way to approach Arendt's thinking is to begin with her study of Europe's institutional, cultural and moral collapse.
8. See Plato's *Republic,* Books 8 and 9; Aristotle's *Politics*, Books 4 and 5; Montesquieu's *Spirit of the Laws*, Books 3 and 8. In her essay, "What is Authority," Hannah Arendt argues for a clear distinction between legitimate authority and tyranny and between despotism and totalitarianism. Her analysis of totalitarianism is partly indebted to Montesquieu's analysis of the forms and principles of government. She treats totalitarianism as an unprecedented form of rule whose animating principle is ideologically justified terror rather than fear.
9. For the critical role of ideology and terror in totalitarian government see chapter 13 in *The Origins of Totalitarianism* (1958; New York: Meridian Books).
10. See the sub-section on Total Domination in *Origins*, pp. 437-459.
11. Ibid. p. 439. Arendt's reflections on human evil undergo a partial change after reporting on the Eichmann Trial. See "Thinking and Moral Considerations: A Lecture." *Social Research* (Fall 1971) and *Thinking*, pp. 3-6
12. Ibid. pp. 447-457.
13. See *Origins*, "The Nation of Minorities and the Stateless People," pp. 269-302. The phenomenon of statelessness, as Seyla Benhabib argues, adds an important dimension to the theory of justice: the dimension of just membership as well as just distribution and punishment. See *The Rights of Others: Aliens, Residents, and Citizens*. (2004; New York: Cambridge University Press).
14. Arendt draws a clear distinction between the impossibility of effective resistance within the death camps and the lost opportunity for significant resistance within the cities and ghettoes of Europe. In her highly controversial report on the Eichmann trial, she criticizes the leaders of the Jewish councils for uncritically complying with Nazi directives. Her argument is partly based on the belief that non-compliance and resistance prior to mass deportation would have severely disrupted the plans for the final solution. See *Eichmann in Jerusalem* (1963; New York: Viking Press).
15. The concept of witnessing is central to Arendt's understanding of the moral life. She bases her analysis of Socratic morality on the thinking person's recurrent self-encounter in solitude; because the thinker is regularly meeting with himself on the occasions of thought, he is made aware of the moral character of his partner in dialogue. The regular practice of thinking has moral importance for it forces a man into a position of repeated self-scrutiny. By contrast, political morality is based not on self-reflection but on the witness of others to a man's public conduct. Action in the space of appearance loses its meaning when there is no one to observe

and appraise it and recount its story. What is clearly lacking in her approach is the concept of a divine witness who sees and recalls all things. See "Thinking and Moral Considerations: A Lecture," *Social Research* (Fall 1971) and "Civil Disobedience," *Crises of the Republic*.

16. For the murder of the moral capacity of the person, see *Origins*, pp. 451-453.

17. Arendt, *The Life of the Mind*, vol. II, *Willing* (1978; New York: Harcourt Brace Jovanovich), p. 272.

18. *Origins*, p. 438.

19. Deception and lying in politics are not new. But totalitarian propaganda was not content with the linguistic distortion of reality. Total domination uses terror to transform reality so that the ideological lies are eventually confirmed by experience. The political ideology asserts that the regime's intended victims are less than human; terror is then used to transform the inhabitants of the death camps into an ostensibly sub-human condition.

20. *Origins*, pp. 296-297.

21. Arendt borrows the redemptive understanding of storytelling from Isak Dinesen: "All sorrows can be borne if you put them into a story or tell a story about them."

22. *Origins*, pp. 446-447. "Nothing perhaps distinguishes modern masses as radically from those of the previous centuries as the loss of faith in a Last Judgment."

23. This is the title that was used, over her protest, when *Origins* was first published in England. Young-Bruehl, *Hannah Arendt: For Love of the World*, p. 200.

24. See "From the Pariah's Point of View: Reflections on Hannah Arendt's Life and Work," Elizabeth Young-Bruehl in *Hannah Arendt: The Recovery of the Public World*, ed. Melvin Hill (1979; New York: St. Martin's Press), pp. 3-26. For a full biographical account of Hannah Arendt's life and work, see *Hannah Arendt, For Love of the World* (1982; New Haven: Yale University Press) by Young-Bruehl.

25. Although Hannah Arendt was reluctant to characterize her philosophical method, she can best be understood as a phenomenologist. She provided a thoughtful account, *logos*, of the human appearances, *phenomena*, in the public and the private realms of human existence. She practiced a linguistically based phenomenology in all of her work though she never thematized it.

26. See Arendt, *Love and St. Augustine* (1996; Chicago: University of Chicago Press).

27. See "Stateless Persons," *For Love of the World*.

28. Arendt, *Men in Dark Times* (1968; New York: Harcourt Brace and World). The threat of existential despair and the refusal to submit to it are recurrent themes in this text and in *Origins*.

29. The actual quote is by J. H. Whitfield, *Machiavelli*, Oxford, 1947. Arendt's support for this reading of Machiavelli can be found in *On Revolution* (1965; New York: The Viking Press), p. 290.

30. Arendt, *Between Past and Future* (1968; New York: The Viking Press), pp. 140-141.

31. Even in *The Life of the Mind*, political themes continue to recur though without pride of place.

32. For the romantic critique of bourgeois society, see *The Second Discourse on Inequality* and *Emile* by Jean-Jacques Rousseau. For Arendt's critique of Rousseau's political romanticism, see especially *On Revolution*, pp. 70-76.

33. These categories and representative mentalities are developed and extensively compared in *The Human Condition* (1958; Chicago: University of Chicago).

34. In the *Republic*, Socrates defines the *ergon* of a thing as its specific function, that operation which the thing alone can perform or which it can perform better than anything else. In the *Nicomachean Ethics*, Aristotle adopts the Platonic language and asks whether man *qua* man has a specific *ergon*. He concludes that the *ergon* of man is to live in accordance with reason, man's highest power. But since reason, *nous*, is shared by men and gods, is there an exercise of *nous* that is distinctively human? Here Aristotle appears to waver slightly. He grants that political activity, *praxis*, is unique to humans; the gods do not constitute a political community. But he encourages human beings to place the theoretical above the practical intellect. The highest human virtue is not practical but theoretical wisdom. The perfection of man, therefore, is not identified with the perfection of his specific *ergon* but with his most god-like activity.

35. The charge of political nostalgia is often directed at Arendt's political thought. While this charge is often unfair, I agree with her critics that she failed to acknowledge the limitations as well as the merits of the classical republic.

36. Aristotle emphasizes that neither the brutes nor the divine need a *polis* as a condition of self-fulfillment. But human beings require the *polis* for the attainment of virtue (*arete*), both moral and intellectual. Life in a *polis* is natural to man since it is the proper site for the perfection of his nature. See *The Human Condition*, pp. 24 and 305; and Aristotle's *Politics*, 1253a, pp. 25-40.

37. Arendt repeatedly claims that our political vocabulary has lost its revelatory character. We no longer know the experiential or historical origins of the basic political terms we employ. This ignorance prompts us to use as synonyms terms that are semantically divergent and to rely on ideological vocabularies that are no longer relevant.

38. Neither classical liberalism with its emphasis on freedom from politics nor Marxism with its call for the replacement of government by public administration really prize active citizenship and participation in public affairs.

39. Tocqueville, *Democracy in America*, vol. II, p. 349.

40. Arendt, *Between Past and Future*, p. 174.

41. Ibid. p. 141. This is another way of asserting our need to rethink the full implications of human plurality.

42. "The 'reconciliation with reality,' the catharsis, which according to Aristotle was the essence of tragedy, and, according to Hegel was the ultimate purpose of history, came about through tears of remembrance." *Past and Future*, p. 45.

43. Arendt, *Men in Dark Times*, pp. 228-229.

44. See chapters 9 and 10, *Origins,* for this pattern of political and social disintegration.

45. For Arendt's fullest discussion of the Roman Trinity, see *Between Past and Future* chapters 1 and 3.

46. "Our tradition of political thought had its definite beginning in the teachings of Plato and Aristotle. I believe it came to a no less definite end in the theories of Karl Marx." *Past and Future*, p. 17.

47. According to Arendt, laws of history do not exist and that the belief that they do is ideological. See *On Revolution*, pp. 51-52, 113-114, 255-261.

48. For the use of representative characters as instruments of social and political analysis, see Alasdair MacIntyre, *After Virtue*, (Notre Dame: University of Notre Dame Press, 1981) pp. 23-30.

49. In *Republic* 8 and 9, Plato sketches the various types of disordered political leadership ranging from timocrats and oligarchs to undisciplined democrats and tyrants.

50. See *Origins*, pp. 79, 144, 255.

51. See Hans Kohn, *Political Ideologies of the Twentieth Century* (New York: Harper, 1966) pp. 3-18. Kohn traces the rise of exclusive nationalism and radical socialism as well as the decline of republican universalism to the abortive revolutions of 1848.

52. Arendt, *Origins*, p. 314. French politics, in particular, were marked by this conflict between national loyalty and divisive class membership. The *union sacré* created by the First World War put a temporary end to partisan rivalries that had dominated post-revolutionary France.

53. See *Origins*, pp. 17; 38-39.

54. See *Origins*, Part Two: Imperialism for her rich and suggestive account of the imperialist project. Nowhere is Arendt's intellectual debt to Rosa Luxemburg greater than in her analysis of the economic origins of nineteenth-century imperialism.

55. See *Origins*, pp. 149-151; 188-189; 197; 200; 457-459.

56. See chapter 5, *Origins*, "The Political Emancipation of the Bourgeoisie."

57. See *Origins*, pp. 152-153. "Hobson was the first to recognize both the fundamental opposition of imperialism and nationalism and the tendency of nationalism to become imperialist."

58. *Origins*, p. 267.

59. Ibid. vii, Preface to the first edition.

60. *Origins*, pp. 300-318. Also, *On Revolution*, pp. 162-164. Arendt sees the basic movement of western history since the political revolutions of the eighteenth century as one of growing world alienation. Human beings became increasingly atomized and isolated as they lost the sensible world as a common matrix of reference. Membership in social classes provided a limited brake on this process of political decline. When the classes lost their stabilizing and unifying power, the political dangers of loneliness and worldlessness struck Europe with fury.

61. See "Antisemitism as an Outrage Against Common Sense," chapter 1 of *Origins*, pp. 3-10.

62. *Origins*, "A Classless Society."

63. *Origins*, p. 317.

64. For the important contrast between isolation and loneliness, see *Origins*, pp. 474-479.

65. Although the history of Europe in the first half of the twentieth century is well known, Hannah Arendt brings it to life through her disciplined passion, her powerful rhetoric, and her interweaving of poetic and factual materials. She recreates the intellectual and spiritual context of the events she is recounting. Hers is not the detached objectivity of the historian, but the spellbinding power of the storyteller. The reader is required, periodically, to disengage from her narrative spell in order to realize that hers is one story among the many that can and need to be told. For the psychological differences distinguishing the people from the social classes, the mob and the masses, see *Origins*, Part III: *Totalitarianism*, chapter 10: A Classless Society.

66. *Origins*, p. 315.

67. *Origins*, pp. 315-318.

68. Ibid. p. 311.

69. Arendt, *The Human Condition*, pp. 58-59.

70. *Origins*, pp. 311-326, 350. In the third section of *Origins*, Hannah Arendt vividly depicted the nature and consequences of worldlessness. Later, in *The Human Condition*, she traced world alienation to its source in the revolutionary events of the modern age. The polar opposition between love of the world and world alienation always remained at the center of her political understanding.

71. See *Origins*, pp. 468-474. Her concept of ideology is rooted in its etymological origins: logically unfolding the implications of a single seminal idea.

72. For the Arendtian contrast between "the need to think" and the "desire to know," see *Thinking*, pp. 11-15; *Past and Future*, pp. 6-15; and *Lectures on Kant's Political Philosophy*, p. 20.

73. *Origins*, p. 477. "Self and world, capacity for thought and experience are lost at the same time."

74. Idem. The original quote is actually Martin Luther's. Hannah Arendt cites it in her investigation of totalitarian ideologies.

75. *Genesis* 2,18. "It is not good that the man should be alone; I will make him a helpmate for him." For the distinction between solitude and loneliness, see *The Human Condition*, pp. 65-69. It is important that the loneliness of the doer of good works be distinguished from the organized loneliness of a mass society. The sources of their world alienation are significantly different.

76. See *The Human Condition*, section 3, "Eternity versus Immortality" and chapter 2, "The Public and the Private Realm," as well as *Past and Future*, pp. 71-73.

77. Hannah Arendt finds inspiration for her political philosophy in the historical experiences of both Greece and Rome. Periclean Athens is her model of the public quest for terrestrial immortality; Republican Rome is the source of fundamental insights into stability and permanence in public affairs. For her richest elaboration of the Roman political spirit, see "What is Authority" in *Between Past and Future*.

78. See *Past and Future*, pp. 129-141 "The famous 'decline of the West' consists primarily in the decline of the Roman trinity of religion, tradition and authority." p. 140.

79. *Past and Future*, pp. 120-121.

80. *Past and Future*, p. 124.

81. *Past and Future*, pp. 125-128.

82. *Past and Future*, pp. 127-128,134-135,138-141.

83. In summarizing this process, I draw on the full range of Arendt's published work. She especially highlights Nietzsche, Kierkegaard and Marx as nineteenth century thinkers struggling with the spirit of suspicion released by the scientific revolution. See"Tradition and the Modern Age" in *Between Past and Future*.

84. Arendt was scandalized by the failure of governments and citizens in all countries to protect the Jews and to oppose the violence of extra-legal political movements. The vaunted moral traditions of Europe no longer provided reliable protection against evil in times of crisis. Neither institutional religion nor conventional morality effectively resisted mass deportation and murder "when the chips were down." See *Thinking and Moral Considerations and Men in Dark Times*.

85. The moral decline of Europe is thoughtfully explored in *Origins, Men in Dark Times, Between Past and Future, and Eichmann in Jerusalem* among other texts.

86. Arendt, *Between Past and Future*, pp. 140-141.

87. See in particular chapter 1, "Tradition and the Modern Age" in *Past and Future*.

88. See *Republic* VII, 514a-521b.

89. Arendt, *Lectures on Kant's Political Philosophy*, pp. 21-24.

90. It is doubtful that these unwelcome alternatives exhaust the possibilities of philosophical citizenship. See chapters 3 and 5 for other ways that philosophers can contribute to the life of the city.

91. This preliminary introduction to the *Republic* will be more fully developed in chapter 3, sections B and C.

92. See *Nicomachean Ethics*, Book 10, chapters 4-8.

93. See *Between Past and Future*, pp. 124-125. There are striking parallels between Arendt's critique of the Platonic tradition in political theory and Heidegger's critique of western ontology in his *Introduction to Metaphysics*. Both of them seek to overcome a tradition of thought founded on Platonic concepts and metaphors and to return, at least partly, to a pre-Socratic mode of thinking and speaking. See Dana Villa, *Arendt and Heidegger: the Fate of the Political*, (1996; Princeton: Princeton University Press).

94. See "The Traditional Substitution of Making for Acting," *The Human Condition*, pp. 220-23.

95. Aristotle, *Nicomachean Ethics*, 1140a, pp. 1-25. "Neither is acting making nor making acting."

96. See Aristotle's *Politics*, Book 1, chapter 1; and Book III, chapter 1; for the primacy of the concept of rule or governing, see Books III and IV of the *Politics*.

97. *Politics,* 138a ; cited by Arendt in *Past and Future*, p. 116.

98. See *Past and Future*, pp. 105-106; 116-118; *Human Condition*, pp. 28-37.

99. *Human Condition*, pp. 196-199.

100. Arendt, *Crises of the Republic* (1972; New York: Harcourt Brace Jovanovich), pp. 142-143.

101. See Arendt's remarks in the Hill volume, *The Recovery of the Public World*, pp. 333-339. "I always thought that one has got to start thinking as though nobody had thought before, and then start learning from everybody else."

102. Herman Melville, *Moby Dick*, chapter 23, "The Lee Shore," for the memorable image of Bulkington as independent thinker and comrade.

Chapter Two

LOOK TO THE GREAT AND COMMON WORLD

If we compare the modern world with that of the past the loss of experience ... is extraordinarily striking.[1]

THE SPIRIT OF ARENDTIAN POLITICS[2]

The first three centuries of the modern era were each dominated by a great revolution. In the seventeenth century the new science of nature destroyed the ancient geocentric cosmology and altered our basic conception of knowledge and truth. In the eighteenth century, the political upheavals in America and France turned the West upside down and accelerated the movement towards democratic social equality. The industrial revolution of the nineteenth century brought productive manufacture out of the home and into the urban factories; it dramatically increased European wealth but at a threatening social and political cost. By the twentieth century the process of historical change had only accelerated. During its first fifty years, there were two world wars, a global depression, the creation of unprecedented totalitarian regimes and the explosion of atomic weapons. The cumulative force of these momentous events overwhelmed our inherited traditions.[3] Western philosophical, theological and political thought had their origin in the Mediterranean basin over two thousand years ago. With numerous adjustments, they survived the transition from the ancient to the medieval world and the transfer of spiritual authority from the empire to the church. The continuity of our intellectual inheritance remained essentially intact until the advent of modern science. The founders of the scientific revolution and their philosophical allies deliberately rejected what the great medieval thinkers had struggled to preserve. They viewed the traditions of the ancients as a major obstacle to their nascent enterprise and systematically attacked their authority.[4] In the eighteenth century the leaders of the French Enlightenment actively embraced this spirit of radical criticism. For the *philosophes* it was the Catholic Church and the inherited aristocratic and monarchical order that had become the *bête noire*. By the 19th century the crack in tradition had widened to the point that no part of the classical inheritance was spared, though the full effects of this rupture were not immediately felt. It is only in the twentieth century that the break in tradition, the discontinuity between past and future, has become the acknowledged starting point of serious human reflection. What had been for centuries a concern of the few has now become the common condition of life[5].

Hannah Arendt shared the pervasive conviction that we cannot restore the broken thread of tradition. There is no returning to an earlier world that has now disappeared. Yet, unlike many of her modern predecessors, she was deeply troubled by the loss of our ties to the past. While she welcomed the release from tradition's authority, she feared that without the guidance of tradition human beings might forget the past altogether. The break in tradition had increased rather than lessened the importance of the past for our thinking. Although we are required to think without bannisters, we must recognize the danger this condition entails; at every moment we are in danger of falling.[6]

Arendt's distance from the classical tradition establishes her modernity without making her its champion, for she was even more critical of modern political thinking than she was of its classical antecedents. Temporally speaking, she was without a cultural home in either the past or the present. This was her self-understanding and it is essentially accurate. Her life experience had convinced her that human dignity and liberty could only be theoretically and practically secure in a stable political order. This deep conviction partly explains her opposition to classical and early Christian political thought. The philosophical denigration of the *polis*, the disproportionate value assigned to the contemplative life and the Pauline emphasis on individual salvation had combined to deny politics an honored place in the post-Socratic world. Later, in the early Christian era, the Church's stress on eternal life had prevented the formation of a genuine political mentality. Only with the separation of church and state during the Renaissance were the conditions for an authentic politics restored. But the great political awakening heralded by Machiavelli and the civic humanists never fulfilled its promise. The scientific revolution subverted the original spirit of politics and the contemplative aspirations of philosophy. In fact, philosophy and politics suffered more from modernity than any other human activities.[7] Both of these forms of life presuppose a temper of mind and spirit incompatible with the dominant culture of the modern world. If the primary crisis of the present age is political, this is largely because the genuine *ethos* of politics and the convictions of modernity are antithetical. In trying to protect human dignity by restoring the original dignity of politics, Hannah Arendt was consciously resisting the spirit of the modern age.

What is the *ethos of politics* to which Hannah Arendt often refers? Put in the simplest terms, it is to love and care for the world more than for oneself, and to treasure the opportunities the world provides for achieving and preserving human excellence.[8] The spirit of Arendtian politics is the spirit of worldliness; it is to examine all things from the perspective of the common world and to measure them in relation to their worldly importance. "In politics, not life but the world is at stake."[9]

It is evident from these initial reflections that the concept of the world is the cornerstone of Arendt's understanding of politics. What does she mean when she speaks of caring for the world and that "world alienation is the essence of the modern age?"[10] She is not using the term 'world' as Wittgenstein did in the *Tractatus* when he asserted that "The world is all that is the case; the world is the totality of facts."[11] Although the Arendtian world is explicitly factual, it is not coextensive with the whole of reality. Yet if it signifies only a limited part of existence, what are its defining boundaries? Where does it begin and end? There is no simple answer to these questions, for Arendt's conception of the world is embedded in a matrix of interdependent categories apart from which it lacks intelligibility. To grasp what she means by the world we have to take an indirect route through this complex categorial terrain.

Human life as it occurs on this earth is inconceivable without sensible appearance.[12] It is essential to human beings that they appear before others and that others appear before them. The only knowable period of human existence begins with our original appearance at birth and ends with our disappearance at death. Mystery surrounds the mortal life span of the individual; our ultimate whither and whence are matters of faith rather than verifiable cognition. A secular philosophy that does not rely upon faith or divine revelation must confine its reflections to the space of appearances. Without denigrating faith or denying religious transcendence, Hannah Arendt's thinking was entirely based on linguistic and phenomenal evidence. In a secular age and culture, she believed the restoration of human dignity depends on what appearances reveal and conceal.

When children are born they enter a pre-existing spatial and temporal order. The space that they enter is divisible into a natural realm symbolized by the earth with its biological species and a humanly constructed realm which Hannah Arendt called the world.[13] These two realms correspond to an irreducible difference in human modes of being. As an animal, the human being is a natural, earthly creature subject to the necessities of biological life.

Like other animals, humans are nurtured by their natural parents, gradually achieve biological maturity, sexually reproduce their kind, and invariably vanish from the earth. The natural pattern of species life is essentially cyclical. Human beings are born and die, but by means of their coming and going the life of the species is preserved. The dominant category we use to think about natural earthly existence is life, initially the life of the individual animal but ultimately the life of the species.[14] The biological interpretation of human existence is in one sense fundamental. Without the stability of the earth, the fecundity of nature and the biological conditions required for preserving life, there would neither be materials with which to build the world nor living agents to do the building. The human world depends upon the earth as the productive arts depend upon nature and the craftsman upon the living animal. But we must recognize both teleological as well as genetic priority. Although human beings are initially natural entities, they inhabit the earth so that they might erect and dwell in a world of their own making. The world built by human hands has teleological priority over nature because the human being is a person as well as an animal, a particular *who* even more than a specific *what*.[15] While other animals can flourish in a natural environment, an *Umwelt*, human persons only flourish in a world, a *Welt*, whose pattern of movement is rectilinear rather than cyclical. Spatially speaking, the world is that region of the earth shaped and bounded by human beings to serve as their mortal home. It is the region they deliberately create to house themselves, the associations they form, and the activities they choose to pursue. What the world contains, how it appears, and what takes place within it all depend on human choice. Human beings construct the world and order their worldly transactions in accord with their governing vision of themselves. The world they make and preserve provides the most striking evidence of their self-interpretation.[16]

The temporal dimension of human appearance is comparable in importance to its spatial aspect. Human beings are born into both the cosmic time of nature and the historical time of the world. These two temporal dimensions are measured by strikingly different units of duration: the significant periods of biological time are demarcated by the origin and perishing of species. But the decisive unit of historical time is the normal span of an individual person's life. Each child is a new person in an old world, a world that antecedes each human birth and survives each human death.[17] Because every human being is mortal the survival of the world requires the miracle of human natality. The *naissance* of the child is always the *renaissance* of the world. The narrative history of the world is composed of the life stories of the persons who formerly dwelt in it. It is these individuals who built and preserved the world and created its distinctive places and buildings as the stage for their memorable actions and passions. The spaces into which the world is divided are differently weighted in meaning and importance. But without a common historical memory transmitted across the generations the spatial and temporal segmentation of the world would remain invisible and unknown. This is a major reason why human beings are liberally educated, to prepare them for life in an old world whose significant past is preserved in the active memories of mortals. Without an effective civic education, without this transmission of communal memory, each generation of humans would inhabit a world lacking in depth.[18] Spatiality is the aspect of sensible appearance that makes living persons visible and present to one another. The passage of time would make their pasts and their lives permanently invisible unless memory and narrative continued their work of rescuing the dead from oblivion. A central purpose of liberal education is to enable the young, the generation of newcomers, to recover a time out of mind.[19] Education balances young people's natural interest in the future by telling them the story of the world. The aim of this story is to engender in the young a deep self-transcendent love, love for the world, respect for the greatness of the past, a yearning to measure up to what has already been said and done. A civic or liberal education transforms the biological animal into an independent adult responsible for the survival and flourishing of the common world. The educational commitments and practices of a culture clearly signify its level of worldliness.[20]

The varieties of sensible appearance also serve to distinguish the different types of human activity. In *The Human Condition*, Hannah Arendt relied on this ontological category to distinguish the various modes of the *vita activa* and to oppose the active life as a whole to the life of the mind.[21] Labor, work and action, the basic forms of the active life, are sensible occurrences that give rise over time to equally sensible outcomes. The life of the mind is partly contrasted with the *vita activa* because it does not appear before others; we learn of its nature and complexity by introspection or by studying its sensible expressions in words, works and deeds. The sensible phenomena that compose the realm of appearance are internally segmented by temporal and spatial criteria. The relevant temporal distinctions are keyed to the life spans of individual persons. Hannah Arendt classifies an appearance as durable if it outlasts the mortality of its agent, and as permanent if it remains intact through the succession of human generations.[22] Tools and instruments are familiar examples of durability; works of art and architecture are the primary examples of permanence. But there are fleeting and transient appearances as well as lasting ones, ranging from human deeds and speeches that disappear as soon as they are enacted to the products of labor that must be consumed and digested before they spoil and rot. The products of labor, the most natural human activity, are contrasted with the artifacts of work, the properly world-building faculty. Labor produces objects of consumption whose life-giving benefit is lost if they are not quickly eaten or frozen. Work fabricates durable and permanent things that serve as a common worldly bond uniting the dead, the living and the unborn. The speeches and deeds emerging from the faculty of action occupy a unique temporal position within the *vita activa*. Unlike work and labor, action and speech leave no distinct phenomenal product behind. Viewed solely as temporal occurrences, they are even more short-lived than the most perishable consumer goods, for they become invisible and inaudible as soon as they occur. Human actions would be the most futile of all appearing activities unless witnessed by peers who can preserve them in memory before transforming them into memorable stories.[23] Although these actions in their purely phenomenal character have no share in worldly permanence, if their chronicler is gifted enough, the stories keeping them and their heroes alive may become immortal. Though the heroic deeds of Achilles deprived him of life, they won for him, thanks to Homer's poetry, everlasting fame.[24] Works of art and the stories that enshrine and transmit memorable action are the most permanent of all human appearances. They bind together the human generations by teaching the world's newcomers the greatness of their ancestors and the splendor of their extraordinary words and deeds. But the preservation of the past relies on the future as well. Without the constant influx of new beings to populate the world, great works would decay, great deeds would be forgotten and the world itself would eventually revert back into nature.

The space of appearances is divisible on different principles from the demarcations of time. In the division of worldly space, the critical distinction is between the public and the private realms, between what should be shown and displayed to every adult person and what should be hidden and sheltered from common awareness and discussion.[25] Human activities and their perceptible outcomes should be made public if they are meant by their nature to appear, to be seen, heard, discussed, understood and judged by a community of peers. If they are not intended for such public scrutiny and appraisal, they should be concealed, hidden from the light and visibility they are not meant to bear.[26] Hannah Arendt believed that each type of human activity pointed to its proper location in the space of appearances. For example, it is an essential aspect of human speech and action that they occur in the presence of peers able to understand their meaning and properly respond to it. It is equally essential for the integrity of good deeds, in the scriptural sense emphasized by Jesus of Nazareth (*Matthew*, 6), that they remain unwitnessed by other persons, even by the one who enacts them.[27] Human beings need to create distinct spaces within the world where the full range of their activities can occur. We have equal need of a brightly lit public realm where human excellence and greatness can shine, and of a darker private domain where intimacy can flourish, children can develop in safety, and our brute animality can function without shame. In ancient Greece, the household, *oikos*, was the designated locus of privacy and the *polis* the privileged place of public assembly and display.[28] Both realms were governed by distinctive mentalities, since the cultural character of a space changes due to the concerns activities admitted within it. A primary task of culture is to create diff spaces within the world where each type of activity can achieve its proper excellence, and to maintain the integrity of that space by restricting admission to those who respect its spirit and requirements. But this puts the main point too negatively. The best way to maintain the cultural integrity of different spaces is to educate the young in the specific arts and virtues each space requires. The guiding cultural insight is that the public and private realms both need education and protection if they are not to be corrupted by alien concerns and demands.

We need carefully to distinguish between what does not appear and what should not appear. Only the latter is private in Arendt's strict use of that term. The principal events in the life of the mind do not occur in the realm of appearances; our interior acts of thinking, volition and judgment do not appear to the senses.[29] For this reason, human beings are not required to choose in which worldly spaces to locate them. But the case is entirely different with the constitutive activities of the *vita activa*. It is a critical cultural decision to confine important aspects of our biological existence within the private realm; it is a decision of equal importance to erect a public space outside the home where domestic considerations have limited validity or relevance. The need for a demarcation of public and private spaces only arises within the context of worldliness. If human beings were exclusively animals, and if the preservation of life were their foremost concern, then the spatial distribution of appearances on the basis of their phenomenal character would be irrelevant. The deliberate division of the world into public and private realms will always seem unnatural if we tend to think of nature and the world as anthropological contraries. Hannah Arendt accepted this provocative conclusion since she contrasted nature and world as the ancient Greeks had contrasted nature and art.[30] But a different strain in Greek thought best expressed in Aristotle considers natural whatever is essential to the flourishing of a living substance. In this sense, politics, education and the spatial differentiation of the world are all natural to human beings because they contribute to our full humanity.[31]

With these Arendtian distinctions in view, perhaps we're ready to answer the original question: What is the world, and what is the spirit of worldliness that it elicits from its devoted inhabitants? The world is the man-made artifice that separates human existence from all merely natural environments.[32] It is the product of human hands, constructed over many generations, and deliberately designed to offer human beings a dwelling place more permanent and stable than their mortal selves.[33] It is composed of distinct and particular things, sensible artifacts, that human beings have built and preserved as the site of their common existence: things like churches, homes, factories, bridges, libraries, monuments, parks, museums, stadiums and universities. Things like desks, tables, altars, beds, instruments, paintings and pieces of sculpture. Arendt divides the fabricated things of the world into two major kinds: objects of use and works of art.[34] Tools are a good example of the first type of artifact. They are made by craftsmen to be used in doing the work of the world. Because it is intended that they should be used repeatedly, they are made to be durable, made to last, until eventually, through the course of repeated use, they are finally used up. In the case of tools, their recurrent use finally overcomes their durability. Even the most well made artifact will eventually become useless unless it is spared the "wear and tear" of human employment. For this reason, certain artifacts, notable for their beauty, grace and revelatory power, are exempted from use and prized solely for the distinction of their appearance. Arendt designates these singular phenomenal objects works of art, the most worldly of all human things; they were created not for durability but for permanence. This distinction helps to explain why the art and architecture of an historical community are the supreme expressions of its spirit. They constitute the most persuasive phenomenal testimony of what a particular culture chose to construct and preserve. This expressive power is, perhaps, more true of architecture than the plastic arts, for the public and private buildings of a world are created both to appear and be used. Even architecture, however, cannot escape the consequences of constant use. The most excellent buildings will eventually decay unless special care is taken to preserve and restore them. The responsibility for conserving these worldly treasures rests with succeeding generations. But unless a building is striking in its appearance or surrounded by the shield of public memory and commitment, the new members of the old world are unlikely to preserve it. Works of art and architecture have only their beauty and their narrated history to protect them from ruin. They perfectly symbolize the old and enduring world that shelters them; both must win the loyalty of each new generation if they are to survive and endure.[35]

The Arendtian world is not merely a collection of things, however useful or beautiful. It is designed to be an earthly home and not a warehouse. Cellars and attics are full of durable things, yet they are not organized and arranged to serve as human dwelling places. If the fabricated things of the world are to constitute a genuine home, they must be so ordered and displayed that human beings feel at home among them. The internal order of the world, the shaping of the spaces it contains, the way it sensibly appears, the harmony of its many distinct parts, its fitness for the full range of human activities—all these serve to constitute its identity and excellence. Although the phenomenal world is not a biological substance, its existence depends on the internal relations among its parts as much as the most complex organism. For the world to elicit our love and allegiance, it must be a well-ordered whole constructed to meet the private needs and public hopes of its past and future inhabitants.

Although Hannah Arendt's rhetoric is occasionally confusing on this point, the world of which she speaks is not identical with the public realm.[36] The distinction between public and private spaces is internal to her concept of the world; these carefully differentiated realms constitute the world's most fundamental spatial division. The world as a whole is composed of sensible appearances, but among these appearances some are deliberately concealed from public scrutiny and protected within enclosures of privacy. The residential home of a family and the solitary study of a scholar are as much a part of the world as the commercial market place and the political assembly, even though the activities that flourish in these private spaces are not public in nature. The humanly constructed world shelters both non-worldly and worldly activities; it shelters the biological life of the human animal and the political intercourse among citizens, the solitary prayer of the monastic and the transfiguring craft of the artist. But the distinctive activities of craftsmen and citizens are more dependent on the public world than are those of their fellows. Craftsmen, because they build the world and use it for displaying and exchanging their works, citizens, because the public world provides the common stage on which they meet, interact and converse.[37] Despite this striking affinity between artists and citizens, there is an important asymmetry between these distinct human types. Craftsmen fabricate the things of the world in isolation; although they are closely connected to the world by the durable objects they make, the process of making itself follows canons that threaten the public realm's integrity. This danger helps to explain why the Greeks, who revered well-made artifacts and lavished praise upon them, distrusted craftsmen and frequently excluded them from citizenship.[38] Within the culture of worldliness, craftsmen are essentially ambivalent figures. The Arendtian world needs productive craftsmen to bring durable objects into being, yet its political culture is threatened by the specific mentality that governs productive work. The process of human fabrication follows the principle of utility, the logic of means and ends. But, Arendt insists, the true spirit of the public world transcends utility with its tendency to convert all things into means, even those things once viewed as ends in themselves. At the heart of craftsmanship is a division of loyalties between the principles governing the fabrication process and the very different spirit needed to care for the works it creates. Only the crafted works have the solidity and stability, the potential permanence that the ways of the world require. Measured by the spirit of worldliness, it is the durable artifact not the utilitarian process of making that has the higher dignity. The modern cultural emphasis on fecundity of the creative process to the neglect of the finished work is a striking decline in the worldly spirit.[39]

Labor and work are the forms of the *vita activa* that a h perform in isolation. They require neither plurality nor n conditions of their occurrence.[40] Examined indep goods they produce, they don't need the public world as a condition of their meaning and importance. In these several respects, they are clearly distinguished from action and speech. *Praxis* and *lexis*, action and speech, are the modes of the *vita activa* for which plurality, publicity and an intelligible worldly background are indispensable.[41] Action is rarer than labor and work, and more susceptible to neglect or denigration because the enabling conditions on which it depends are far more complex.[42] Action, in Arendt's sense of the term, presupposes a stable and enduring world, clearly divided into public and private spaces, and inhabited by adults freed from the illiberal mentalities of labor and work.[43] It presumes that these citizens have been drawn together by their love of the world and by their desire to participate in public affairs. In their discursive exchanges and transactions, human agents constitute a changing web of personal relations against the background of a stable world. The stability of the world serves as a needed counterpoint to the manifest instability of the interpersonal web. A reliable network of enduring things and fabricated structures provides the common background for the fragile alliances of human beings and their otherwise futile deeds. Within Arendt's picture of the *bios politikos*, both the stable world of artifacts and the unstable web of persons depend on each other for meaning. "Without being talked about by men and without housing them the world would not be a human artifice but a heap of unrelated things." . . . "Without the human artifice to house them, human affairs would be as floating, as futile and vain, as the wanderings of nomad tribes."[44] Action and speech are needed to humanize the durable world; the stability and permanence of their places of assembly are needed to draw human beings together and to keep them from drifting apart. To use a geometrical metaphor, the world is concurrently within the human circle and outside it. From the outside it provides the stage or background against which the drama of human action unfolds; from the inside it provides a major topic of public discourse and deliberation. Political agents, who design the world so that they can interact within it, soon find the world itself at the center of their mutual concern.

If we extend the semantic scope of "the world" so that it includes not just the enduring human artifice but the web of human relations and the actions and speeches inserted into that web, then the spirit of Arendtian politics as love of the world comes into full view. The republican citizens, who embody this *ethos*, voluntarily leave the darkness and privacy of the household or the study to enter the brightly lit public realm. In foregoing the shelter of their private homes, they enter a space in which necessity and utility are no longer the governing principles.[45] From the perspective of Greek political thinking, the private home was the antithesis of the public realm. Within the household concern for biological life was primary, while in the *polis* life and security were repeatedly risked for the sake of the city.[46] Today, the privacy of the ⁀ontinues to provide a dark place where birth, nurture, growth and intimacy can flourish. But the home has always been a pre-political realm because it is structured by human inequality; historically, this was the inequality between masters and slaves, old and young, male and female; in the contemporary West, where slavery has been abolished and gender equality insisted upon, the structural contrast between parents and children remains. Natural inequality based on differences of age and experience is inescapable here. Parents are called to love their children and to exercise authority over them until they mature and become adults. The bonds of the household are still rooted in nature, though the love of the couple and the affection of the family clearly transcend what is merely biological. To a great extent the natural basis of the home makes it a realm of necessity, a place where the demands of biological life are constantly addressed. For the ancient Greeks, this was the dominant feature of the household and its defining purpose. Modern cultures have emphasized another aspect of privacy, its connection with intimacy, affection and a richer conception of family life.[47] At its best, the home fulfills both ancient and modern requirements. What the home cannot do is provide a sphere of civic equality and freedom, a gathering place for peers united in their quest for excellence and their concern for the fate of the world. To address these ends one must abandon the protections of privacy and risk the challenge of public life.

The communal character of the public realm has two related aspects. First, it signifies what citizens share as a common trust and responsibility in contrast to their private possessions and concerns.[48] The intimacy of husbands and wives, the affection of parents and children and the internal relations within a family are properly private concerns, as is the use they make of the durable objects within their own homes. The public bond among citizens is not a shared curiosity about the private lives and passions of others but a mutual concern for the well being of the world and the web. It is the common world, with its blessings, burdens, obligations and opportunities that belongs to all of them equally and for which they are collectively responsible. Citizens also share the common visibility that results from their assembling in an illuminated public space. Drawn from their private households by hatred of despotism, or a sense of obligation, or hope for personal greatness, or opposition to injustice, or concern for the commonweal, they now stand revealed as adults before their peers.[49] In the bright public light they can show *who* they are and what they can do, as they appear before others to whom they are bound by neither natural necessity nor the intimacy of love. In the public arena, human beings are connected by their common concern for the world rather than their personal attraction to one another. Their mutual relations are properly governed by civility, the respect that one citizen shows to another in recognition of their worldly fellowship. Human plurality makes possible many different types of interpersonal relations. Civic fellowship is distinguished from other forms of human connection by the mediating role of the world. Were the stable human artifice to be destroyed and the web of citizenship to come unraveled and the greatness of the past to be forgotten so that the places of the world lost their historical importance, then civility could no longer survive as a bond of human association. Human beings would continue to live together, but the great public potential arising from their plurality would have been lost.[50]

We have emphasized what the Arendtian spirit of worldliness excludes: a preoccupation with natural necessity, unequal inter-personal relations, exclusive attachment to individual life and security, an absorption in what is private and needs to be hidden. But worldliness is not hostile to privacy as such. On the contrary, it recognizes the deep human need for a privately owned place in the world. "A life spent in public, in the presence of others, becomes, as we would say, shallow. While it retains its visibility, it loses the quality of rising into sight from some darker ground which must remain hidden if it is not to lose its depth . . . the only sufficient way to guarantee the darkness of what needs to be hidden against the light of publicity is private property, a privately owned place to hide in."[51] Indeed, the abolition of private homes and property would not leave the public realm unharmed. The loss of privacy would obscure the most basic worldly distinction we possess. If human beings are to acquire and exercise the specific *ethos* of politics, they need phenomenal reminders that they are passing between realms governed by conflicting mentalities.[52] Hannah Arendt's constant reliance on visual contrasts such as light and dark, manifest and hidden, as a way of distinguishing public and private, is meant to emphasize striking phenomenal differences that symbolize equally profound differences of outlook. The visual appearance of a human space should indicate appropriate action and speech within it.

The durable human artifice, the unstable web of political relationships and the fleeting actions and speeches of individual citizens are meant to be seen and heard in common. Taken together they constitute the defining boundaries and the interior life of the public realm. Spatially, they form a series of concentric circles, with the frame of the world enclosing the assembly of persons and the actions of its individual members occupying the dramatic center of interest and attention. But the human circle of speech and action is transparent, so that the spectators observe the actors in the center against the background of the common world. The actors in their turn are focused on the spectators whom they frequently address, and are dependent on the stable artifice that provides them with a common place of assembly and dialogue. Hannah Arendt regularly relied on theatrical images to capture the spatial dimension of politics.[53] But politics is the consummate living theatre, where actors and spectators are constantly changing roles, where there is no common script or orchestrating director, and where improvisation is king. However helpful the dramatic metaphor, it is important to remember that the theatre is an imitation of action rather than the reverse.[54] Were politics actually to become theatrical, to become a play with well-defined parts and a pre-ordained script, then both sets of activities would lose their reason for being. Politics and drama are similar in their mutual dependence on the common space created when human beings come together to see and be seen, to hear and be heard. In the theatre as in the civic assembly, human beings are judged by the way they appear to their peers.

Hannah Arendt often emphasized a further clarifying parallel. For a theatrical work to succeed, to come dramatically to life, both the actors and the audience must rise above the pressing concerns of personal life. The actor must fully assume the mask of his character, thereby concealing his own face and fortune. The members of the audience must detach themselves from the cares of everyday life to enter sympathetically into the lives of strangers whose origins and destinies are independent of their own. For the duration of the drama, disciplined self-transcendence is required on both sides of the proscenium arch. The obligatory disinterestedness is assisted by a series of conventions. The audience enters the theatre having left their private affairs behind them at home or at work; the unfolding action of the drama engages the audience's attention keeping private concerns at a distance. The communal atmosphere created by the play informs the spirit of the audience, while the audience by its disciplined attention sustains the actors in their dramatic roles.[55] Both audience and actors submit to this complex discipline for reasons that are elusive and hard to articulate. The public life of the theatre is neither necessary nor useful for the people who sustain it. It does not feed our animal appetites; nor can it advance our personal projects, unless put to a use for which it was not properly intended. To identify the specific human goods the theatre achieves, we need to transcend the familiar horizon of necessity and utility. We need to recognize the importance of human practices whose meaning and value are internal to engagement in the practice itself. Our only access to these internal goods is through the shared activity that brings them into being.[56] In the case of the theatre, the relevant activity and the internal goods it promotes are inherently communal. As an imitation of action the theatre discloses the awesome potential of human plurality itself. Through their sustained interaction, the characters in the drama reveal to the assembled community its collective capacity for greatness and tragedy. Across the spatial and aesthetic distance of the theatre, the audience can discern what private life often conceals: the great range of human diversity, the rich spectrum of human relationships, and the splendor and wretchedness that belong to our common world.

Hannah Arendt's normative conception of politics is based on a mutual love for the world that takes time to acquire. This self-transcending love is the affective complement of what she calls an "enlarged mentality."[57] This mentality is created in the theatre by sympathetic entry into the lives of fictional characters. In politics it is achieved by progressive liberation from the restrictive claims of privacy and self-interest. Human beings must voluntarily transcend their private concerns in order to adopt the public mask of citizenship.[58] The *persona* or mask of the citizen allows each individual to reveal his or her own uniqueness in the company of disinterested peers. What the citizen masks are the cares and concerns of private life. These are covered over, hidden, so that what they normally obscure and conceal might become visible—the promise and perils of the common world for which all citizens are responsible. The fate of the world only comes into view as the center of shared attention when the concerns of the private ego or the partisan interest group cease to be the dominant reference point. For the world to arrest and retain the attention of its members, it must be phenomenally striking. It must win the allegiance and loyalty of citizens through its beauty, importance and depth. The Greeks understood that the phenomenon of beauty, as the arresting power of pure appearance, is neither biologically necessary nor technically useful. Beauty constitutes a third dimension of existence, beyond the spheres of instrumentality and self-preservation. To be free to enjoy things of beauty, one must be free from the urgent claims of the body and the absorbing requirements of privacy. It is these claims and requirements that one deliberately masks on entering the public world. In one sense, the legal or political mask of citizenship equalizes all persons who wear it, for it establishes the world as the common reference point of every citizen. Having a shared world to which everyone thoughtfully attends and for which all are responsible causes private inequalities to decline in importance. As Hannah Arendt's passionate critique of bourgeois liberalism revealed, citizenship is compromised when the politics of self or class interest prevent the world from equalizing private differences rooted in nature or personal misfortune.[59] Only actively belonging to a common world can create true political equality; one law applied equally to all, one realm of action and interaction to which every citizen has equal access, one shared conversation in which all are entitled to speak and be heard.

The common world draws citizens together and at the same time it keeps them apart. In the world's gathering or assembling function, it does not conceal differences of individual fortune, but it equalizes their relevance for public activity. In its separating function it actualizes the existential differences among humans and endows them with public importance. The uniqueness of individuals, *who* they really are as particular persons, is hidden from others in the darkness of private life. No one knows a person's true identity, what she can do, or what he has to say as long as they remain within the shelter of privacy. It requires courage to leave that shelter, to place oneself visibly against the historic background of the world, to enter a circle of critical peers and step into its center knowing one shall be judged by the normative standards of excellence and greatness.[60] Politics is based on an

LOOK TO THE GREAT AND COMMON WORLD

essential complementarity between equality and individual difference equality of civic condition created by belonging to a common world is anced by each citizen's unique perspective upon it. The same world appears differently to all of its members when they view it from their distinct personal perspectives. Liberated from our common biological destiny and from the uniform interests of class or group, citizens are free to form their opinions of the world and to voice them to others in shared conversation.

Although authentic political speech is always unscripted and personal, it becomes intelligible to others by referring to a common world. This community of reference is the essential condition for combining discursive uniqueness with mutual intelligibility. In Arendt's conception of politics, distinct individuals look to the great and common world as the source of their enduring community. They speak and act together with the greatness of the past and the beauty of the world to inspire them. In their shared civic life, they experience a distinctively public happiness rooted in the joy of acting and appearing together with other adults. As long as they remain meaningfully connected, they sustain a public realm committed to excellence where the deeds of human beings and the work of their hands can survive the relentless passage of time. In the humanistic politics Hannah Arendt celebrates, the passion for personal distinction, the love of the common world, the enjoyment of cooperative action, the aspiration to historical greatness, and the pleasures of public friendship are combined. "When man takes part in public life he opens up for himself a dimension of human experience that otherwise remains closed to him and that in some way constitutes a part of complete happiness."[61]

THE CULTURAL CONVICTIONS OF MODERNITY

The human capacities of labor, work, action, speech, thought, cognition and contemplation are given us by nature, but the relative importance accorded them varies in different cultural settings and historical epochs. It is quite improbable that a specific activity will flourish in a culture that does not prize it highly. The best evidence of strong cultural esteem for a human capacity is a community's resolve to create the conditions required for its excellence. This is particularly true for the political faculties of action and speech, because they clearly depend on a complex set of institutional and cultural conditions. A common world for which all citizens share collective responsibility cannot be assumed, nor can the political *ethos* of worldliness and liberality that transcends the needs of the private self and the canons of instrumental reason. Human beings must freely create the enabling conditions of Arendtian politics, and because they depend on free human choice, they can easily decline or disappear. In the history of the West two major reasons account for our failure to sustain an authentic public realm: the pre-modern attraction to the transcendence and eternality of God and the modern invasion by life concerns from below.⁶² In post-Socratic antiquity, the most promising human beings ceased to enter political life, partly because the classical *polis* had lost its vaunted independence and partly because the *bios politikos* was subordinated to the life of theory. When political life lost its cultural centrality, the ablest human beings ceased to honor it by their voluntary participation. They tended, instead, to bear the obligations of citizenship as a burden imposed by temporal necessity. The singular importance assigned to contemplation (*theorein*) blurred the internal distinctions within the *vita activa*, so that the characteristic mentalities of labor (necessity), work (utility) and action (public liberty) were no longer recognized as distinct. All non-contemplative forms of life now appeared similar because they commonly lacked the stillness and solitude that theoretical communion with the divine required.⁶³

Early Christian thought did not restore the *bios politikos* to its pre-Socratic eminence. The missionary church depicted in Paul's letters and in the *Acts of the Apostles* clearly anticipated the end of historical time and the triumphal return of Christ in glory. The apocalyptic expectations of apostolic Christianity were antithetical to the Arendtian spirit of worldliness. In classical antiquity, mortal citizens hoped to win everlasting fame in an immortal world through political remembrance. Pauline Christianity, by contrast, promised eternal life to everyone who placed his/her faith in the risen Redeemer. Although the ancient concern for personal immortality was thereby preserved, individual salvation through faith differed fundamentally from the terrestrial rewards of political heroism.⁶⁴ As Christianity became more widely accepted and its apocalyptic emphasis weakened, the Church's original opposition to political engagement did not radically alter. Christians still saw themselves as pilgrim travelers on earth in provisional exile from the Kingdom of God, their true home. Since human beings had their created origin and final destiny in God, they should live in the world without fully belonging to it.⁶⁵ While charitable ministry to those in need was strongly encouraged, the "good deeds" of Christians were not to be done in the public light. Because genuine glory and honor belong properly to God, "When you practice charity, your left hand must not know what your right hand is doing, so that your charity will be in secret."⁶⁶ The good deeds of Christians respond generously to the sufferings of their worldly neighbors, but they are done in the name of the world to come.

The Roman Empire, where most Christians lived, was the provisional home of their fallen nature; the empire was ruled by a love of self (*cupiditas*) that implied contempt for or indifference to God. But the City of God to which true Christians aspire is ruled by the love of God (*caritas*), even unto contempt for self.[67] Both ancient politics and authentic Christianity continued to demand self-transcendence, but for the Christian, it is the wholehearted love of God and neighbor rather than devotion to the common world that effectively silences human egoism. The original Christian attitude towards the world was therefore ambivalent. While Christians recognized the need for public service and for responsible political authority, they tended to view imperial (Roman) politics as a necessary consequence of sin. When the faithful depart this valley of tears, they leave the burdens of worldly citizenship behind, for it is the joyful vision of God not obligatory political activity that constitutes the deepest human fulfillment. "We see now through a glass darkly but then face to face."[68]

Philosophical respect for contemplation and the Christian love of self-concealing goodness subvert the *ethos* of Arendtian politics by challenging human beings to live like God. Both of these powerful cultural currents provide a paradigm of divine activity as the model for human life at its best. While the philosophical and Christian visions of existence permit limited political engagement, they no longer assign politics a place of cultural distinction. A shared knowledge of eternal truth or a common faith in God's redemptive ministry constitutes the new center of human fellowship. Political affairs were displaced from their privileged position in the hierarchy of human concerns and gradually lost their power to join human beings together across the generations. The fellowship of inquiry or the Christian community of worship and belief replaced the unifying web of citizenship, while political *praxis* was reduced to the mundane level of labor and work, activities required because of sin or necessity. "If reason is divine, then, in comparison with man, the life according to it is divine in comparison with human life. But we must not follow those who advise us, being men, to think of human things and being mortal, of mortal things, but must so far as we can make ourselves immortal and strain every nerve to live in accordance with the best thing in us."[69] Christians would later amend Aristotle's exhortation in the *Ethics* by emphasizing faith in divine revelation rather than the perfection of theoretical reason. Yet, both philosophers and Christians agreed that the political summons to human affairs must be superseded by the call to a higher and nobler life.

The dignity of theoretical contemplation may have kept philosophers from engaging in political activity, but the appeal of the *bios theoretikos* was always limited to the few. The Christian gospel, by contrast, was intended for human beings of all nations; the good news of salvation first preached by Jesus and later by Paul and the apostles explicitly transcended the social divisions of the ancient world. In the fellowship of Christ, there is neither Jew nor Greek, male nor female, slave nor free.[70] The shared Christian culture that eventually emerged in the middle ages did not prevent the formation of a public realm, but medieval thinkers remained uncertain whether practical politics could or should comply with the gospel imperatives. Machiavelli deliberately dramatized the historic tension between the evangelical counsels of the Sermon on the Mount and the stern requirements of competitive politics.[71] Machiavelli wanted to restore the humanistic spirit and political mentality of republican Rome. He was certain that the pressing demands of the political world could not be reconciled with the normative standards of authentic Christianity. In Machiavelli's judgment, unless the Christian religion was effectively separated from Renaissance politics, both were certain to lose their integrity. Because the commands of the gospel don't apply to politics, only deception and hypocrisy could result from demanding their observance. Although Machiavelli is notorious for his alleged amorality or immorality, Arendt believed that his goal was to restore the political culture of the Roman republic that Augustine had sharply criticized in the *City of God*. Like his ancient republican ancestors, Machiavelli celebrated the political realm as the site of human glory and the theatre where human *virtu* could be displayed.[72]

He was an early proponent of modern secularization, the institutional separation of church and state and the explicit recognition of their mutual autonomy and independence. It was not Christianity that he opposed but the intrusion of its normative standards and other worldly concerns into public affairs. Renaissance politics would never recover its republican greatness until it was liberated from the transcendent expectations of the Catholic Church. Those expectations were as alien to the Roman republic as the private cares of the household had been to Athenian citizenship. Though the Christian call to goodness and the householder's absorption with biological or species life are profoundly dissimilar, both cultural outlooks are apolitical in nature; and, according to Arendt, they become anti-political when they penetrate the realm of human affairs.[73]

A useful way to mark the evolution of modernity is to trace this growing process of political secularization.[74] The greatest of the medieval thinkers, like Thomas Aquinas, had wanted to integrate the realms of nature and grace without conflating their ontological differences. To achieve this integration, Aquinas relied on the Aristotelian principle of hierarchical pluralism. He recognized several distinct but complementary human goods that were ordered hierarchically in accord with their intrinsic perfection. Divine grace and created nature were internally complementary, as the gift of grace perfected and completed our natural created capacities. Aquinas claimed that divinely revealed faith perfected human reason, as sacred theology, faith's articulate expression, perfected philosophy, reason's finest work. In the realm of practical conduct, the moral and intellectual virtues emphasized by Aristotle in the *Ethics* were brought to perfection by the theological virtues of charity and hope.[75] As a Christian theologian, Aquinas subordinated created human capacities to unmerited divine gifts. But he also recognized a relatively autonomous order of created nature regulated by the operation of secondary causes and effects. The pagan philosophy of Aristotle and the high culture of classical antiquity symbolized for Aquinas the remarkable achievements of which humans are capable without reliance on divine revelation. Wherever possible he sought to harmonize the teachings of the Christian tradition with the achievements of classical humanism. Although Aquinas was hardly a secular thinker in the modern sense, he implicitly acknowledged the relative autonomy of important human practices. Natural science and philosophy were able to develop without relying on the truths of faith, just as political communities had their own integrity apart from revealed religion. He never encouraged this independent pattern of development, because human nature unaided by grace was inevitably sinful and imperfect. Like Aristotle, Aquinas tended to emphasize the complementarity of human practices and human virtues. Although neither denied the reality of conflict, they did not believe that irreconcilable differences were permanently inscribed in the nature of things.[76]

The leading thinkers of the modern age, whatever their personal religious convictions, took an emphatically secular line in declaring their disciplinary goals. Machiavelli and Hobbes in politics, Descartes and Spinoza in philosophy, Galileo and Darwin in science, Adam Smith and Marx in economics, all conceived of their new fields of inquiry as autonomous self-governing practices. Neither church leaders nor the relevant scriptural texts were granted authority over their independent research. By the end of the eighteenth century, the theoretical and institutional life of the West had become predominantly secular. The major enterprises of modernity no longer appealed to religious authority for insight or justification. In its increasing independence of Christian scripture and theology, the modern world had begun to resemble the culture of antiquity. However, Arendt insisted that the pervasive secularization of modernity failed to restore the political *ethos* of the ancient Greeks and Romans. What she found especially striking in modernity was the occurrence of world alienation in the midst of an increasingly secular culture. The historic renaissance turn from otherworldly transcendence was never effectively reversed in the West, but modern secularization, to which the Renaissance gave rise, should not be confused with the Arendtian spirit of worldliness.[77]

After the Greek *polis* lost its political independence, contemplative and religious concerns assumed a new importance in the cultures of the Mediterranean basin. They overshadowed the active life to such a degree that its significant internal diversity was no longer recognized. When the *vita activa* finally reasserted itself under the auspices of Florentine humanism, both Renaissance art and politics were rejuvenated by the recovery of classical models of excellence. At the inception of the modern age, it seemed that all the great cultural practices of antiquity would once again flourish. Modern

Chapter 2

...d modern science clearly fulfilled this original promise in a way that ...ern politics has not. To explain their strikingly uneven destinies Hannah ...endt appealed to the phenomenon of world alienation. Her historical genealogy is intended to account for the diminished stature of politics in an openly secular age. While fabrication and labor were elevated in modernity to unprecedented levels of cultural importance, modern politics fell deeper and deeper into crisis. When the deepest convictions of modernity had taken root, they proved to be incompatible with the political humanism Arendt hoped to restore.

What does Hannah Arendt mean by world alienation? The cultural reality to which she refers is just as complex as its contrary, the spirit of worldliness. Human beings cease to love and care for the common world when they no longer feel at home in it. This sense of collective estrangement can result from several interrelated causes[78]: the collapse of a stable and durable world clearly divided into public and private realms; the forgetfulness of the past which endows the enduring things and places of the world with their historic meaning and importance; the disintegration of the web of citizenship that forms around and within the boundaries of a common world; the political failure to honor action and speech by creating the cultural and institutional conditions required for their excellence; the decline of common sense and its role in disclosing a shared objective world; the adoption by Galilean science of a cosmic perspective that threatens the distinctively political way of perceiving space and time; the invasion of the public realm by biological and private concerns so that the disinterested *ethos* of the republican citizen is effectively lost; the limitless growth of a waste economy that relentlessly depreciates all durable, worldly things; the heuristic focus of historians on invisible lawful processes, so that the intrinsic worth of particular objects, persons and events is no longer recognized. When human beings become estranged from the world and its narrative history, they lose their connective bonds and their sense of continuity with past and future. In the resulting isolation, they no longer strive to honor their ancestors or to accept their fiduciary obligations to posterity. Deprived of their common earthly home, they turn either to private and solitary joys or to the fictional worlds created by ideology. World alienated beings tend to be deeply disoriented and dangerously lonely.

If the political story of modernity is centered on world alienation, then three events assume major importance in the narrative: the European discovery of America, the expropriation of ecclesiastical property during the Protestant Reformation, and the rise of modern science and the technology it inspires and employs.[79] The voyages of exploration in the fifteenth and sixteenth centuries, which led to Europe's historic engagement in Asia and the Americas, were the beginning of a much greater process of discovery. European adventurers began by surveying the surface of the earth and eventually directed their attention to the entire universe. The process of terrestrial discovery reached its climax in the mapping of the earth as a whole. From the geographic and scientific perspective, this was a remarkable accomplishment, but its political implications were far more ambiguous. In order to survey the earth as a single entity, cartographers must place themselves at a theoretical distance from it. They must adopt, at least in their thought experiments, an extra-terrestrial standpoint that requires deliberate disengagement from earthly affairs. Voluntary detachment from a human context or practice is the price demanded by intellectual mastery of it. This theoretical principle had been known since Pythagoras, who contrasted the active contestants in the festival of life with the solitary spectators, who refrained from participating in order to understand what was really going on.[80] Although the exploration of the Americas soon led to the earth's political transformation, Arendt explicitly emphasized its enduring impact on theoretical inquiry. The great modern discoverers began to think about the earth from an extra-terrestrial standpoint. This allowed them to survey its spatial parts as a comprehensive whole, but it radically changed the way in which earthly affairs appeared.

The keys to this radical shift in perspective are distance and angle of vision. As previously noted, the political standpoint on human affairs is in many respects analogous to that of the theatre. The audience views the actors across a limited distance that allows both parties to see, hear, and respond to each other. The actions and speeches on the stage retain their full particularity and the spectators apprehend the dramatic protagonists as distinct persons. The aesthetic distance required for dramatic meaning to appear leaves the appropriate human scale intact. Men and women are seen against the background of the world within the same plane of vision that they enjoy in their inter-relations. This shared visual space allows the spectators to become actors and the actors to become spectators as they rotate positions within the web of relations they constitute together. Although each person in the political web occupies a unique standpoint, citizens, in their mutual relations, share a common space of appearances and a common language for discussing what occurs within it.

Given a single plane of vision, a common world at a limited but observable distance, and similar sensory faculties, those who act and speak and those who bear witness to their actions occupy the same phenomenal space. But this is no longer true for the extraterrestrial surveyor whose perspective is analogous to that of the airplane traveler observing the city from a space far above it. What the traveler gains in comprehensive vision, he evidently loses in concrete detail. He is no longer able to observe his peers in an appropriately human way. The significant phenomenal differences among them disappear at this distance, and the vertical line of sight flattens out the heterogeneity of the world. The result is a phenomenal uniformity that conceals whatever is of striking importance in the political realm. The extra-terrestrial observer has lost the common sense world as the shared medium of interaction with others. Human beings no longer appear to him in their uniqueness and particularity against the background of the human artifice. Phenomenally speaking, they have become like so many indistinguishable insects moving meaninglessly across the surface of the earth. If human beings and events are judged politically by the way they appear, then the standpoint of the earthly mapmaker is fundamentally anti-political. For there is nothing in the appearances granted from on high to indicate the dignity and importance of what he observes.

Mapmakers retain the ability to coordinate the intra-worldly and extra-terrestrial perspectives and to connect intelligibly their correlative sets of appearances. The opposing perspectives are of course complementary for they ultimately refer to a common set of sensible objects. But to use a contemporary semantic idiom, they fix their reference in opposing ways so that the languages they use to speak about the same objects no longer have a common meaning.[81] Were the intra-worldly standpoint of politics to be lost or neglected, the extra-terrestrial surveyor would be completely unaware that he was observing human beings engaged in the shared pursuit and preservation of excellence. Now, every human perspective and linguistic description conceals as well as reveals. This dual epistemic function is the inevitable consequence of our finitude.[82] The most effective remedy for this limitation is discursive plurality, the cultivation of many perspectives and vocabularies for speaking about the world as a whole. In the *Pensées*, Pascal succinctly articulated the normative principle for finite beings: "Unity without multiplicity is tyranny; multiplicity without unity is confusion."[83] Even if human beings were to leave the world just as they found it, they would still transform their grasp of its meaning and importance by altering the way it appears to them. In itself, the adoption of the cartographer's perspective did not cause human beings to care less for the world. But it revealed how political awareness and concern depend on the world's way of appearing to those who belong to it. The dignity and importance of politics were threatened by this disengaged manner of seeing even before it was radicalized in the new theoretical science of nature.

A shift in theoretical perspective alters our way of thinking and speaking about what exists. Profound intellectual changes often have an important but indirect influence on the world's internal order and contents. But the most direct way of transforming the world is to create significant new artifacts or to destroy those with the greatest historical resonance. A change of comparable importance occurs when the worldly balance between the public and the private realm is upset. From Arendt's political perspective, such a lasting imbalance was the most salient effect of the Protestant Reformation. This momentous religious event, generally remembered for fragmenting Christian unity in Europe, appeared to her in a very different light. Her genealogical

emphasis was on the expropriation of ecclesiastical and m̲͟ ͟ ͟ ͟ ͟ ͟
the militant reformers and their political allies, a process th̲ ͟ ͟ ͟ ͟
to the expropriation of peasant land and to a denial of the ͟ ͟ ͟ ͟ ͟
private property.⁸⁴ Hannah Arendt spoke of property in hallowe͟ ͟ ͟
cause she believed that a privately owned place in the world is a ͟ ͟
condition of a good human life. Human beings need a private and inv͟ ͟ ͟
home where they can regularly retreat for shelter and quiet before f̲ ͟ ͟ y
emerging to participate in public affairs. The expropriation of property deprives them of this critical privacy and accelerates the disappearance of
worldly buildings and places of assembly. It is essential to remember that
Arendt was defending private property and not the limitless accumulation of
individual or corporate wealth.⁸⁵ As a source of stability and temporal continuity, property is an essentially worldly phenomenon. In its tangible worldliness it differs significantly from creating and amassing wealth, which in
modernity has often depended on confiscating property and destroying durable artifacts. The most important forms of private property are inheritable
lands, homes and use objects that can be preserved and transmitted through
the history of a family. Taken together they ensure the spatial and temporal
continuity that human beings seek in a meaningful home. Private property
plays an essentially conservative role in human affairs. It establishes settled
boundaries within which human beings can securely move, and it fortifies the
world against natural processes and the destructive capacities of action and
work. Given the mortality of human beings and the threat of futility affecting
all their words and deeds, they need reliable frameworks of security and
permanence to raise them to the level of worldliness. Private property, a
common set of enforceable laws, a shared liberal education, a secure fund of
historical memories and the Roman trinity of religion, tradition and authority
are the basic conservative elements on which worldly permanence is
founded.⁸⁶

The pursuit of limitless wealth, by contrast, sacrifices the worldliness of
property to the ideal of productive abundance. Both modern capitalists and
socialists see worldly stability as an obstacle to their goal of unlimited material production.⁸⁷ The constant expansion of wealth depends on a cyclical
process of production and consumption that devours durable artifacts and
transgresses the boundaries of privacy. In the global economy, the purpose of
fabrication is no longer to create a durable world of artifacts as a common
source of inter-generational continuity. The evaluative priority has clearly
shifted from the objective worth of the thing made to the relentless expansion
of the production process itself. The deliberate depreciation and destruction
of worldly objects has become a necessary condition of unlimited economic
growth. Unless private consumption keeps pace with collective production
the machinery of abundance creation will grind to a halt. The unquestioned
commitment to economic growth is regularly justified by appeals to the

public good, since the continuing expansion in social wealth depends on a steady rise in economic productivity. The political and cultural outcome of this process is the dubious equation of the common good with the production, distribution and consumption of nonworldly objects. Promoting the life process of society, therefore, takes precedence over every other public concern; to the inexhaustible demands of this process non-economic goods must be regularly sacrificed. It is as though biological nature had invaded the human world, transforming durable and permanent things into objects of consumption. The insatiable modern appetite for wealth has created a waste economy in which the worldly spirit of conservation and protection spells ruin. Within the cultural and spiritual atmosphere of a waste economy, the *ethos* of Arendtian politics declines to the zero point.[88]

The most serious source of world alienation is modernity's proudest achievement, the continuing revolution in science that officially began in the sixteenth century though its roots are traceable to the late middle ages. For Arendt, no event is more significant for advancing that revolution and for revising our sense of human existence than the invention of the telescope and its use by Galileo in the creation of a universal physics.[89] Galileo's deliberate alliance of mathematics and technology makes him the true father of modern science and the best representative of its revolutionary spirit. Galileo's originality was twofold. He rejected Aristotle's division of natural science into celestial and terrestrial physics, with each field of inquiry distinguished by its own laws and principles. He proposed, instead, to create a universal science of nature whose governing principles would apply throughout the cosmos. The new physics would overcome the phenomenal dichotomy between earth and sky that had dominated western poetry and reflection since Homer and Hesiod. This traditional dichotomy, which Aristotle largely accepted, was based on the way things naturally appear to a terrestrial observer. Since the origin of human history, individual mortals had stood on the earth, their natural home, and looked to the sky in their yearning for immortality. Premodern poets and cosmologists had agreed that the heavens were somehow nobler than the earth, more lasting, more beautiful and more harmonious in their orderly motions; as sensible appearances seemed to confirm, they belonged to a different order of being from terrestrial substances.[90] But Galileo deliberately opposed the principle of mathematical and physical simplicity to the obvious fact of phenomenal difference. He reasoned that the *cosmos* was uniform in its elements and laws and that this underlying mathematical uniformity was ontologically more basic than the diversity of sensible appearance. Galileo's commitment to cosmic homogeneity allowed him to create a universal science with mathematical laws of unrestricted scope.

Galileo fortified his mathematical challenge to the testimony of the senses by using the telescope, the first purely scientific instrument in western history. He thereby forged an enduring bond between the modern practice of science and the use of technical instruments deigned to enlarge our native capacities.[91] As Galileo argued, the telescope disclosed the untrustworthiness of sensory evidence and the inherent relativity of the terrestrial perspective. Since he aspired to an absolute knowledge of nature, equivalent to that of God nature's Creator, he rejected the reality of the sensory world as it appears to human perceivers on the earth. True being and sensible appearance part company in the metaphysics of Galileo, and they remain estranged or in conflict to the present.[92] Galileo supplemented his scientific discoveries with the problematic distinction, also to be found in Locke, between primary and secondary qualities. Despite the questionable merits of this philosophical dichotomy, it had the intended effect of further reducing confidence in our sensory powers. On Galileo's account, the unaided senses present us with a veil of misleading appearances concealing the true geometrical structure of nature. The ancient Heraclitean dictum, that nature (*physis*) loves to hide, became the oracular key to interpreting modern science. Since nature conceals its truth behind misleading appearances, it must be compelled to yield through force what it fails to offer to the theoretical observer. The purpose of scientific instruments and experiments, therefore, is to put nature on the rack, to reject its deceptive sensible testimony, and to extract through coercive ingenuity and pressure the hidden truth it withholds.

In their impact on human self-esteem, modern scientific discoveries had a double edge. They seemed to confirm the Cartesian fear that prior to the modern age human beings had been living in a dream world. Pre-modern men and women had accepted the reality of the world as disclosed through sense perception, but in this uncritical trust they had been profoundly deceived. Scientifically enlightened minds were finally liberated from this primordial deception. By refusing to accept the reality of appearances, the reliability of the sensory given and the validity of the terrestrial standpoint, modern thinkers were now in a position to discover ultimate truth. This belief was the source of their enlightened pride and their unprecedented contempt for their intellectual predecessors.[93] The rapid rise of faith in mathematical physics and technology was accompanied by an abrupt loss of confidence in tradition, common sense and whatever owed its authority to the natural or historical given. But the distrust of the given was not confined to human sensory powers. All metaphors of knowledge and truth based on receptivity and revelation lost their former credibility. If ocular vision could no longer be trusted, then the eye of the mind was no more reliable than its sensory analogue. If the voice of tradition should be met with suspicion, then so should the inner voice of conscience, scripturally understood as an authoritative encounter with God's prophetic word.[94] As long as human beings accepted the framework of terrestrial appearances, they would remain intellectual children divorced from the cosmic perspective of science and the absolute knowledge of nature it claimed to offer.

In her critical reading of the scientific revolution, as in her earlier appraisal of the Protestant Reformation, Arendt's outlook was emphatically political. She was principally concerned with how these historic events affected the cultural requirements of authentic politics. Despite his evident theoretical greatness, Galileo seemed to her a problematic figure because the cognitive vision he proclaimed was politically disastrous. His epistemic privileging of the cosmic perspective undermined the phenomenal order on which politics depends. The political mentality of the citizen is formed within the space of sensible appearances as they present themselves to terrestrial beings. The active citizen, always one among many equal persons, sees the world from a perspective that is intrinsically limited. Each citizen seeks to overcome the limitations of his standpoint, not by ascending to a cosmic perspective that invalidates the reality of the phenomenal world, but by freely exchanging opinions with his peers so that through their shared conversation all aspects of the appearing world might become known and acknowledged. The citizen deliberately refuses a political Archimedean point, whether Platonic, Galilean or Cartesian, that would introduce absolute knowledge, abolishing the plurality of perspectives and opinions from the public realm. For the Arendtian citizen acknowledges that the conduct of politics is essentially relative, based on the finitude of a plurality of persons, whose fragile community depends on their devotion to a common world and their memory of its particular history. The entry of the absolute into politics means the abolition of this plurality of perspectives and opinions, and therefore, the disappearance of public freedom, the *raison d'être* of political life.[95] Galileo's epistemic strategy for liberating modern science from common sense could only bring tyranny if applied to the city and its citizens. While he sought to eliminate sensible appearances, diversity of opinion and relativity of perspective, the goal of Arendtian politics is to achieve concerted action and agreement through their free and open interplay. A theory of knowledge based on Galilean principles poses a mortal threat to the practice of politics and to the dignity and importance human beings are prepared to accord it. "Compared with the earth alienation of modern science, the withdrawal from terrestrial proximity in the discovery of the globe and the twofold process of expropriation and wealth accumulation are of minor significance."[96]

In seeking a universal cosmic standpoint, modern philosophers and scientists deliberately tried to distance themselves from the earth. By locating the earth within a centerless universe, they rejected the privileged position it had enjoyed in Ptolemaic astronomy. The ontological reduction of the earth in modern physics foreshadowed the later reduction of particular human beings in nineteenth-century biology. From the cosmic perspective of Darwinian evolution, the unique human person is reduced to a type specimen of organic life, confined to existence on a small and spatially insignificant planet. Human words, works and deeds are comparably diminished in stature; construed in exclusively scientific terms they become the transient phenomenal effects of invisible cosmic processes. If the spatial and temporal perspectives adopted by modern physics and biology were granted canonical status, the critical Arendtian distinctions between nature and world, animal and person, biological survival and historical greatness, instrumental utility and political liberality would all be effaced. The exclusively scientific image of the human being directly threatens Arendtian politics and her understanding of human dignity and uniqueness. And it raises the critical question, how the new sciences of nature can be credibly combined with a comprehensive account of the human person.[97]

Arendt considered Descartes the father of modern philosophy because he gave articulate expression to the dominant spirit of modernity. The defining aspects of that spirit are deeply informed by the discoveries and prejudices of Galilean science: distrust and suspicion of the human faculties and of the historical traditions that had relied on their epistemic validity; the flight from the sensibly given world into the interior recesses of the self and the subsequent subjectivization of philosophy; the exclusive acceptance of mathematical physics and Cartesian introspection as reliable sources of truth coupled with a relentless critique of common sense; the continuing search for a secure Archimedean point that would restore the lost harmony between appearance and reality. Only from the perspective of the "true Archimedean point" would things again appear as they really are.[98]

Radical Cartesian doubt was the initial philosophical response to the new science of nature. In fact, the history of modern philosophy can be told as the articulation and exhaustion of the potentialities of hyperbolic doubt.[99] In this narrative of cultural suspicion, Descartes and the later Wittgenstein would serve as the terminal figures, the first inaugurating and the second repudiating unrestricted critical reflection. Cartesian doubt is radical because it extends not only to the truth claims of particular judgments, but to the human faculties themselves, particularly the senses and common sense. In rejecting the epistemic reliability of the senses, Descartes generalized the position of Galileo and laid the groundwork for all specifically modern thought.[100] He memorably expressed the enduring modern suspicion that the senses are not adequate to the experience of reality.[101] Yet in putting the senses and their intentional objects into question, Descartes undermined more than he had originally intended. He unleashed a general spirit of suspicion that subverted all of our receptive capacities. This systemic distrust of receptivity and givenness helps to explain the low esteem of religious faith, divine revelation and contemplative activity in the modern age. All forms of intentional awareness that depend on vision, the reception of the given or the apprehension of appearance will remain cognitively suspect, as long as perceptual awareness is regarded as invalid or untrustworthy. Descartes overlooked this unintended consequence of hyperbolic doubt since he confidently relied on his own clear and distinct intuitions as guarantors of truth. But the point was not lost on his critical successors whose radical exercise of doubt undermined the "self-authenticating intuitions" with which Descartes hoped to silence scepticism and permanently ground the construction of science. Within Descartes' own philosophical project, hyperbolic doubt was practiced to achieve epistemic certainty. Yet, his lasting cultural contribution was not the serene assurance of certainty but the spirit of pervasive suspicion that undermined nearly everything human. By the nineteenth century the acids of hyperbolic doubt had been extended to religion, morality and politics. They subverted the foundations of the Roman trinity and gave the problem of political and moral authority a new and unprecedented urgency.[102]

Galileo jeopardized the dignity of politics by shifting the standpoint of reliable cognition from the earth to the universe. In his quest for absolute knowledge, he criticized the relativity of the terrestrial perspective and the sensible appearances it offered to human perception. Sharing Galileo's dream of a universal physics, Descartes endorsed the ideal of a scientific Archimedean point. But he soon realized that an absolute standpoint could be neither sensory nor spatial in character. As long as human knowledge depends on the mediating operations of the body and the senses, it is subject to corporal finitude and to an inevitable relativity of perspective. Descartes therefore proposed a method for achieving scientific cognition in which the body played no causal role. Rather than placing the Archimedean point in the heavens, he located it in the pure disembodied ego, the extensionless Cartesian self.[103] His selection of the disengaged rational ego as an absolute standpoint had two clear advantages: it liberated the attainment and formulation of knowledge from causal dependence on the body, and it grounded the expanding edifice of science on a foundation of indubitable certainty. In this way, Descartes hoped to satisfy two epistemic goals with one principle. The Cartesian ego would serve simultaneously as the first object of incontrovertible knowledge and the privileged subject of all justified cognition.

To ensure the absolute sovereignty of the ego, Descartes had to redescribe the nature of human experience. On his revisionary account of perceptual awareness, human beings are no longer able to perceive a common world through their senses. Rather, each finite subject is confined to a private space of appearances from whose objective contents all other persons are excluded. In each conscious episode, the solitary subject always encounters an aspect or feature of himself. The sensible world no longer enjoys an objective, or intersubjective, status independent of the particular perceiver, but is ontologically reduced to an inner state of the individual's private awareness. Its *esse*, or being, as Berkeley later insisted, is merely to be perceived (*esse est percipi*).[104]

The relocation of sensible phenomena within the private consciousness the subject has the advantage of rendering the ego immune from error. Cartesian subjects cannot be mistaken as long as they confine their perceptual judgments to describing what they immediately perceive. As the perceived object has no other reality than its immanent presence to the subject in thought, the ego cannot mistakenly judge it to be other than it is. But there was an ontological as well as an epistemic purpose to Cartesian revisionism. Since Descartes denied the formal or mind independent reality of the proper sensibles like color or sound, by reducing them to private states of consciousness he could preserve their status as appearances without acknowledging their true being or reality. The Galilean depiction of nature as pure mathematical extension was effectively vindicated and the specter of universal skepticism laid permanently to rest. Descartes' flight from the sensible world into the interior privacy of the disembodied self established the intellectual framework of modern thought. Most of Descartes' successors accepted his account of human consciousness although they forcefully challenged the metaphysical and epistemic conclusions he had drawn from it.[105]

Arendt's objections to Cartesian subjectivism were far more radical than those of his philosophical critics. If Descartes' account of sense perception were taken literally, as it rarely is even by philosophers, it would subvert the elemental conditions of political existence. It is simply not possible to identify political agents or citizens with disembodied Cartesian egos. The former belong to a web of adult persons united in their collective concern for the common-sense world. The latter are solitary beings confined within the private enclosure of consciousness and incapable of shared discourse and action with others. Descartes maintained that his disembodied egos were causally united through belonging to the natural world, a membership based on a mysterious connection to the bodies with which they were contingently joined. But at the level of intentional awareness each subject is locked within an exclusively private space; there is no common world that appears to them all providing the shared background and reference for their public speech and debate.

Descartes attempted to preserve the dignity of the solitary ego by endowing it with freedom and causal agency. He opposed the consciousness of the thinking self to the brute extension of mindless nature,[106] trying in this way to integrate the Galilean account of the physical universe with a moral and theological description of the human being. Viewed from the cosmic perspective of the new science, the earth, the human body and the human senses shrink to insignificance within the vastness of the indefinite universe. But the true self is metaphysically independent of the body and the body's trivial position in cosmic space and time.[107] The bearer of human freedom and dignity is not the finite incarnate person with whom we share our public and private lives, but the invisible self in its splendid and sovereign isolation, the

Archimedean knower of the universe and the rock of epistemic certainty. Far more is at stake here than the ontological bifurcation of the human person. For the metaphysical division of the human being into *res extensa* and *res cogitans* is the logical consequence of a more fundamental decision about the valid modes of intentional awareness. In Cartesian philosophy, methodology regularly determines metaphysics. What Descartes sought to establish in his philosophy was the exclusive legitimacy of two epistemic perspectives on reality: the cosmic perspective of mathematical physics for the understanding of nature and matter (*res extensa*) and the introspective awareness of the disembodied ego for the comprehension of mind and humanity (*res cogitans*). On this epistemic fiat rests the uneasy division between natural science and modern philosophy. As we know from their subsequent histories, each of these ambitious rivals demanded imperial authority in the realm of knowledge. The interminable metaphysical debates between scientific materialists and philosophical idealists merely reflect this deeper methodological struggle for supremacy. The relentless pressure for ontological reduction in the modern age is ultimately based on the antecedent will to epistemic uniformity.

From Arendt's political perspective, the ontological quarrels of modern philosophy are largely parochial. They unfold within a framework of uncritical assumptions to which she was resolutely opposed. The simplest way to summarize her objections is with the following historical judgments: modern science has abandoned the earth for the universe; modern philosophy has rejected the world for the self.[108] What was lost or excluded through these cultural upheavals was the epistemic validity of common sense, the distinctively political mode of thought and cognition. Hostility to common sense was a central feature of both the Galilean and Cartesian traditions. Since their critique of common sense was ambiguously expressed, it is important to recall the depth of their opposition. It was not the common sense judgments of a particular culture or historical period that were rejected but a distinctive way of thinking and speaking about the sensible world. The epistemic content of common sense varies, of course, with differences in history, geography and culture, but this recognized diversity coexists with a similarity of intentional standpoint.[109] Whenever human beings live together in a stable community, common sense is their method of relating to the concrete and particular objects that serve as the center of their public life. Since modern science and philosophy aspired to absolute knowledge, universally valid for all times and places, they rejected the legitimacy of common sense, whose practical judgments are undeniably relative in scope. In one sense, of course, Galileo and Descartes were right. Common sense is prone to a general bias against the theoretical aspirations of science; its cognitive interest is limited to what can be said here and now in the resources of ordinary language. When this bias interferes with legitimate theoretical pursuits, it should be actively resisted and overcome.[110] But the "enlightened" leaders of modernity failed to demarcate the scope and limits of common sense and to define its complementary relation to scientific theory. Instead, they placed common sense under an epistemic quarantine, threatening the dignity of every human practice that depends upon its operation. No human activity suffered more than politics from this epistemic stigma, for the decline of common sense portends a related decline in allegiance to the common world.

Let us briefly examine the internal connection between rejecting common sense and fostering world alienation.[111] In the individual person, common sense is the cognitive capacity through which the disclosures of the separate senses are integrated. Perceptual objects appear to us as unified things, rather than as discrete sensible elements, because common sense coordinates their different sensible aspects into a unified whole. Human beings orient themselves in the world by means of these enduring and identical objects; they provide our daily touchstone of reality and reference. The durable objects of common sense are also the source of temporal continuity linking the past to the future for successive generations of mortals. We have noted the special importance of works of art, the most permanent of all worldly objects, in this critical generational bonding.

In communal life, the exercise of common sense plays a parallel role. To appreciate its epistemic contribution, consider the following analogy. Common sense allows individual persons to coordinate the different sensible aspects of a single perceptual object, so that they may deal with it as a unified whole. But individuals are always members of a community of persons, just as the objects they experience are discrete things in a common world. Each person occupies a unique spatial and temporal standpoint with respect to this common world of objects. Each of them apprehends a limited set of phenomenal aspects under which the world appears. Contrasting perceptions of the world are articulated in the diverse opinions the members of a linguistic community reciprocally exchange. Once again, we are confronted with the tension between plurality and unity. How are different persons to coordinate their distinctive opinions to achieve an enlarged understanding of their world as a whole? It is the common sense of a community that allows its differently situated members to comprehend one another, to judge the worth of their opposing opinions, and to coordinate their collaborative actions. In the individual, common sense provides cognitive access to the unity and stability of particular objects; in public life, it assures access to a common world for a plurality of persons.[112] When the credibility of common sense is denied, human beings lose faith in their perceptual experience and in the cooperative activities that depend on a shared sensible realm. Modern art and modern science have effectively exploited this distrust of common sense, but its effect on modern politics has been disastrous.[113]

A stable objective world disclosed through the senses to several human generations is an essential condition of a fully human life. It provides the necessary framework of shared intelligibility within which human beings can speak and act together. This common world exists in between its unique members, simultaneously separating and connecting them; it provides the familiar public matrix where they learn their native language, acquiring a community of allusion and reference. As young people master the languages and traditions of their community, they also master its inherited practices, institutions and forms of life.[114] They appropriate a common standard of reality based on their inter-subjective experience and discussion of public objects. Gradually, they achieve an understanding of history through their encounter with a world more durable than the mortal beings now living within it. With the knowledge of history comes an acceptance of their obligations to the world, a growing awareness that this complex public achievement transcends the lives, interests and concerns of its present inhabitants. But if this man-made world is to provide a stable dwelling place for posterity, it must be cared for and conserved. The limited interests of particular persons and groups are often at odds with the stern demands of the world. But who shall speak and act for the common world against the pressure of interest groups or the claims of the ego, if the spirit of worldliness declines, or the world undergoes such constant transformation that it loses its power to elicit human loyalty and allegiance? The modern hunger for wealth and the limitless demands of a waste economy are effectively depriving the old world of its durability and permanence. Our Galilean and Cartesian inheritance have weakened respect for common sense and subverted our trust in sensible appearances. These powerful cultural forces have accelerated the process of world alienation, severely eroding our shared commitment to the destiny of the world.[115]

THE VICTORY OF THE *ANIMAL LABORANS*

The profound cultural oppositions between old and new have their deepest source, perhaps, in contrasting appraisals of the basic human powers. For modernity has deliberately reversed the hierarchical judgments of its ancestors. Both the Platonic and Christian traditions assigned the highest ethical priority to the contemplative life.[116] In defending this supremacy claim, Aristotle and Aquinas treated contemplation as the most god-like human activity, the source of our deepest beatitude. The purest and most complete happiness shall be found in the beatific vision of God, "in seeing Him who sees all things."[117]

In the *Human Condition*, Arendt argued that the classical tradition had blurred the distinctions within the active life through its one-sided attachment to contemplative activity. She openly welcomed the newly restored dignity the Renaissance accorded to the *vita activa*. At the beginning of modernity, it seemed that the West might provide a balanced account of the different human capacities and that the Platonic opposition between *theoria* and *praxis* would finally be overcome. Unfortunately, the modern age shared the classical assumption that a single "central, human preoccupation must prevail in all the activities of men."[118] If this restrictive assumption were true, then the full range of human powers must be subordinated to a single highest power and function for the sake of its flourishing. In Plato's *Republic*, this meant that human beings must labor, erect a durable public world and engage in political activity solely to enhance theoretical contemplation and the incomparable joys it affords. On this model of hierarchical subordination, the several forms of the active life are simply different means to a final contemplative end. Since classical culture was explicitly teleological, this would partly explain why the internal differences within the *vita activa* often went unremarked. The phenomenal diversity among the various "means" was occluded by focusing attention on the end they allegedly served.

The special dignity ascribed to the *vita contemplativa* in classical and medieval culture did not survive the triumph of Galilean science and the Cartesian spirit of radical doubt. Both modern philosophers and physicists agreed that true being was concealed from the receptive faculties of sense and intellect. Humanly designed instruments and coercive experiments were needed to unveil the secrets of nature; pre-critical thought must undergo a methodological catharsis in order to satisfy the demands of Cartesian certitude. For the leading moderns, certain truth can only be grasped through active extortion and never through receptive contemplation. Etymologically, the contemplative person is a spectator, one who withdraws from the active life to witness in stillness the unfolding spectacle of time and eternity.[119] The contemplative spectator is a person of vision in an age deeply suspicious of sight and the cognitive metaphors dependent upon it. Drawing on Plato's epistemic imagery, Arendt claimed that the traditional concept of truth was based on the experience of revelation.[120] Once theoretical inquirers turned away from the active life and the transient spectacle of temporal becoming, eternal truths would appear to their minds with an infallible immediacy and directness. In these solitary acts of contemplative vision, whether sensory or intellectual, the being of reality and its mode of appearing are one and the same.

In modernity, however, being and appearance have permanently parted company; uncritical acceptance of the phenomenal given is the least reliable guide to truth. The active powers of the ego, especially fabrication, must be critically employed to penetrate beneath appearances to the invisible reality they conceal. This strategic reliance on making explains the importance assigned to experiments in the new scientific method. Carefully designed experiments are intended to compel nature to answer the questions of greatest interest to the scientific community. In Kant's famous metaphor, scientists are critical judges compelling nature's response to unwelcome questions she would prefer to evade. Being and truth no longer reveal themselves freely to the attentive observer; they must be extracted from nature through ingenious experiments and coercive force. The crafting of technical instruments, the deliberate design of evidence yielding experiments and the creation of scale models replicating invisible natural processes have become fundamental aspects of scientific practice. Kant accurately expressed modernity's epistemic spirit in the core principle of his Copernican revolution. "Human reason has insight only into that which it produces after a plan of its own."[121]

The unprecedented dignity accorded fabrication partly derives from its role in experimental science. But the new importance of making also depended on the insistence of Baconian pragmatism that knowledge be verified by the testimony of fruits and works.[122] Bacon claimed that classical philosophy had been sterile and useless because it failed to increase human mastery of nature. For Bacon, the ultimate purpose of science is the expansion of technical power, the increasing control of natural processes in the service of human needs and desires. Genuine knowledge is invariably productive, relying on the instruments of *homo faber*, the human toolmaker, while progressively supplying him with new instruments and methods for dominating the world. The cultural triumph of *homo faber*, the elevation of making or fabrication over every other human capacity, is clearly signaled in Bacon's teleology. In Bacon's philosophy, theoretical inquiry has lost its inherent dignity and purpose and become simply a means to technical mastery and power. In the new pragmatic canon, fruits and works, the tangible objects of consumption and use, have become the ultimate test and goal of human inquiry.

The cultural supremacy of *homo faber* constitutes a double reversal of the Greek understanding and appraisal of the human capacities. Even before Plato had subordinated *praxis* to *theoria*, Hellenic culture had rendered an unambiguous verdict on the comparative merits of action and fabrication. Political activity was superior to craftsmanship because a public life devoted to beauty and greatness was more fully human than one based on the principle of utility.[123] Although craftsmen produce durable worldly objects, the exercise of their craft is imbued with the *banausic* spirit.[124] They reduce natural substances to serviceable materials that they shape and mold in the light of their guiding ideas. Craftsmanship is governed by the principle of utility that treats all natural and human things as means or instruments to the controlling end of the finished work. The Greeks judged the artisan to be politically dangerous because he was constantly tempted to extend the mentality of his craft to the public realm. He was habitually inclined to subvert the political principles of greatness and beauty by applying the principle of utility beyond its legitimate scope. The *polis* clearly depended on *homo faber* to construct private homes and public assemblies for its citizens, but it distrusted the mentality of craftsmen, more attached to the process of fabrication than to its durable worldly products. The spirit of public freedom animating the *polis* was explicitly distinguished from the governing *ethos* of fabrication.

"To be what the world was always meant to be—a home for men during their life on earth—the human artifice must be a place fit for action and speech, for activities not only useless for the necessities of life but of an entirely different nature from the manifold acts of fabrication by which the world itself and the things in it are produced."[125]

The political capacities of action and speech are constantly threatened with futility. Unlike fabrication and productive labor, they leave behind no visible trace of their occurrence. Without an enduring world to shelter their transient appearance and a web of witnesses to preserve them in public memory, they would disappear from human awareness as though they had never been. The same threat of mortal oblivion hangs over the human person. The unique individuals who enter the world at birth will gradually be forgotten by their temporal successors unless they can distinguish themselves through their memorable words, deeds and works. Arendt believed that the discourse and actions of human beings disclosed their unique identities in a way that their labor and work could not. To know who human beings are you must attentively observe them in action; you must see and hear them speak, act and interact in the presence of their peers. Only in the bright light of a public realm culturally regulated by normative standards of excellence, can the greatness of the human person appear. For the classical Greeks, haunted by their awareness of human mortality and constantly faced with the danger of oblivion, historical greatness offered the highest promise of worldly survival.[126] Through great words and deeds inserted into the public realm, a mortal citizen could arrest the attention of his peers, secure their grateful remembrance and preserve the narrated memory of his name and his being as long as the *polis* endured.[127]

With the eventual decline of the independent Greek cities and the Roman republic, and the cultural ascent of the Christian religion, the classical understanding of politics lost its hold on the West. The recovery of pre-Christian political ideals during the Florentine Renaissance, however, created a new respect for the republican tradition. But why did the promising resurgence of civic humanism prove so fleeting? As the political capacities of action and speech were no longer eclipsed by contemplation, what kept them from reclaiming their traditional honor and dignity? Beyond the various reasons already examined in this chapter, it was the cultural priority assigned to fabrication, to the works of *homo faber*, which explains their comparative neglect. Modern appraisals of the cultural rivalry between politics and craftsmanship are directly opposed to those of antiquity. The moderns explicitly elevated fabrication above action and speech; they celebrated the mentality of the artisan and toolmaker and never really embraced Arendt's spirit of worldliness. As respect for the *vita contemplativa* effectively disappeared, a new form of political life, the modern nation-state, began to emerge. But politics within the nation-state no longer enjoyed the importance and dignity granted it in classical Greece and republican Rome. The utilitarian standards of fabrication were directly imposed on political activity to the comparative disadvantage of action and speech as distinct capacities in the active life.[128]

Four criteria internal to the practice of craftsmanship helped to cast modern politics in a negative light: productivity, durability, sovereignty and utility. Craftsmen are inherently productive; they use their tools and skills to build the durable things of the world. Once they have completed their work, they can publicly exhibit the objective goods it has produced. Because the visible products of fabrication survive the production process, the creativity and talent of the craftsman remain open to public display. The finished works are available to bear witness to the excellence of their craft. But the speeches and deeds of political agents survive only in the memory of witnesses; they leave no visible, phenomenal trace of their prior existence. The conduct of politics does not produce durable goods open to continuous public inspection. Moreover, in politics it is the excellence of the agents themselves that is judged, rather than their art or their skill. The political virtues of citizens or statesmen are not separable from the political actions and speeches that embody them, as the merits of the well-made artifact are separable from the personal qualities of its maker. The impersonal standards by which artifacts are judged are inappropriate to politics where personal excellence (*arete*) rather than craft (*techne*) is decisive.[129] In the realm of art we judge the excellence of the work rather than the virtues of the artist, but in politics the decisive judgment is always a personal appraisal of the statesman or citizen.[130]

Although the finished works of craftsmen are ultimately intended for public inspection, artisans generally practice their craft in isolation. An evident tension exists between the privacy required for the process of making and the public nature of the thing that is made. Craftsmen need isolation so that they can focus attention on their creative or inventive ideas. They use these antecedent mental images to guide the unfolding of the fabrication process; in practicing their craft, artisans are not lonely because they have their ideas and the emerging artifacts to keep them company. In fact, the deliberate isolation of craftsmen guarantees their sovereign control over the finished work. If they don't admire what they have made, they can modify their work or even destroy it. The fabricating life of *homo faber* is the closest human approximation to the modern ideal of individual sovereignty. Only the resistance of the raw materials they selected and their deficient skill can limit the realization of their original plans. And even these limits are not rigid, for craftsmen can build or buy tools to supplement their native powers and to transfigure the resistant materials with which they work. When human beings aspire to sovereignty, to complete independence in executing their projects, they invariably picture themselves as artists or builders, the makers or shapers of the human world. But the ideal of sovereign control is structurally unattainable in politics, the domain of human plurality par excellence.[131] When human beings participate in public affairs, they are never alone but always in the company of their civic peers. Although their speeches and deeds are intended to win the support and approval of their fellows, their powers of mastery and coercion are limited. In the political sphere, citizens are free to give or withhold support for the initiatives of others as they choose. The realization of a favored political project or plan therefore is always uncertain, not only because of chance (*tyche* or *fortuna*), but because the continuous interaction of free beings regularly has consequences no one could antecedently foresee. Anyone who enters political life hoping to execute a utopian project is likely to be frustrated. Either they will see their original plans transformed through the free responses of other persons or they will be tempted to use coercive force so that the purity of their original vision might be preserved. The modern ideal of individual or collective sovereignty, modeled on the practice of *homo faber*, is essentially anti-political. It relies on a form of mastery and power that only applies to isolated artisans rather than to free citizens joined in political community.[132]

The political limitations of sovereignty are indirectly related to the constraints on the principle of utility. The creative life of *homo faber* actively fosters the utilitarian mentality. In the process of making, artisans look upon blueprints, models, tools, raw materials, even on their own skill, as means to completing the finished work; these disparate resources simply exist, in reserve, for the artisans' use. The craftsman, *qua* fabricator, instrumentalizes reality, depriving natural or worldly things of their intrinsic dignity and worth. Only the completed work is treated as an end in itself, and even the finished product risks becoming a means once it is effectively detached from the production process. The utilitarian spirit of craftsmanship seriously devalues the things of the world, particularly those phenomena of intrinsic worth that exist to be judged for their beauty or greatness. Instrumentalism is particularly dangerous in politics, for when consistently applied to the public realm, other persons become disposable means in the service of cherished political ends. The internal logic of utility clearly entails this unwelcome consequence. Strict adherence to its canons confronts political agents with a difficult dilemma: either they coerce or manipulate other people to achieve their political aims, or they discover a practical alternative to technical reason, the dominant form of modern rationality. Immanuel Kant, who saw clearly the threat to human dignity entailed by the principle of utility, attempted to circumscribe its validity in his second formulation of the categorical imperative. "So act as to use humanity, both in your own person and in the person of every other, always at the same time as an end, never simply as a means."[133] But Kant's ethical language, explicitly designed to restrict the scope of utilitarian thinking, was itself stamped with the metaphor of use. Thinking of interpersonal relations in the artisan's categories of means and ends is inherently dangerous. The manipulation of other persons through physical or psychological coercion is inconsistent with treating them as ends. For both moral and political reasons, the utilitarian mentality must be excluded from public affairs without excluding teleology from the appraisal of public policies and practices.[134] But lacking normative criteria for assessing political agents and actions and a viable concept of political rationality, this exclusion of technical reason appears to leave politics in limbo. This is where political thinking has tended to remain, torn between a Kantian morality of intention divorced from the concrete demands of reality and a utilitarian ethic of consequences modeled on non-political forms of the active life.[135]

Despite the isolation of *homo faber* and the seclusion in which artisans normally work, they remain bound to the public world through the durable artifacts they display and exchange there. The desire to display what they make maintains their interest in the public realm as a space of appearances where things can be judged by the standards of beauty and greatness. Although craftsmen deliberately distance themselves from others in the course of production, they ultimately welcome the presence of peers as an audience or market for their finished work. While their utilitarian prejudices make them critical of action, their desire to preserve a public space of appearances makes them potential allies of responsible citizens. Politically speaking, *homo faber* remains an ambiguous figure; political existence is impossible without the durable world craftsmen build, but politics is threatened by the utilitarian mentality with which they build it.[136]

The cultural triumph of *homo faber* rested on the early modern conviction that making is the highest human activity. This cultural victory was achieved at the expense of both philosophy and politics; when judged by the normative standards of fabrication, both contemplation and action are found wanting. Throughout the eighteenth century, even until the outbreak of the French Revolution, the supremacy of making as the dominant human capacity was nearly uncontested. But intellectual and social forces were already working to deprive *homo faber* of his cultural glory. By the late nineteenth century, the mentality of the productive laborer, the *animal laborans*, had become so pervasive that the classical distinction between labor (*ponos*) and work (*poiesis*) was no longer fully intelligible.[137] Work was deprived of its essential connection to worldliness and subordinated to the interests of individual and species life. Although productive activity continued to be celebrated, the intrinsic worth of the worldly artifact, the durable thing produced, no longer greatly mattered. The sheer abundance of humanly produced objects, the fecundity of the production process itself, had become the paramount public concern, reducing the question of the artisan's merit to the margins of interest.

The three great modern revolutions, scientific, democratic and industrial, indirectly contributed to this cultural conflation of labor and work. The concept of a lawful recurrent intelligible process is the most important heuristic notion in the new science of nature. The epistemic ideal of modern scientific inquiry was to discover universal patterns among functionally related events that could be expressed in mathematical equations. Aristotle's heuristic focus on the formal and final causes of substantial change was superseded by Galileo's model of causal explanation through mathematically expressible functional laws. The lawful explanation of recurrent natural events became more important to science than discovering the what and the why of a particular thing. This theoretical preoccupation with explanatory processes gradually altered our thinking about human affairs. The new scientific paradigm also revised the concept of fabrication, for it shifted attention from the finished product to the recurrent process of production. The thing-like character of the finished work, the aspect of fabrication that bound it to the public world, eventually lost its importance. In assessing productivity what mattered was the cycle of production itself and the sheer abundance of objects it could yield.[138] The structural differences between work and labor are far more evident in the character of the things they produce than in the nature of their productive processes. The temporal durability of use-objects and the intended permanence of art works contrasts strikingly with the perishable nature of consumer goods. At their best, artisans and craftsmen build lasting and beautiful objects to enhance human life in the world. But *homo faber*'s cultural rival, the *animal laborans*, only produces objects of consumption to meet the demands of biological life. "Considered in their worldliness the things needed to sustain the life process are the least worldly and most natural of all things."[139] Because the inescapable demands of nature and life are cyclical, labor must continually reproduce what human beings need to survive. These cyclical biological demands account for the repetitive nature of laboring; its rhythmic pattern of production and consumption mirrors the natural movement of the life process itself. As long as the life span of the mortal individual served as the cultural measure of historical time, the traditional distinction between labor and work was relatively secure. But evolutionary biology explicitly substituted the life span of the species for that of the individual in its most important temporal calculations. From the cosmic perspective of species life, even the production and replacement of use-objects began to appear cyclical; for over many generations the human species regularly consumes the durable products of work just as the individual person survives by consuming the products of labor. Both evolutionary biology and Galilean cosmology effectively obliterated the important cultural distinctions between nature and history. The cosmic perspective of the new sciences obscured the phenomenal differences separating the human world from nature and setting the web of citizenship apart from the biological kinship of *homo sapiens*. When the *animal laborans* eventually displaced *homo faber* in the cultural hierarchy of modernity, human beings were reconceived as productive animals, but the only goods such animals produce are those needed for biological life.

The evolving culture of modernity has gradually eroded a set of ethical distinctions that were fundamental to the ancient world. In Aristotle's *Ethics*, liberal activities are explicitly contrasted with those that are necessary or useful.[140] *Ponos*, the activity of productive labor, was understood to be necessary because the maintenance of individual and collective life depended on it. *Poiesis*, the activity of fabrication, was considered useful, because it produced the artifacts and instruments human beings employ in the conduct of their daily affairs. The properly free or liberal activities, such as *theoria* and *praxis*, could only occur when the demands of necessity and utility had already been satisfied. In the order of their temporal appearance, politics and philosophy are evidently dependent on labor and work.[141] But in the teleological order the priority is reversed; human beings are not born simply to live but to live well. For the ancient Greeks, living well meant liberation from the incessant demands of one's animal nature for the sake of those higher, freer, more human activities that are desirable in themselves and for their own sake. In the liberal realm of free activities, beauty and excellence are the appropriate standards of judgment. Here, human beings, together with their works, deeds and discourse, are judged on the basis of their intrinsic merit. To paraphrase an idiom in Kant's moral theory, the realm of freedom is a kingdom of ends where the standards of nature and the demand for utility no longer hold sway.

The cultural supremacy of *homo faber* first imposed utilitarian standards on politics. Political action and speech lost their intrinsic dignity, as they were reconceived as technical means to extra-political ends. Politics ceased to be a privileged realm of public liberty and excellence regulated by its own standards and purposes, as it increasingly fell under the influence of economics. Nothing could be more foreign to the Greek understanding of politics than its present subordination to economic imperatives. For the classical Greeks, economics meant the rule of the private household.[142] It referred to that dark sphere of human existence governed by inequality, necessity and coercion. Only when released from the burdensome cares of household management, was the family head free to participate in the life of the *polis* from which private concerns and biological demands were effectively excluded. Human existence was deliberately ordered so that economic goods served as pre-conditions of liberal activities. When the demands of their animal nature had been satisfied, human beings were free for the distinctively human activities of citizens and thinkers.

During the French Revolution at the close of the eighteenth century, economic necessity first became an important political concern.[143] The great political revolution in France brought the poor and the destitute, *les misérables*, into the very center of the realm of freedom. The industrial revolution that followed brought productive manufacture out of the household and into the space of appearances. These historic events radically reversed the traditional understanding of publicity and privacy. In the classical world, the private realm had been the sphere of necessity and the public realm the space of genuine freedom. But from the mid nineteenth century onward, a major reversal in human priorities occurred. Satisfying the life requirements of society became the basic political obligation. As politics inherited the heavy burden of responding to natural necessity, so private life, in the intimacy of the home, became the new sphere of individual liberty.[144] These startling cultural reversals help to explain why Greek political terms have so radically changed their meaning in the modern age. For our contemporaries, the *telos* of the human city is primarily commercial and economic, while the goal of one's private existence has become preserving and exercising individual freedom. This dramatic restructuring of communal life coincides with the elevation of labor to cultural supremacy in the hierarchy of human powers. Labor has become the noblest and most important human activity because the life of the species that it effectively sustains has become the highest recognized good.[145] The first duty of modern political leaders is to organize the public realm as a center of production and distribution yielding the maximal number and diversity of consumer goods. Political activity can still claim to promote public happiness, now understood as the aggregative sum of private satisfactions of the individual members of the consumer society. The mentality of the *animal laborans* dominates this public culture of production and consumption. Human happiness has lost its traditional association with excellence, with activity in accordance with virtue.[146] Happiness is now identified with easing the burdens of the human animal, with increasing the pleasures and reducing the pains of the laboring life. There has been an undeniable increase in cumulative wealth, but the cost in human aspiration and self-understanding has been immense.

> It is frequently said that we live in a consumer's society, and since labor and consumption are but two stages of the same process, imposed upon man by the necessities of life, this is only another way of saying that we live in a society of laborers. The point is not that for the first time in history laborers were admitted and given equal rights in the public realm but that we have almost succeeded in levelling all human activities to the common denominator of securing the necessities of life and providing for their abundance.[147]

NOTES

1. Arendt, *The Human Condition*, p.321.
2. Although Arendt based her normative conception of politics on actual political activities, much that is considered "political" today does not satisfy her normative criteria. In fact, most of contemporary politics is "anti-political" when judged by her standards. The phrase "Arendtian politics" is meant to signify her civic republican understanding of political existence.
3. Arendt tended to emphasize the rupture of tradition caused by the signature events of the modern age. In this chapter, I follow her lead, but in the opening section of chapter 5, I question whether the discontinuity she emphasizes is overstated.
4. The philosophical critique of the Aristotelian and Scholastic traditions is clearest in Descartes, Bacon, Hobbes, and Spinoza.
5. See *Thinking* p. 11 and *Past and Future*, p. 9, 14, 93-95.
6. See *Past and Future*, p. 193-195 and *Thinking* p. 12. For the condition of thinking without banisters, see *Hannah Arendt: The Recovery of the Public World,* ed. M. Hill (New York: St. Martin's Press, 1979), 314.
7. *Human Condition*, 294.
8. See *Hannah Arendt: The Recovery of the Public World*, p. 311. "The decisive thing is whether your own motivation is clear-for the world-or for yourself."
9. *Past and Future*, 156. In *The Human Condition*, the contrast between life and the world undergirds the distinction between the private and public realms and the related distinctions among labor, work and action. In *On Revolution*, the contrast between life and world serves to distinguish the social and political objectives of revolutionary action.
10. Chapter 6 of *The Human Condition,* "The *Vita Activa* and the Modern Age," clarifies the concept of world alienation and explains its historical sources. This theme, which first surfaced in *The Origins of Totalitarianism*, later served as a fixed reference point in Arendt's political reflection.
11. Ludwig Wittgenstein, *Tractatus Logico-Philosophicus* (1963; London: Routledge and Kegan Paul), p. 7. Arendt's concept of the world is clearly rooted in the phenomenological tradition of Husserl and Heidegger, particularly Husserl's concept of the *Lebenswelt* and Heidegger's concept of *Dasein*, as the human way of being-in-the-world.
12. In her political thought, Hannah Arendt concentrated on the public realm of appearances and on the words, deeds and works it was designed to evoke and display. Later, in the *Life of the Mind*, she offered an ontological defense of appearance against both classical and modern critics, see Volume one, *Thinking, The Life of the Mind*, pp. 19-65.
13. For life, worldliness, and plurality as structural features of the human condition, see *The Human Condition*, 7-11.
14. I explore the political implications of the temporal shift from the life span of the mortal individual to the life span of the human species in the final section of this chapter.
15. For the anthropological distinction between *who and what*, between person and nature, see *The Human Condition*, 10-11, 175-182.
16. For an incisive account of human beings as self-interpreting animals, see Charles Taylor, "The Self in Moral Space," *Sources of the Self* (1989; Cambridge: Harvard University Press) 25-52.
17. For the newborn's dual relationship to life and the world, see "The Crisis in Education," *Between Past and Future*, pp. 185-193.
18. For memory as the faculty of depth, see *Past and Future*, 94.
19. John Dunne in *A Search for God in Time and Memory* articulates the dimensions of time that are ordinarily out of mind: the existential time of the person's life conceived as a whole; the historical time of the world in which individual life is embedded; the cosmic time of nature which serves as the scientific background to human history; the divine time, or timelessness of God that provides the ultimate context for all modes of temporality. In Hannah Arendt's politically oriented approach to education, the emphasis is on historical time, the memorable past of the old world.

20. Conversely, systemic failures of education point to a pattern of world-alienation retreat from political responsibility. *Past and Future*, 190.

21. There are evident parallels between *The Human Condition*, devoted to a phenomenological analysis of the active life, and *The Life of the Mind* with its division of mental activities into thinking, willing and judging. For Arendt, the essential difference is between activities constituted by their phenomenal character and those that are invisible and do not appear.

22. See *The Human Condition*, section 18, "The Durability of the World" and section 23, "The Permanence of the World and the Work of Art."

23. See *Between Past and Future*, 41-48.

24. See *The Human Condition*, 192-195; *Past and Future*, 44-46.

25. Arendt, *The Human Condition*, p. 64. "The distinction between the private and public realms, seen from the viewpoint of privacy rather than of the body politic, equals the distinction between things that should be shown and things that should be hidden."

26. The brightness of public light, though it illumines greatness and excellence, can be too intense for persons and activities requiring darkness and shelter. As growing beings, the young need the cover of darkness as the roots of plants need the protection of depth. The good deeds commanded by Jesus and experiences of personal intimacy also require privacy as a condition of their authentic occurrence.

27. See *The Human Condition*, 73-78.

28. See Section 5, "The Polis and the Household," *The Human Condition*, 28-37.

29. See *Thinking*, "Mental Activities in a World of Appearances."

30. See Aristotle's *Physics* Book II, chapter 1, 192B 8-37.

31. "For what each thing is when fully developed we call its nature, whether we are speaking of a man, a horse or a family" Aristotle, *Politics*, I, 2, 1252b 32-35. Aristotle's concept of nature is ultimately teleological. *Eidos* is revealed in *telos*; the nature of a thing is fully disclosed only in its flourishing or attainment of perfection. Those things are natural to man on which his achievement of perfection depends. Hannah Arendt largely follows the moderns in leaving teleology aside; she often associates the natural with the biological dimension of man, that which links him to the animals and makes him a subject of scientific inquiry.

32. Arendt, *The Human Condition*, p. 7. Her distinction between the world and the natural environment corresponds to the difference in German between *Welt* and *Umwelt*. Nature is transformed into a habitable world through the deliberate exercise of human art (*poiesis*).

33. Ibid. p. 152.

34. See *The Human Condition*, 153-174.

35. For education as the humanizing process through which the young are introduced to the world and its history, see *Past and Future*, 188-193.

36. "The term 'public' signifies the world itself, insofar as it is common to all of us and distinguished from our privately owned place within it." *The Human Condition*, 52.

37. For the tension and complementarity between politics and craftsmanship see *Past and Future*, 215-219.

38. *Between Past and Future*, p. 215. "To be a philistine, a man of *banausic* spirit indicated . . . an exclusively utilitarian mentality, an inability to think and judge a thing apart from its function or utility. But the artist himself being a *banausos* was by no means excluded from the reproach of philistinism; on the contrary, philistinism was considered to be a vice most likely to occur in those who had mastered a *techne*, in fabricators and artists."

39. See *The Human Condition*, 296-297; 306-309; 313; 320-323.

40. See *The Human Condition*, 7-10; 22-28.

41. *The Human Condition*, 175-181.

42. See Alexis de Tocqueville's *Democracy in America*, vol II, "Why democratic nations show a more ardent and enduring love of equality than of liberty." "Men cannot enjoy political liberty unpurchased by some sacrifices, and they never obtain it without great exertions," 101-102.

43. Major parts of *The Human Condition* are devoted to contrasting the specific mentalities of the *animal laborans* and *homo faber* from the republican spirit of the *zoon politikon*.

44. *The Human Condition*, p. 204.

45. The demands of biological necessity permeate the household; the canons of utility govern the craftsman's activity in his private studio.

46. This is one reason courage was considered the cardinal political virtue. See *The Human Condition*, 36; 186-187.

47. *The Human Condition*, 38-39.

48. "Now every citizen belongs to two orders of existence; and there is a sharp distinction in his life between what is his own (*idion*) and what is communal (*koinon*)," Werner Jaeger, *Paideia* (1945), III, p. 111. Today, we are surprised to discover the etymological connection between the English word 'idiotic' and the Greek term *idion*. For the Greeks, those things were idiotic whose significance was exclusively private.

49. For the range of principles that can inspire participation in the public realm, see *Past and Future*, 152-153 and *On Revolution*, 88-89; 97-98.

50. *The Human Condition*, 214-215. For Aristotle's account of civic friendships based on a shared sense of justice, see *Nicomachean Ethics*, Book VIII, chapter 9.

51. *The Human Condition*, p. 71.

52. See "The *Polis* and the Household" *The Human Condition*, p. 28-38.

53. See *Past and Future*, 137,153-155; *On Revolution*, 86, 97-98, 101-103, 106-109.

54. "The objects the imitator represents are actions." See Aristotle, *Poetics,* 1148a 1-2.

55. Both theatrical and political activities depend on the "public spirit" of participants and witnesses. See *On Revolution* 221-229.

56. For the important concept of goods internal to a practice, see Alasdair MacIntyre, *After Virtue* (1981; Notre Dame, Indiana: Univ. of Notre Dame Press), pp. 175-189.

57. A concept she borrowed from Kant's *Critique of Judgment*; see *Past and Future*, 220, and *Lectures on Kant's Political Philosophy*, 43-46.

58. *On Revolution*, 106-109.

59. For Arendt's explicit critique of bourgeois politics, see *Origins*, chapters five and nine.

60. *Human Condition*, 36-37; 186-187.

61. Arendt, *Crises of the Republic*, p. 203.

62. Arendt believed that the autonomy of politics was compromised in antiquity by the transcendent concerns of philosophy and theology, and in modernity by the commercial and industrial concerns of economics. Antiquity compromised politics from above, modernity from below.

63. *Human Condition*, 14-21.

64. *Human Condition*, 21, 314-316.

65. Early Christian references to the world are not entirely negative. On many occasions, the world symbolizes human nature resisting God's grace. But there are other contexts in which the world refers to the redemption of human nature. "God so loved the world that He sent His only begotten son to redeem it." Through Jesus, God sought the redemption of the world rather than its abandonment to the forces of evil.

66. St. Matthew's Gospel, chapter 6. For Arendt's radical understanding of Christian goodness, see *The Human Condition*, pp. 65-69.

67. For St. Augustine, the two symbolic cities are dominated by the erotic priorities of their citizens. There is an evident parallel between the Augustinian division of men and their deepest allegiances and the Platonic distinction between the lovers of true being and the lovers of visible spectacles. In the Platonic framework, the true philosophers are really citizens of an ideal Republic while the nonphilosophers attach themselves to an earthly *polis*.

68. St. Paul, Corinthians I, chap. 13.

69. Aristotle, *Nicomachean Ethics*, Book 10, 1177b30.

70. In *Romans*, Paul emphasizes that the saving power of Christ reduces the significance of all traditional distinctions. United by their faith in the risen Lord, Jew and Gentile, slave and free, male and female are equal at the deepest level human beings can attain. This is the common inheritance that constitutes the community of the universal church.

71. See chapter 18 of the *Prince*. "And it must be understood that a prince, and especially a new prince, cannot observe all those things which are considered good in men, being often obliged, in order to maintain the state, to act against faith, against charity, against humanity, and against religion." For Arendt's political defense of Machiavelli see *Past and Future*, 136-138, *On Revolution*, 36-39, 286-287, *The Human Condition*, 77-78.

72. For Arendt's description of Machiavellian *virtù* see *Past and Future*, 137 and 153.

73. "Goodness, therefore, as a consistent way of life, is not only impossible within the confines of the public realm, it is even destructive of it." See *The Human Condition*, p. 77.

74. For Arendt's political analysis of secularization, see *Human Condition*, 253, 320; *Past and Future*, 135-141; *On Revolution*, 159-161.

75. For the complementarity of the cardinal and theological virtues, see Joseph Pieper, *The Four Cardinal Virtues, and Faith, Hope and Love*, See also, chapter 13 of Alasdair MacIntyre's *After Virtue*.

76. See MacIntyre, *After Virtue*, p. 153 and 167-168.

77. *Human Condition*, 253-254, 320-321.

78. These Arendtian themes are drawn from *Origins*, *The Human Condition*, *Past and Future*, and *On Revolution*.

79. See Section 35, "World Alienation" in *The Human Condition*, 248-273.

80. See Nicholas Lobkowicz, *Theory and Practice*, (1967; Notre Dame, Indiana: Univ. of Notre Dame Press), pp. 5-9.

81. Michael Dummett interprets the Fregean distinction between *sinn and bedeutung* so that the *sinn* of a referring expression is a particular way of fixing its reference. See Dummett's *Frege: Philosophy of Language* (1973; New York: Harper and Row).

82. The theme of finitude as limitation is critical to Arendt's thought. It is a dangerous sign of *hubris* when we neglect human limits and seek to overcome them. In her consistent emphasis on finitude, Arendt is indebted to both Heidegger and Jaspers.

83. Blaise Pascal, *Pensées* #510.

84. For the role of private property in preserving worldliness, see *The Human Condition*, pp. 53-65; pp. 96-101; 230-233. ". . . the privately owned share of a common world...is the most elementary political condition for man's worldliness."

85. For the distinction between property and wealth, see *The Human Condition*, 61-67, 252-253.

86. For the critical importance of stability and durability, see *On Revolution* 222-225. "The effort to recapture the lost spirit of revolution, must, to a certain extent, consist in the attempt at thinking together and combining meaningfully what our present vocabulary presents to us in terms of opposition and contradiction." 223-224.

87. See *Crises of the Republic*, 211-219.

88. *The Human Condition*, 133-135.

89. *The Human Condition*, 257-268.

90. Aristotle, *The Parts of Animals*, 644b2-645a37.

91. "What Galileo did and what nobody had done before was to use the telescope in such a way that the secrets of the universe were delivered to human cognition with the certainty of sense-perception; that is, he put within the grasp of an earth-bound creature and its body-bound senses what had seemed forever beyond his reach." *The Human Condition*, p. 259-260.

92. "If Being and Appearance part company, forever, and this—as Marx once remarked—is indeed the basic assumption of all modern science, then there is nothing left to be taken on faith; everything must be doubted." Ibid. p. 250. For Arendt's spirited defense of appearance as "true being" see *Thinking*, chapter 1.

93. It is striking to compare Aristotle's critical appropriation of his predecessors with the cavalier dismissal of their importance by Descartes, Hobbes and Bacon.

94. *The Human Condition*, 274-280, 319-320; *Past and Future*, 29-32.

95. *Past and Future*, 146. "The *raison d'etre* of politics is freedom, and its field of experience is action."

96. *The Human Condition*, p. 264.

108 Chapter 2

97. We can trace this urgent concern in modern philosophers from Descartes and Kant to Wilfrid Sellars and Charles Taylor. Like Kant, Sellars wants to combine the scientific understanding of nature and man with the preservation of moral freedom and ethical discourse. Taylor explicitly opposes the ontological and methodological reduction of human beings to the assumptions of scientific naturalism.

98. For the modern search for the Archimedean point and the dangerous consequences of applying it to human affairs, see *The Human Condition*, 257-284, 322-323.

99. *The Human Condition*, 273.

100. The history of hyperbolic doubt would open with the dreams and demons of Descartes' *Meditations* and close with the linguistic therapy of Wittgenstein's *On Certainty*. For a decidedly arch version of the story see Richard Rorty's *Philosophy and the Mirror of Nature*.

101. Both Galileo and Descartes rely on the example of touch to raise doubts about the objective validity of perception. But this is a dubious choice for reasons that Arendt makes obvious. "The pain caused by a sword or the tickling caused by a feather indeed tells me nothing whatsoever of the quality or even the worldly existence of a sword or feather. Only an irresistible distrust in the capacity of the human senses for an adequate experience of the world—and this distrust is the origin of all specifically modern philosophy—can explain the strange and even absurd choice that uses phenomena which, like pain or tickling, obviously prevent our senses from functioning normally, as examples of all sense experience. . . . If we had no other sense perceptions than these in which the body senses itself, the reality of the outer world would not only be open to doubt, we would not even possess any notion of a world at all." *The Human Condition*, pp. 114-115.

102. See "What is Authority," *Between Past and Future*, pp. 91-141.

103. *The Human Condition*, 284.

104. See George Berkeley, *Principles of Human Knowledge*, Part one, section 3.

105. For Descartes' successors, intentional awareness is typically construed as the subject's perception of an immanent object within the consciousness of the perceiver. The direct object of awareness exists in and for the act of perception; at the same time it represents a cause external to the perceiver's consciousness that served to bring it into being. Given this model of human perception, the representational account of awareness, the epistemic and ontological problems of modern philosophy naturally follow. But the credibility of the model itself is another matter.

106. See Descartes' *Meditations*, Meditation II.

107. See Michael Polanyi, *Personal Knowledge*. "For as human beings, we must inevitably see the universe from a center lying within ourselves and speak about it in terms of a human language shaped by the exigencies of human discourse. Any attempt rigorously to eliminate our human perspective from our picture of the world must lead to absurdity," *Personal Knowledge*, 3.

108. *The Human Condition*, 6.

109. For an excellent account of common sense as a legitimate intellectual standpoint, distinct from but complementary to the standpoint of explanatory science, see Bernard Lonergan, *Insight* (1958; New York: Harper and Row, 1978), pp. 173-181.

110. For the general bias of common sense against the mind's inherent theoretical desires see *Insight*, pp. 225-242.

111. This theme pervades several of Arendt's most important texts: *Origins, The Human Condition, Past and Future, On Revolution, Lectures on Kant's Political Philosophy*.

112. Any human practice that depends essentially on public discourse and argument will require a common field of reference and meaning. Descartes' representational model of awareness subverted the requirements of intellectual community and drove philosophers, as diverse as Frege and Arendt, to defend the basic conditions of inter-subjectivity. For common sense, the existence of a common world guarantees a plurality of opinions potentially intelligible to all participating members.

113. Arendt is particularly interested in the uneven cultural histories of the different human capacities. One factor uniting modern art and science is their reliance on ingenious fabrication; a second is their conscious refusal to accept the appearances of the sensible world. Science

seeks the invisible causal processes underlying phenomena; modern art creates an alternative set of appearances deliberately designed to undermine confidence in the way things "normally" appear.

114. The later Wittgenstein emphasized the essential connection between learning a language and assimilating a common form of life. When human cognition is considered linguistically, rather than in terms of Cartesian ideas, the plausibility of Descartes' account quickly fades. In both the *Philosophical Investigations* and *On Certainty*, Wittgenstein sought to recover the validity of common sense. Parallel efforts were undertaken by Husserl and Heidegger.

115. Arendt's narrative in *Origins* showed how political alienation in Europe contributed to the rise of totalitarianism. In *The Human Condition*, she emphasized the historical sources of modern world alienation and the cultural reversals to which they led. The two works are complementary though distinct in their topical emphasis.

116. See Lobkowicz's *Theory and Practice* for changing historical appraisals of the *vita activa and the vita contemplativa*. It is important to recognize the semantic evolution of terms like *theoria and praxis*.

117. That blessedness, beatitude, is to be found in the vision of God is the common conviction of such diverse thinkers as Aristotle, Aquinas, Spinoza and Hegel. In subordinating theoretical to practical reason, Kant and Marx challenge the contemplative bias of the philosophical tradition.

118. Arendt, *The Human Condition*, p. 17.

119. See Lobkowicz, *Theory and Practice*, pp. 5-9 for the etymological roots of *theoria and theorein*. The term originally referred to the spectators at athletic festivals who refrained from participating in the games themselves.

120. *The Human Condition*, 15, 17. Arendt appears to follow Heidegger here with his understanding of truth as *a-letheia or unconcealment*. Though she leaves many of her epistemic claims undeveloped, aspects of her epistemology are presented in "Truth and Politics," in *Past and Future*, and *Thinking, Vol 1 of The Life of the Mind*.

121. Kant, *Critique of Pure Reason* (1781; New York; St. Martin's Press, 1961), p. 20.

122. Francis Bacon, *Novum Organon*. "For fruits and works are as it were sponsors and sureties for the truth of philosophies."

123. For the opposition of the beautiful to the necessary and the useful see Aristotle, *Politics* 1333a30-1333b10.

124. See "Instrumentality and Homo Faber," *The Human Condition*, pp. 153-159. "The issue at stake is, of course, not instrumentality . . . as such, but rather the generalization of the fabrication experience in which usefulness and utility are established as the ultimate standards for life and the world of men," p. 157.

125. *The Human Condition*, p. 173-174.

126. See *Past and Future*, 41-48.

127. See *The Human Condition*, 21, for justified doubts about the immortality of the polis and of the Roman Empire. For the revolutionary concern with permanent institutions of liberty, see *On Revolution*, 222-231.

128. See section 42, *The Human Condition*, "The Reversal within the *Vita Activa* and the Victory of *Homo Faber*."

129. The critical distinction between *arete* (personal excellence) and *techne* (craft or skill) is central to those Platonic dialogues where Socrates dialectically engages the Sophists and their pupils. See *Protagoras, Gorgias, Meno and Republic*.

130. A striking feature of Arendt's political philosophy is the attention she gives to the disclosure of the human being in speech and action. She seeks to locate in the phenomenal realm of action the reality of personal dignity that Kant had assigned to the noumenal order. She wants to restore freedom and action to the realm of appearance from which Kant had systematically excluded them. See "What is Freedom" in *Past and Future*.

131. For the incompatibility of sovereignty with human plurality, see *The Human Condition*, 234-235; *Past and Future*, 163-165; *On Revolution*, 153, 156, 160, 168.

132. Ibid. Fabrication itself is not anti-political. What is anti-political is transferring the norms of fabrication into the realm of human affairs.

133. Kant, *Foundations of the Metaphysics of Morals*, p. 96 in the Harper Torchbook edition.

110   Chapter 2

134. One can follow Arendt in rejecting utility as a norm of public policy, without adopting her *atelic* conception of political action. Aristotle's conception of *praxis* unites the nobility of action with its explicit orientation to the common good. I defend Aristotle's teleological approach to politics in both chapters 3 and 5 of this volume.

135. See Max Weber's famous distinction between a Kantian ethic of intention and a Weberian ethic of responsibility in Politics as a Vocation. But Weber ties his ethic of responsibility too closely to technical reason and a voluntarist conception of political ends.

136. See *Past and Future*, 215-219 and *The Human Condition*, 159-163.

137. See "The Defeat of Homo Faber and the Principle of Happiness" section 42 of *The Human Condition* and section 11 "The Labor of our Body and the Work of Our Hands" in the same volume.

138. Whenever the quantity of objects produced is privileged over the quality of what is made, then the standards of labor have gained priority over those of work. This altered priority is precisely what happens in the cultural shift from craftsmanship to mass production.

139. *The Human Condition*, p. 96.

140. See the earlier reference to Aristotle's *Politics* in note 123 and the countless references to this classical distinction in *The Human Condition*. Arendt's political thinking seeks to restore the ancient spirit of liberality to our understanding and appreciation of public life.

141. Aristotle's *Politics*, 2, 1252b26-37 "The state comes into existence, originating in the bare needs of life, and continuing in existence for the sake of a good life." *Metaphysics*, 1, 2, 982b 11-27 "For it was when almost all the necessities of life and the things that make for comfort and recreation had been secured that philosophical knowledge began to be sought."

142. "We therefore find it difficult to realize that according to ancient thought on these matters, the very term 'political economy' would have been a contradiction in terms: whatever was 'economic,' related to the life of the individual and the species, was a non-political, household affair by definition." *The Human Condition*, p. 29.

143. *On Revolution*, particularly chapter 2, "the Social Question," closely examines the problematic role of necessity in the political revolutions of the modern age. Arendt has been sharply criticized for attempting to separate the political and economic objectives of revolutionary action. For a reappraisal of the "social question" from the civic republican perspective, see chapter 5 of this volume.

144. See "The *Polis* and the Household," section 5 of *The Human Condition*, 28-38 and 70-71.

145. For Arendt's argument that life has become the *summum bonum* in the late modern world see *The Human Condition*, pp. 313-320.

146. In the *Nicomachean Ethics*, Aristotle defined *eu-daimonia* in this way: "he is happy who is active in accordance with complete virtue and is sufficiently equipped with external goods not for some chance period but throughout a complete life." N. Ethics, Book I, chapters 7 and 8.

147. *The Human Condition*, p. 126.

Chapter Three

OUR TRADITION OF POLITICAL THOUGHT

> Our tradition of political thought began when Plato discovered that it is somehow inherent in the philosophical experience to turn away from the common world of human affairs; it ended when nothing was left of this experience but the opposition of thinking and acting, which, depriving thought of reality and action of sense, makes both meaningless.[1]

OVERCOMING TRADITION

This chapter is concerned with two types of thinking, the recollective examination of past experience and the critical scrutiny of the narratives and theories to which recollective thinking leads. The first type of thinking is the source of tradition, the shared understanding of the past that is transmitted across the generations. The second type puts tradition itself into question, challenging its fidelity to the past, its adequacy for the present, and its practical relevance for the future. Hannah Arendt was an openly critical thinker who radically challenged the traditions of political thought she inherited. Our purpose here is to examine the substance and validity of her criticism, to present the heart of her case against her theoretical predecessors and to judge it for accuracy and balance.

Hannah Arendt believed that human beings "need to think" if they are to make sense of what they see and hear.[2] It is sensible events and concrete experiences that provide human thought with its focus and reference. Although thinking is an invisible activity, it is bound to the sensible world for its original impetus and its ultimate confirmation. Thinking requires a withdrawal from the world of appearances in order to understand and articulate what specific appearances have disclosed or revealed. Human actions and lives are incomplete without thinking; unless they are remembered and reflected upon they disappear from the world as though they had never existed. The human spirit resists the futility of time's passage by seeking the meaning and intelligibility of the past. By attending carefully to what we perceive, by recalling it, questioning it, by seeking to connect it to our implicit sense of how things are, we transform lived experience into meaning. In Goethe's language, we turn the truth of life and time into poetry, as Plato did with his memories of Socrates or the evangelists with the life and death of Jesus of Nazareth.[3] Through remembrance and reflection we seek to comprehend what has already occurred; through story telling and conceptual discourse we articulate our understanding of experience and invite others to respond to what we say and write.

We think, therefore, in order to understand and then share our understanding with others in conversation and writing. Public discourse by objectifying thought, by making it tangibly present in space and time, also renders its conclusions subject to judgment. We learn to understand and judge the world by comparing our account and appraisal of it with that of our parents, teachers, and friends, and finally with the privileged accounts of the thinkers and storytellers our culture particularly honors. It is useful to distinguish two different ways in which we communicate about the past. We rely on stories, narratives, to preserve a factual record of historical events and individual lives. Through these stories, we establish a common remembrance of our human ancestors and determine what was truly important in what they did and said, endured and suffered, completed or left unfinished. Without these narratives the unique persons and singular events of the past would be forgotten and we, their earthly descendants, would lack a shared standard of reference by which to understand and appraise the world of the present. Without them, our public life would lack depth and discernment.[4]

But the past is not confined to the particular events and agents that are the subject matter of narrative. It also contains recurrent human activities, like thinking, speaking, acting and making, which are among the topics of philosophical thought. Philosophical thinking clarifies the nature of these activities by describing what they are, by distinguishing them from one another, by exploring their complementarity or opposition, by articulating the criteria appropriate to their appraisal, by assigning them a place of importance in the larger pattern of human life. The task of philosophical clarification is advanced by contrast. To understand a specific form of human conduct, like action (*praxis*), we need to distinguish it from other activities along a broad range of comparable dimensions.[5] In what worldly space does the activity properly occur: the public realm of political engagement, the privacy of the familial household, the interiority of the mind or the heart? In what temporal pattern does it regularly unfold: the cyclical pattern of labor, the rectilinear pattern of making with its determinate beginning and end, the unfinished pattern of action whose unforeseen consequences continue endlessly into the future? Is it an activity that occurs in solitude like thinking, or isolation like making, or does it require the presence of peers like action and speech? What are the sensible outcomes in which the activity reveals its occurrence: the durable objects of fabrication, the short lived consumer goods of productive labor, the invisible trains of personal thought that remain hidden from public scrutiny unless transformed into articulate speech and text? And what is the characteristic mentality of those who regularly engage in the activity? Do they have the laborer's absorption with necessity and survival, the artisan's utilitarian outlook, or the free citizen's commitment to public liberty and excellence? As her appreciative readers know, Hannah Arendt excelled at these extended comparisons among the different human capacities. For her, as for the English moralist Bishop Butler, the first principle of thought was simple. Each activity is what it is and not something else; it is to be described in a vocabulary suited to its nature; and it is to be judged by normative standards that are specifically its own.[6]

Political thinking is concerned with what occurs in the public realm, with political events and activities, with the enabling conditions they require, with the relationships they establish or dissolve, with the specific culture and education that prepare human beings for public life. Political narratives commemorate the words and deeds of earlier heroes, like Pericles, Caesar or Lincoln, the momentous events that structure historical time, like the Peloponnesian War or the bombing of Hiroshima, and the rise and fall of great political communities, like classical Athens or imperial Rome. These narratives both inspire and caution us; they teach us the best and the worst that human beings have done when they joined together to pursue common ends.[7] The complementary task of political philosophy is to examine, understand and conceptualize such recurrent political phenomena as action, speech, power, citizenship, debate, judgment, the founding and sustaining of cities. Political realities need to be carefully distinguished from each another and from non-political activities like fabrication or violence. Political thinking develops by attending to events in the public realm and by relying on the revelatory power of political language. According to Arendt, the familiar expressions of natural language and the disclosures of common sense are better guides for political reflection than our inherited theories, because Western political theories, both ancient and modern, have tended to level rather than respect significant phenomenal differences. The natural languages citizens speak are the historical repository of reflection on experience; where an inherited linguistic difference exists, it is reasonable to expect that it marks an enduring phenomenal difference. Most political theories, by contrast, have tended to scorn common sense discourse, and sought to replace it with causal explanations that treat phenomenal differences as surface expressions of an underlying unity.

Arendt's political thinking is oriented to understanding and preserving the past. In this respect, it differs from modern scientific thought, which, since Bacon and Descartes, has wanted to predict and control the future. For Arendt, the purpose of political thinking is to understand and judge the realm of human affairs not to master and rule it. In fact, political thinking becomes ideological when it adopts the pragmatic purposes of modern science and conflates the critical distinction between nature, the realm of lawful necessity, and history, the locus of human freedom and choice. For Arendt, genuine political thinking rests on the validity of that ontological distinction, but pragmatic prejudices have made its observance increasingly difficult.[8]

What is the dynamic connection between political thought and tradition? As its etymology indicates, tradition is a Latin rather than a Greek cultural category. Together with religion and authority it constitutes the Roman Trinity to which we referred in the opening chapter. These three principles complemented the ancient Roman belief that the founding of their eternal city was a sacred and unique occurrence. Religion, tradition and authority were three ways of insuring continuity in historical time, of preserving the unifying bond between Rome's heroic beginning and its subsequent political history.[9] Our inherited concepts of the past and tradition are closely related but not identical. The past signifies the totality of events that have already occurred in time. Tradition is the articulate fruit of sustained reflection on what has been. It is the inherited story of the past that each generation teaches its children as a way of incorporating them into its common life. Tradition selects from the immensity of the past what is worthy of preservation and transmission. It identifies what is memorable, gives it a name and description, and assigns it a place of importance in the storehouse of public recollection.[10]

The evolving language of a community is the cultural carrier of its enduring traditions. When thinking becomes articulate in symbol, story, concept, extended comparison, theory and criticism, it assumes a tangible form that can be passed from one generation to another like a piece of land, a home or a treasured heirloom. Children assimilate the traditions of their parents and ancestors by learning the languages they speak, by listening to their stories, by acquiring a framework of categories and principles for making sense of their common world. This process of generational transmission is neither static nor secure, for the newcomers usually modify and revise what they receive from their elders. They augment and revise the inherited treasures in the course of making them their own. As Alasdair MacIntyre has said, "a living tradition is an historically extended, socially embodied argument" that transcends through criticism and invention the limitations which it inherits.[11]

But traditions can lose their vitality as well as preserve it. They can become rigid, resistant to criticism and unwilling to address the doubts of the young about their continuing relevance.

While no one can live apart from shared traditions, we can orient ourselves towards them in strikingly different ways. In the medieval Christian world, the patristic and conciliar traditions enjoyed the authority of a renowned teacher whose superior insight was tacitly assumed and revered. With the medieval recovery of Aristotle's texts and their translation into Latin, his philosophical principles acquired a special authority among the medieval schoolmen though ecclesiastical critics often condemned them as unorthodox. The cultural currents of modernity were deeply antithetical to the Roman trinity. The modern sciences of nature and politics prided themselves on their radical novelty and dismissed the classical inheritance as an obstacle to intellectual progress.[12] This spirit of hostility to the historical given persisted in the Enlightenment; the *philosophes* generally treated traditional beliefs as a complex of prejudices to be cast away. The nineteenth century masters of suspicion, Marx, Nietzsche and Freud, openly rebelled against the hierarchical frameworks transmitted by classical and Christian thought. In celebrating the causal priority of productive labor, sensuous vitality and the libidinal unconscious, they were deliberately inverting the Platonic hierarchies that Christian theology had largely preserved. Marx's critique of capitalism, Nietzsche's genealogy of morals and Freud's debunking of religion subverted the authority of tradition across a broad cultural spectrum. Recent decades have witnessed a more balanced approach to our intellectual and cultural inheritance. Gadamer and MacIntyre have both challenged the Enlightenment's cavalier rejection of tradition; Paul Ricoeur and Charles Taylor have opposed to the hermeneutics of suspicion an equally necessary hermeneutics of retrieval. These nuanced approaches to the legacy of the past offer an attractive alternative to medieval docility and postmodern suspicion.[13]

How should we describe Hannah Arendt's approach to the western tradition of political thought? She did not think within the tradition by accepting its authority, or outside the tradition by rejecting its relevance. She chose instead to think against tradition by challenging its prejudices, distortions and omissions. Her stance was foundational and critical; she questioned the basic assumptions and principles of western political theory, both classical and modern, arguing that they failed to respect the truth of political phenomena. Her interpretive strategy was modeled on the example of earlier German philosophers. She followed Kant by rejecting the metaphysical prejudice against the realm of sensible appearance; she followed Husserl by reverting directly to observable phenomena in order to break the grip of unexamined convictions; she followed Nietzsche by uncovering the biases that had deformed the traditional understanding of politics; she followed Heidegger in charging the western tradition with a neglect of action and speech analogous to the "forgetfulness of being."[14]

Unlike her Enlightenment predecessors, she did not believe that we could lessen the power of tradition by simply rejecting its validity. Unless we exposed and refuted inherited prejudices they would continue to dominate our thought and speech. The cultural legacy of two millennia had burdened practical inquiry with unexamined assumptions, misleading metaphors, and automatic thought patterns. Only sustained critical thinking could free the mind from these distorting prejudices and allow it to approach political phenomena afresh. Moreover, she insisted that our political theories have been created by opponents and rivals of politics rather than its friends and supporters. Even where explicit distortion had not occurred, the work of articulation had been highly selective. Many authentic political experiences, such as mutual promising and the forgiving of trespasses, had never been properly thematized. To retrieve what had been forgotten, neglected or misrepresented, it was necessary to probe beneath traditional theory to its hidden roots in language and experience.

It is essential to distinguish between critiquing the tradition and retrieving the past. Hannah Arendt shared the Enlightenment's opposition to our premodern political inheritance, but she did so for radically non-modern reasons. She opposed the tradition not because it bound us to the past, but because it concealed what the past most needed to teach us. In this work of selective retrieval, she was also guided by a well-established German paradigm. Recall Nietzsche who attempted to revive the warrior ethic of the Homeric heroes, or Heidegger who wanted to recover the pre-Parmenidean sense of Being as *physis,* or the Protestant reformers who demanded a return to the earliest forms of Christianity before its distortion by Greek and Roman culture.[15] Hannah Arendt excavated the linguistic fragments of the ancient past, in search of a pre-philosophical understanding of political life. She sought in Greek and Roman poetry, history and rhetoric, an understanding and appreciation of politics that the classical philosophers had been reluctant or unwilling to acknowledge.

Because the past and tradition are not the same, it is important to distinguish the stories we tell of them. Hannah Arendt's narrative account of the past is a retelling of memorable political events: the Spartan victory over Athens, the fall of imperial Rome, the rise of the nation state, the French and American Revolutions, the emergence of totalitarian movements and governments.[16] By contrast, her genealogy of our political tradition is a critical examination of inherited metaphors, concepts, arguments, and theories. The two story lines are distinct though often intersecting; the history of political theory is clearly dependent on the correlative history of politics as Plato,

Augustine and Machiavelli bear witness. But the causal relations are often reciprocal, with tradition shaping the human response to historical events as well as interpreting their meaning.

Despite the evident diversity of Western political theories, Hannah Arendt regularly referred to "our tradition of political thought" as a unified whole.[17] She described this tradition as having a definite beginning in Plato's *Republic* and an equally definite end in Marx's reversal of the Hegelian dialectic. On her account, the unifying theme of the tradition was the oppositional relation between theory and practice, thought and action, contemplation and speech. Our tradition began with Plato's critique of the Homeric warrior ethos and his elevation of philosophy to the highest form of human life. It ended when Marx inverted the normative Platonic hierarchies and recast philosophical theory as the servant of revolutionary *praxis*. For Arendt, Plato is the founder and father of political philosophy and his allegory of the cave the most influential description of politics ever composed.[18] The myth of the cave deliberately reversed the Greek understanding and appraisal of politics. It depicted the political realm, the realm of human affairs, as dark, disorienting and shadowy, a realm of appearance and opinion where true being and knowledge cannot be found. To discover what is genuinely real, the philosopher must withdraw from the cave and engagement in political life; he must leave speech and action completely behind before he can contemplate and enjoy eternal truth. After leaving the cave, growing slowly accustomed to the sunlight and taking possession of the truth, he is obliged by anonymous mentors to reenter the *polis* to impose extra-political standards of appraisal on the conduct of his fellow citizens. The eternal forms of speechless contemplation are externally prescribed as the normative measures of political activity, and life in the *polis* is restructured to support the philosophical quest. The compact republican symbol of the philosopher-king expresses Plato's radical proposal that the thinker's solitary discoveries govern the collective action of the city for the benefit and protection of philosophy.

According to Arendt, the declared supremacy of contemplation (*theorein*) as the god-like human capacity ruled western metaphysical and political thought from Plato to Hegel.[19] Marx brought that influential tradition to an end by deliberately subordinating theory to practice, by making philosophy an instrument of revolutionary *praxis,* in open rebellion against the Platonic paradigm. In fact, Marx explicitly inverted the conceptual hierarchies that the philosophical tradition had used to disparage the active life. He glorified labor and violence that had traditionally been denigrated and cast suspicion on the independence of reason and speech. "The philosophers have only interpreted the world in different ways; the point is to change it." Marx converted Hegel's philosophical insight into the dialectical structure of history into a program of revolutionary struggle. Plato's transcendent ideas, which served the philosopher-king as the evaluative measure of human affairs, were deliberately given temporal embodiment by Hegel and then transformed by Marx into blueprints for the making and molding of history.[20]

What did Arendt mean when she claimed that political philosophy ended with Marx? She certainly did not mean that political thinking was no longer important, or that the answers to our political questions had all been discovered. What ended with Marx was the viability of thinking within the set of conceptual parameters that Plato had established. The Platonic tradition that opposed theory to practice, thought to action, and contemplation to political engagement had exhausted its revelatory potential. Marx, although he deliberately inverted the classical hierarchies, still remained bound by the traditional dichotomies. In the Arendtian story, Marx's subversive retention of the traditional framework led to serious contradictions that thwarted his laudable intention to restore the dignity of the *vita activa*.[21] To fulfill that intention, political thinking must abandon Plato's metaphysical and epistemic hierarchies and reconceive theory and practice as complementary activities of equal gravity and importance. Completing this re-conception is a primary goal of Arendt's political humanism.

Hannah Arendt's genealogy of political thought was highly selective and deeply polemical. In her many books and essays, she regularly returned to the same themes and criticisms: that philosophical reflection had failed action and speech by distorting their nature and purpose, that philosophers had denigrated political activities by denying the greatness of human affairs, that the public realm had been invaded by biological concerns leading to the victory of economics over politics. In her critique of the tradition, we find a recurrent appeal to the same theoretical benchmarks. In the ancient world, Greek philosophy and Christian theology disparaged politics in the name of nobler motives and ends. Plato opposed Socrates' love of wisdom to Pericles' quest for imperial power and glory; he opposed philosophical dialectic to political rhetoric and the contemplation of eternal truth to the active pursuit of worldly immortality. Early Christian thought was dominated by apocalyptic expectations that subverted the classical contrast between mortal individuals and immortal cities. By proclaiming the mortality of the world and the immortality of the individual soul, Christianity abolished the immortalizing *telos* of the ancient republic. As Plato had questioned the visible splendor of Periclean Athens, so Augustine cast doubt on the glory of republican and imperial Rome. Augustine claimed that the great deeds of the Roman heroes had been motivated by love of honor rather than love of God, that their ambition for glory far exceeded their devotion to justice. With the collapse of imperial Rome and the gradual acceptance of political responsibility by the Church, the dignity of political activity was not restored. The various forms of the active life were still subordinated to the *vita contemplativa,* and Christian works of charity were to be done in secret rather than the public light.

Augustine interpreted imperial power as a legacy of original sin and Rome's coercive governance as a flawed but necessary means of securing public order.[22]

In the Florentine Renaissance of the fifteenth century, the Christian hostility to power politics was openly challenged by Machiavelli's civic humanism. Machiavelli deliberately reversed the Augustinian critique of republican and imperial Rome; he glorified active citizenship in a political community and denied the supremacy of the speculative life. He praised the Roman passion for honor and glory, advocating a love of country greater than the love of one's individual soul. In retrieving the Roman political mentality, he sought to secularize public life, to judge political agents and actions by the attainable standards of this world rather than by the transcendent norms of Christianity. Augustine rejected the Roman quest for worldly distinction and honor as a sign of vanity and pride, but for Machiavelli this starkly secular ambition was the source of political greatness and glory.[23]

In Arendt's genealogy, the political renaissance Machiavelli initiated was extremely short lived. Although the leading moderns repudiated the metaphysical prejudices of antiquity and spoke scornfully of classical political thought, they created an intellectual and cultural atmosphere incompatible with Machiavelli's humanism. They denied the supremacy of contemplation and honored the dignity of the *vita activa*, but chose fabrication and labor rather than action and speech as their models of worldly activity.[24] They embraced the new science of nature based on material and efficient causes and developed a science of politics to complement their naturalistic vision. In modern political theory, the untutored passions and interests of the self were given precedence over intellectual, moral and civic virtues, and government was reconceived as a collective instrument of private happiness and survival.[25] Bourgeois liberalism, with its emphasis on self- interest and the unlimited acquisition of wealth, created a public culture in which the spirit of the artisan and the commercial trader ruled supreme. The utilitarian categories of means and ends became entrenched in political discourse; rational egoism gradually subverted the *ethos* of republican citizenship; and the commercial transactions of the labor and exchange market became the model for all interpersonal relations. When Marx revolted against the inhumanity of the bourgeois vision, he did so in the name of the laboring animal rather than the republican citizen. While classical liberalism had its roots in the new naturalistic cosmology, European socialism was inspired by Hegel's philosophy of history. Marx embraced Hegel's dialectical conception of historical change, his strong emphasis on associative belonging and group conflict, and his vision of actualized freedom as the ultimate *telos* of protracted human struggle. But he rejected Hegel's concept of Absolute spirit and his vision of human beings as instruments of divine self-knowledge. Marx made social production the principal cause of historical progress, and, according to

Arendt, he bought the mentality and concerns of the laboring animal into the center of modern politics. Although Arendt admired Marx's integrity as an independent thinker, she deeply condemned his baneful influence on our political tradition. "Marx strengthened the politically most pernicious doctrine of the modern age, that life is the highest good and that the life process of society is the very center of human endeavor."[26]

Since the mid-nineteenth century, western political thinking has been confined within the ideological horizon that grew out of the French Revolution. Arendt believed that political conservatism, bourgeois liberalism and Marxian socialism are rival philosophies of history inspired by the revolutionary upheavals in France that lost their limited credibility at the time of the First World War.[27] The Great War set in motion a series of catastrophes that shattered the institutional continuity of Europe. In the dark decades between the wars, the collapse of tradition, which had been essentially a problem for theorists, became the common concern of all thinking adults. When that historical rupture occurred and civic humanists, like Arendt, turned to the received tradition for guidance what they found were a plethora of political theories, ancient and modern, that were basically anti-political. In their urgent concern for the future of Europe, their thoughts were driven back into the past. But between them and the retrievable past stood the formidable barrier of tradition, which had to be lifted before the past could become a source of renewal and insight. The urgency of Europe's political crisis explains why Arendt saw overcoming tradition as a practical requirement rather than a theoretical option. We "need to think" critically about the tradition before we can understand the true meaning of the past, or plan wisely and responsibly for the future.[28]

Our goal in this and the following chapter is to present Hannah Arendt's critical arguments against the "tradition." We will follow her genealogy of political thought, orienting ourselves by her benchmarks, and correlating when necessary her intersecting stories of tradition and the past. What have been the specific failures of western thought in understanding and appraising political action and speech? What prejudices, rivalries and systematic deformations were the causes of these errors? Why have philosophy, theology and the natural and social sciences all viewed politics in a distorted or antagonistic light? These are the primary questions we shall address as we reconstruct Arendt's critical path through ancient and modern political theory. To avoid misunderstanding, I want to be clear that the plot of this story is hers and not mine. I am offering a synoptic account of Arendtian thought rather than aligning myself with its judgments. In some cases, I have dissented from her arguments openly in the text, but the bulk of my critical reservations are confined to the endnotes and to subsequent chapters.

GREEK POLITICAL PHILOSOPHY

> "It is the distinctive mark of Greek philosophy that it broke entirely with this Periclean estimate of the highest and most divine way of life for mortals."[29]

Arendt contended that the ancient Greeks and Hebrews had contrasting perceptions of the worth of human life. While the Jews saw earthly life as a divine gift for which to be grateful, Greek thinkers and poets seriously questioned why anyone would choose to be born. Deeply conscious of human mortality, they pondered whether the certainty of death did not confer futility on every human life. For the Greeks of the Homeric age, human beings were the only conscious mortals in a cosmic order whose gods, celestial bodies and living species were all immortal, *athanatos*.[30] Goaded by this contrast, their poets created a distinctive model of heroic nobility: the *telos* of the Greek hero was to strive for personal immortality, to overcome the equalizing power of death through heroic words and deeds that distinguished their author from all other mortals. But if *praxis* and *lexis*, human action and speech, were to achieve a form of deathlessness, they would need to be witnessed and remembered by peers. In themselves, words and deeds were even more fleeting and transient than the mortal lives they sought to redeem from futility. The hero's quest for immortality, therefore, essentially depended on the public tales of poets and historians to rescue human greatness from oblivion. For Arendt, it was this deliberate quest for worldly immortality that led to the founding and sustaining of the Greek *polis*. The *telos* of the ancient city, as she described it, was to create an agonal competition for excellence (*arête*) among its citizens, to inspire them to words and deeds of singular greatness and to insure their lasting remembrance after death.[31]

Why did ancient citizens enter the public realm of the city and risk its many dangers and demands? They did so in pursuit of the worldly permanence that only an enduring *polis* could offer them. They acted out of love for their city and for the opportunity it provided to excel, to distinguish themselves, to reveal who they really were in the company of their civic peers. Arendt largely based her account of the *bios politikos* on Pericles' celebrated funeral oration in Thucydides' history of the Peloponnesian war.[32] Pericles' task, on that solemn occasion, was to justify the deaths of Athenian soldiers who had fallen in battle. In commemorating and praising the fallen, he argued that their deaths were noble and beautiful (*kalon*) because they occurred in defense of a *polis* that the dead had loved even more than their brief earthly lives. It was the collective greatness of Athens as a political community (*koinonia*) that inspired its citizens to acts of individual greatness, acts that would be remembered as long as their city preserved its freedom. But, for Pericles, in what did the celebrated greatness of Athens consist? In the courage of its ancestors who had preserved the independence and freedom of the *polis*; in the ambition of its people who had extended the Athenian empire throughout the Aegean; in their zeal and energy that had created lucrative wealth and trade; in the daring of its citizens who had left their mark for good and evil throughout the world. For Pericles, the Athenian polis had effectively replaced Homer as the leading teacher of Hellas and as the guarantor of human remembrance. The heroic city no longer needed epic poets to immortalize the greatness of its citizens by insuring them their due mead of glory.[33]

In creating Greek political philosophy, Plato explicitly rejected this Periclean portrait of the ancient city. According to Arendt, Plato did this for historical reasons that were highly specific and for metaphysical reasons that were essentially timeless. In assessing her claim, it helps to begin by recalling the historical context in which Plato's political philosophy emerged. Plato came of age in the course of the Peloponnesian War, a war that culminated in the defeat and subsequent political decline of Athens. Shortly after the war's end, he witnessed the trial and death of his beloved teacher Socrates. Plato's native city had turned against its most virtuous citizen and the life of public inquiry he visibly embodied. In response to the killing of Socrates, Plato withdrew from the political career he had planned to pursue and devoted himself to the philosophical life. He memorialized Socrates and continued his critical work of public interrogation and argument (dialectic) by composing the Socratic dialogues, dramatic recreations of intellectual encounters between Socrates and the cultural and political elite of his time. Plato's dialogues were not the beginning of Greek philosophy, whose origins are traceable to the cosmological thought of the Ionian naturalists, but, for Arendt, they were the beginning of Greek political philosophy; and they bear the stamp of the emotional atmosphere in which they were composed.[34]

From its inception, Arendt believed, political philosophy was not concerned with understanding and appraising political phenomena in their own right. It was not a disinterested study of political reality but a partisan contribution to the cultural rivalry between philosophy and politics written from the perspective of a deeply engaged participant. Its primary purpose, she argued, was either to protect philosophers from the dangers of political activity or to transform the city into a reliable servant of philosophical inquiry. Absorbed in the struggle between the virtuous few and the ignorant many, Plato created a non-Socratic opposition between philosophy and citizenship, between the life of thought and the life of action.[35]

Plato was sharply critical of the political culture that sustained the Periclean city.[36] That culture, an extension and refinement of the Homeric warrior ethic, encouraged love of honor and fear of shame as the psychological basis for civic conduct. It openly appealed to the irascible *thumos* within the human soul rather than the principle of directive reason, and made the spirited warrior rather than the critical thinker the primary model of human excellence. The Platonic Socrates, the central character in the maieutic dialogues, represented a new pattern of human *arete* based on love of wisdom rather than honor, and fear of injustice rather than shame. Plato also challenged the criteria of political greatness that Pericles invoked.[37] For Plato, cities were properly judged by the virtues or vices they cultivated in their citizens rather than by their armaments, wealth and imperial power. Great statesmen were to be judged by the truth of their public rhetoric rather than its persuasive influence over the uninformed *demos*. Did their speeches promote the lasting good of the city or did they flatter the untutored passions of the majority? If the affairs of the *polis* were governed by speech, would it be the speech of the sophist intent upon victory or the speech of the philosopher intent upon truth? And in the *agon* for civic leadership between sophists and philosophers, could the true philosopher ever prevail if the final decision were left to the democratic multitude?[38]

Plato's most serious philosophical criticism challenged the explicit *telos* of Periclean politics. While Plato acknowledged the human longing for immortality, he no longer believed that citizens could immortalize themselves though great words and deeds. He did not reject the *eros* for immortality as such, but he denied that it could be satisfied within the political life of the Periclean city. To achieve true immortality, the citizen must turn away from the realm of human affairs, from its flattery, disorder and rivalry, in order to contemplate eternal and invariant truth. In the silent contemplation of eternal forms the soul experienced genuine immortality and discovered *nous* the only psychic power that was truly divine. When *nous* replaced *logos* as the highest human faculty and contemplation displaced speech as the supreme human activity, the traditional dignity of politics was permanently compromised. Before the emergence of Plato's philosophy, the most important experiences for the Greeks had been political. But for Plato, those same experiences were viewed as obstacles to the supreme good or as provisional instruments for its attainment.[39]

Is there an intrinsic hostility between philosophy and politics, between theorists and statesman, or is their cultural rivalry a tragic misfortune traceable to the Athenian execution of Socrates? Can theory and *praxis* coexist as complementary activities, or are they irreconcilable enemies engaged in inevitable conflict? According to Arendt, Plato skewed the subsequent history of political thought by treating philosophy and politics as diametrical opposites.[40] He starkly contrasted the citizen's changing opinions about human affairs with the philosopher's secure knowledge of the invariant intelligible ideas. He opposed the vanity and pettiness of orators and sophists to the noble concerns of the true philosopher. The ordinary citizen is immersed in the partisan speech and debate of the political assembly. The philosophical citizen withdraws into solitude in search of immutable being. Politics engages human beings in the tumultuous center of the human circle; philosophy disengages them from the disorder and confusion of the civic cave. For Arendt, the critical moment in Plato's story occurs when the philosopher ends his contemplative silence and reluctantly returns to his civic peers.[41] Are ordinary citizens genuinely threatened by philosophical truth so that they inevitably turn against the philosopher as an alien or traitor? Or does the *polis* only become hostile when the philosopher seeks to impose his transcendent norms on the discussion and conduct of human affairs? Do the eternal truths discovered by philosophy illumine political life, or do they coexist in a separate realm that the *polis* can tolerate as long as its autonomy and integrity are respected?

For Arendt, Plato should have acknowledged that thought and action, contemplation and speech, philosophy and politics are complementary but separate activities with an equal claim to human concern and respect. Instead, he sought to escape from the intrinsic perplexities of politics, by imposing extra-political standards and principles upon public life. He compromised the integrity of politics and philosophy, requiring philosophers to govern their native cities as benevolent despots and requiring citizens to act in the service of non-political ends.[42] Arendt believed that political hostility to philosophy was largely a reaction to this coercive proposal, though the fate of Socrates, whom she exempted from the charge of tyranny, surely requires a more complex explanation.

The historical origins of Greek political thought, however, cannot fully account for the tension between philosophy and politics. There are systematic biases against the political that are rooted in the nature of philosophical experience. Philosophers suffer from a *deformation professionelle* that disposes them to rank the soul over the body; interior mental activities over public action and speech; intellectual solitude over communal involvement; intercourse with oneself over discussion with others; a life of theoretical detachment over active engagement in human affairs. Hannah Arendt did not reject these traditional ways of distinguishing between philosophy and politics, but she did oppose the hierarchical order that Plato imposed upon them.[43]

At the core of Greek political philosophy is an elaborate hierarchical ordering of the powers, operations, objects and virtues of the soul.[44] The hierarchy is explicitly teleological with lower elements subordinated to higher ones and existing and functioning for their benefit. *Nous* or intellect is the noblest human faculty and the ontological source of affinity between divine and mortal beings. The human intellect is explicitly contrasted with sensibility, the capacity to perceive and feel, which humans share with the other animals. *Logos*, the capacity for articulate speech, is intermediate between sense and intellect; it is a distinctively human power and, according to Arendt, the political faculty *par excellence*. The basic operations of intellect are thinking, understanding and judging; the climax of the intellectual life occurs in the silent, motionless act of contemplation (*theorein*) in which the receptive mind apprehends the disclosure of invisible and invariant truth. In the classical hierarchy of human activities derived from Plato, thought is ranked higher than action and contemplation given precedence over speech. Discursive thinking at its best prepares the mind for contemplative silence, as action and speech create the political conditions for undisturbed philosophical thought.

Sentient, intellectual and linguistic operations are essentially intentional in nature; through their unimpeded occurrence human beings become aware of a range of entities independent of their own existence. As the soul's operations are ordered hierarchically, so are their intentional objects. The nobler an intentional operation the more excellent the set of entities it can apprehend. The intentional objects discerned in acts of contemplation are the very highest modes of being. They are pure intelligible forms or ideas (*eide*) whose constitutive properties include the supreme metaphysical perfections; they are ungenerated, indestructible, immutable, universal and necessary. Transcending the boundaries of space and time, eternal forms are inaccessible to sense perception and inconceivable by those whose ontological horizon is confined to sensory awareness.

The metaphysical excellence of the forms casts a negative light on the political realm. Political actions and events lack the defining perfections attributed to the forms. Human affairs are subject to constant change; they exhibit a radical contingency and unpredictability; and they consist of sensible particulars confined to a limited region of space and time. What the contemplative intellect seeks in intentional objects cannot be found in political phenomena among the most transient of all sensible things. But the hierarchical contrast between eternal forms and fleeting human events is not confined to the order of being. The cognitive states of the soul that result from intentional activity systematically reflect the excellence of their objects. The mind's apprehension of intelligible forms generates knowledge or *episteme* in the knower, a true certain grasp of invariant necessity. By contrast, political awareness is restricted to fallible opinions, *doxai*, about constantly changing human affairs. Political "knowledge" lacks the epistemic excellence of theory, just as its intentional objects lack the metaphysical perfections of the intelligible forms. Moreover, the apprehension of theoretical truth is radically non-perspectival. To take a geometric example, there is a single, invariant intelligibility that is grasped by all thinkers who understand the Pythagorean theorem, regardless of their spatial or temporal location. But the political opinions of citizens are inherently perspectival; they are as diverse and variable as the worldly standpoints of the thinkers who form and exchange them. For Plato, there is a *chorismos*, a radical ontological separation, not only between intelligible forms and sensible things, but also between knowledge and opinion, the cognitive states they engender in the human soul.[45]

To complete this extended hierarchical contrast, theoretical understanding is a liberal activity, an intrinsic good, pursued by the soul for its own sake and deeply enjoyed whenever it occurs. But political inquiry pursues practical insight as a means to an external end. Its grasp of human affairs is ordered to a *telos* beyond itself, namely the course of action it recommends for this place and time. And action (*praxis*), unlike theory, is not an exclusively intrinsic good; in the well-ordered *polis* it is commanded by the philosophical ruler to create a favorable setting for the *bios theoretikos*. Political action, though clearly inferior to theory, can justify its importance by creating a *polis* where philosophy can flourish and the ablest philosophers will rule.

The avowed supremacy of philosophy over politics rests on this series of hierarchical contrasts. But the distinctions are framed from the perspective of the spectator, rather than the political agent; and they assume that immutable transcendent ideas are an appropriate measure for the appraisal of human affairs. Arendt explicitly rejects that assumption and the epistemic and metaphysical prejudices it is invoked to support.[46] Those prejudices include the following anti-political beliefs: only eternal and invariant objects are worthy of the intellect's sustained attention; because contingent and mutable particulars are not objects of theoretical *episteme*, they lack ontological dignity; true excellence, beauty and greatness cannot be found among sensible phenomena; the validity of theoretical insights undermines the judgments of common sense rather than revealing their limitations. Arendt's purpose is not to reverse these prejudices by inverting the hierarchical order and privileging what the tradition disparaged. This is the self-defeating strategy she attributed to Marx and the nineteenth century rebels against the tradition.[47] The best way to elevate action and speech is not to denigrate contemplation and thought, but to insist on their autonomy and complementarity. If we approach political phenomena without philosophical prejudices, we can find excellence, freedom, beauty and greatness in the public realm. But to do this, we need to abandon the Platonic bias against the sensible world.[48]

The dignity of politics depends on the dignity of sensible appearances, on the reliability of common sense, on the importance of debate and persuasion among political equals, on the acceptance of thoughtful opinion as a rational capacity with its own evaluative criteria and sources of revision. Common sense judgments and theoretical truths are not antagonistic rivals but complementary forms of human knowing, though they easily become rivals when the evaluative standards of each are imposed on the other, or when the defining properties of theory are erected as measures of political opinion. For Arendt, the plurality and mutability of civic opinions derive from the ontology of human affairs and are not evidence of epistemic inferiority.

The deepest source of the problem, according to Arendt, is not the philosopher's attachment to thought and contemplation but the teleological monism of the Tradition—the uncritical assumption that the unity of human life requires a single unifying purpose to which all other human concerns must be subordinated.[49] It is not the importance of the contemplative life, but the hierarchical order erected upon it that she rejects. The philosophical discovery of eternal truth constituted something very different from the political quest for terrestrial immortality, but not something better or more worthy of respect. Plato treated that legitimate difference as an irremediable and fatal opposition; while Aristotle's approach was far more conciliatory, even he insisted on a single hierarchy of excellence culminating in the supremacy of the contemplative life. The theoretical understanding of eternal reality was accorded such importance that crucial differences among human relationships were not attended to. As a result, Greek political theory substituted pre-political, non-political, even anti-political relationships for the mediated interaction of civic peers that constitutes the *bios politikos*. Significant differences internal to the practice of politics were disregarded or overridden, and an influential tradition was created that distorted the nature of action and speech.

THE PLATONIC INHERITANCE

Plato's political philosophy is dominated by his memory of the trial and death of Socrates. In the context of Athenian political history, that trial had a double meaning; it represented the city's indictment not only of an individual man but also of his distinctive way of life. Athens, acting in the name of Greek politics, charged Socrates and Socratic philosophy with endangering the city's well being. Both were accused of impiety, of subverting the ancestral myths about the divine, and of corrupting the young through the discursive practice of sophistry. While the life of the ancient *polis* depended on a shared agreement about justice, Socratic inquiry challenged that cultural consensus and the inherited myths (*mythoi*), opinions (*doxai*) and laws (*nomoi*) on which it was based. By discrediting the traditional sources of justice, Socrates subverted the foundations of the *polis* and weakened the citizens' allegiance to its common way of life.[50]

Plato responded to the political critique of Socrates by reversing the Socratic indictment. He depicted Athens, the exemplary Greek *polis*, as hostile to true philosophy and its quest for comprehensive truth. Moreover, he argued that genuine philosophers greatly benefitted their native cities and were indispensable to their struggle for justice. Created in a deeply polemical context, Plato's political philosophy, therefore, had two intersecting aims: to criticize persisting political prejudices as barriers to the discovery of philosophical truth and to defend authentic philosophy as the most reliable remedy for the city's persistent and intractable ills.

Plato's immanent critique of the classical *polis* emphasizes its failure to achieve justice, the specifically political excellence; his external critique stresses the city's propensity to choose the apparent rather than the true good. In many instances, the two perspectives overlap, for the city's habitual resistance to truth is often the major cause of its internal disorder. In his political dialogues Plato faults the ancient city for its theology, its account of the divine, its mimetic poetry, its representation of the heroic, its *paideia*, the psychagogic effects of its public culture on the souls of young citizens. The dominant mentality of patriotic citizens is shown to be provincial and partisan; they love a small part of being to the exclusion of the whole and care more deeply for what is their own (*idion*) than for what is truly good.[51]

Plato depicts Athenian politics as anti-philosophical because its common notions of reality, truth, virtue and discourse are restrictive and radically incomplete. From the prevailing political perspective, reality coincides with the sensible world, that which appears to a plurality of citizens in a common space of disclosure and discussion. But philosophical inquiry requires an ontological conversion (*periagoge*), a radical liberation from the horizon of sensibility and the painful discovery that being and sensible appearance do not coincide.[52] Plato is not content, however, to disclose the ontological and ethical limitations of the political realm; according to Arendt, he tends to denigrate sensible appearance as such and to emphasize its power of diversion and concealment. To discover the truth about being, to know what is genuinely real, truth-seeking citizens must withdraw their attention from the sensible world and redirect it gradually to the purely intelligible realm. This graduated withdrawal from the political cave climaxes in the act of speechless contemplation, in the intellectual vision of the eternal and transcendent forms (*eide*). These forms are invisible and completely unknown to everyone absorbed in the agonal spectacle of politics. The biases of the city divert the inquiring mind from the pursuit of truth and thwart the philosophers' attempt to make that saving truth known when they descend from the sky to the public square.

Political debate, for Arendt the very essence of public life, is effectively dominated by the opinions and judgments of the *polis*'s ruling party.[53] But these opinions are fallible and, as Socratic inquiry consistently shows, often in error about the most important human concerns. Many influential opinions are based on rumor and hearsay; their credibility tends to be as ephemeral as their evidentiary sources are unreliable. Enduring opinions frequently solidify into unexamined prejudices that fiercely resist challenge and scrutiny. Both kinds of conviction express how things seem not how they are. They are the intellectual currency of the democratic majority who cannot transcend the realm of appearance or the unquestioned authority of the civic consensus. For true philosophers, however, commonly shared opinions constitute the critical mind's starting point not its final allegiance. The *telos* of human inquiry is not common opinion (*doxa*) but knowledge, *episteme*, the true, certain, infallible grasp of immutable being.

Plato accepted Pericles' description of the *polis* as a school of civic virtue.[54] But he insisted that the "virtues" cultivated in Periclean Athens were counterfeit rather than real. These "virtues" were counterfeit because they shaped the souls of ordinary citizens in ways that obstructed their capacity for justice. The erotic pursuit of wealth, honor, victory and power was openly admired and publicly encouraged; poverty, shame and rhetorical defeat were to be avoided by the ambitious citizen at all costs. In opposition to Pericles, Plato argued that the true purpose of the virtues was to bring harmony and normative order (justice) to the human soul and the republican city, but the Athenian counterfeits of virtue had the opposite psychological effect. In the Platonic dialogues, the philosophical virtues of Socrates are dramatically contrasted with traditional models of heroism: the fear driven courage of Achilles, the partisan cleverness of Odysseus, the hedonistic moderation of Eryximachus, and the short sighted *phronesis* of Pericles.[55] True justice is shown to depend upon wisdom, on knowledge of the Good itself, rather than on uncritical adherence to popular custom and law. Without philosophical rulers to oversee and direct the *paideia* (culture) of the republic, the city cannot fulfill its authentic educational mission, the creation of virtuous citizens and statesmen.

Although Plato subordinates speech (*lexis*) to the contemplative silence of the mind (*nous*), his dialogues confirm the importance he attributed to public inquiry and argument. His philosophical hero, Socrates, was a master of dialectical conversation. But there are limits to the power of persuasive speech even for someone with Socratic virtuosity. Socrates' dialectical arguments may logically refute the false beliefs of his interlocutors, and yet fail to transform their souls (the cases of Callicles and Thrasymachus exemplify this revealing pattern of dialectical success and rhetorical failure).[56] In addition, the *polis* is filled with numerous sophists who deliberately flatter the *demos* and corrupt their souls with the pleasing power of rhetoric. Political speech may be persuasive without being true; it may cater to what people desire or fear rather than lead them to what is genuinely good; to quote the Aristophanic maxim, it can easily make "make the worse appear the better cause." The judicial condemnation of Socrates by the majority of the Athenian court appears to have shaken Plato's faith in the power of democratic political debate to disclose what is just or to reveal who is good.

In her rejoinder to Plato, Arendt generally depicts his critique of Periclean politics as a loss of faith in the classical republican ideal.[57] But this is a highly selective way of characterizing Plato's opposition to the Periclean *ethos*. Pericles was the chief architect and defender of Athenian imperialism. In expanding and justifying the Athenian empire, he combined the honor and shame ethic of the warrior tradition with an explicit appeal to power and self-aggrandizement. His celebrated rhetoric showed that he made Athenian power and glory rather than justice the aim of both domestic and foreign policy.[58] Arendt fails to acknowledge the explicitly moral basis of the sustained Platonic criticism of Periclean Athens. In Alasdair MacIntyre's terms, Pericles conflated the goods of victory and social effectiveness with the goods of true human excellence.[59] Plato's political dialogues are designed to display and critique this fundamental confusion as well as to articulate and defend the cardinal virtues in a genuine form. Plato repudiated Pericles' claim to effective political leadership, arguing that he sought to create a well-fortified city rather than a virtuous one. Under Pericles, Athens became the feverish city of luxury and greed described in *Republic* II.[60] The interpolitical struggle between Athens and Sparta and the intra-political conflict between Athenian oligarchs and democrats are both traceable to *pleonexia*, to an inordinate attachment to nonsharable goods. Arendt's celebratory rhetoric about Athenian freedom and greatness completely avoids and obscures Plato's normative criticism of Periclean politics. It also fails to address two inescapable questions at the core of political philosophy. What are the appropriate criteria by which to judge political agents and actions? In what does the well being of a free republic consist?

Plato's most devastating indictment of the *bios politikos* occurs in his allegory of the cave.[61] Arendt treats this parable of the inquisitive philosophical citizen as the very heart of Plato's political philosophy. The cave story deliberately reverses Homer's account of Odysseus' journey to the underworld; it is the dramatic narrative of a *periagoge*, a conversion, in which the convictions of Homer and Greek common sense are systematically inverted. In the *Odyssey,* Homer had favorably contrasted bodily life on earth with the wraith-like existence of the soul in the shadowy underworld of death. But Plato's counter-myth in the *Republic* suggests that earthly life may be the true underworld and that the living body is really a shadow of the more substantial soul that animates and governs it. For Greek common sense, nothing was more real than the sensible objects human beings can actually see and touch. For ordinary citizens, then and now, durable artifacts and lasting natural substances provided the credible standard of worldly reality. In the myth of the cave Plato deliberately unsettles these familiar ontological assumptions; sensible objects are described as the shadows of phantoms and the sensible world is portrayed as a theatre of illusion. The true philosophers emerge as the antagonists of common sense, turning its unexamined convictions upside down.[62]

Plato's reversal of Athenian political assumptions is no less dramatic than his censure of Homer. For the classical Greeks, the public realm was meant to be a place of illumination and remembrance, a place where human excellence could shine forth and personal distinction appear. But the *polis* loses its putative splendor when transformed by the myth into an obscurely lit cave that conceals what is truly excellent and hides it from view. Over time, loyal citizens become deeply attached to their *polis*, treating it as their permanent earthly home. Plato, however, depicts the *polis* as an underground prison in which human beings are shackled and immobilized by their dependence on the senses and common opinion. If what is noblest in themselves, their god-like intellects, are ever to discover what is noblest in being, they need release from the bondage of their civic convictions and attachments. From the philosophical perspective, the highest purpose of human existence is to see, to know, to understand, to contemplate immutable being. The excellence of human knowing depends on the metaphysical excellence of its objects. But what is fairest and most brilliant in the order of being cannot be discovered in the shadowy darkness of the city. Civic justice, when it exists, is a pale reflection of the perfect form of justice itself; and political discourse about what is good fails to reveal or even acknowledge the eternal source of intelligibility and perfection.

To turn the captive soul's attention from the sensible to the intelligible, from the cave to the sky, requires protracted struggle and personal discomfort. It requires the cessation of action and speech; it means becoming perfectly still, withdrawing from the company of peers, radically revising one's notions of truth, beauty, goodness and divinity.[63] Nonphilosophical citizens cannot endure and accomplish this painful transition from darkness to light, from sensible appearance to invisible reality. The true philosophers who can and do undergo *metanoia* experience incomparable joy in the emerging vision of the intelligible forms. Completely absorbed in the vision of justice itself, they have no desire to return to the imperfect justice of the human city. The incessant political struggle for honors and prizes, the disorderly competition for power, strike these emancipated citizens as profoundly illiberal. The *bios politikos*, which the pre-Socratic Greeks had considered the noblest of human activities, is now depicted as burdensome and base, a harsh imposition of mortal necessity like the forced labor of slaves.

But according to the myth, the philosophical citizen is not permitted to enjoy his hard-won solitude; he is compelled to re-enter the cave by his former liberators, to bring the light of truth down into the public darkness.[64] However, the fate of the truth-seekers and truth-tellers in politics is sobering. When they remain outside the cave, the philosophers are ridiculed as useless; when they re-enter the cave they are threatened with death. The majority of their fellow citizens are strongly attached to the city's political culture, to its deepest convictions about justice, nobility and honor. They are unwilling to accept the philosophers' critique of their way of life, or to believe in perfect metaphysical forms they are unable to see or imagine. For them, the philosopher's "emancipatory truth" endangers their city and threatens its future security. Out of loyalty to the *polis* they reject the returning philosophers and attempt to kill them. The historic destiny of Socrates is dramatically re-enacted in Plato's symbolic parable of the ascending and descending philosophical-citizen.[65]

To Plato, it seemed deeply unjust that the most virtuous citizens should be condemned to death for loyally serving their city. If dialectical arguments are unable to persuade the multitude, and the true philosophers are unwilling to coerce their civic peers, how can the fate of Socrates be avoided? There seem to be only two alternatives: either the genuine philosophers keep silent and remain aloof from the political struggle, or they become the ruling party in the city and establish the civic consensus on justice by which the majority of citizens live. In exploring the second alternative, Plato created the provocative fiction of philosopher-kings who govern the city in speech through the insights of contemplative reason. But according to Arendt, Plato distorted his metaphysical theory of the forms in order to give it substantive political relevance. She construes the Platonic forms as objects of intellectual beauty that satisfy the mind with their unequalled illuminatory power; they are the intellectual analogues of pure aesthetic phenomena. As objects of beauty they have no referential or practical function beyond displaying their own intrinsic excellence and perfection; the human mind finds delight simply in knowing and admiring them. But in order to grant the forms political significance, Plato had to transform his pure *eide* into normative measures of the sensible world. Under this practical reconception, the forms became transcendent yardsticks of perfection, in comparison to which all sensible phenomena are found wanting. Using the forms as metaphysical standards of perfection, Plato justified his negative ontological appraisal of political affairs; using them as legislative models to be copied or imitated, the philosopher-rulers sought to impose their timeless order on the constant flux of human existence. Through the despotic imposition of these eternal norms on spatio-temporal particulars, the political realm lost its autonomy and dignity, its capacity to conduct and appraise public life using immanent criteria that are uniquely and properly its own.[66]

In Plato's myth, the philosophers return to the darkened city with their saving insights in order to reform it, to make it more just. But Arendt contends that philosophical rule serves the benefit of the rulers rather than the citizens. On her revisionary account, Plato has designed a hypothetical *politeia* whose primary aim is the security of the philosophers and the protection and promotion of their distinctive way of life. In effect, he has proposed a non-violent despotism, a city deprived of public liberty and political equality in which an intellectual elite governs without the constraint of laws for their own benefit. The Platonic city in speech is really a philosophical tyranny that the tradition has fatefully and mistakenly described as an ideal republic.[67]

Let us conclude by summarizing Arendt's critical assessment of Plato's political legacy.

Plato systematically devalued four important aspects of the *bios politikos*. He deprived political phenomena of metaphysical dignity because they lacked the perfection of immutability. He rejected the epistemic reliability of common sense and subverted the political opinions that depend upon it. He opposed the philosophical *eros* for wisdom and justice to the political longing for worldly recognition and terrestrial remembrance. He denied the human capacity to establish justice by means of democratic persuasion and argument.

For Plato, the best human beings, the wisest and most virtuous, desire to be free from the unwelcome burdens of citizenship. They view political activity as an imposition of necessity, as an onerous hardship they are compelled to accept, as a dangerous immersion in a sphere of partisan ignorance. According to Arendt, Plato has re-described the life of the classical citizen in the language traditionally reserved for depicting the condition of a slave.

When the most virtuous citizens do enter politics, their declared purpose is not to debate and persuade their peers but to rule, to govern their fellow citizens with the infallible authority of eternal truth. Under the rule of philosophical reason, which is made the essential requirement of political justice, the *polis* becomes a benevolent despotism where the philosophical few reluctantly command and the nonphilosophical many, once they acquire the mandated moderation and docility, voluntarily obey.

Plato conceives the practice of statesmanship on the model of the fabricating arts. He describes political action (*praxis*) in alien categories imported from the realm of making (*poiesis*) and substitutes the mentality of the craftsman for that of the free citizen. By treating practical knowledge as a craft, a *techne*, he reduces political activity to an instrumental good, a subordinate means to an extra-political end.[68] On Arendt's critical indictment, the cultural fruits of Plato's political reflections are distinctively anti-political. At its worst, the political life is reduced to the status of slavery; it bears the ancient curse of necessity and coercion. At its best, it has the instrumental value of a useful craft in the service of higher non-political goods.

Chapter 3
ARISTOTLE'S PRACTICAL PHILOSOPHY

Let us begin our reflection on Aristotle by contrasting two approaches to political thought, the descriptive and the revisionary.[69] Descriptive thinking takes its bearings from existing political language and practice. In its account of political reality, it attempts to honor the opinions, conduct and customs of the people it is investigating. Revisionary thinking is usually more normative than empirical. It seeks to reverse or oppose existing practices and principles because they fall short of its critical standards. In immanent criticism, the standards adopted are internal to the practice of politics, but applied with unusual rigor; in an external critique political discourse and conduct are subject to prescriptive criteria more exigent than prevailing custom requires.

Arendt depicts Plato as a revisionary theorist in open rebellion against the culture of the ancient city. His polemical aim in the dialogues was not to understand Greek political life but to disparage its importance by contrasting the conduct of existing *poleis* with the norms of his philosophical republic. Metaphysical and epistemological standards drawn from contemplative activity were unjustly imposed on political affairs, and the immanent criteria of appraisal developed by pre-Socratic culture were ignored or suppressed. However, Arendt presents Aristotle as a more descriptive thinker who follows the lead of Greek public opinion in most of his political writing. In fact, Arendt's own portrait of the ancient city is heavily dependent on Aristotle and Thucydides, who both emphasize the intrinsic importance of politics and the distinctive Greek way of conducting it. Yet even Aristotle is not immune from Arendt's polemical criticism; she views his *Politics* as an uneasy compromise between authentic Greek political insight and revisionary Platonic theory.[70]

Perhaps the best way to read the *Politics* is as a critical response to Plato's political dialogues. In his practical writings, Aristotle repeatedly emphasized the most fundamental Platonic questions and themes: citizenship, law, property, friendship, justice, education, virtue, the distribution of political functions and responsibilities. But he had deep reservations about the literal proposals advanced in the dialogues, especially those found in the *Republic*. Aristotle defended private property, opposed the utopian community of wives and children, revised the Platonic conception of statesmanship and often suggested that Plato misunderstood the specific nature of the political community.[71] For Aristotle, a *polis*, a political *koinonia*, is not an enlarged and extended family; it has much greater internal differentiation and quite different sources of cohesion and commonality. These notable criticisms do not, however, make Aristotle Plato's theoretical antagonist. He refined and revised his Platonic inheritance, attempting to perfect and complete what Plato had already begun.

One of Arendt's deepest objections to Plato is that he burdened political philosophy with a series of hierarchical oppositions: thought vs. action, contemplation vs. speech, philosophical solitude vs. political community, knowing vs. doing. Aristotle shared Plato's predilection for hierarchical orders, but he tended to treat as functional complements what Arendt perceives as antithetical polarities in Plato. A relevant example is Aristotle's careful distinction between theoretical and practical inquiry.[72] Aristotle explicitly affirmed the ethical supremacy of theory over practice, but he also granted the *bios politikos* a dignity and excellence of its own. For Aristotle, it is a serious mistake to impose the normative criteria of demonstrative science on the study of human action. The norms of each field of inquiry should be correlated with its distinct subject matter; essential differences in the order of being must be duly reflected in the order of knowing.

Theoretical and practical inquiry differ in their objects, methods, aims, virtues and outcomes. The proper objects of scientific theory are the invariant causes and principles of natural substances; the theoretical method of inquiry is to advance from sense perception through disciplined questioning to the intellectual apprehension of explanatory causes; the aim of theory is demonstrative knowledge of the universal and invariant properties of sensible entities in the natural world; the virtues of the speculative intellect are forms of irrevocable insight: *episteme* (science) and *sophia* (theoretical wisdom); the climax of the theoretical life is a permanent grasp of invariant truth in which the inquiring mind finds disinterested joy. By contrast, the proper object of practical inquiry is the domain of human agency and action; this important field of being is marked by variable causation and is subject to unpredictable change. It exhibits the contingency arising from human choice rather than the necessity of invariant natural law. The appropriate method in practical philosophy is the dialectical examination and refinement of existing opinions, those of the many as well as the wise. The ultimate goal is not demonstrative knowledge of invariant causal patterns, but the reform and improvement of human *praxis* itself.[73]

There are three distinct but interconnected levels of insight that arise from practical reflection: 1) the political wisdom (*phronesis*) of the statesman that guides deliberation and judgment on particular courses of action; 2) the political knowledge (*politike*) of legislators and rulers who oversee the comprehensive good of the political community; the legislator also requires knowledge of the many partial goods that need to be integrated in a well-ordered commonwealth; 3) the comparative insights of the practical philosopher into the merits and limitations of existing *politeia*.[74] For Aristotle, practical philosophy is an empirical and normative inquiry which classifies the different types of political association, explains their sources of persistence and perishing, and judges their proximity or distance from the most excellent constitutional order. Its ultimate purpose is to provide informed advice to educated citizens and statesmen charged with the care of existing political communities. Practical political decisions are always situation-specific; they tell people what to do and avoid in these circumstances at this time. But particular courses of action aimed at limited contextual goods must be coordinated with a network of policies aimed at quite different but equally legitimate goods. The responsibility of the statesman, the highest political authority, is to coordinate this complex pattern of recurrent goods required for the city's comprehensive well being. The political philosopher advises the statesman on the normative ordering of public goods, seeking to correct each city's tendency to view its own practices and institutions in a partisan and uncritical light. The goal of practical reasoning is not utopian innovation in an historical vacuum but highly specific cultural and institutional reforms matched to the history of a particular city and its people.

Aristotle's analysis of political reality is based on his causal matrix of inquiry.[75] All four of the causes are politically relevant, but primary emphasis is given to formal and final causation. Among the significant material causes Aristotle recognizes are the number of citizens, the size, climate and location of the *polis*, the patterned distribution of property and wealth. The well-constituted city should be large enough to be self-sufficient but not so large it cannot be governed with justice. The relevant efficient causes include the economic, military, religious and cultural activities (*erga*) on which the specific goods of the *polis* depend. Political greatness is properly measured by effective power, by a city's capacity to achieve its specific *telos* or end. The *polis* is a purposive association established to ensure the comprehensive good of all its citizens. To accomplish this aim, it distributes political offices and responsibilities (martial, legislative, deliberative and judicial), and cultivates in its citizens the virtues required for achieving the communal good. The formal and final causes of a *polis* must be carefully integrated so that its *politeia*, its patterned distribution of political powers and functions, will be adequate to attaining its ambitious ethical ends.

Arendt credits Aristotle with several political insights of lasting importance. He recognized the dignity of political life and explicitly honored the human capacities required for effective citizenship. For Aristotle, the *polis* is the highest form of human association, and the human being is by nature a political animal, a *zoon politikon*.[76] The fulfillment or perfection of human nature depends on the exercise of virtues that only the *polis* is capable of cultivating. Possessing these virtues, especially justice, humans are the best of animals, but deprived of them, sadly, they are the worst.[77] Reason and speech are the human capacities on which political life essentially depends. To live together justly through speech and persuasion is the mark of free persons; to conduct human affairs through coercion and violence is the practice of tyrants and uncivilized peoples. Political speech is essentially concerned with justice and injustice, with human benefit and harm, with the multiple dimensions of communal wellbeing. By deliberating together about the public good, deep and lasting connections are created among citizens as they gradually develop a shared agreement about what is excellent and right.

Unlike Plato, Aristotle is generally respectful of inherited Greek opinion. What is believed by many and by men of old, and especially by eminent men is rarely without merit.[78] But the validity of received opinion is inherently limited. Citizens are naturally inclined to exaggerate the worth of opposing claims; there is a persistent tendency to individual and group bias that must be checked and corrected by those in authority. Still, the views of the many are likely to be right in at least one respect and those of the wise in several or nearly all. The common sense of the community must be critically appropriated by its political leaders and not treated as a systematic source of error. Aristotle's epistemic disposition towards the sensible world is equally flexible. All human knowing begins with sense perception; the apprehension of intelligible forms essentially depends on the fashioning of sensible images; to reach a causal understanding of things imperceptible we must rely on empirical evidence. Although intellect is a nobler faculty than sensibility, the two cognitive powers are functionally complementary in contributing to human understanding. Though the senses cannot perceive divine being, knowledge of God is philosophically achieved through the causal explanation of celestial phenomena. In the field of cognition, Aristotle did not reject the distinctions he inherited from Plato; he presented lower cognitive operations in the Platonic hierarchy as pre-conditions of higher functioning rather than barriers to its attainment.

Aristotle also emphasized the plurality of human beings and the diverse partnerships they are able to create. The earliest alliances are based on biological necessity, the common need for survival, but humans seek to live together even without the demand for mutual assistance.[79] There are several forms of human association, *koinonia*, rising in dignity from the household (*oikos*) to the *polis* and including the different levels and types of friendship. In his practical philosophy, Aristotle relied on the following questions to distinguish the different forms of community: who are their members; what do they share in common (*koinon*); for the sake of what goods have they agreed to associate; what holds them together in the face of centrifugal pressures; how have they delegated responsibilities among their members; to what degree of unity can they reasonably aspire? The basic Arendtian distinctions between private and public spaces and relationships, between *oikos* and *polis*, household and city, are heavily dependent on the associative taxonomy Aristotle presented in the opening books of the *Politics*.[80]

Not surprisingly, human *koinonia* also admit of hierarchical ordering. The *polis* is the best and most complete association, the only one to achieve true self-sufficiency. It is composed of free adult citizens who share in the exercise of political power and responsibility. They must be numerous enough for the city's economic and political independence, but few enough for the citizens to know each other's characters and personal histories. Political as opposed to tribal unity is not based on blood, kinship or property. What citizens share in common are language, culture (*paideia*), law and territory. Of greatest importance is their shared sense of justice that is most clearly reflected in the city's *politeia* or constitution. The *telos* of the *polis,* its very reason for being, is the comprehensive good of the whole civic community. As a self-sufficient city includes less comprehensive communities within itself, so it also embraces the limited goods at which they aim. Health, victory, prosperity and peace are genuine goods with which the *polis* is legitimately concerned. But its deepest commitment is to the moral and intellectual virtues whose exercise constitutes *eudaimonia*.[81] A city cannot live well without living justly, without entrusting its highest offices and honors to its most virtuous citizens, to those who make the greatest contributions to the commonweal. It is their shared sense of justice, their common fund of virtues, their mutual love for the *polis* and its history, that holds the citizens together in the face of domestic faction and war. Civic friendship and civility are essential to the city's enduring concord; these distinctively public virtues allow ordinary citizens to rise above narrow self- interest and to identify their personal good with that of the larger community.[82]

Lasting civic cooperation is not due to chance and spontaneous agreement. Political associations must be well governed if they are to be peaceful and just. But the political governance of citizens should be clearly distinguished from the two familiar forms of household rule. The master-slave relationship is generally despotic in nature. The master of the household governs his slaves through physical coercion for the master's benefit. In contrast to slavery, the royal rule of parents over children is based on authority; it exists to serve the needs of the child rather than the well being of the parent. Both royal and despotic rule assume marked inequalities of competence, virtue and power between governors and governed. These inequalities are absent from the political rule that obtains among citizens who, in the just city, voluntarily cooperate for their mutual benefit and wellbeing. While Arendt explicitly rejects the concept of political rule as a contradiction in terms, Aristotle deliberately retains it, carefully distinguishing the constitutional rule of free citizens from both royal and despotic governance. In a free city, citizens alternately adopt the positions of ruled and rulers; in fact, they learn how to govern others by first learning to obey the common laws binding on everyone.[83] Aristotle agrees with Arendt that the governance relations of the household are not those of the *polis*. The city is not an extended family where wives, children and property are held in common. It is a carefully differentiated partnership, with considerable economic and functional specialization. Its internal order and peace are based upon justice and mutual respect not the compliance of inferiors with the master's binding commands.

When citizens argue and debate public policy, their contrasting opinions emerge within the framework of a civic consensus on justice. This shared agreement about justice, about what the citizens owe to each another and to their common *polis*, is the primary source of political friendship (*philia*) and the ultimate ground of civic cooperation.

Despite her high regard for Aristotle, Arendt identifies three critical areas where Plato's political philosophy compromised his pupil's practical insight: the assimilation of action (*praxis*) to making (*poiesis*); the reliance on rule as the central category of political analysis and appraisal; the teleological primacy accorded to the contemplative life.[84] In each case, Arendt believes, Aristotle followed Plato's theoretical guidance rather than the patterns of Greek civic culture. The result, to her mind, was an erosion of important distinctions that the Greeks had embodied in their political practice but had failed to articulate conceptually.

POIESIS AND *PRAXIS*

Arendt repeatedly criticized traditional theories for failing to provide an unprejudiced account of human action. While human beings can think in solitude and produce durable artifacts in isolation, they can only act politically in concert with others. Their freedom of action is inseparable from human plurality and from the perplexities, limits and dangers that acting with others entails. By identifying these limits and dangers, we can begin to understand why many political thinkers have sought to replace action with making as the central activity in the *vita activa*.[85]

Human action is inherently irreversible. Whatever is publicly said cannot be unsaid; whatever is done in the presence of others cannot be undone. Once an action has begun, it sets in motion a chain of reactions that the initiating agent is unable to cancel or control. The risk of futility attending action also makes it suspect to political theorists. Whenever we act, it is deeply uncertain whether we will achieve our intended purpose or even determine the meaning that witnesses ascribe to what we have done. The results of action are essentially unpredictable, not only by the initiating agent, but also by the spectators who observe and comment on each action's commencement and unfolding. Although human beings are free to initiate action, they are never sovereign masters of its development; they cannot control how their peers and successors will respond to what they say and do.[86] The free response of other persons determines the course action takes and helps to account for its boundlessness. The numerous parties to an action do not have the power to end it conclusively nor to secure its provisional results in a permanent outcome. Moral theorists, therefore, are understandably troubled by the anonymity of political action, by the difficulty of tracing clear lines of causal responsibility. While they can sometimes identify who started an action, they cannot hold the initiating agent morally responsible for all of its consequences. Those who begin an action do not and cannot control the course of its subsequent unfolding. Although the concept of collective responsibility should be cautiously retained, it lacks the clear definition that attends the activity of a single, sovereign masterful agent. Because of their multiple authorship, human actions often appear haphazard and incomprehensible; the carefully designed plans of those who initiate an action are often submerged in the short term passions and goals of whoever sustains or diverts its momentum. And even when action is provisionally effective, the web of relationships it establishes is inherently unstable. Decisive action can transform a climate of opinion and create new centers of power and agency, but it cannot ensure their endurance. The cooperative alliances action establishes easily dissolve, and climates of opinion often prove as unstable as the weather itself.[87]

Arendt contends that political philosophers since Plato have wanted to escape the constitutive limits of engaging with others in human affairs. But in seeking to discover a substitute for action, for the unpredictability resulting from a plurality of interacting persons, they have inevitably sought an escape from politics itself. The monotony of the replacements proposed for action indicates the simplicity of what is at stake.[88] Unwilling to accept a cooperative activity in which equal persons freely interact and unpredictably respond, western theorists have preferred the fiction of a single agent, isolated from interference by others, who remains the master of the political process from beginning to end. In classical terms, they have substituted *poiesis* (fabrication) for *praxis* (action) and applied the standards and principles of *poiesis* to their assessment of the political realm. When measured by the normative criteria of fabrication, action fares no better than it did when compared to the norms of contemplative insight. In contrast to the boundlessness of action, the fabricating process of the craftsman has a definite beginning and end; if completed successfully, it produces an independent object with its own durability and identity. The masterful craftsman is personally accountable for the thing that is made, and he is free to destroy his work if it fails to satisfy his standards of excellence. A talented artisan has full control of the fabrication process; the exercise of his art makes the stages of that process intelligible and affords a high degree of reliability to the finished product. When the play is by Shakespeare or the portrait by Rembrandt, we know in advance, that it will be well made. Good craftsmen are reliable, predictable, and individually accountable for what they make, and when they fail, as they occasionally do, they simply destroy the results of their abortive effort.[89]

Human fabrication is a non-political activity, normally conducted in relative isolation and governed by the principle of utility. The tools and raw materials, even the technical craft of the artisan, are instruments in the service of the finished product. For craftsmen, these are instrumental rather than intrinsic goods deriving their importance from the worldly object they help to produce. Despite their structural differences, fabrication and action are not incompatible activities. Human making only becomes anti-political when its defining properties, utilitarian intention, the isolation of the craftsman, and the coercive control of materials, are inserted into the political realm, or when pre-political activities that appear to resemble fabrication are raised to the highest political rank. Arendt classified legislative activity as a pre-political occurrence, in direct contrast to Plato and Aristotle, who treated legislation as one of the essential political arts. They did this, she believes, because an influential lawmaker, like Solon, can easily be compared to a political craftsman; his legislative activity has a definite beginning and end, and it seems to yield a tangible product, a code of written laws, when it concludes.[90]

Arendt accuses Plato of patterning his analysis of political leadership on the fabrication model. The alleged source of Plato's confusion was the important affinity he noted between contemplation and creative production. Both the thinker in solitude and the artist in isolation deliberately withdraw from the company of others. There is a further striking parallel between the thinker's contemplative vision of the eternal ideas and the craftsman's careful attention to the model or image guiding the production process. Arendt believed that, for political purposes, Plato transformed his metaphysical *eide* into imaginable prototypes that the philosopher ruler could use to direct and measure the crafting of tangible things. In this way the objects of theoretical insight were given a practical function as models and measures of human production. The fragile web of interpersonal relations that emerges from the free interaction of peers was mistakenly treated like a durable artifact and subjected to the standard of a perfect, immutable idea.[91] The well-made objects produced by talented craftsmen often closely resemble the prototype's perfection. The ontological gap between governing image and finished artifact is predictably negligible when compared with the distance separating political intention from practical result. Arendt accused Plato of wanting to close that disturbing distance by severely restricting the number of political agents and by converting political leadership into a species of sovereign craftsmanship.

Did Aristotle commit a similar error to the mistake Arendt attributed to Plato? He repeatedly distinguished *praxis* and *poiesis* as types of practical activity, and explicitly recognized the preeminence of action and speech in political life.[92] Arendt's structural distinction between action and fabrication is an explicit retrieval of Aristotle's conceptual and linguistic position. Yet she accuses Aristotle of failing to honor his own practical insight; by emphasizing the political purposes of action and the public goods it seeks to bring about, he obscures the sharp contrast to which Arendt is deeply committed.[93] Arendt wants actions to occur and be judged in their own right as pure instances of sensible appearance. Aristotle, however, treats virtuous actions as the rational outcome of prior deliberation and choice; for him, they occur to promote the public good and are subject to critical appraisal by the norms of justice.

Although Arendt sets acting and making in sharp opposition, she does recognize an important similarity between fabricated objects and political words and deeds. Both political events and finely crafted artifacts need a brightly lit public space in which to appear. They both exist to be seen, talked about, and eventually appraised by those who can appreciate them impartially, those who are able to enjoy these arresting appearances simply for their own sake.[94] Yet, while actions and artifacts are both revelatory, what they reveal is strikingly different. A well-made object bears witness to the craft of its maker, to the skill he possesses and to the care and attention that governed its production. But the craft of the artisan should not be confused with his personal identity. We repeatedly encounter Shakespeare's unparalleled art in his plays and sonnets, but they never tell us who he is. The personal uniqueness of a human being is never reducible to the range of arts and skills he or she possesses. But according to Arendt, public speech and action in the appropriate settings are the fullest disclosure we ever receive of the personal identities of others. Humans distinguish themselves as unique beings by their free conduct and discourse in the company of peers. They actualize their personal uniqueness by publicly expressing who they are in the constant give and take of human communication. As the public architecture of an age is the highest revelation of its worldly culture, so the words and deeds of its public men and women bear clearest witness to the personal greatness or mediocrity of its citizens.[95]

Arendt's epiphanic conception of political activity has had few important defenders. The majority of theorists have been more impressed by the limitations and dangers of action. Arendt's rejoinder to their critical unease is uncompromising. Action is irreversible, often futile, unpredictable and boundless in its consequences, and incapable of generating stable and lasting results; these sources of exasperation, however, are inseparable from human plurality, freedom and agency. The desire to escape from action and politics is a desire to escape from defining features of the human condition itself. The theoretical substitution of fabrication for action does not alter their ontological differences, but it has led to deep misunderstanding of the nature and dignity of political life.[96]

The mentality of the artisan, as we have noted, is inherently utilitarian. The categories of means and ends not only dominate the process of production, but they also determine the public's attitude towards its finished product. The artisan is a toolmaker, a crafter of use objects, whose durable artifacts are commonly valued as instrumental goods. But when action is confused with fabrication, it also becomes instrumentalized. Politics then loses its standing as a realm of human activity transcending the legitimate concern with necessity and utility. Political activity is degraded into a subordinate means to allegedly higher non-political ends. In classical antiquity these "higher" ends were philosophical and religious; in modernity they eventually became economic and social. In both settings, the *bios politikos* lost its importance and dignity as a genuinely liberal activity, and its constitutive elements and underlying requirements were denied just and precise articulation.

But far more than the cultural importance attributed to politics is at stake. When the principles of fabrication are inserted into human affairs they threaten the very integrity of action and speech. In the course of production, the artisan regularly does violence to the raw materials of nature: wood is cut; stone is hammered; hemp is twisted; iron is smelted and reconfigured. The governing design of the craftsman rules the production process; material obstacles and resistance are repeatedly overcome with force. Although the finished product is spared the coercive effects of productive violence, as a use object it too is subject to continuous manipulation. Tools and instruments are not degraded by repeated use since that is the reason for which they are made. But when the violence applied to natural materials is directed against human beings, or when the manipulation of things is extended to the treatment of persons the political consequences are ominous. Action and speech effectively establish the relations of human beings with one another. When human action is modeled on making, the probability of coercion and violence is greatly increased; when political speech is employed as a means to extrapolitical ends, it easily becomes an instrument of manipulation and deceit.

These dangers are particularly acute for utopian and revolutionary political thinkers. Plato acknowledged that the exile of adult citizens would be necessary in order to establish his true republic on earth; Machiavelli insisted that force was essential in creating a new body politic; Marx claimed that the historical *telos* of a classless society justified the resort to revolutionary violence.[97] To bring the anticipated utopia into being, all available measures are legitimate, including despotism, coercion and terror. "You can't make an omelet without breaking eggs." "You cannot repair the body politic without removing the diseased organs." The utopian thinker does not have to glorify violence to embrace its practical utility, but merely to comply with the logic of fabrication itself.[98]

Arendt is often criticized for excessive scholasticism, for articulating distinctions without a difference, but in this case, I believe her warnings are of cardinal importance.[99] *Praxis* and *poiesis* are fundamentally different; the mentality of the citizen should not be that of the productive artisan; the utilitarian logic of the craftsman does lead to violence in human affairs. Human beings should never be treated like things no matter how exalted the revolutionary cause. The inescapable gap between the intention and outcome of action is genuinely troublesome, but because of human plurality and freedom, it cannot and should not be eliminated.

In action unlike fabrication the intended end does not justify the means. "Since the end of human action as distinct from the end products of fabrication can never be reliably predicted, the means used to achieve political goals are, more often than not, of greater relevance to the future world than their intended goals."[100]

The complex and uncertain relation between intention, action and outcome also affects the criteria of political appraisal. The significance and worth of action and speech do not depend on their ultimate consequences. It is legitimate to judge *poiesis* by the quality of the thing that is made, for in craftsmanship the excellence of the result is what matters. But important human actions have many authors and respondents, and their outcomes are under no single agent's control. Lee's conduct in the Civil War is no less heroic because the South was eventually defeated, Lincoln's presidency no less praiseworthy because it was cut short by assassination. Even when carefully chosen action is successful and achieves its original aim, the human relationships it establishes are essentially fragile. Successful craftsmen produce durable and useful artifacts; remarkable statesmen enact policies subject to continual revision and amendment. In human affairs, the consequences of action are boundless, without internal completion, and one never knows when memories of past initiatives and injuries will return to haunt or grace the life of the present.

Arendt is surely right to emphasize the nobility of politics, the dignity of the public realm, the significance of public liberty, the "enlarged mentality" demanded of citizens and statesmen. Politics can never escape the tangled knot of human greatness and wretchedness, but the goods it seeks to promote and the evils it strives to deter are of lasting importance. The institutional and cultural requirements of enduring political excellence are exceedingly hard to establish and maintain. Future generations are blessed by their creation and cursed by their predecessors' failure to sustain and support them.

Arendt found limited support in the intervening tradition for her pre-Socratic understanding of politics. She criticized Plato and Aristotle for failing to defend the Periclean concept of the *polis*. Pericles had revitalized the Homeric warrior ethic by endorsing an amoral politics of greatness and glory. He depicted the public realm as a theatre of daring and risk where citizens could strive for worldly immortality. Arendt's concept of action as epiphanic disclosure, as a fleeting enactment of beauty whose greatness creates lasting memories, was essentially modeled on the Periclean ideal. Arendt describes action as a pure actuality, as an *atelic* occurrence that aims at no outcome beyond its self-manifestation.[101] This ontological description clearly avoids the conflation of *praxis* and *poiesis*. Action is now patterned on the performing rather than the productive arts. In Arendt's concept of action, as in theatrical performance, the achievement consists in the event of appearance itself. Great action is like great flute playing or dancing, rather than like great sculpture or painting. To make the comparison clearer, it is like improvisational jazz performed without a score, where the musical performers respond spontaneously to each other's initiatives.[102]

Arendt's concept of action as pure appearance without a purpose has marked aesthetic overtones.[103] Politics becomes effectively separated from ethics and from the central ethical categories of virtue and the good. Beauty replaces justice as the proper measure of political excellence; there is an explicit shift from practical wisdom to virtuosity as the defining merit of the statesman.[104] The appraisal of action, like the appraisal of works of art, transcends the accepted norms of good and evil. It is the greatness of action, its capacity to evoke lasting memories in those who witness and speak of it, that is finally decisive for historical judgment. Only Kant, among the major Western philosophers, provided adequate categories for defending this atelic politics of honor and glory. Arendt's appropriation of Kant, however, was highly selective. Although her most explicit debt was to Kant's third critique, one aspect of his moral philosophy greatly impressed her. Kant was committed to preserving the purity and autonomy of the moral realm. He wanted to ground the categorical imperatives that constitute the moral law in the autonomy of practical reason. To ensure the purity of moral judgments, he rejected as heteronomous every attempt to base them on metaphysical, theological or naturalistic principles. Natural inclinations and purposes, divine commands and rewards, had no legitimate place in his carefully circumscribed moral sphere. With the elimination from ethics of natural and supernatural ends of action, practical wisdom lost its directive moral authority. The purpose of Kantian ethics was no longer to discover and actualize the comprehensive human good. Kant's moral aim was not to promote human happiness, but to render human beings worthy of it.[105]

While Arendt does not endorse the goals of Kant's moral theory, she does seek to create a pure and autonomous politics of her own. Her opposition to any trace of political heteronomy parallels Kant's attempt to protect the moral realm from every type of external influence. Thus Plato is criticized for imposing transcendent measures on the exercise of political judgment, and Aristotle is faulted for basing his politics on a theory of human teleology. Aristotle's practical philosophy is inseparable from his understanding of the human good. The *telos* of politics is the rational discovery and actualization of the comprehensive and enduring good of the civic community.[106] Achieving that noble purpose greatly depends on the cultivation and exercise of the intellectual and moral virtues, especially practical wisdom and justice. Arendt excludes these basic Aristotelian categories from political analysis, just as Kant had excluded them from his moral theory. By doing this, Arendtian actions become ends in themselves; they are no longer rationally ordered to the promotion and protection of intrinsic goods. Purified of all natural and religious teleology, Arendt's political theory risks becoming as formalistic and empty as Kantian ethics. Does keeping politics Arendtian pure require the loss of its traditional ethical substance?

To avoid this dilemma, Arendt turns from Kant's moral philosophy to his critique of judgment. Unexpectedly, she discovers there the necessary categories to defend the Periclean politics of greatness and glory. It was the critical thrust of Kantian ethics, its sustained rejection of moral heteronomy that supported Arendt in her critique of the tradition. Her positive account of political action derives not from Kant's ethics, however, but from his philosophical analysis of aesthetic phenomena. Arendtian actions are directly compared to the pure sensuous appearances that constitute the aesthetic realm. Both free human actions and aesthetic objects are concrete, phenomenal particulars that exist to be seen and judged by disinterested spectators. Aesthetic rationality is a faculty of taste and discernment; it is the capacity to decide what is worthy of appearance in a public realm designed for that singular purpose.[107] The greatness of action resembles the beauty of sensible appearance; both are measured by the disinterested pleasure they give to discerning and impartial spectators. The depth and duration of that pleasure effectively determine whether a particular action is remembered and preserved in a meaningful story. Memorable greatness is crucial, for it is the only reliable protection for action against the threat of temporal oblivion. Deprived of public honor and glory, *praxis* and *lexis* disappear from the world without leaving a trace of their being.

Arendt's distinctive account of action and politics is a curious hybrid. A pre-Socratic politics of worldly immortalization is articulated and defended in Kantian aesthetic categories. Aristotle's political philosophy, by contrast, developed within a radically non-Kantian metaphysical and anthropological framework. Aristotle was deeply attentive to traditional Greek practice and opinion, but his categories of analysis and appraisal have their source in Platonic intellectualism and his own naturalistic teleology.

Aristotle was a hierarchical pluralist in metaphysics and ethics. He assigned human beings an intermediate ontological position, above the beasts, the non-rational animals, and below the gods, the immortal divinities of his theology. The hierarchical structure of being was essential to his ethics for the human good is distinct from both animal survival (mere living) and uninterrupted divine blessedness.[108] Aristotle's metaphysical horizon is clearly in view whenever he addresses anthropological matters. By contemporary standards, his ordered ranking of human agents and activities is markedly aristocratic. The most excellent activities are the most god-like; the least excellent and most burdensome are those human beings share with the beasts. Aristotle typically connects a form of conduct with a category of agency, so that human lives as well as the activities that shape them are hierarchically ranked and defined. Natural slaves are the lowest types of human being. Their bodies dominate their lives and practical reason plays a limited directive role in their existence.[109] The characteristic activity of slaves is *ponos*, labor, the most necessary and least excellent form of human behavior. Labor is necessary because it produces the food and executes the repetitive tasks essential to sustaining biological life. Subject to the necessity of their bodies and the coercion of their masters, the lives and mentalities of slaves are ignoble even if they live in comparative comfort and ease.

Artisans, mechanics and merchants are not under the control of a human master, but according to Aristotle, these wage laborers also lead lives that are not fully human.[110] The political cast of Aristotle's anthropology colors his critique of these agents of technical reason. Lives devoted to instrumental production and trade are typically preoccupied with acquiring money and external goods. While the good life requires arms, tools and financial resources those who immerse themselves in their production and exchange acquire a *banausic* mentality. They are unsuited for citizenship because their way of life is illiberal and without adequate leisure, lacking sufficient opportunities to acquire and exercise the virtues.[111] Although Aristotle accepts the servile and useful arts, he values them primarily for the instrumental goods they produce. Strikingly, he does not honor the process of production but the worldly excellence or utility of the thing that is made. Like Arendt, Aristotle sharply distinguishes the mentality of the craftsman from that of the active citizen. *Poiesis*, in its many and various forms is essentially different from *praxis* and *lexis*. No less different are the characteristic lives of producers and traders from those of freemen. Slaves are excluded from the *bios politikos* because of their absorption in bodily necessity; artisans and merchants are considered imperfect citizens and incomplete humans because they are immersed in utilitarian enterprises.[112]

For Aristotle, it is citizens and statesmen who lead lives of freedom. They are free from slavish necessity and banausic utility; they are free for the noble and honorable actions of citizenship. In Aristotle's ethical hierarchy, the *bios politikos* is the distinctively human life, the one most suited to our composite nature. Neither beasts nor gods require a *polis* for their wellbeing, their *eudaimonia*. Humans, by contrast, are political animals, doers of deeds, speakers of words, and sharers in a common and elevated form of life.[113]

While Arendt is surprisingly vague in giving examples of political action, Aristotle is explicit about the range of activities to which classical *praxis* refers. The core of political action includes: just acts, like keeping promises and observing contracts; brave acts, like confronting dangers and taking risks in battle; magnificent acts, like bestowing generous gifts on one's city and friends; wise acts, like offering good counsel in deliberative assemblies and debates. The life of *praxis* and *lexis* consists of communication with and interaction among one's civic peers. Although essentially linked to the citizen's embodied existence, it is more liberal, nobler and more praiseworthy than *ponos* or *poiesis*. When human action is done well, it is based on perfection of character and guided by practical wisdom. Physical, moral, and intellectual excellences converge in virtuous *praxis*, which depends as well on a moderate number of external goods.[114]

Aristotle insists that virtuous actions are intrinsically noble; they are desirable in themselves and worthy of honor and praise. But he also insists they are useful, that they serve to bring about important human goods internal to the practice of politics.[115] Goods like security, justice, internal and external peace, the transmission of virtue, the wise use of public wealth and prosperity. In Aristotle's practical philosophy, intellectual distinctions do not imply dualistic separations. Virtuous actions are desirable in themselves and for the sake of the political goods they promote and protect.[116] *Pace* Arendt, they are simultaneously noble and useful. But they are not stripped of their dignity because of their utility. They are not mere subordinate instruments serving extra-political ends, but essential sources of the common good, the specific *telos* of political association.

If human beings were the highest substances in existence, then the *bios politikos* would be the supremely happy life.[117] Yet, the life of the gods is more blessed than that of mortals, and according to Aristotle, we should not assume that the gods make contracts, fight battles and deliberate about war and peace.[118] Aristotle's philosophical theology attributes only contemplative activity to divine beings. In his metaphysics, the gods are incorporeal and eternal substances, continuously engaged in theoretical self-understanding. They represent the summit of ontological and ethical perfection. While human beings are clearly not divine, they do have the god-like capacity for contemplation, *theoria*. When they engage in the philosophical life, the *bios theoretikos*, they become closest to the gods in being and happiness. Theoretical wisdom, the contemplative knowledge of god as the first cause and principle of all being, is the most excellent and least necessary human activity. If the forced labor of slaves constitutes the perigee of human existence, then the contemplation of the divine is the apogee. No other human activity is more liberal, leisurely, self-sufficient and pleasurable; no other so effectively narrows the metaphysical gap between god and human.[119]

Aristotle's political philosophy is based then on three levels of hierarchical pluralism: the metaphysical hierarchy that extends from beasts to gods; the anthropological hierarchy that extends from slaves to contemplative metaphysicians; the ethical hierarchy that extends from the preservation of life to the highest and most complete happiness. The necessary goods like food and shelter are required for biological survival; the instrumental goods like tools and weapons are indispensable objects of use, not desirable in themselves, but for the sake of some higher activity to which they contribute. The virtuous actions of citizens are both noble and useful—they are pursued and praised as both intrinsic and instrumental goods. The contemplative understanding (*theorein*) of God is the most perfect human good—it aims at no end or excellence beyond itself. Because human beings are natural mortal substances, they achieve contemplative perfection only rarely and at the end of a long process of intellectual and personal development. In Aristotle's practical philosophy, hierarchical pluralism is regularly balanced by functional complementarity. Human beings must live in order to produce, produce and consume in order to act virtuously, and think and act nobly in order to be godlike. The most excellent life depends on the fully ordered array of human goods, so that *eudaimonia* entails both the perfection and completion of human nature.

What are the implications of this background analysis for Aristotle's practical philosophy? Does he obscure the distinction between *poiesis* and *praxis* as Arendt contends? My reflective conclusion is that he does not. He consistently asserts that production and action are structurally different in character. But the acknowledged distinction between them does not preclude their sharing important similarities. Both making and doing are similar in the following respects: they depend on the exercise of practical reason; they deal with contingent particulars not invariant universals; they treat of things that lie within the scope of human power; they both are purposive, although the ends they pursue can be brought about in a number of ways; they involve some form of means-ends reasoning; they require close attention to the concrete circumstances in which they are performed or enacted.

However, the differences between *poiesis* and *praxis* are even more important than their similarities. Metaphysical differences: *poiesis* is a *kinesis* , a type of movement that remains ontologically indeterminate and incomplete until its end has been actually achieved. Making is an activity that reaches completion only by stopping and leaving behind an independent artifact different from itself. *Praxis* is an *energeia*, an actuality whole and complete at any moment of its occurrence. As an ontological event, it does not lack anything (even if it fails to achieve its intended end); nor is it augmented by extended duration.[120]

Different types of ends and results: although making and action are purposive, the ends at which they aim and the results to which they lead are radically different. When the process of making is finished, it leaves behind a well-made product, a durable artifact with its independent existence and merit. By contrast, the appropriate ends of action (peace, justice, liberty, security for example) are never permanent achievements. When action is successful, it establishes or preserves a web of human relations that is inherently fragile. The virtuous actions that contribute to justice and peace must be continually renewed and repeated. While the process of fabrication has a definite beginning and end, the need for virtuous action is never satisfied and its provisional results are never complete or secure.

Different criteria of appraisal: *Poiesis* is judged by the phenomenal quality of its product, by the excellence or utility of the thing that is made. The fabrication process is generally hidden from public view and is considered irrelevant to the assessment of the fabricated outcome. *Praxis* and *lexis*, however, essentially occur in the public realm and are subject to appraisal from several different practical perspectives: was this the right course of action under these circumstances; did it deliberately aim at a virtuous end; did it emerge from a sound line of reasoning; was it performed as the person of virtue (the *phronimos*) would do it? Although virtuous actions are done to promote the public good and are subject to appraisal by the norms of practical wisdom, they may fail to achieve their intended purpose and still be worthy of praise.[121]

The requirement of different virtues: *techne*, the virtue of the productive intellect, clearly differs from *phronesis*, the virtue of practical intelligence.[122] *Techne* enables the artisan to produce well-made objects with economy and skill. *Phronesis* enables the citizen or statesman to discern the right course of action in the contested thicket of public life. Although *phronesis* is distinct from the moral virtues, it is impossible to be practically wise without being good.[123] Some moral virtues, though certainly not all, are required of the skillful artisan, for bad men are clearly able to produce good things. As Aristotle noted, the skillful physician has the power to kill as well as cure. The arts by themselves, however, are morally incomplete; they require the direction of the virtues to ensure their employment for the common good.

To preserve the dignity and self-sufficiency of action, Arendt endorsed an *atelic* politics of glory patterned on aesthetic phenomena. Aristotle insisted that virtuous praxis is an intrinsically good activity performed in the service of the commonweal. He carefully integrated ethics and politics through the overlapping categories of *arete* and *eudaimonia*.[124] Arendt rejected his political teleology because she feared it would instrumentalize action and thereby deprive it of inherent worth. This decision was supported by a political theory that emphasized taste, virtuosity and artistic performance to the serious neglect of practical wisdom, the moral virtues and justice. What Arendt hoped to avoid by this unorthodox strategy is reasonably clear. But is her revisionary approach to political conduct (legislative, judicial, deliberative, cultural and martial) actually required to preserve its dignity? Three apparent non-sequiturs at the heart of Arendt's developed position suggest it is not. Because action does not have an end in the same sense that making has, it does not follow that action is purposeless or without an appropriate goal. By distinguishing between productive ends, in the sense of temporally finished artifacts, and practical ends, in the sense of legitimate public goods for the sake of which we deliberate and act, we can affirm that action is purposive and yet clearly distinguish it from fabrication. Because virtuous *praxis* is an intrinsic good desirable in its own right, it does not follow that it must lack instrumental value. Aristotle's carefully graded ethical pluralism avoids the sharp Arendtian dichotomy between the noble and the useful. Because action should not be judged solely in terms of its practical consequences, it does not follow that the ends at which it aims and the manner in which it pursues them are irrelevant to its appraisal. What properly matters in the evaluation of action is the wisdom and justice of what is done and the intellect and character of those who do it.

I have pursued this argument at length because it is central to Arendt's critique of Greek political philosophy. As she correctly insists, it is a serious mistake to confuse *praxis* with *poiesis*, a mistake with especially dangerous political implications. We are collectively in Arendt's debt for the exceptional light she cast on this recurrent confusion. The disputed question, however, is whether Aristotle also conflated the distinction between making and doing. While I believe that he did not, I have tried to show why Arendt thought that he had. If political conduct is truly an *atelic* activity, then Arendt's criticism of Aristotle stands. But if citizens and statesmen have a discernible set of goods for which they are practically responsible, then Aristotle is essentially vindicated and Arendt's own position becomes subject to serious challenge.

RULING AND BEING RULED

Greek political philosophy is largely based on the description and appraisal of the Athenian polis. Athens provides the dramatic setting for nearly all of Plato's dialogues and serves as an important model for Aristotle's portrait of the ancient city. Arendt accused Plato and Aristotle of misrepresenting the *polis*'s character by substituting pre-political or nonpolitical experiences for traditional Athenian practices. She pressed this criticism with three examples: the replacement of *praxis* with *poiesis*; the substitution of political authority and command for rhetorical persuasion; the abandonment of public debate and argument for the rule of experts.

Arendt's depiction of the ancient city is a study in contrasts. She sharply divides its spatial arrangements into two opposing spheres: the private realm of the household (the *oikos*) that is organized for the preservation of life, and the public realm of the *polis* that is deliberately designed for greatness and glory. In the darkness of the household inequality prevails. Slaves and women labor to meet the requirements of biological necessity under the rule of the household master. In the brightly lit public realm, liberated male citizens are equal and free. Liberated from the coercion and necessity of the *oikos*, they freely engage with their civic peers in the agonal competition for political excellence.

Arendt insists that the pattern of relationships in the classical household was explicitly pre-political. A threefold inequality obtained in the *oikos*, separating masters from slaves, parents from children and husbands from wives. The governance of the *oikos* was based upon rule, which, according to Arendt, was a structure of discipline explicitly confined to the private realm. There were two distinct types of household rule corresponding to the household's disparate inequalities. Masters ruled despotically over slaves, resorting to violence and coercion against them as circumstances required. The rule over family members, by contrast, was royal or authoritative in nature and intended for their benefit and wellbeing. Given the *oikos*' structure of inequality, freedom was absent from the classical household, because public freedom in the ancient city depended on the presence of recognized peers with whom one could liberally speak and act.[125]

There was a separate sphere of authority outside the canons of the *oikos* and the *polis*. This was the authority belonging to the realm of learning, teaching and knowledge. Epistemic authority governed the relations between masters and apprentices in the arts and between teachers and students in the theoretical disciplines of mathematics and physics. In the educational realm, as opposed to the household, the relevant inequalities were not based on strength, age and gender but on mutually recognized differences in knowledge and skill.[126] Both education and family life stand in marked contrast to the *bios politikos*. In the public space of civic equality, of *isonomia*, the household heads meet one another as peers.[127] Within this restricted domain of shared citizenship, all forms of rule are deliberately excluded. The equality of citizens is based upon mutual agreement. Free citizens consent to live together as equals and to conduct their public affairs in a uniquely political way. Arendt insists that coercion and violence, authoritative command and obedience, as well as reliance on the epistemic authority of experts are all non-political strategies for ordering human existence. The *bios politikos* is based on debate, public argument, the free exchange of opinions and judgments among recognized peers. The political alternative to rule and command is personal initiative and persuasive leadership. The most daring and courageous citizens undertake a new course of action and solicit the support and assistance of their peers in carrying it forward. Cooperative action arises from voluntary consent and mutual agreement, not authoritative command or the threat of force. There is no government or state, in the modern sense of these terms, authorized to use public power against visible violators of the law. In the place of ruling, governing and teaching, we have persuasive argument and debate, freely created consent and cooperation or dissent and resistance.[128]

In Arendt's narrative, the trial and death of Socrates decisively altered the republican commitment to political liberty. Plato, in particular, lost faith in the capacity of free citizens to live together wisely through persuasion and dialectical argument. Raised in the political culture of Athens, Plato did not want, however, to base public life on coercion and violence. Disillusioned by the folly of his contemporaries, but anxious to avoid resorting to despotism, he proposed a nonviolent replacement for classical civic equality. Arendt believes that Plato tried to escape from the dilemmas of politics by replacing *praxis* with *poiesis* and political debate with the rule of experts. In Plato's *Republic*, the concept of normative authority was transferred from the household and the sphere of education into the public realm, fatefully reversing the earlier Greek understanding of political life.[129] Because of Plato's unparalleled influence, the modalities of rule became the central concern of political analysis. The particular form of rule Plato recommended in the *Republic* was explicitly distinguished from two recognized patterns of coercion, those of masters over slaves and of educated Greeks over barbarians. To find a non-despotic model of human rule, Plato turned to the fields of education and the technical arts. Platonic political rule was modeled on the normative relations between teachers and students, doctors and patients, navigators and passengers. This was the rule of directive reason and knowledge over ignorance and opinion; it was hierarchical, non-violent, based on a shared recognition of epistemic inequality, and clearly exercised for the benefit of the ruled. In his specifically political dialogues, Plato experimented with different forms of governing authority: the philosopher king, the adaptive statesman, the rule of law.[130] No one was authorized to govern other persons who had not first learned the art of self-government. The Platonic requirement of self-mastery required the soul's authority over the body and reason's hegemony over the passions and appetites. Psychic and political justice were critically connected so that the normative order of the best *polis* had to be patterned on that of the genuinely philosophical soul.[131]

Three distinct notions of legitimate authority can be traced to the ancient Mediterranean world. The first derives from the Jews; it is based on their faith in a transcendent, law-giving Creator who issues commandments, divine imperatives, to the chosen people of Israel. The second derives from the Romans; it is based on the sacred and authoritative character of the Roman foundational experience. The third derives from Platonic philosophy; it is based on the recognized inequalities of knowledge and competence that separate teachers and students, masters and apprentices in all fields of learning. In Arendt's judgment, only the Roman notion of authority was genuinely political in origin. The Hebrew distinction between God and God's people, between transcendent creator and God's mortal creatures, has no credible analogue in human affairs. The Platonic model of directive authority based upon the superior knowledge of masters and teachers is declared illegitimate by Arendt because it imposes an extra-political paradigm on the conduct of politics.[132]

To secure the stability of the city and the safety of its philosophical citizens, Plato reconceived the nature of the political life. In his *Republican* thought experiment, he deliberately excluded the majority of citizens from direct participation in politics. In limiting political agency to a small class of virtuous philosophers, he followed the historical example of the Greek tyrants. He wanted, however, clearly to separate the despotism of coercive violence from the authoritative rule of superior knowledge. For Plato, true political authority rests on the relevant inequalities of knowledge and virtue. These inequalities simultaneously justify the rulers' right to command and the ordinary citizens' obligation to obey. The demonstrated wisdom of the statesman, the voluntary consent of the citizens, and the ministerial nature of philosophical governance, are clearly intended to distinguish the legitimate rule of the wise from the tyrannical imposition of force.

Arendt strongly rejects the Platonic attempt to create a political intermediary between persuasion and coercion, between the conventional equality of citizens and the marked inequality of despots and subjects.[133] She does not deny the legitimacy of human authority as such; but she does oppose the insertion of epistemic inequality into properly political relationships. There is a genuine inequality of knowledge between parents and children, teachers and students, doctors and patients. Shared recognition of this inequality is an essential condition for the exercise of authentic authority. It is tempting to seek its equivalent in the political sphere, to envisage a *techne* of statesmanship analogous to the arts of navigation and medicine. Arendt consistently resists this "temptation" in the name of political equality and freedom. For her, the liberty and equality of citizenship are incompatible with any form of rule and the dignity of concerted political action with any structure of command and obedience.

Where did Aristotle stand on the issue of political authority? Let us first examine Arendt's critique of Aristotle before comparing it to his actual position. Arendt acknowledges Aristotle's critical distance from Plato on several major points: he draws a much sharper distinction between *oikos* and *polis* than Plato did in the *Republic;* he recognizes the existence of equality and freedom among active citizens; he stresses the importance of persuasion and the exchange of differing opinions in the conduct of political argument; he clearly distinguishes *phronesis* from *episteme* and *techne* as species of rational knowledge. Despite these significant contrasts, Aristotle's Platonic allegiances often lead him into contradiction or *aporia*. On Arendt's critical account, Aristotle's *Politics* is compromised by a profound inconsistency.[134] On the one hand, he defines the *polis* as a voluntary association of equal citizens united in the pursuit of the best life. On the other, he accepts the ruling relationship as the basic category of political analysis. He elevates rule to conceptual eminence by classifying the *politeia* of the numerous Greek cities based on their distribution of political authority. Thus, we have rule of the one, the few or the many; rule with or without the constraint of law; rule for the sake of the governors or the governed; despotic, royal and constitutional rule.[135]

For Arendt, these combined Aristotelian claims are in fact contradictory, because an association of equals is incompatible with any type of rule. Even authoritative rule exercised for the sake of the governed, presupposes a type of inequality precluded by citizenship. Aristotle recognized that constitutional rule among free citizens is fundamentally different from the despotic and royal rule occurring in the household. To justify political authority he based it upon the educational model of teachers and students. In most forms of education, the natural and evident differences between old and young structure the teaching-learning relationship. Yet, Arendt insists, "Nothing is more questionable than the political relevance of examples drawn from education."[136] The practice of education is properly hierarchical because it rests on relevant inequalities of knowledge and responsibility, whereas in politics, we deal with adult citizens, peers, who are beyond the age and need of education. Authentic citizenship actually begins when education and authority come to an end, and young adults assume their share of responsibility for the common world.[137]

Arendt is suspicious of political rule and authority and of the hierarchical principles invoked to justify them. Aristotle, however, takes hierarchy for granted and looks upon rule as natural and good. For him, the ruling principle is not restricted to human affairs for it originates in the constitution of the universe. There is a natural ruler in all well-ordered wholes: the *kosmos*, the human *psyche*, the *polis*, the classical *oikos*. Hierarchy and rule pervade the order of being to which we mortals belong. At the same time, he recognizes important differences in the types of rule and in the internal relations between rulers and subjects. Analogous patterns of governance can be found within the soul, the household and the political realm. Examples of despotic rule include that of the soul over the body, masters over slaves, and tyrants over their fellow citizens. Royal rule obtains in the directive authority of reason over the passions, parents over their children, and virtuous kings over their obedient subjects. Aristotle offers no example of constitutional rule within the rational soul. However, the ruling pattern within the *polis* among free men and citizens is constitutional in nature; sibling and spousal relations provide a limited analogue to it within the classical household.

For Aristotle, rule is legitimate when it is based on the relevant inequalities and exercised for the good of the composite whole. Natural substances and artifacts, human partnerships and associations are well ordered when they are well designed and well governed. By nature, the superior principle within the composite should rule its subordinate elements. This criterion of sound order requires the soul's rule of the body, and, within the soul, reason's governance over the passions and appetites. In human *koinonia* like the *oikos* and the *polis*, it justifies the authority of those who excel in reason and virtue. Anarchy, the absence of directive rule, or the subordination of greater to lesser elements within the whole, corrupts the composite's development and prevents the achievement of its appropriate *telos*.

To determine correctly who should govern whom and in what manner, it is essential to distinguish several types of inequality. Inter-specific inequality constitutes a difference among natural kinds; familiar examples include the ontological divisions between gods and humans and between shepherds and sheep. Members of a common natural kind differ in the degree of their operative power and virtue. They exercise the same natural capacities but more or less well. Inequalities within a species can be either provisional or permanent. Children generally differ from their parents and teachers in a provisional way; but according to Aristotle, the sexual difference between men and women has permanent political implications. The striking inequality between masters and slaves can be either natural or conventional in origin. "Natural slaves" lack the directive capacities of practical reason; they can understand and obey the rational commands of others but cannot issue them. Conventional slaves have the ability to govern themselves but are prevented from doing so by the coercive power of their masters.[138]

Aristotle's philosophical dependence on Plato is evident in his moral psychology. For both of them, the constitution of the soul guides their conception of legitimate rule. Although they differ in their detailed portraits of the human psyche, they agree that its internal structure is hierarchical. Reason is the noblest part of the soul and its natural ruler; sensibility is a nonrational psychic power able to follow the directives of reason. Reason and sensibility exist in all human beings, but their effective operation differs from person to person and from one stage of life to another. "Nature has given to young men strength and to older men wisdom." While sensitive desires and emotions should comply with reason's rule, they cannot follow its directives without the relevant moral virtues. The moral virtues are acquired excellences of character that habituate the soul's desires and passions to the governing authority of the practical intellect. In the well-ordered soul, practical wisdom commands and the virtuous sensibility obeys. But without the cooperation between reason and desire that the virtues of character establish, the interior life of the soul is contentious. Lacking practical wisdom and moral virtue, the human soul is at war with itself and unable to act with insightful authority.

Arendt repeatedly criticizes Plato and Aristotle for collapsing the contrast between *oikos* and *polis*, for inserting the ruling patterns of the household into the free exercise of public affairs. Is this important criticism justified in Aristotle's case? I don't think it is for the following reasons. Aristotle insisted on the need for rule in all complex wholes as a condition of their good order. But he insisted as well on the need to distinguish different types of rule: despotic and royal in the household, constitutional in the polis. For Aristotle, the polis is a voluntary association of free and equal citizens for the sake of the best human life. Despotic rule does occur within actual cities, but it constitutes a perversion of their normative order. Royal rule is justified only as a rare exception, when the statesman's wisdom is so remarkable as to make him a god among his fellow men.[139] Constitutional rule is the appropriate norm in political affairs and it clearly differs in kind from both forms of household governance.

But what is the nature of constitutional rule? Aristotle believes that human beings are born for citizenship, that they need to belong to a just *polis* in order to live virtuously and well. In a constitutional *politeia,* citizens share in the exercise of political power. Within the ancient Greek context, this means that they engage in deliberative, judicial and military activities with their peers. When the distribution of political functions is properly ordered, the citizens act in concert for the common good. Constitutional rule, the government of free citizens by free citizens is a carefully acquired art. "Those things we need to learn before we can do them we learn by doing them." In the case of constitutional governance, we only learn how to govern freely by first learning how to obey. "He who has never learned to obey cannot be a good ruler."[140]

The shared exercise of power in a free city does not eliminate the political relevance of hierarchy. Just as he combined noble and useful goods in his ethical account of *praxis*, so Aristotle integrates hierarchy and equality in his political analysis of government. However, the civic equality that Aristotle favors is geometrical and not arithmetic.[141] Distributive justice requires that all citizens share in political power in proportion to their merit and qualifications. It is one thing to serve on a jury and another to act as a judge, one thing to exercise elective suffrage and another to hold the most important political offices. Age, experience, tested virtues of character and practical wisdom, these are the relevant criteria in distributing political responsibilities. When the criteria are equally satisfied, then the designated responsibilities should be equally shared. Citizens rightly recognize the superior virtue of their peers by granting them positions of authority and leadership. While moral virtue is expected of all adult citizens, in a well-ordered *polis* discernible differences in excellence correspond to distinctions in the assignment of office and *ergon*.

The most basic and important political arguments concern a city's constitution, its *politeia*. In Aristotle's practical philosophy, the *politeia* is the formal cause of a *polis*, the enduring source of its identity and unity. Within natural substances, their formal causes are internally ordered to their *telos*. In the analogous case of the *polis*, this means that the *politeia* is explicitly designed by the city's founders to promote the comprehensive good of the whole community. In the *Politics* of Aristotle, *politeia* explicitly refers to the organization and distribution of a city's political powers and operations; Aristotle's causal focus is on the reality of generated power, on citizens cooperating effectively in institutional and cultural affairs. Since human beings cooperate for a purpose, the creation and preservation of power is not an end in itself. The various forms of political cooperation are designed to achieve specifically political goods: peace, justice, security, public freedom, the cultivation and exercise of the virtues. The task of the genuine statesman, the *politikos,* is to coordinate the actions of these different centers of power and to integrate the goods they promote and preserve for the common good.

Pace Arendt, Aristotle believes in multiple ways of generating political power. In actual cities, there are at least three ways of achieving effective cooperation among citizens. Persuasion: the debate among equals can lead to agreement on a shared course of action or support for a broad range of policies. Authority: citizens can recognize the superior virtue of their political and military leaders and voluntarily obey their commands and directives. Lawful coercion: those driven by passion to resist rational persuasion can reluctantly comply with the law to avoid the threat of justified punishment. Historical cities, with morally and intellectually diverse populations, regularly rely on all of these strategies to achieve their legitimate ends.[142]

The core of the *Politics* is an empirical and normative study of political power. As an empirical study, it emphasizes the generation, distribution, exercise and maintenance of power; as a normative study, it distinguishes between legitimate and illegitimate uses of power. Illegitimate power consists in the covert or overt resort to violence against the body politic. Civic coercion, however, may take several forms: sophistical rhetoric is an abuse of persuasion as a source of collective agreement; counterfeit virtue an abuse of authority by aspiring political leaders; and the lawless resort to coercion or force an abuse of the rule of law. If power and violence are not carefully distinguished, the normative concern for justice and legitimacy disappears, and political power is treated as inherently coercive and despotic. But uncritical opposition to power is an anti-political prejudice, for the antithesis of power is impotence, and an impotent *polis* cannot act for the common good.

Aristotle's *Politics* provides several ways of classifying and appraising Greek *politeia*. Who governs: Does the governing authority belong to a single ruler, a select body of designated citizens, or to the whole adult population? How is government exercised: Is the conduct of government constrained by law or does it operate lawlessly; do the citizens freely consent to the rule of their leaders or are they regularly subject to force and coercion; is political leadership based upon the relevant knowledge and virtue or does it merely express the prevailing opinion of the ruling body? Who is governed: under despotic rule, unequal slaves and mistreated citizens; under royal rule, provisionally unequal family members and children; under constitutional rule, the alternation of ruling and being ruled among free consenting citizens. For whose benefit does governance actually occur: legitimate government pursues the good of the whole political community; illegitimate government aims at the restricted wellbeing of the ruling class. Procedures of selection, succession and accountability: How are particular offices and functions regularly distributed; what is the procedure for alternating and replacing political leaders; when and how do public officials account for their conduct to the whole body politic?

In the course of the *Politics,* Aristotle examined the merits and limitations of both actual and imagined *politeia*.[143] He reached the sober conclusion that reasonable objections could be raised against all of them. But he followed his accustomed tendency to rank constitutions hierarchically from the best to the worst. The despotic rule of a single tyrant who governs lawlessly for his own benefit is the worst form of *politeia*. Since the opposite of the worst is supposedly best, does it logically follow that a lawful monarchy ruled by a virtuous king is the political ideal?[144] In some passages in the *Politics,* Aristotle seems to make that assertion, but his actual position is more nuanced and subtle. Since politics is a practical art, properly sensitive to existing political conditions and constraints, there is no *politeia* that is unconditionally best *sans phrase*. We need, therefore, to distinguish between what is best: under the most desirable conditions of education and virtue; under normal or typical conditions; under this set of concrete historical circumstances. What is best under the most desirable conditions is the appropriate measure for appraising political practice. However, articulating a normative measure of appraisal is no substitute for developing a concrete program of action for this time and place. It would be mindless to attempt to establish an aristocracy of virtue when the exigent conditions such a *politeia* requires have not first been met. In both constitutional design and political reform several practical considerations are relevant: the qualifications of the potential rulers; the equitable distribution of political offices; the stability of the polis through time; generating sufficient power to achieve legitimate and attainable ends; workable provisions for lawful succession in office; the avoidance of crippling political factions; the development of the required virtues among the citizenry as a whole.

It is very difficult to summarize Aristotle's political teaching. In some contexts, his outlook is clearly hierarchical and aristocratic; in others the importance of civic equality is explicitly recognized. Arendt reads this tension as a sign of internal contradiction, but she neglects the thematic of virtue, from which the tension usually arises. When Aristotle focuses on virtue, *arete*, as a qualification for rule, he tends to be hierarchical, because the attainment of virtue is difficult and the combination of virtues required of the exemplary statesman is exceedingly rare.[145] But when he thinks of the *polis* as a school of *arete*, and cultivating virtue as the *telos* or aim of political practice, his emphasis shifts to developing the citizenry as a whole. His hierarchical judgments are clearest when he classifies monarchy and aristocracy as the best *politeia* because they provide a ruling principle of practical wisdom coupled with adequate external resources. But then he questions whether it is just for a single person or set of persons to have supreme and unqualified power.[146] If all citizens are educated in virtue and entitled to share in political power, is it wise or fair to curtail or restrict their engagement in public life? From this political perspective, the hierarchical emphasis on command and obedience appears one-dimensional, for during their civic careers ordinary citizens engage in numerous political activities: they prepare and fight battles; propose, refine, accept and obey legislation; participate in lawful judicial proceedings; debate and reach decisions in deliberative assemblies; perform the administrative functions of magistrates; share in their city's highly diverse cultural life. In some cases they exercise leadership, in others they follow the lead of their peers or comply with the rule of law. Through their civic education, they learn to obey, to debate, to propose, to criticize, to judge and to assign public offices on the basis of recognized merit. In a word, they exercise the arts and virtues essential to political association.

Aristotle recognizes the numerous benefits that flow from an active and informed citizenry. The wise sharing of political power generally strengthens the stability and unity of the polis. While the principle of civic equality favors the distribution of power, the hierarchical principle matches *ergon* to *arete*, specific function to excellence, and places a premium on the outcomes of civic education. The appropriate political education is normative and critical, for power cannot be responsibly shared unless the citizens are prepared to use it wisely and well. Aristotle integrates the claims of hierarchy and equality in his concept of the polity or mixed regime.[147] While the mixed regime is not the most excellent *politeia*, it is the most stable and least crippled by faction. In its blending of diverse political elements, the polity takes account of three important and essential practical realities: the competing claims to rule of the different classes, the existing distribution of external goods, the multiple sources of public power. Since each factor influences the city's wellbeing, Aristotle recognizes their legitimate place in the just constitution. The democratic parties base their claim to rule on military grounds; their adherents provide the majority of the soldiers needed to defend the city and its people. Oligarchs assert their political preeminence on the basis of property and wealth, since their personal affluence gives them the leisure participatory politics requires. When aristocratic gentlemen seek political authority, they emphasize their exceptional virtue and breeding. For Aristotle, all of these partisan claims have a limited validity, though each class tends to overstate the merits of its case.

The divisive enmity between rich and poor is a major cause of political instability.[148] Democratic parties typically support the civic aspirations of the poor while their oligarchic rivals favor the concerns of the rich. These recurrent factional struggles should be offset by deliberately creating a broad middle class whose political moderation (*sophrosyne*) strikes the mean between democratic envy and oligarchic arrogance.[149] Civic virtue tends to be strongest in those with a moderate economic position; they have limited desires for personal possessions and property but sufficient external goods to give them a stake in the existing regime. Aristotle applies his doctrine of the mean to the city's economic arrangements with subtlety and realism. While recognizing the political importance of economic inequality, he clearly subordinates economic policy to larger public purposes and goods.

Aristotle's tendency towards moderate realism is also reflected in his position on political power. Wisdom and consent, persuasion and command, coercion and the threat of force all play a legitimate role in the political dynamics of the mixed regime. Effectively governing the polity requires successfully combining several political factors: the practical wisdom of the virtuous few, the common sense of the moderate many, the compulsive rationality of law with its explicit threat of punishment for those lacking in virtue and tempted by immoderate desires. Although he does not invoke "the balance of power," a clear recognition of political tensions and the need for a flexible dynamic constitution shapes Aristotle's portrait of the mixed regime.

The *Politics* also contains a qualified defense of the political competence of the ordinary citizen. Unlike Plato, Aristotle does not emphasize the epistemic limitations of the democratic multitude. He affirms the political importance of plurality, and acknowledges that the collective virtues within a community often surpass the excellence of a few. The collective judgment of the majority should not be arbitrarily dismissed. Ordinary citizens are competent to judge the effects of public policies, just as those who dwell in a house can appraise its adequacy better than the architect and the builder. But the analogy with the productive arts points to the limitations as well as the strengths of the democratic majority. In the most important public offices, personal virtue is at a premium. It is one thing to approve a wise course of action, quite another to discover and articulate it persuasively. We should not ask the majority for brilliant initiatives in public affairs, but informed appraisal and provisional consent to policies conceived and enacted by their leaders.[150]

Aristotle's assessment of democracy, therefore, is characteristically moderate. Democratic *politeia* are rarely excellent, but their internal corruption is less dangerous than that of monarchical or aristocratic regimes. In practice, democracy tends to favor the rule of the poor, who are envious of the rich and suspicious of citizens with exceptional virtue. The recurrent democratic fallacy is to insist on arithmetical equality in all things. But equality of citizenship does not entail equality of merit nor an equal claim to political authority. Distributive political justice is based on geometrical equality, on unequal rewards for unequal contributions to the commonweal. The most important public offices should be assigned to the most eminent and qualified citizens. Political eminence is rooted in several sources of discernible inequality: age, experience, moral virtue and mastery of the political arts, especially practical wisdom.[151]

Phronesis, practical wisdom, is the distinctive virtue of the statesman and the specific excellence of deliberative reason.[152] It occupies the strategic center of Aristotle's political theory but is strangely absent from Arendtian thought. Given its centrality in political life, it is important to ask: Who are the practically wise? In ordinary life, they are the people whose counsel we seek when confronted with important but difficult decisions. We turn to them for advice periodically on what ought to be done or avoided here and now. In a good society, based on just laws and a sound and effective civic education, it is possible for the majority to be morally virtuous. Through long experience and consistent training and practice they can acquire the moral virtues needed to act responsibly in public life. However, *phronesis*, the characteristic excellence of the legitimate ruler, is not reducible to these commonly shared civic virtues. For Aristotle, it is an elemental fact of human nature that only a few can be wise. *Phronesis* is the result of a rare conjunction of favorable factors: strong native intelligence, sound moral and civic education, sufficient experience and maturity, remarkable goodness of character, unusual foresight in practical affairs. It is a virtue lacking in the young and inexperienced and those who live without comprehensive moral excellence.

Political wisdom is directly concerned with achieving the specific ends of the *polis*. We have already identified several of the common goods at which a legitimate *politeia* aims. But agreement on political goals is consistent with two types of spirited political debate. In one type, exemplified by Socrates' dialectical practice, citizens disagree about the nature of the human good itself. In pursuing their arguments, they seek to distinguish: the true from the apparent good; the greater from the lesser good; the comprehensive from the partial good; the enduring from the ephemeral good. The citizen or statesman with *phronesis* must be able to make these critical moral discriminations. Yet even when substantive agreement on the human good is reached, there are usually several ways to pursue legitimate political ends. Rational deliberation attempts to determine the best way to achieve a specifically desired good under existing conditions. The *phronimos*, Aristotle's practically wise person, excels in rational deliberation, in discerning the best course of action for this place and time. The political excellence of qualified rulers, the only legitimate source of their political authority, combines moral virtue, practical insight and a deep knowledge of one's *polis*, its citizens and the practical world they inhabit.

For Aristotle, the exercise of *phronesis* was either architectonic or deliberative.[153] Practical wisdom is required of those who design and reform constitutions, as they match the governing laws of a people to its history, culture and geographical and political circumstances. Practical wisdom is also essential in deliberative and judicial contexts, in the conduct of public affairs in the assembly and the courts of justice. The specific function of statesmen in politics is to provide just and effective leadership on a consistent basis. Sound political judgment is always carefully attuned to the situation at hand. It means knowing when to push for full performance and when to compromise; when delay is wisdom and when it is disaster; when widespread consent is necessary and when action must be taken despite substantial opposition. *Pace* Arendt, the wise statesman must know when to persuade, when to command and when to employ legitimate force.[154]

The *phronesis* of the statesman is more morally demanding than Arendtian virtuosity for it is explicitly exercised for the common good. Aristotle's reasoned approach to political matters can best be described as critical normative realism. Aristotle is an empirical realist who consistently appeals to the testimony of experience and history. "The truth in practical matters is discerned from the facts of life."[155] People of great and enduring virtue are rare, and no *polis* can count on having large numbers of them among its citizens. The springs of human conduct are varied, with motives for civic action ranging from the noble to the base. All human beings are capable of evil, and even the most virtuous citizens are occasionally blind or bad-tempered. The rule of law has its evident shortcomings, but lawless societies are invariably despotic and harmful. Aristotle is never tempted by the speculative idyll of anarchism. The achievement of justice requires strong and effective government; good government requires knowledge and virtue on the part of its leaders; and responsible citizens are formed through sound civic education and the prescriptions and prohibitions of law. Human beings are the best of animals when perfected by art and virtue and the worst when separated from law and justice.[156]

In Arendt's republic of liberty, citizens conduct their political lives on the basis of persuasion and argument alone. But Aristotle is explicit about the limited effectiveness of persuasion in human affairs. Authentic persuasion has weight with virtuous people, who are moved to act or refrain from acting by appeals to nobility and shame. It also has weight with ordinary citizens, who already have the required moral excellences and respect the wisdom of their experienced leaders. However, moral argument is neither sufficient to make human beings good nor to reform their characters later in life.[157] For those citizens lacking in virtue, whose conduct is guided by their passions and appetites, legal warnings and sanctions are often necessary as corrective measures. The best statesmen are students of the human soul who understand the subtle continuum of virtue and vice that exists among their peers. Politics, the art of the humanly possible, is never easy and often disappointing. It requires doing the best that you can under difficult, often trying, sometimes tragic conditions. It is shadowed by the fact and threat of mortality, for the *polis'* most experienced and trusted leaders are continually passing from the public scene. It is challenged, as well, by the fact of natality, by the newcomers and strangers who must learn how to live together justly as citizens. Within this fragile and intricate web of diverse and unequal human beings, the statesman presides, speaking and leading as circumstances require, exhorting the citizens to do what is best, and protecting the community against external and internal threats to its well-being. The virtuous governing of free persons by free persons: Aristotle's constitutional rule.

THE BEST WAY TO LIVE

For Aristotle, the purpose of practical philosophy is to discover and actualize the human good. In the first book of the *Nicomachean Ethics,* he identifies this good with *eudaimonia,* the best and most complete human life.[158] As his developing argument makes clear, Aristotle's ethical judgments are based on a carefully articulated anthropology. There is an explicit theory of human nature that underlies and supports his account of personal wellbeing. The anthropological theses are not arbitrarily assumed, but presented as a refinement and completion of traditional Greek common sense. Because human nature is exceedingly complex, prevailing conceptions of the good are a mixture of insight and oversight. There is broad agreement on the most obvious features of living well, and understandable disagreement about the relative importance of pleasure, virtue and wisdom. For Aristotle, these disagreements are not simply expressions of subjective preference; they rest instead on more or less adequate conceptions of what it means to be fully human.[159]

On what aspects of the human good had the ancient Greeks reached consensus? They agreed that the best life is neither available to slaves nor to those who live under despotic rule. To live under tyranny or the mastery of another person is to lack full rational agency; such lives are constrained by biological necessity and human coercion. Artisans, mechanics and merchants were also perceived as not living well. Their lives were chiefly spent in making, using and selling external goods, such as weapons, clothing and tools. While external goods surely belong in a well-balanced life, they are not the focus of a free person's attention and concern. For the classical Greeks, then, human lives constrained by necessity and immersed in utility were judged to be lacking in freedom.[160]

To live well is to live freely, to enjoy a way of life selected and chosen for its own sake. On these basic principles, both the many and the wise are agreed. However, practical wisdom diverges from conventional opinion on the life that is freest and most desirable. After critically surveying a broad range of Greek ethical opinions, *endoxa,* Aristotle submits three rival accounts of the good life to thoughtful inspection.[161] Each account is based on a specific understanding of the *summum bonum*, the supreme human good. Aristotle's dialectical strategy is to present the three positions in ascending orders of adequacy, so that a deeper and richer understanding of human existence gradually emerges from the extended argument. We can identify these different lives, *bioi,* by the animating loves that give them direction and purpose: pleasure, honor and wisdom.

According to Aristotle, base or vulgar people desire a free but non-virtuous life devoted to the enjoyment of sensual and bodily pleasure. Impressed by the example of Oriental tyrants, like the rulers of Sardanapallus, they think of freedom as the license to do and enjoy whatever they please. They therefore seek wealth, power, and external goods as enabling conditions for their despotic conception of liberty.[162] Aristotle severely criticizes the advocates of the voluptuous life, not because he condemns the body and disparages pleasure, but because this form of life, available to beasts as well as to mortals, is unworthy of human beings.

More refined citizens are prepared to sacrifice physical pleasure and comfort for the political life devoted to virtue. Loyal members of the *polis*, they willingly support the excellence of their city through heroic and liberal actions. In a just *community*, their peers reward their demonstrated virtues by granting them public honors and offices. These honors, in turn, confirm the nobility of their character and the exceptional merit of their conduct. Although honorable deeds chiefly depend on civic virtue, they also require a limited set of external goods; soldiers, for example, need weapons and armor, public benefactors need to possess moderate wealth. While the vulgar seek worldly possessions as instruments of pleasure, the noble require them in moderation as instruments of virtuous activity.[163]

Aristotle acknowledges that the life of virtuous political activity is well suited to our composite nature. The *bios politikos* would be the freest and best way to live, if human affairs were really of paramount importance.[164] But in the metaphysical hierarchy of being and perfection, mortals are clearly subordinate to the divine. The lives of the gods are perfect models of blessedness and excellence; and their lives are not burdened by the demands of the body nor the passions and desires of the soul. According to Aristotle, the gods are purely noetic beings engaged in continuous self-contemplation. Humans are metaphysically linked to the divine through *nous*, the highest power of the rational soul. While the gods are intrinsically wise, humans have a natural desire for wisdom that leads them to engage in theoretical inquiry. The culminating *telos*, or climax, of human inquiry is contemplative knowledge of the first causes and principles of being. At the theological summit of the theoretical life, humans become closest to the gods, enjoying, if only briefly, a glimpse of divine happiness. Theoretical wisdom, *sophia*, is the supreme human virtue, and the life which it crowns, the *bios theoretikos*, is the most godlike of those to which humans can aspire.[165]

Aristotle draws this synoptic conclusion from his extended dialectical argument: *eudaimonia* is a life of the best and most complete virtue enjoyed over a long and full existence.[166] It is the best life because it culminates in wisdom, the highest virtue, but it is most complete because it contains the full array of goods that comprehensive wellbeing requires. Humans are mortals, not gods, who seek to achieve *eudaimonia* during their limited existence on earth. In the *Politics*, Aristotle recognized the merits of a mixed regime that took realistic account of the city's economic and social complexity. In the *Nicomachean Ethics*, he similarly recognizes the merits of a mixed life that combines in the proper proportions external goods with physical, moral and intellectual excellences. In both contexts, Aristotle is a hierarchical pluralist who consistently subordinates the necessary to the useful, the useful to the virtuous and the morally virtuous to the godlike.[167]

While Arendt never rejected the theoretical life, she did oppose the Greek philosophers' interpretation and appraisal of it. The special attention they devoted to contemplation tended to obscure articulated distinctions within the *vita activa*.[168] When politics was confined to the practice of governing others, it ceased to be the province of free and equal citizens and became an unwelcome burden imposed on the virtuous against their will. Philosophers replaced statesmen and military leaders as exemplars of human excellence, but in the myth of the cave, these new cultural heroes now looked with contempt upon human affairs. They described themselves as strangers, involuntarily exiled within the *polis*. Only their mortal bodies sojourned in the earthly city; their souls' allegiance belonged to an invisible eternal republic.[169]

These other worldly prejudices are most pronounced in the discourse of Pythagoras, Parmenides and Plato, but Arendt contends that even Aristotle failed to overcome them. His hierarchical account of the best human lives is clearly guided by the contemplative ideal. Although Aristotle praised the *bios politikos* in the *Ethics*, he did not prize it as an unconditional and final human end.[170] Moreover, he allowed the alien categories of utility, rule and hierarchy that he inherited from Plato to distort his account of political conduct. As war is properly conducted for the sake of peace, so *praxis* exists for the sake of *theoria*, a godlike existence superior to its political rival. Though Arendt is silent about Aristotle's theological claims, we know from her Kantian background that she questions the validity of metaphysical knowledge and presumptive comparisons between human and divine agency. Aristotle's ethical subordination of politics to philosophy depends on a theology Arendt does not accept; but her critical suspicions extend to Aristotle's anthropology as well. His discussion of the best life relies on a theory of human nature based on a detailed account of the *telos* of inquiry and science. For Aristotle, science (*episteme*) is superior to historiography as a form of human knowledge because it deals with invariant universals rather than contingent particulars.[171] Scientific inquiry is concerned with causal necessity, the study of history with unpredictable human agency, science with the what-ness (the essence) of natural substances, historical reflection with unique persons and their variable and free interactions. But Arendt strenuously objects to these classical assumptions of metaphysical and epistemic privilege. Why should causal necessity be privileged over freedom, scientific demonstrations over historical narratives, the what-ness of a thing over the who-ness of a person or invariant teleology over free self-constitution?

In the dialectical spirit of Aristotle, it is wise to respond to these Arendtian criticisms by drawing some important distinctions. Let us begin by clarifying the complex relations Aristotle affirms among the *polis, politike* and the *bios politikos*. Aristotle repeatedly claims that the *polis* is the most perfect human association. When governed by justice and virtue, cities become self-sufficient and lacking in no human good. As Pericles asserted in his celebrated funeral oration, the *polis* is a school of *arete,* where all the human virtues can be acquired, exercised and communally remembered. This ensemble of excellences includes the civic virtues of ordinary citizens, the moral and intellectual virtues of statesmen, and the godlike virtues of theoretical inquirers. Within the just city, there is a legitimate place then for both the political and the contemplative life.

Politike, political science, is the most important part of practical philosophy. It is an architectonic knowledge of the common good based on a profound understanding of human nature and teleology. Drawing on theoretical insights into the human *eidos* and *telos*, the statesman effectively integrates the plurality of goods that are required for the city's wellbeing.[172] Two types of leisure, *schole*, are included among these politically important goods: the leisure of ordinary citizens allowing them to engage in the conduct of public affairs; the leisure of genuine philosophers allowing them to live the *bios theoretikos* without interference. Despite its critical role in governing the *polis*, *politike* is not the highest form of rational knowledge. Cosmology and theology are epistemically superior to political science, because their subject matters, the heavens and the divine, are ontologically superior to the words and deeds of mortal citizens.[173]

The *bios politikos* is a noble form of life devoted to establishing justice and securing peace in the realm of human affairs. At its best, politics consists of rational discourse (*lexis*) and virtuous actions (*praxis*) directed towards the common good. In classical Greece, their political engagement chiefly engaged adult male citizens in deliberative, martial and judicial activity.[174] In openly criticizing Greek political practice, Aristotle insisted that the *telos* of the just city is not pleasure, wealth, conquest or empire, but cultivating within the body politic the best and most complete virtue. For the great majority of citizens, virtuous participation in politics provided their chief opportunity for attaining *eudaimonia*.

Aristotle does not treat the honorable life of the citizen and the theoretical life of the philosopher as incompatible rivals. But he does contrast them at length in order to determine the best way for humans to live. Their polemical rivalry is a contest for supremacy rather than a struggle for coexistence. As the good *polis* provides a home for philosophical citizens and a comprehensive *politike* recognizes the special place of speculative wisdom among the virtues, so the *bios politikos* creates communal conditions in which theoretical inquiry can develop and flourish.

In what does the philosophical life, the *bios theoretikos* consist?[175] Although all humans have a natural desire to know, only a few make it the effective center of their existence. They pursue knowledge disinterestedly, for its own sake, because of the joy that increased understanding brings. Their inquiry originates in wonder (*thauma*) and progressively unfolds through sense experience and reasoning to reach the apprehension of explanatory causes. The path of theoretical inquiry ascends from terrestrial substances to knowledge of the heavens and culminates in the contemplative knowledge of god. The metaphysical knowledge of divine causality is the least necessary and most excellent achievement of mortal man. *Sophia*, philosophical wisdom, is the supreme form of virtue and the climactic fulfillment of the intellectual life. Fullness of being consists in the theoretical contemplation of cosmic and divine order.

Contemplative wisdom constitutes the *telos* of the *bios theoretikos*, as comprehensive justice constitutes the *telos* of political activity. But why is the philosopher's contemplative life superior to the active life of the statesman? In Aristotle's philosophy, all things are finally understood and judged with reference to the divine. But the more we learn about the gods, the more we realize how different they are from ourselves. The gods do not have bodies or passions; they don't form alliances and engage in commercial transactions; they never suffer the slings and arrows of fortune and are completely immune from both birth and death. The divine life is blessed, perfect and completely contemplative in nature. Although we mortals are not divine, we are most akin to the gods when we contemplate their being and causal power. The *bios theoretikos* is the best way for humans to live because it is the most godlike existence available to them. Aristotle supports this ethical conclusion by arguing that the contemplation of God is the most liberal, leisurely, continuous, pleasurable and perfect activity in which human beings can engage.[176]

To keep Aristotle's ethics in perspective, we need to distinguish two forms of perfection or closure. One is the closure or completion of a hierarchical order that advances from lesser to greater goods culminating in a supreme excellence, a *summum bonum*. Aristotle's strategy in *the Nicomachean Ethics* is to articulate a hierarchical order of excellence that rises from the goods of the body to those of the soul and culminates in the virtue of theoretical wisdom. Contemplative wisdom is the highest human good; it is the summit of the ascending ethical quest and serves no end or purpose beyond itself. The other relevant form of closure is completeness or wholeness. For the life of a natural substance to be complete, it must include all the goods required by the substance's *telos*. Because human beings have a composite nature, because they occupy an intermediate ontological position, above the brutes but below the gods, they need many different goods in order to live well. Theoretical wisdom is the climax, but certainly not the whole of human wellbeing. External and internal goods, physical, moral and practical excellences, are all pre-conditions of attaining and enjoying wisdom. While they combine to make wisdom possible, wisdom gives them their ultimate purpose and point.[177]

In choosing how to live, humans confront three distinct and serious dangers. If they choose the voluptuous life centered on physical pleasure, they become less than human. If they choose the political life based on the love of public honor and praise, they remain merely human. If they choose the philosophical life, they risk forgetting that they actually are human. *Hubris*, transgressing the ontological boundary between mortal and divine beings, is the great philosophical temptation. Pleasure seekers and lovers of honor seriously err by failing to perfect the divine presence within them. While true philosophers respect that presence, they need concretely to remember the complex mortal substance in which it is deeply embedded. Cicero later expressed Aristotle's ethical vision in deliberately paradoxical terms; when human beings are at their best, they live like mortal gods.[178]

What is Aristotle's considered view of philosophical citizenship? He does not encourage committed philosophers to withdraw from the life of the *polis* (there is no hint in his teaching of allegiance to an eternal republic). Nor does he favor a neglect of *phronesis* and *politike*, and exclusive attention to theoretical pursuits and concerns. True philosophers do not require immunity from political obligations but freedom from exclusive attention to human affairs. The well-ordered *polis* creates room for several ways of life that go beyond the *bios politikos*. Because humans are mortal and finite, they cannot do two things at once. The leisure, solitude and stillness demanded by theoretical inquiry are typically interrupted by war and political turmoil. To think well, especially to understand and contemplate invisible realities, requires ceasing normal physical activity. This limitative truth partly accounts for the symbolism of philosophical withdrawal so prominent in Plato's cave analogy. It is one reason both Plato and Aristotle subordinate the *bios politikos* to the contemplative life. At the same time, it is only the *polis*, the comprehensive school of the virtues, that makes the contemplative life possible at all; and only the statesmen, with their *politike* and *phronesis* who establish a community in which philosophy can develop and flourish.

The relationship between philosophy and politics is genuinely complex. The philosophical life transcends the defining activities of citizenship, but it also depends upon their full execution. Recognizing the depth of this dependence, Aristotle does not countenance the complete secession of philosophers from political engagement. Characteristically, he opts for an intermediate position between those of Plato and Pericles. Philosophers should not become kings or rulers of the *polis*, but they should serve as practical advisors and counselors to those who govern. With their comprehensive knowledge of being and humanity, they are well positioned to correct the distorting biases that polarize political life and to encourage political leaders to take the long and inclusive view in setting their priorities and policies.

I have tried in this section to show how Aristotle blunts the force of Arendt's criticism by deliberately seeking a normative mean between Plato and Pericles. He accepts the Periclean concept of the *polis* as a school of virtue, but he also accepts the Platonic indictment of Athenian imperialism. Aristotle is clearly sympathetic to the Platonic hierarchies of excellence, ontological, epistemic and ethical, but he checks Plato's tendency to treat functional complements as antithetical contraries. Aristotle's practical philosophy is a remarkable synthesis of Ionian naturalism and Platonic formalism. By combining the material and efficient causes of the Greek Naturalists with the formal and final causes of his revered teacher, he preserves both excellence and wholeness in his persuasive account of the human good.

Although Arendt's appraisal of Aristotle often misses the mark, his practical philosophy is not without serious problems. Let us conclude this chapter by identifying some of his most telling weaknesses.

1. Aristotle uncritically assumes the normative character of ancient institutions and practices. Thus, he takes for granted slavery, the inequality of women, and highly restrictive qualifications for citizenship. He also assumes without question the absolute priority of the *polis* as a setting for the good human life.[179]
2. His abiding attachment to Greek cultural practices coincides with a general blindness to whatever is not Greek. By contemporary standards, he is deeply ahistorical in his neglect of alternative ways of conceiving and organizing human affairs.
3. By supporting a closed secular teleology in which *eudaimonia* may be attained in this life, Aristotle avoids the mysterious questions of death and immortality and fails to engage the serious Platonic reflections on the ultimate destiny of the soul.[180]
4. Aristotle is blithely aristocratic in his approach to the human race. Greeks are superior to barbarians, men to women, free citizens to slaves, philosophers to everyone else. He does not seem troubled or uneasy that the many shoulder burdens and sacrifices in order that the few might become wise and free.
5. Aristotle's intellectual strategy is heavily weighted towards harmony, unity and order. He combines unity with order through the device of hierarchical pluralism and unity with harmony through the strategy of functional complementarity. While these irenic approaches generally serve him well, they lessen his alertness to conflict, tragedy and the profoundly agonal character of political life.[181]
6. Aristotle's sharp separation of theory and practice is deeply oversimplified and his classical conception of science unduly restrictive. His theory of knowledge was effectively undermined by the modern empirical sciences with their systematic commitment to theoretical and applied research.[182]
7. "Human beings live in the image of the god(s) whom they serve."[183] Aristotle's account of the best way to live is heavily dependent on his philosophical theology. The contemplative life is supremely good because of its unique kinship with divine activity. But Aristotle's concept of God is deeply unorthodox and his proof for God's existence and nature rests heavily on mistaken cosmological premises.

After Aristotle's death, when the Hellenic culture he so brilliantly synthesized began to interact with the cultures of Jerusalem and Rome, many of these limitations came into sharper focus. Mediterranean peoples to the east and west of the classical Greeks developed new conceptions of human order and excellence. With the dramatic emergence of Christianity and the extension of the Roman Empire into Europe and Asia, Greek philosophy lost its cultural dominance in the Western world. And very different conceptions of nature, man, God and citizenship began to transform our tradition(s) of political thought.

NOTES

1. Hannah Arendt, *Between Past and Future*, (Viking, New York: 1968) 25.
2. For the potential futility of action and speech see *The Human Condition*, 173, 197. For "immortal fame" as a remedy for the futility of human life see *Between Past and Future*, 46, 71, 74.
3. See John Dunne, *The Way of all the Earth* (4-26) for the reciprocal bonds between poetry and truth.
4. "For memory and depth are the same, or rather, depth cannot be reached by man except through remembrance." *Past and Future*, 94.
5. See chapters 3-5 in *The Human Condition* for an extended contrast between labor, work and action.
6. In her Gifford lectures on *The Life of the Mind*, Arendt carefully distinguished among thinking, acting and judging as she had earlier distinguished among *ponos, poiesis, and praxis*.
7. Arendt's narrative of totalitarianism reminds us of the worst that human beings can do and suffer. Her account of the American and French Revolutions celebrates the colonial founding of freedom and explains the French failure to establish lasting liberty. Her stories of "men in dark times" show what human beings can do faced with political and cultural decline.
8. Arendt was critical of pragmatism both as a theory of science and as a theory of action. See *The Human Condition*, 272, 306 and *Past and Future* 100-104.
9. See *Past and Future*, 120-135, for the dependence of religion, tradition and authority on the Roman experience of a unique political foundation.
10. "Without testament or to resolve the metaphor, without tradition—which selects and names, which hands down and preserves, which indicates where the treasures are and what their worth is, there seems to be no willed continuity in time." *Past and Future*, 5.
11. Alasdair MacIntyre, *After Virtue* (Notre Dame, Indiana: University of Notre Dame Press, 1981) 206.
12. Descartes and Bacon in their philosophies of science and Hobbes in his political philosophy exemplify the cavalier dismissal of tradition.
13. See Michael McCarthy, "The Critical Appropriation of Tradition," *Soundings*, Fall/Winter 1999.
14. Heidegger's insistence on the "ontological difference" between being (*sein*) and beings (*seiendes*) invites comparison with Arendt's insistence on the "phenomenological difference" between action (*praxis*) and fabrication (*poiesis*). See Heidegger's *Introduction to Metaphysics*.
15. "And that is the opportunity, provided by the very fact of crisis—which tears away facades and obliterates prejudices—to explore and inquire into whatever has been laid bare of the essence of the matter." *Past and Future*, 174.
16. See chapter 1, "The City in Ruins," Totalitarianism as a Limit Situation.
17. See *Past and Future*, "Tradition and the Modern Age," 17.
18. Arendt returns repeatedly to Socrates' myth of the cave (*Republic* VII) in interpreting Plato's political teaching. See *Human Condition*, 20, 75, 226, 292 and *Past and Future*, 17-19, 35-38, 39-40, 68, 106-115, 229-231, 237-238, *On Revolution*, 229, 318. For the myth itself see *Republic* VII, 514a-521a.
19. See *Human Condition*, 14 and 222-240. ". . . the enormous superiority of contemplation over activity of any kind, action not excluded, is not Christian in origin. We find it in Plato's political philosophy, where the whole utopian organization of the polis is not only directed by the superior insight of the philosopher but has no other aim than to make possible the philosopher's way of life." See *also Past and Future*, 107-115.

20. "Marx, when he leaped from philosophy into politics, carried the theories of dialectics into action, making political action more theoretical, more dependent upon what we today would call an ideology, than it ever had been before." *Past and Future,* 30.

21. *Past and Future,* 21-25; *Human Condition,* 12, 17.

22. Arendt correctly distinguishes two different aspects of Augustine's political thought. The coercive power of the state, its reliance on the sword, may be a legacy of sin, but the associative character of human existence is rooted in human sociability itself. *Past and Future,* 73.

23. See Machiavelli's defense of the Roman political *ethos* in the *Discourses and the Prince.* For Machiavelli's reliance on Roman political experiences, see *Past and Future,* 136-141 and *On Revolution* 36-39 and 286-287.

24. This is the central theme of chapter VI in *the Human Condition,* "The *Vita Activa* and the Modern Age."

25. See *The Human Condition* 294-326 for the initial triumph and subsequent defeat of *Homo Faber.*

26. *On Revolution,* 64.

27. *On Revolution,* 11.

28. "The end of a tradition does not necessarily mean that traditional concepts have lost their power over the mind of men." *Past and Future,* 26.

29. *Thinking,* 133.

30. See "Life as the Highest Good," section 44, chapter VI, *The Human Condition* and "The Concept of History," chapter 2 of *Between Past and Future and On Revolution,* 280-281.

31. *Past and Future,* 70-72.

32. Thucydides, *History of the Peloponnesian War,* II. 41.

33. Thucydides—ibid. "Thus requiring no Homer to sing our praises nor any other whose verses will charm for the moment."

34. For Arendt's account of the origin of Greek political philosophy, see *The Human Condition, Between Past and Future, On Revolution,* and *Thinking.* "The growing apoliticism of the philosophers after Socrates' death, their demand to be freed from political activities and their insistence on performing a nonpractical, purely theoretical immortalization outside the sphere of political life had philosophical as well as political causes." *Between Past and Future,* 72.

35. See *Human Condition,* 17-18 and *On Revolution,* 319. Arendt agrees with Cornford's claim that "the death of Pericles and the Peloponnesian War mark the moment when the men of thought and the men of action began to take different paths." *Human Condition,* 17.

36. For Socrates' critique of Pericles, see *Gorgias* 514-522.

37. Plato, *Gorgias,* 514-516.

38. Plato, *Gorgias* 481b-486e and *Republic, Book VI.*

39. *Human Condition,* 14-21. For the true philosophers' desire to be free from the burdens of politics, see Plato, *Republic* 517-521b.

40. Arendt reads the myth of the cave as confirming this oppositional judgment, metaphysically, epistemologically, rhetorically, and psychologically. The volatile realm of human affairs is unfavorably compared to the realm of immutable being that the true philosophers love and seek.

41. See *Past and Future* 112-115, 228 and "the traditional substitution of making for action," section 31, *The Human Condition,* 220-230.

42. For Arendt's interpretation of Plato's philosopher kings as not so benevolent despots, see *Past and Future* 104-115, and *Human Condition,* 220-230.

43. See "Mental Activities in a World of Appearances" section II of *Thinking.* "My use of the term *vita activa* presupposes that the concern underlying all its activities is not the same and is neither superior nor inferior to the central concern of the *vita contemplativa*." *Human Condition,* 17.

44. I have based this hierarchical ordering on Aristotle's *De Anima* and *Nicomachean Ethics.*

45. *Republic* VI and VII. The ontological and epistemic *chorismos* between forms and things, and between knowledge and opinion is marked by the central division in the divided line and in the mythical contrast between cave and sky.

46. Arendt rejects this assumption whether the transcendent norms are Platonic or Christian in nature. Her commitment to political autonomy requires that political agents and actions be judged by the immanent criterion of "greatness." *Past and Future*, 46-47 "action can be judged only by the criterion of greatness because it is in its nature to break through the commonly accepted and reach into the extraordinary." *Human Condition*, 205.

47. See Tradition and The Modern Age, chapter 1 of *Past and Future*.

48. For the restoration of dignity to the phenomenal world, see Appearance, Part I of *Thinking*.

49. *Human Condition*, 17.

50. This sharp critique of philosophical citizenship is dramatized in Aristophanes' comedy *The Clouds*. It is further developed and then forcefully rebutted by Socrates in both *The Apology* and *The Republic*.

51. Socrates uses the construction of a just "city in speech" to highlight his criticisms of Athenian political culture and practice. The radical forms of communism proposed in the 2nd and 3rd waves of paradox dramatize the contrast between political partisanship and authentic devotion to the common good.

52. Socrates had already acknowledged this contrast in responding to his old and new accusers in the *Apology*. In the *Republic*, the contrast is thematized in the ontological distinction between intelligible being and sensible becoming structurally elaborated in *Republic* VI and VII.

53. Socrates shows how this distortion occurs in the diverse forms of nonphilosophical rule: timocracy, oligarchy, democracy, and tyranny. See *Republic* 8 and 9 and numerous passages in the *Apology and Gorgias* .

54. Thucydides, *The Peloponnesian War* (Hackett Publishing: Indianapolis) 94.

55. For the critique of Achilles and Odysseus, see *Republic* II and III. For the contrast between philosophical and hedonistic *sophrosyne* see *The Symposium*. For the critical assessment of Pericles as an authentic statesman see the *Gorgias*. The virtues of Socrates have a different psychological origin and a different psychagogic effect from the *aretai* of his heroic predecessors.

56. Both Callicles in the *Gorgias* and Thrasymachus in the *Republic* actively resist Socrates' efforts at dialectical healing. The art of medicine, for bodies or souls, requires the cooperation of the patient to be effective.

57. *Human Condition*, 204-207.

58. Thucydides, *Peloponnesian War*, 91-97.

59. MacIntyre, *After Virtue*, 125-137; 175-187.

60. *Republic* 372d-374b.

61. *Republic* 514a-519.

62. *Republic* 515a-518d.

63. *Republic* 508d, 516a-521.

64. *Republic* 519c-521.

65. The trial, imprisonment and death of Socrates are dramatized in the *Apology*, *Crito*, and *Phaedo*. The fatal return of the true philosopher to the cave is depicted in *Republic* VII. In nearly all the dialogues Socrates is threatened for challenging deeply held opinions or for criticizing publicly revered leaders. It is unclear whether Socrates' reasons for returning to the cave are really compulsory. What is the psychagogic effect of experiencing the Good in an erotic soul devoted to philosophy? The infinite power of the Good diffuses itself ontologically, philosophically and politically.

66. For Arendt's critique of Plato's political use of the forms, see *Human Condition* 221-230; *Past and Future* 104-115.

67. *Past and Future*, 107-115. "The philosopher announces his claim to rule, but not so much for the sake of the polis and politics . . . as for the sake of philosophy and the safety of the philosopher."

68. *Human Condition*, section 31, "The Traditional Substitution of Making for Acting"; *Past and Future*, 110-115.

69. I have borrowed this distinction, in slightly amended form, from P. F. Strawson, *Individuals* (London: Methuen, 1959) 9-11.

70. See *The Human Condition* 24-27, 31-33, 37, 83, 206-207 and *Past and Future* 115-118.

71. Aristotle, *Politics*, Book II, chapters 2-6.

72. Aristotle, *Metaphysics I*, chapters 1 and 2; *Nicomachean Ethics* VI, chapters 3-13; X, chapters 7-8.

73. I am drawing for this summary on *the Posterior Analytics, Physics, Metaphysics, De Anima, Nicomachean Ethics and Politics*.

74. For Aristotle's account of *phronesis*, see NE, Book 6, chapters 5, 7, 8 and 12. For the architectonic character of the political art, see NE, BK 1, ch. 2. Aristotle's *Politics* taken as a whole provides an excellent example of comparative political philosophy.

75. For Aristotle's account of the four causes see *Physics* II, chapter 3, and *Metaphysics* I, chapters 3-10.

76. See *Politics*, Book I, chapter 2. "Man is the only animal nature has endowed with the gift of speech." *Human Condition*, 27.

77. *Politics*, 1253a 32-36.

78. Aristotle begins both his theoretical and practical inquiries with a dialectical examination of the opinions (*endoxa*) of his predecessors, the many, the few and the wisest of these. Even the opinions of the many contain an aspect or part of the comprehensive truth Aristotle seeks. See *Metaphysics* II, chapter 1.

79. See *Politics*, 1278b 20-25, as well as Aristotle's account of friendship, *philia*, in Book 8 of the *Nicomachean Ethics*. ". . . for without friends no one would choose to live, though he had all other goods."

80. See Aristotle's *Politics*, Books 1 and 2; *The Human Condition* II, 5, 28-38. "The *Polis* and the Household."

81. ". . . the human good turns out to be activity of soul in accordance with virtue . . . the best and most complete" NE. 1098a 12-20.

82. See Aristotle's account of justice, in NE Book 5, chapter 1, as the virtue concerned with another's good. Also, *Politics* 1276b 28-30 "one citizen differs from another, but the salvation of the community is the common business of all."

83. *Politics*, 1277b 7-27.

84. See *The Human Condition* 17, 220-230 and *Between Past and Future* 115-120.

85. For the inherent merits and limitations of action see chapter 5 in *The Human Condition*.

86. For the critical distinction between human freedom and sovereignty see *Past and Future* 163-165 and *On Revolution* 153, 156, 159-160.

87. For the unstable and despotic nature of public opinion, see On *Revolution* 76, 93, 221-228.

88. *The Human Condition*, 220.

89. The following asymmetry illustrates a crucial difference between making and acting. Whatever is made can be unmade, but whatever is done cannot be undone. Arendt refers to this difference as the irreversibility of action.

90. See *The Human Condition* 63, 188, 194-195 and *On Revolution* 186-187.

91. See *The Human Condition* 225-230 and *Past and Future* 110-115.

92. *Nicomachean Ethics*, Book 6, chapter 4 ". . . neither is acting making nor is making acting."

93. *The Human Condition* 205-207.

94. *Between Past and Future* 216-224.

95. *The Human Condition* 39, 91, 157; *Past and Future* 208-226.

96. "The substitution of making for acting and the concomitant degradation of politics unto a means to an allegedly 'higher' end . . . is as old as the tradition of political philosophy." *The Human Condition* 229.

97. *Past and Future* 139-141; *Human Condition* 228.

98. ". . . the very substance of violent action is ruled by the means-end category, whose chief characteristic if applied to human affairs, has always been that the end is in danger of being overwhelmed by the means which it justifies and which are needed to reach it" *Crises of the Republic* 106, see also *Past and Future* 215-216.

99. Many of the traditional justifications of political violence depend on the conflation of action and fabrication. See the chapter "On Violence" in *Crises of the Republic and Human Condition* 229.
100. *Crises* 106.
101. *Human Condition* 206-207.
102. For the relevant analogy between action and creative performance see *Past and Future* 153-156 and *Human Condition* 207.
103. See *Past and Future*, 218-226.
104. *Past and Future* 137, 152-156; *Human Condition* 204-207.
105. Kant, *Groundwork of the Metaphysics of Morals*, 61.
106. *Nicomachean Ethics* 1094b 1-11 and *Politics* 1252a 1-5, 1252b 26-35, 1278b 37-42, 1279a 16-21.
107. *Past and Future* 220-224; and several sections of Arendt's *Lectures on Kant's Political Philosophy*.
108. *Nicomachean Ethics*, Book I, chapters I and 7; N.E. Book x, chapter 7; *Politics* 1252b 27-35.
109. *Politics* 1254b-1255a 2, 1260a 12.
110. *Politics* 1258b 25-38; *Politics* Book 3, chapter 5; *Politics* Book 7, chapter 8. See also Arendt's commentary *The Human Condition* 81-84.
111. *Politics* 1265a 32-37, 1326b 26-32; NE 1177b 1-25.
112. Arendt borrows from Aristotle the classical distinction between activities necessary for the preservation of life, activities useful for the attainment of some higher good, and liberal activities, that are good in themselves and desirable for their own sake. Leisure *(schole)* makes liberal activities possible. *Nicomachean Ethics* 1176b 1-8.
113. *Politics* 1252b 27-1253a 40.
114. NE, Book 1, chapter 8 and NE Book 10, chapter 8.
115. See MacIntyre, *After Virtue* 175-180 for his account of goods internal to a practice and their dependence on the exercise of genuine virtues.
116. See *Republic* 357b-358a where Glaucon classifies human goods into three types: instrumental, intrinsic, and those that are both intrinsic and instrumental. For Aristotle, virtuous political actions are good in themselves, but they also contribute to the specific goods for which the *polis* is collectively responsible.
117. "... of the highest objects, we say; for it would be strange to think that the art of politics, or practical wisdom, is the best knowledge, since man is not the best thing in the world," NE 1141a 20-23; 1141b 1-7, and NE 1145a 7-12.
118. NE X, chapter 8.
119. NE X, chapters 7 and 8
120. For Aristotle's contrast between *kinesis* (motion) and *energeia* (actuality) see *Physics* 201b 24-202 a2; *De Anima* 417a 15-21 and 431a 6-8; *Metaphysics* 1050a 22-1050b5 and *Nicomachean Ethics* 1094a 1-15 and NE Book X, chapter 4.
121. For Aristotle's critical distinction between doing what and doing as the virtuous person does, see NE Book 2, chapter 4 and NE Book 6, chapters 12 and 13.
122. NE, Book 6, chapters 4, 5, 7, 8
123. NE, 1144b 30-33 "it is not possible to be good in the strict sense without practical wisdom, nor practically wise without moral virtue."
124. "For even if the end is the same for a single man as for a state, that of the state seems at all events something greater and more complete whether to attain or to preserve." NE 1094b 7-11. See *Politics*, Book 7, chapters 1-2.
125. See *The Human Condition*, 28-37. Aristotle's *Politics*, Book I, chapters 3-13.
126. See *Past and Future* 111, 116-120, 182-185, 189-193.
127. *The Human Condition* 32-33, 215; *On Revolution* 30, 285.
128. *On Revolution* 119-120, 131-132, 235-237, 250-253; *Crises of the Republic* 73-102.
129. *The Human Condition* 222-230; *Past and Future* 104-115.
130. *The Human Condition* 222-230; *Past and Future* 106-108.
131. See *Republic*, Books IV-IX.
132. See chapter 3, "What is Authority" in *Past and Future*.

133. *Past and Future* 92-93.
134. *Past and Future* 116-120; *The Human Condition* 183, 222, 230.
135. *Politics* Book 3, chapters 6-18; Book IV and Book VI.
136. *Past and Future*, 119.
137. *Past and Future*, 183-196.
138. For Aristotle's distinction between natural and conventional slavery see *Politics* Book I, chapters 4-6, Book 7, chapter 3.
139. *Politics* 1284a 2-18, 1288a 1-25, 1332b 16-24.
140. See NE 1103a 23-1103b7; *Politics* 1277a 24-1277b 30, 1333a 1-5.
141. For the distinction between arithmetical and geometrical equality (and justice) see NE Book V, chapters 3-6; *Politics*, Book 3, chapters 3 and 12.
142. See *Nicomachean Ethics*, Book X, chapter 9; *Politics*, Book VII, chapters 7, 14-15.
143. See *Politics*, Books 2, 3, 4, 6 and 7.
144. *Politics*, Book 3, chapters 7, 13-18.
145. NE Book 6, chapters 5, 7, 8, 9, 12-13; *Politics*, 1277b 25-30.
146. *Politics*, Book 3, chapters 4-10. "Ought the good to rule and have supreme power? But in that case, every body else, being excluded from power, will be dishonored." *Politics* 1281a 27-35.
147. See *Politics*, Book 3, chapter 7, and Book 4, chapters 8-9, 11-12, Book V, chapter 7.
148. See *Politics* Book 3, chapters 7-13, Book 4, chapters 3-6, Book V, chapters 5-6, Book 6, chapter 5.
149. *Politics*, Book 4, chapters 11-12.
150. *Politics* Book 3, chapters 11-13.
151. "Now what is just or right is to be interpreted in the sense of 'what is equal'; and that which is right in the sense of being equal is to be considered with reference to the advantage of the state, and the common good of the citizens." *Politics* 1283b 40-1284a 11.
152. See NE Book 6, chapters 8, 9, and 13; *Politics* 1277a 15-25. "The good ruler is a good and wise man, and he who would be a statesman must be a wise man."
153. NE 1141b 22-1142a 10, NE, Book 6, chapters 5, 7 and 8.
154. NE Book X, chapter 9.
155. NE 1179a 15-23, NE 1098b 9-12.
156. *Politics* 1253a 31-33.
157. NE 1179b 4-20.
158. See NE Book 1, chapter 7.
159. NE 1097b 23-1098a 20.
160. *Politics*, Book 7, chapters 8 and 9.
161. NE, Book 1, chapters 4 and 5.
162. NE 1095b 13-21, NE 1176b 8-1177a.
163. NE 1178b 33-1179a 15, NE Book IV, chapter 1 and Book X 1178a 25-1178b 8.
164. NE 1141a 20-1141b 8.
165. NE 1177b 26-1178a 8.
166. NE 1098a 16-20.
167. *Politics*, Book 7, chapter 3.
168. *The Human Condition*, 15-16.
169. *The Human Condition*, 16; *Republic* 591c-592b.
170. For the distinction between praising and prizing see NE 1, chapter 12. For the correlative subordination of practical to theoretical wisdom, see NE, Book 6, chapter 7.
171. NE, Book 6, chapters 3-6; *Poetics* 1451a 37-1451b 32.
172. NE, Book 1, chapters 2 and 13, Book X, chapter 9; *Politics* Books 7 and 8.
173. See *Parts of Animals* Book 1, chapter 5; *Metaphysics* Book 1, chapters 1-2; NE 1140a 20-1141b 23.
174. See Arendt, *The Human Condition* 25-26 for the Homeric emphasis on "doing great deeds and speaking great words" and MacIntyre's *After Virtue* chapters 10-11 for the transition from heroic to political virtues in classical Greek culture.

175. Aristotle introduces the *bios theoretikos* in NE Book 1, chapter 5. He then clarifies its nature in NE Book 10, chapters 7 and 8. He also offers a brief sketch in *Metaphysics* 1, chapters 1-2.

176. NE 1177a 19-1177b 25.

177. NE Book 10, chapter 8.

178. See Lobkowicz, *Theory and Practice,* 33. "Just as it has made the horse for racing, the ox for tilling and the dog for hunting, nature has made man for two things, as Aristotle says, for thinking and acting—as if man were a mortal god." See also NE 1177b 26—1178a 8.

179. See *Politics*, Book 1, chapter 2, Book 2, chapter 1, Book 7, chapters 1-3. See MacIntyre, *After Virtue* 139, 149, 152. "Aristotle who saw the forms of social life of the city-state as normative for essential human nature was himself a servant of that Macedonian royal power which destroyed the city-state as a free society. Aristotle did not understand the transience of the *polis* because he had little or no understanding of historicity in general."

180. See *Republic* X, the whole of the *Phaedo*, and parts of the *Apology*. Even in the *De Anima*, Aristotle only touches briefly on the immortality of active *nous* "When mind is set free from its present conditions it appears as just what it is and nothing more: This alone is immortal and eternal . . . and without it nothing thinks." *De Anima* 430a 20-25.

181. See MacIntyre, *After Virtue*, 153.

182. See Bernard Lonergan, *Collection,* 238-241 and *A Third Collection*, 41-44.

183. A remark attributed to the psychiatrist Clemens Benda. Aristotle bases his argument for the superiority of the theoretical life on the contemplative nature of the divine activity. See NE 10, chapters 7 and 8.

Chapter Four

THE MARXIST REVERSALS OF TRADITION

> Marx knew that the incompatibility between classical political thought and modern political conditions lay in the accomplished fact of the French and Industrial Revolutions, which together had raised labor, traditionally the most despised of all human activities, to the highest rank of productivity and pretended to be able to assert the time-honored ideal of freedom under unheard of conditions of universal equality.[1]

Plato and Marx are the central characters in the Arendtian narrative of western political philosophy. She claimed that "our tradition of political thought" began with Plato and came to an end in Marx.[2] As we have seen, this does not mean that she asserted the end of politics, or of political reflection and judgment, but rather that a governing set of evaluative assumptions and conceptual oppositions had lost their traditional authority so that we are now required to think about human affairs *ohne Geländer*, without inherited banisters.

Arendt admired Plato and Marx as deeply as she disagreed with them. For her, they were great thinkers, unavoidable thinkers with whom we must constantly struggle. We cannot overcome their tremendous influence on our understanding and conduct of politics by neglecting or dismissing them. Rather, we must identify the central experiences and events that shaped their political thinking and critically challenge the interpretive legacy they bequeathed us.

As we begin this chapter on Marx, we need to remember Arendt's overriding conviction that the western tradition has been basically antipolitical. It has largely been framed not by the friends and supporters of politics, but by its intellectual adversaries who wished to subordinate political activity to some allegedly higher purpose. Four pivotal moments dominate Arendt's genealogical narrative. In classical Greece, Plato attempted to subordinate politics to the superior life of philosophy. In the early Christian era, St. Paul urged the disciples of Jesus to withdraw from the affairs of the world for the sake of their personal salvation. At both the advent and climax of modernity, the liberal bourgeoisie placed politics and government in the service of capitalist economic ambitions. And the centuries-old tradition finally collapsed when Marx substituted an ideological philosophy of history for a genuine theory of political governance and action.

Arendt's critical engagement with Marx occurs in several different textual settings. In *The Human Condition*, she criticizes his theory of labor and the teleological primacy he assigned to the value of species life. In *On Revolution*, she criticizes his philosophy of history, "the murderous dialectic of necessity and freedom" he effectively promulgated. In *The Crises of the Republic*, she criticizes Marx's endorsement of revolutionary violence and his uncritical reliance on material abundance as a guarantee of universal freedom. But the interpretive key to her appraisal of Marx can be found in "Tradition and the Modern Age," the opening essay in *Between Past and Future*.[3] In that seminal essay, Arendt situates Marx in direct relation to Plato and connects the beginning of political philosophy with its putative demise. While this chapter will draw liberally on several Arendtian texts, at its structural center is her placement of Marx at the end of our political tradition.

Through mythical symbols and stories, and memorable philosophical arguments, Plato established the hierarchical contrasts at the heart of the western tradition.[4] In these carefully correlated Platonic oppositions, sensible becoming is subordinated to intelligible being, transient opinion to unalterable knowledge, rhetorical discourse to contemplative silence and political action to philosophical understanding and thought. In the pre-Socratic *polis*, classical citizens forcefully liberated themselves from necessity and coercion in order to share in political liberty. In Plato's deliberate cultural reversal, true philosophers escaped the burdens of politics in order to contemplate intelligible being. When they reluctantly returned to the *polis*, they used their privileged epistemic authority to prevent the recurrence of Socrates' fate by making the cave safe for philosophy.[5]

Aristotle refined and developed the hierarchical distinctions he inherited from his teacher. He retained Plato's belief in the ethical supremacy of the contemplative life, but he argued that the active life had a hierarchical structure of its own. Thus *praxis* and *lexis*, the fundamental political activities, were ethically superior to *poiesis*, the productive activity of the craftsman, while both *praxis* and *poiesis* were superior to *ponos*, the burdensome labor of the slave. Aristotle justified his hierarchical contrasts on both ethical and metaphysical grounds. Ethically, human activities should be ranked based on their freedom, nobility and excellence. Properly free or liberal activities are chosen for their own sake because they are intrinsically good. They are explicitly contrasted with those lesser endeavors undertaken from necessity or as a means to some higher end. Ethical and metaphysical criteria converge in Aristotle's influential appraisal of the free lives that transcend biological necessity. For Aristotle, the philosophical life is best because it is godlike in nature; the political life is noble because it actively engages the highest practical capacities of mortal citizens; the hedonistic life devoted to the enjoyment of sensual pleasure is vulgar because it is available to brutes as well as to humans.[6] At the base of Aristotle's evaluative hierarchy is the laboring existence of the slave. The slave's life lacks freedom, nobility and excellence. Immersed in biological necessity and enforced through the master's coercion, it is not fully human by Aristotle's standards.

Hierarchical inequality, both metaphysical and ethical, shapes the Greek cultural tradition. The philosophical life is accessible only to the most virtuous citizens; the political life is available only to the male masters of private Greek households; while the life of sensual pleasure is open to everyone freed from the burdens of slavery. The higher and freer the form of life, the fewer the people able to enjoy it.

Karl Marx deliberately rebelled against these classical hierarchies articulated in Greek philosophical thought and transmitted to the Latin West through scholastic theology and pedagogy. By the mid-nineteenth century, the principal realities of European life were no longer compatible with Greek and medieval ethical and political theories. Although Marx was conversant with classical thought, he was an essentially modern thinker, deeply attuned to the historical realities of his age. Thus he embraced defining aspects of modernity deeply inconsistent with Plato's and Aristotle's anthropological vision: 1. Marx strongly endorsed the process of modern secularization; he rejected philosophical and religious other worldliness, asserting the exclusive dignity and importance of human affairs on this earth.[7] 2. He shared the modern distrust of theoretical contemplation and disinterested knowledge. For Marx, genuine science begins with suspicion of sensible appearances and common opinions; it proceeds to uncover the invisible causes underlying sensible phenomena and unreflective belief. Having discovered these lawful patterns of causal necessity, humans can finally become masters of their destiny, strategically allying their efforts with the ruling forces of nature and history.[8] 3. Marx strongly endorsed the democratic aspirations of the French Revolution. The revolutionary ideals of liberty, equality and fraternity were no longer restricted to the privileged few but meant for the entire human race. In fact, until liberty and justice were universally "realized," the historical project of modernity would remain incomplete.[9] 4. The industrial revolution had transformed the scale and scope of human history. It had created a dynamic urban society based on international commerce and innovative technology, and animated by the profit maximizing ideology of capitalism. With the rise of the factory system, productive manufacture and commercial exchange, increasingly dominated Europe's public affairs.

A revisionary anthropology supported these powerful revolutionary currents. The leading moderns glorified what the ancients had disparaged, and treated with contempt and suspicion what their classical predecessors considered noble and godlike. The supremacy of disinterested knowledge was denied; the importance and dignity of the *vita activa* were affirmed; and productive endeavor was exalted as the highest expression of human freedom and power.

Marx was deeply aware of these historical changes and their incompatibility with traditional hierarchical beliefs. In Arendt's view, "he tried desperately to think against the tradition while using its conceptual oppositions."[10] This polemical strategy led him to overturn or invert the ancient Platonic antitheses. Arendt chooses three revealing examples to highlight Marx's iconoclastic approach: his conception and reappraisal of labor, violence, and philosophical reflection. Each of these reversals is succinctly expressed in a provocative statement intended to contradict an important traditional belief. "Labor created man." "Violence is the midwife of history." "Philosophers have only interpreted the world. The point is to change it."[11]

In asserting that labor created man, Marx challenged the biblical conception of God and the philosophical and scriptural appraisals of labor. For the ancient Greeks, labor had its origin in human animality, in the endemic struggle of mortals with biological necessity and the demands of survival. In Hebrew scripture, labor is depicted as a punishment imposed on Adam and Eve for the original sin. In both the Greek and biblical traditions, human freedom and happiness require liberation from the pain and burden of labor. By deliberately glorifying labor, by making it the creative source of the human species itself, Marx espouses a Promethean humanism openly defiant of the biblical and classical assessment of the human condition.

In describing violence as the midwife of history, Marx challenged the Greek conceptions of politics, action and speech. According to Herodotus, the father of western historiography, the purpose of historical narrative is to preserve from oblivion the great words and deeds of mortals, both Greek and Persian alike.[12] These glorious actions worthy of enduring remembrance are essentially political in nature. Politics is an affair of shared *logos*, of persuasive speech among equals, the free interaction of citizens in a lawfully constituted public realm. Coercion and violence (*bia*) were specifically excluded from the conduct of political life. While they governed pre-political relations in the private household and dominated the transactions between Greeks and barbarians, they functioned within the *polis* itself as an *ultima ratio*, as an instrument of last resort when all appeals to persuasion and argument had failed.[13]

Marx believed, however, that class struggle and conflict were the essence of history and that violence was pervasive in historical politics. Greek society had been effectively divided between masters and slaves, feudal society between nobles and serfs, and industrial society between capital and labor. The dominant economic class at each stage in history used its political power, its legal control of the means of violence, to oppress and subdue the class beneath it. Government and law primarily functioned to protect inequalities of power rooted in exploitative economic relations. Beneath the surface civility of politics the state was despotic and coercive, using ideology and law to conceal its oppressive intent.

For Marx, the turning points in history occurred when the exploited class revolted successfully against its economic and political oppressor. These violent revolutions transformed existing social and political relations. The decline and death of the ruling class coincided, however, with the birth of a new but structurally similar class rivalry, as the historical pattern repeated itself. Thus violence governs political history in both pre-revolutionary and revolutionary times. But while the normal political violence of the state sustains the oppressive status quo, revolutionary violence moves history closer towards its ultimate goal: a classless and stateless society no longer burdened by oppression, coercion and rule.

In his eleventh thesis on Feuerbach, Marx takes critical aim at the history of western philosophy. "The philosophers have only interpreted the world in various ways; the point is to change it."[14] The philosophical tradition from Plato to Hegel had emphasized the epistemic priority of *theoria*, the disinterested knowledge of being. In classical Greece, the *theoros* was a disengaged observer, a person of leisure (*schole*) who silently discerned the true order of things. The speculative vision of the *theoros* left existing reality unaltered, whether the objects of *theorein* were Plato's immutable forms or history's dialectical telos(Hegel). The rhythm and spirit of the *vita contemplativa* are succinctly expressed in Aquinas' lovely description: "to rest and see, to see and love, to love and praise."

Although Hegel was an innovator who made the history of human affairs the new focus of philosophical thought, in one crucial respect he remained quite traditional. He continued to believe that the philosophical quest climaxed in the contemplative knowledge of the divine. The *telos* of history, the autonomous freedom of absolute spirit, was brought to fulfillment in the rational self-knowledge of the Hegelian philosopher. For Hegel, the true meaning of history is fully disclosed in the teleological development of western philosophy.[15]

A critical student of Hegel, deeply influenced by his dialectical account of the historical process, Marx openly dissented from important aspects of Hegelian philosophy. For Marx, the end or meaning of history is the actualization of human rather than divine freedom, an actualization achieved by deliberately "making history" rather than contemplatively observing its passage. Marx clearly subscribed to the Baconian principle that true knowledge is power that proves its worth in the fruits and works it helps to produce.[16] For Bacon, this epistemic revision was designed to ensure technical mastery of the natural universe; for Marx it was meant to ensure mastery of the historical process; and for both, to promote the radical transformation of the human condition through the alliance of science and technology.

The modern cultural emphasis on increasing "fruits and works" clearly reversed the Platonic hierarchies. In Plato's well ordered *polis*, all practical activities, from agriculture to legislation, occurred in support of philosophical inquiry. Human existence culminated not in the opinion-based practices of the shadowy cave but in the vision of eternal truth by the liberated few. As *nous* was the godlike power in the soul, so contemplative understanding of the divine was the supreme activity in the well-ordered life. The whole *vita activa* was politically organized to support the philosophical quest.[17]

For Marx, the philosophical tradition inspired by Plato had inverted the causal order of reality. The true purpose of theoretical inquiry was to understand the lawful dynamics of nature and history. The historical process is teleological, as Hegel had claimed, but its *telos* is entirely practical and not theoretical. Human history is moving dialectically, irresistibly, towards universal freedom and equality. But dialectical motion is highly complex and does not follow a linear progression. This complexity entails that material progress coexists with radical alienation, for human beings have become neither equal nor free in modern capitalist societies. Marx attributed radical alienation to both capitalist reality and thought; only a critical philosophy that grasps the causal connections between being and consciousness could overcome it. The philosophical tradition had been practically impotent and productively fruitless because it misunderstood the true relation between cause and effect. It is only economic forces (the increasing productivity of labor) and social struggle (revolutionary violence) that drive human history forward. These material and efficient causes operate from below, *pace* Hegel, creating and then transforming the forces of production that advance the historical wheel.[18]

The critical stages in human history are properly defined in economic terms. Marx refers to the ownership and control of economic forces as "the relations of production." On his account, the great historical revolutions occur when these economically structured relationships are overturned by the previously oppressed economic class. Prior to an economic revolution, it is the dominant socio-economic class that exercises political authority and controls the institutions of culture and pedagogy. The philosophy, art and religion of the pre-revolutionary period invariably express the material interests of the ownership class, but they normally do so clandestinely. The ruling class conceals the full extent of its oppression by falsely representing its hegemonic power. Marx designates these distorted and self-serving portraits of historical power ideologies. Their strategic purpose is to justify the legitimacy of those who command and to pacify the anger and resistance of those who obey.[19]

Marx's critical philosophy of history, therefore, has two closely related objectives: to reveal class based ideologies for what they are, distorted expressions of interest based consciousness; and to arouse and channel the revolutionary energies of the economically oppressed. The critique of ideology undermines the cultural and political authority of established power; the explanatory science of historical change enables revolutionary theorists and their working class allies to align their efforts with the real causes of social transformation.

According to Arendt, Marx not only challenged the traditional estimates of labor, violence and philosophy, he also implicitly endorsed them.[20] On her reading of Marx, he was a self-consciously modern thinker working within an ancient intellectual tradition, for whom the convergence of classical and modern ideals generated internal contradictions. For Arendt, these unintended contradictions become clearest in the utopian society Marx claims will emerge from the overthrow of capitalism. She questions what human existence will be like after the meaning of history has been "realized" in a classless society? In theory, economic activity will be so productive that every one will be liberated from alienated labor and the coercive rule of the state. All human beings, without exception, will now enjoy the leisure and freedom available only to citizens in the Athenian *polis*.[21] But in classical Athens, citizens forcefully freed themselves from labor and coercion so that they could engage in the higher activities of philosophy and politics. Arendt then addresses this seminal question to Marx. If the actual purpose of philosophy is to promote the classless society, a society in which philosophy and politics are no longer necessary, what are socialized citizens to do with their precious leisure and liberty? What is their bitterly won freedom for?

Arendt traces these unresolved tensions in Marx to a fundamental conflict in his intellectual loyalties. As a Promethean humanist, Marx glorified labor for its limitless creative potential, while implicitly treating it as a curse from which socialized humanity would be liberated. As a revolutionary activist, he strove to eliminate the bourgeois state and to end its coercive authority, but he could find no trace of excellence or greatness in the bureaucratic distribution of benefits, the principal form of "political" activity in a stateless society. Finally, as a radical philosopher of history, he deliberately subordinated the contemplative to the active life, but left no credible task for philosophy to perform after its historical commission had been fulfilled.

Arendt believed that Marx confronted unprecedented modern realities that he tried to address using traditional concepts that no longer aligned with them. Inadvertently he demonstrated the ensnaring power of "the tradition" in the process of seeking to overcome and reverse it.[22]

We need to gain some critical distance from Arendt's reading of Marx before attempting to appraise its validity. To this end, we shall use sections A–C of this chapter to develop an independent account of Marx as a student and critic of modernity. We shall focus on three aspects of his thought: the scandalous contradictions in modern society, the dialectical nature of history, and his many-sided critique of capitalism. With this background in place, we shall revisit Arendt's placement of Marx in the history of the western tradition and evaluate her assessment of him as the last great political philosopher.

PROGRESS AND DISILLUSION

Karl Marx and Hannah Arendt were both humanistic thinkers. Each was deeply concerned about protecting human dignity and extending human liberty. Each was openly hostile to the conditions of existence that emerged under bourgeois capitalism. They were strikingly united in what they opposed, and profoundly divided by contrasting anthropological visions. Arendt was a political humanist committed to restoring the dignity of republican citizenship, and preventing ideology and terror from destroying human life on this earth. Marx was a Promethean humanist committed to defending the dignity of productive labor and overcoming the scandalous contradictions in modern society. His socialized humanism is culturally rooted in the intellectual revolutions of modernity, the radical reconceptions of nature and history that began with Copernicus and Galileo. Among the leading scientific naturalists, he is closest to Darwin, whose evolutionary account of species genesis and perishing parallels Marx's theory of historical change. And while Hegel awakened Marx's historical consciousness, his mature philosophy of history defiantly challenged Hegel's philosophical and cultural authority.[23]

The enduring power of Marx's analysis is grounded in its synoptic character. Marx combined the critical suspicion encouraged by Descartes with the enlightenment's alliance of scientific knowledge and technical power. In fact, he treated that alliance as the principal source of modern progress and pride. At the same time, he embraced the social and historical awareness of the romantic tradition. He supported the romantic critique of liberal individualism and explicitly rejected the Cartesian theory of the disembodied, disengaged subject. Marx insisted that human beings are always embodied agents belonging to specific economic classes with their particular historical identities and prejudices. These classes belong to distinct stages in history differentiated by their economic, political and cultural institutions and beliefs. Conceived as an intelligible whole, human history exhibits a dialectical pattern of movement and conflict, as human beings constantly change their relations to nature and to one another.

Although Marx would have rejected the description, he was a deeply romantic thinker. Like other nineteenth century Romantics, he aspired to an integral form of humanism that would overcome the philosophical and practical dichotomies enshrined in enlightenment liberalism.[24] Thus he sharply opposed Kant's bifurcations of subject and object, mind and nature, freedom and necessity, individual and society. His theoretical and practical ideal was a humanized naturalism or naturalized humanism that overcame these provisional dichotomies within a comprehensive dialectical synthesis.[25]

This convergence of contrasting cultural currents helps account for Marx's unique sensibility. He shared the enlightenment's confidence in unlimited historical progress through the technical mastery of nature. But he also endorsed the profound romantic critique of the bittersweet fruits of the modern age. For Marx, mid-nineteenth century Europe was a tangled knot of greatness and wretchedness, of unprecedented hope and severe disillusionment. But how to explain this unhappy conjunction of practical and emotional opposites? Marx believed that modernity had created secular expectations it had manifestly failed to satisfy, expectations about universal freedom, equality, and expressive fulfillment. I call Marx a romantic because he failed to question the plausibility of these extravagant hopes, seeking instead to fulfill them by joining strategic violence to the scientific mastery of history.

The secular aspirations of modernity were concretely embodied in the struggles and dreams of the French Revolution. Marx saw this still unfinished revolution as the decisive event in modern history, the watershed moment that ended an old institutional and cultural order and gave rise to a new one.[26] The revolution marked the end of the *Ancien Regime*, the hierarchical ordering of human society rooted in medieval feudalism. Under the old regime, the source of political power and legitimacy was inherited land and title. The accepted authority of kings, nobles and clergy rested on their established position in a hierarchical structure sanctified by religion and tradition. But with the deliberate execution of Louis XVI, the unleashing of the Jacobin terror against the nobility and the eventual acceptance of Napoleon's radical reforms, the traditional structures of feudalism were swept away never to return.

The new liberal capitalist order that replaced those structures was not based on inherited status, but on money, finance, credit and commercial and legal expertise. Under early modern capitalism, fluid and exchangeable wealth replaced tangible property as the source of economic power and influence.[27] The newly dominant capitalists defended an alternative model of social existence based on the voluntary exchange of goods and services for personal profit. For the liberal defenders of capitalism, sweet commerce, *le doux commerce*, would make traditional forms of public authority, both political and religious, no longer necessary. In Marx's judgment, it was the European bourgeoisie, the champions and beneficiaries of commercial capitalism, who really emerged victorious from the great revolution. Economically, they now owned the capital and controlled the credit in post-revolutionary Europe. Culturally and politically, their influential theory of *laissez faire* provided public justification for this novel experiment in economic and political order.[28]

Throughout the nineteenth century, political reflection in Europe centered on the French Revolution. Conservatives were nostalgic for all that the revolution had violently destroyed: divinely sanctioned monarchy, the spiritual and temporal authority of clerics and nobles, the ancestral customs, mores and landmarks of the European past. Both political and cultural conservatives viewed the liberal rejection of political and religious authority as a recipe for chaos and eventual despotism.[29]

Economic and political liberals, for the most part, celebrated the new bourgeois ordering of society. They argued that voluntary economic exchanges among enlightened individuals would eventually promote the well being of all. Liberated from the archaic structures of the *Ancien Regime* and the traditional moral and religious prejudices against commerce, Europe would experience a future of international peace and prosperity.[30]

Radical social thinkers like Marx were openly contemptuous of bourgeois liberal complacency. They forcefully insisted that new forms of exploitation and violence had replaced the despotism of nobles and kings. It was now bourgeois capitalists rather than landed aristocrats and clerics who piously justified their inordinate power and privilege. The autocratic ideology of the divine right of kings had simply been replaced by the liberal ideology of *laissez faire*.

Marx aspired to leadership of the radical camp. He hated bourgeois society and rejected the principles and policies of classical liberalism. He insisted that the Revolutionary promise of universal emancipation and freedom remained, in the language of Hegel, "unactualized." Without a far more radical social and economic transformation, the defining aspirations of modernity would remain "abstract and disembodied." The limited freedom and restricted equality supported by bourgeois liberalism failed to match the utopian promises of the Revolution. Although Marx ridiculed the effectiveness of moral norms and ideals, he was profoundly committed to the secular ideals of the revolutionary cause: the fullest measure of liberty, equality, and fraternity for the whole human race.

Marx warned his contemporaries that until the demands of 1789 were actualized in a new social order, Europe would remain in a state of civil war.[31] This conflict was unlike the wars of religion that brutalized the seventeenth century, or the wars of national expansion and consolidation that eighteenth century monarchs had conducted. For Marx, the decisive historical struggle was not rooted in confessional differences or dynastic ambition, but in the deepening antagonism between the bourgeois owners of industrial capital and the urban laboring class that Marx called the proletariat. The coercive power of the bourgeois state actively protected the property rights of capital and invoked the dominant liberal ideology in their defense. For Marx the protracted conflict between capital and labor was the ultimate historical struggle, because it was rooted in the fundamental contradictions of modernity.

What were those revolutionary contradictions as Marx understood them? The key to his dialectical analysis is what Arendt calls "the social question," the scandal of dehumanizing poverty in the midst of unprecedented wealth and material abundance.[32] Human poverty, of course, was not a uniquely modern phenomenon. Both ancient and modern societies had failed to overcome the persisting division between the rich and the poor, between the affluent few and the indigent many. Throughout western history, that evident social division had been considered part of the nature of things, a result of natural necessity or an unalterable consequence of original sin. Even compassionate Christians who sought to alleviate the sufferings of the poor accepted the admonition of Christ, "The poor you will always have with you."

Marx transformed the question of poverty by analyzing it in essentially modern terms. The modern alliance of science and technology had given human beings intellectual mastery over nature. The industrial and agricultural revolutions allowed them to produce far more than they needed to live. The democratic upheavals in Europe and North America had destroyed hierarchical institutions and heightened expectations of both public and private equality. The historic convergence of these several revolutions had raised human hopes for a *novus ordo saecolorum*. But the demoralizing reality of industrial capitalism had shattered this inspiring secular dream. Capitalism had extended human mastery over nature while creating new patterns of social and political oppression.

Marx believed that proletarian poverty was not due to natural necessity but to systemic exploitation. Capitalism's scandalous inequalities were sustained by the coercive power of the state and the legal protection of property rights. Marx dramatized the mid-nineteenth century as an era of scandalous contrasts, "the best of times and the worst of times" *à la fois*. The oppressive contradictions were inescapable: power and impotence, liberty and slavery, interdependence and isolation, abundance and impoverishment. The most radical injustices darkened the industrial cities of Europe, as the working class, whose labor had created the collective abundance, lived under conditions of material and spiritual deprivation.

Although Marx considered himself a critical social theorist and historian who scorned all appeals to religious and moral idealism, his self-image is somewhat misleading. His power and prestige depend heavily on his prophetic critique of industrial capitalism.[33] Like the ancient Hebrew prophets, Marx fiercely criticized the indifference and hypocrisy of established power. He defended the poor and oppressed, he excoriated the idolatry of money and profit, he condemned the inhumanity of the capitalist bourgeoisie. He combined unrelenting hostility to capitalist oppression with utopian hopes for the future. In the classless society that will replace bourgeois capitalism, as in the prophetic vision of the kingdom of God, the lion will lie down with the lamb and justice and peace will prevail evermore.[34]

How did Marx articulate his utopian vision of universal equality and freedom? It has three interrelated aspects, each remedying a structural flaw in the bourgeois capitalist order. In the classless society, all forms of human alienation and oppression would cease. In traditional Biblical language, both sin and the enduring sources and consequences of sin would completely disappear. With alienated labor abolished, everyone would enjoy meaningful work and express their humanity through productive social achievement. With the abolition of the capitalist state, everyone would enjoy meaningful citizenship, deliberating, choosing and acting cooperatively for the benefit of the whole human race. With the contradictions of capitalism overcome, everyone would enjoy meaningful leisure and liberty, the cultural benefits of productive abundance and just distribution. Marx's secular dream, his vision of comprehensive human fulfillment, would become the common reality of the species. In the classless society, all men and women "would hunt in the morning, fish in the afternoon . . . and read Plato after dinner."[35]

Marx was deeply indebted to Hegel, the great modern philosopher of history. By redirecting philosophy's focus from Newtonian science to universal history, Hegel radically changed the western tradition. The temporal sequence of human affairs had been a marginal concern of his predecessors.[36] History had been considered an haphazard collection of disconnected events without immanent meaning or intelligibility. By insisting on the intelligible significance of history, Hegel challenged this powerful philosophical prejudice. Because the cumulative passage of time is meaningful, it is open to theoretical understanding and articulation. History not only changes but actually develops, though the intelligible structure of its development is not evident to common sense. The historical process does not follow a linear pattern. Its motion, instead, is dialectical. This means that history has developed concretely by erecting its own oppositions, contradictions, antagonisms, before actively overcoming them within a dynamic and concordant whole. Hegel also believed that the dialectical logic of rational thought governed the movement of history. All temporal and historical sequences were rational and purposive, advancing dialectically to an immanent end or goal. Until that goal was "actualized," history remained incomplete, lacking in its full reality and truth.[37]

Hegel believed that the *telos* of world history was the fulfillment of the divine nature. Absolute spirit, Hegel's heterodox conception of God, required the temporal emergence of space and time, the lawful processes of nature and history and the cooperation of individual persons and civilized cultures, to achieve its full actualization. Hegel called the full actualization of the divine, freedom or spiritual autonomy. Its highest expression was the rational self-knowledge of God achieved in and through Hegel's philosophy of history. This supreme spiritual achievement was the ultimate purpose of temporal becoming, the implicit goal to which every significant historical event had partly contributed.

Hegel distinguished three levels of spirit in history, the subjective spirit of the finite individual, the objective spirit of particular national cultures or communities, the absolute spirit of the infinite Hegelian God. The three levels were intelligibly connected for finite spirits only actually developed within historical cultures, while both lesser forms of spirit indirectly contributed to actualizing the divine plan. Although subjective and objective spirits are not identical with the reality of God, they are finite expressions of the developing divine nature. Hegel's Absolute Spirit "creates" them and then employs them providentially to fulfill its own teleological requirements.[38]

In each of its ascending forms, the life of spirit also follows a dialectical pattern. Spirit develops, it progressively actualizes its essence, through productive expression. By means of these concrete expressions, spirit embodies itself externally in what appears to be an independent object. This provisional and apparent independence of spirit's expressive life is the key to Hegel's concept of alienation. Spirit becomes alienated from its temporal expressions when it fails to recognize them as essential moments in its necessary lawful development. During this period of alienation, both space and time, both nature and history, appear to exist independent of God and unrelated to God's ultimate purpose. Hegel seeks to overcome this provisional alienation by reconceiving the concrete expressions of spirit as essential moments in its life of dialectical becoming. Thus, for Hegel, the divine life of God that is universal history climaxes in the philosophical grasp of this holistic teleological process. God's climactic self-knowledge, God's "actualized" freedom, is only achieved through philosophical spirits whose intellectual and moral development is shaped by culturally specific historical communities. Thus for Hegel, subjective spirits only develop in and through objective spirit, as the Divine Spirit only actualizes itself through its concrete human expressions, both communal and individual. Philosophical theology remains the supreme form of human activity; in fact, Hegel has assigned the history of philosophy an unprecedented place within the developing reality of God.[39]

Marx retained many structural features from Hegel's philosophy of history. Under Feuerbach's influence, however, he openly repudiated the Hegelian conception of God.[40] Deliberately reversing Hegel's causal analysis, Feuerbach argued that the Judeo-Christian idea of God is an alienated projection of humanity's unfulfilled historical potential. It is not God who actualizes the divine essence through natural and human creation, but alienated humans who reveal their restricted spiritual development by creating the idea of God. The only real, causally effective spirits are concrete human beings who pour their deepest hopes and longings into an external religious idea. Because their hopes have remained "abstract and unfulfilled," humans have expressed them in compensatory theological fictions.

Marx also accepted Hegel's belief in a historical process that develops dialectically towards actualized freedom. But he openly rejected the religious dimension of Hegelian thought. The socialized humanism Marx embraced is explicitly and defiantly atheistic. There are no divine agents; there are only alienated humans unable to recognize that they are the ultimate makers and masters of history. For Marx, all forms of religious humanism, including Hegel's unorthodox theology, are products of an alienated humanity. In its different historical expressions, religion is "the sigh of the oppressed creature, the soul of a heartless and soulless world, the opium of the people."[41] The human need for religious consolation will decisively end, according to Marx, when human alienation is fully overcome, not through philosophical criticism but through revolutionary violence and action.

In 1841, several years after his exposure to Hegelian ideas in Berlin, Marx received a doctorate in philosophy from the University of Jena. His doctoral thesis was devoted to ancient Greek and Roman atomism. For Marx, as for the classical atomists who shaped his ontological naturalism, humans discover at the causal origin of the world not the God of creation, nor cosmic *nous*, nor absolute spirit, but the existence of chance and necessity. At the beginning of cosmic time, there is no ruling intelligence, but only lifeless, mindless matter and inexorable causal laws. Through the lawful motion of these mindless particles the world-order gradually arises and the natural universe becomes intelligible. For Marx, nature's intelligibility exclusively depends on its law governed material structure.[42]

From the Jena period forward, Marx was a comprehensive naturalist in his metaphysical convictions. He accepted the causal primacy of matter in motion; he emphasized the animal body with its biological needs and demands; he endorsed the power of natural necessity as the mother of human invention. Human language, thought, and orderly social relations all gradually emerge from natural causes to satisfy basic bodily needs.[43] He scorned all forms of idealism and theology, Platonic, Christian, Kantian or Hegelian. In asserting the ontological primacy of spirit over matter, western philosophers had confused intelligible effects (ideas, concepts, intelligible forms) with their underlying physical or biological causes. This idealistic tendency was especially pronounced in Hegelian philosophy which attributed supreme explanatory power to the Absolute Idea and reduced the material universe to that idea's derivative expression. For Marx, the only causally effective ideas are human creations which appear at a very late stage in nature's evolutionary development.[44]

In Marx's naturalistic narrative, human beings first emerge from sheer animality, not through reason, speech, contemplation or moral choice, but through engaging in productive labor. It is the evolution of agriculture from hunting and gathering societies that marks the first occurrence of the specifically human. The biological animal becomes a human being when it produces the means of its own subsistence.[45] By deliberately producing their own food, by no longer receiving it directly from natural sources, human beings began to humanize nature, to make it an instrument of their evolving needs and desires, to bring it increasingly under their social control. This evolving process of rationally guided material production is the clue to Marx's defiant claim that labor, not God, had created man.

Marx's ontological naturalism supported his reliance on economic causality in understanding human affairs. He focused his heuristic attention on patterns of economic development. For Marx, the basic economic activities are producing, distributing and consuming material goods. As economic history unfolds, humans develop their productive capacities by extending and refining their technical knowledge and skill. But growth in the forces of human production always occurs within a social matrix of ownership, control and distribution. These social relations of production and distribution are invariably characterized by exploitation and violence. The human struggle for existence historically advances within a societal framework where the strong dominate the weak. At the critical turning points in history, the weak successfully overthrow their economic masters, creating new patterns of oppression and conflict in their stead.[46]

In the Marxian story, the history of class struggle reached its definitive climax under capitalism. Never had the forces of production been so dynamic and powerful; never had the relations of production been so needlessly oppressive and inhuman. The bourgeoisie controlled unprecedented economic and political power; the urban working class controlled only the laboring potential of their individual bodies. Driven by the profit maximizing imperatives of capitalism, the industrial owners paid their workers minimum subsistence wages. This dehumanizing social condition starkly revealed the true basis of human alienation. Productive labor, the specifically humanizing capacity in history, had become, paradoxically, the root cause of alienation.

Marx viewed the radical expansion of capitalist forces of production as a sign of genuine progress, made possible by the Baconian alliance of science and technology. It was, therefore, capitalist relations of production and the bourgeois ideologies invoked in their defense that needed to be unmasked and destroyed. The socialist revolution Marx predicted as a theorist, and demanded as a revolutionary, would begin with the critique of liberal ideology and culminate in the proletariat's violent destruction of the bourgeoisie. Revolutionary violence would indeed be the midwife of history, since the goal of Marx's philosophy is to abolish human alienation by identifying and eliminating its principal causes.

Marx's philosophical anthropology precariously synthesizes many disparate cultural elements.[47] His socialized humanism seeks to combine: the scientific naturalism and materialism of the radical enlightenment, the pragmatic instrumentalism of Bacon, the world historical dialectic of Hegel, the Romantic aspiration to expressive unity and wholeness, the democratic struggle for greater equality and justice, the economic interpretation of history, the romantic and socialist critique of capitalism, the Jacobin commitment to revolutionary violence, prophetic concern for the victims of oppression, and the secular utopianism of the European left. Within his grand synthesis, distinct causal elements account for modern hope and disillusion. His ultimate goal is not explanatory adequacy but world transforming power. Marx's revolutionary aim was to develop a science of human existence, discovering the laws of history in the political and ideological struggles among economic classes, before turning that explanatory science into an irresistible weapon of human equality and freedom.

DIALECTICAL MATERIALISM

"In the wake of the French Revolution, what we received was not 'a new science of politics for a new world' but a series of philosophies of history and of historical necessity."[48]

What is the internal connection between Marx's socialized humanism and his dialectical philosophy of history? Marx's philosophical anthropology is strikingly explicit in what it affirms and denies. Intellectually rooted in enlightenment naturalism, in the disenchanted universe of modern physics, it openly rejects the Cartesian *res cogitans*, the disembodied rational subject. Within Marx's scientific materialism there is no place for independent spiritual causes, whether human or divine. Human beings are not incarnate persons created in the image of the Biblical God. Their causal genesis and development are based entirely on natural processes; their proximate historical ancestors are the higher primates rather than the gods. In several respects, Marx is an ally of Darwin, the father of evolutionary biology. Both men are students of organic life and of the natural processes by which living organisms develop and change. Both treat human beings as complex animals immersed in the struggle for existence that dominates the biological universe. Both are more concerned with the human species as a whole than they are with the destinies of individual persons.[49]

For Marx, humans distinguish themselves from other animals through their productive labor. While non-human species find their means of subsistence within the natural universe, humans gradually produce their own food and shelter. Through their productive activity, they begin to humanize the natural world, to make the natural environment serve their changing needs and desires. Marx emphasizes that this species-defining labor is inherently social. Human beings produce the material conditions of their common life within historically determinate social settings. Marx agreed with the liberal economists that the production and exchange of material goods is the basis of human existence. But he strongly rejected the atomistic biases of liberalism. Human beings neither produce nor exchange in isolation, as solitary, self sufficient individuals. Rather, they produce with others and for others in diverse social frameworks historically demarcated by a specific set of property relations. The critical variables of human existence include the developing forces of production, the legalized ownership and control of productive resources and the patterned allocation of what is produced. The totality of these social relations, the specific manner in which ownership, control and distribution are organized, constitute the economic structure of society.[50]

Both the forces and relations of human production are historically variable. They change and develop over time, and they differ from one economic community to another. Individual human beings conduct their lives within a social and historical matrix over which they have limited control. For this reason, neither economic agents nor the social classes to which they belong are capable of significant autonomy. As situated laboring subjects, humans exercise their limited agency within an economic and natural environment they largely inherit. There is, of course, a reciprocal causality operating here. Both natural and historical forces shape the character of human existence, while the economic and political decisions of humans simultaneously transform nature and history. Still, Marx does not completely abandon the goal of human autonomy. While economic agents and the socioeconomic structures in which they produce and consume are conditioned by external causes, Marx insists that the definitive *telos* of history is the autonomy of the human species as a whole. Both the parallels and the contrasts with Hegelian teleology are striking. Hegel's dialectic made the actualized freedom or autonomy of God depend on the contributions of subjective and objective spirits. The Hegelian God achieves fullness of being through the largely unreflective agency of his finite creations. Marx preserves Hegel's dialectical teleology while deliberately naturalizing the causal agents in the historical process. Hegel's finite spirits became Marx's individual laborers; Hegel's objective spirits became Marx's socioeconomic classes; and the developing autonomy of absolute spirit is replaced by the universal liberation of the evolving human species.[51]

Hegel's theology was heretical because he made human history a constitutive part of the divine reality. The rationally conceived God of Hegel is not eternal and unchanging perfection as in Christian metaphysics; God is rather the infinite spirit that fulfills its *telos* through historical struggle and human cooperation. Following Hegel's example, Marx modeled the historicity of human nature on the pattern of the Hegelian God. For Marx, human nature is not a trans-historical, trans-cultural essence. It is neither created by God nor determined by exclusively natural causes. Unlike the immutable essences of classical metaphysics, human nature changes and develops through time in a lawful dialectical manner. For a classical thinker like Aristotle, human nature was always and everywhere the same. It aimed at an unchanging natural *telos* that only the virtuous few actually achieved. Individual development consisted in moving consistently towards that immutable and attainable goal. In a genuinely virtuous adult, like Socrates, the full potential of human nature was actually realized. *Eudaimonia*, Aristotle's name for actualizing the human essence, was causally dependent on terrestrial nature, the political community, the deliberate cultivation of our highest natural capacities, as well as individual striving and excellence. Only through a common *paideia*, the education in art and virtue offered by the *polis*, were human animals transformed into full human beings.

In Marx's revisionary anthropology, human nature is not fully actualized in exemplary individuals, however gifted or virtuous. The true subjects of historical becoming are not particular persons but economically structured societies. In any concrete historical period, human nature is constituted by supra-individual economic forces over which individual persons have minimal influence. The actual potential of human nature therefore is dynamically variable. It is measured historically by the level of productive capacity achieved in a particular socioeconomic order. This productive capacity is determined by both natural and human causes, but as history progresses and the economy develops the human causes become increasingly important. In the industrial societies of nineteenth century Europe, scientific knowledge, technological skill and systematically organized labor power had raised the productive potential of the species to unprecedented heights. Marx designated the scandalous contrast between the collective wealth of industrial societies and the oppressive poverty of their laboring class the central contradiction of capitalism.

For Marx, the economic interpretation of history is the key to a credible anthropology. To say that "labor created man" does not mean that the individual laborer creates himself, nor that a particular historical economy is entirely self-generated. Individual autonomy is inconsistent with human sociality and social autonomy with human historicity. Marx's thesis of human self-creation is a provocative assertion about the evolving human species considered as a whole. Human beings collectively, in the course of their dialectical history, have transformed the natural universe through their developing knowledge and productive capacity. Now they are finally able to transform industrial society itself, so that it may express and embody rather than obstruct the universal aspirations of 1789. The actual completion of the French Revolution requires the destruction of capitalist relations of production and their replacement by a utopian socialist economy in which property is collectively owned and controlled.

Marx's philosophy of history, like his socialized humanism, is also explicit in what it affirms and denies. What did Marx explicitly affirm in his theory of dialectical materialism?[52]

1. The economic structure of society, the social forces and relations of production, are the real causal determinants in history. On this economic foundation, the legal and political institutions of society are based. The substantive content of the law, the organization and operation of government, cannot be explained in isolation from political economy. Nor can the cultural beliefs and values that receive public expression in a society's art, religion and philosophy be properly understood as autonomous. In Marx's philosophy of history, as in his naturalized anthropology, the causal dynamic operates from below rather than above. It is economic causes that effectively determine institutional and cultural realities. As Marx memorably phrased it, "The mode of production of material life determines the general character of the social, political and spiritual processes of life. It is not the consciousness of men that determines their being, but on the contrary, their social being determines their consciousness."[53]

How radically should Marx's assertion of economic determinism be read? It is reasonable to claim that a community's political and cultural life cannot be understood in isolation from its economy. This is a sound heuristic principle for all forms of historical inquiry. But Marx's more radical claim would require that economic causes uniquely determine the forms of government and legal protections within a community, as well as the philosophic convictions and religious allegiances of its leading citizens. Radical economic determinism is a provocative philosophical thesis, but it suffers from very limited plausibility.[54]

2. The historical development of a society's forces of production heavily depends on human rationality, scientific, technological and economic. In this respect, the rational insights of individual thinkers, inventors, and planners

already determine the character of social existence. At a predictable stage of development, however, the material forces of production begin to conflict with existing property relations. Productive relationships that had earlier enhanced the growth of capacity have now become obstacles to economic progress. They block historical development in two different ways. They fetter the expansion of economic growth, but they also obstruct the revolutionary drive towards productive and meaningful work, authentic citizenship, and satisfying leisure and liberty for all. Let us critically examine Marx's commitment to economic growth. Would the creation of material abundance justly distributed guarantee full human development for every person? Or would it, rather, increase the probability of higher standards of living for the majority of those residing in affluent countries? Faced with Marx's utopian optimism, we need to ask: Are there negative as well as positive consequences, human and environmental, to the modern project of unlimited economic growth?[55]

3. Violence is the midwife of history, of every old society pregnant with a new one. Marx was not a proponent of violence as such. To be effective, revolutionary violence must occur under highly specific economic conditions. Only when the developing forces and relations of production have become incompatible can a successful social revolution occur. But the relevant economic determinants are not by themselves sufficient. The oppressed class, the causal agents of the impending reversal, must acquire the appropriate revolutionary consciousness. They must liberate their minds from the reigning ideologies used to legitimate established power. They must realize collectively that the source of their alienation is the prevailing system of economic oppression. For Marx, it is futile to strike at the leadership of the state or the princes of the church while leaving the economic structure of society intact. True revolutionary change requires new relations of production, new collective forms of ownership, distribution and control. When the economic foundation of society has been transformed, then the institutional and cultural superstructures will inevitably follow.[56]

The dominant economic class will resist revolutionary change, not only politically and legally but ideologically as well. They will defend their privileged position with arms and ideas, using the coercive power of the state as well as its cultural resources to preserve the *status quo*. In this fierce and comprehensive struggle, the radical role of the revolutionary theorist is critical. He must awaken and discipline the oppositional consciousness of the oppressed. He can do this effectively only if guided by the Marxian science that discovers the dialectical laws of social change and reveals the ultimate *telos* of history. To shape the consciousness of the working class, the theorist must offer a causal and ideological critique of the existing society, articulating the economic causes of the workers' alienation and unmasking the material interests behind specious defenses of the established order.

But the revolutionary leader must also discipline the hatred evoked by systemic injustice. The violent assault on existing symbols of power is useless, even counter-productive, if it occurs prematurely. The historical insights of dialectical materialism are therefore imperative, for no social order will collapse until its productive potential has been fully developed. Only when existing relations of production thwart economic growth can revolutionary violence become effective. Human history follows an invariant pattern of dialectical conflict that successful revolutionaries must learn to obey. To become the masters and makers of history, human beings must learn to comply with its laws.[57]

Hegel structured his theory of history around the "cunning of reason." He clearly distinguished the infinite purpose of absolute spirit from the particular goals and passions of historical individuals. Infinite spirit was cunning in using the passions and interests of concrete human beings to achieve its own ends, ends beyond the awareness of the contributing agents. Only in the reflective knowledge of the Hegelian philosopher does the cunning of divine reason reach full human consciousness. In contemplating history as a whole, Hegel discovered the essential role human agents and societies have played in achieving the hidden purposes of God.[58]

A parallel process occurs in Marx's dialectical materialism. All references to the divine are excluded, but Marx's historical *telos*, though now fully naturalized, is no less ambitious than Hegel's. The autonomy of the collective human species has replaced the autonomy of God. But a biological species is not a conscious intentional agent capable of thinking and planning for itself. Although Marx recognizes only human causation in history, until now the decisive agents of change, scientific theorists and inventors, productive laborers and social revolutionaries, have not really known what they were doing. The dialectical laws of history have operated through and yet beyond human influence. Like Hegel, Marx is committed to a dialectical necessity in history that requires human effort while transcending individual recognition and purpose.[59]

Only the scientific historian can discover this remorseless dialectic. But for Marx, the critical revolutionary, this momentous disclosure is not meant to remain unproductive. The true purpose of philosophy is to understand world history in order to master it. Guided by the insights of Marxian science and carefully attuned to the cunning of history, revolutionary leaders cooperate with dialectical necessity by directing the class struggle towards universal fulfillment.

A profound paradox lies at the heart of Marx's materialism. Like his political rivals, the capitalist bourgeoisie, Marx embraced the imperial assumptions of economics. He affirmed the primacy of material interests in human motivation and social dynamics. Yet he deviated from classical liberalism by emphasizing the economic interests of historical classes rather than the individual pursuit of material gain. To support this critical anthropological shift, he replaced Adam Smith's benevolent "invisible hand" with the Hegelian inspired "cunning of history." For Marxists, as for classical liberals, the well being of the communal whole is mysteriously achieved through the narrow self-interest of its parts. Marx differs, of course, from his bourgeois antagonists, insisting that the collective good will only be achieved at the end of history, when the material interests of the proletariat coincide with the aims of the whole human species. Still, it is not the moral aspirations of the proletariat that drive them to revolt but the pursuit of their collective self-interest. Marx stresses that the proletariat is historically unique because it is the first social class whose material interests coincide with the causal requirements of human emancipation as such.[60] He therefore believes that the proletarian victory over the bourgeoisie will not be just another revolt in an endless historical series. On the contrary, the overthrow of capitalism and the emergence of a communist society are celebrated as the climax of human history. Why? Because this apocalyptic transformation will miraculously: create the social conditions for unfettered economic development; bring the history of class struggle and human exploitation to a close; destroy human alienation in all of its forms (concretely, this will mean the end of capitalism, the abolition of the state and the elimination of cultural ideologies);enable all members of the species to actualize their full potential as workers, citizens and individually creative species beings.[61]

For Marx, these utopian outcomes are not romantic dreams but scientific certainties, guaranteed by a theory of history whose economic premises are immune from critical suspicion and whose dialectical structure creates universal harmony out of continuous historical strife. The proletariat functions in Marxist prophecy as a messianic class whose paradoxical role is to achieve utopian ends though dystopian means. Is this yet another dialectical paradox or a practically repugnant contradiction? To embrace Marx's vision of history, we need to believe that freedom only emerges through dialectical necessity, peace through revolutionary violence and genuine autonomy through centuries of collective alienation.[62]

THE CRITIQUE OF CAPITALISM

"Marx's political economy is built on the inevitable collapse of capitalism."[63]

What is capitalism, the form of modern political economy Karl Marx admired and abhorred? How should we understand and appraise its existence as a complex historical phenomenon? To begin at the most basic level, capitalism is a dynamic and evolving economic system based on private ownership of property, the voluntary production and exchange of goods and services, a market-based allocation of resources, and shared acceptance of the profit motive as the engine of economic life. An important symbiosis exists between capitalist theory and practice, for capitalist theories explain and to some extent justify the economic behavior of individuals, social classes, international corporations and governmental institutions, both national and global. Several competing theories correspond to the different forms of capitalism, but the great majority are versions of economic liberalism. Capitalism, like bourgeois liberalism its political partner and ally, is best understood as an historical construct of western modernity.[64]

In classical Greece, 'economics' referred to the art of household management. Although the Greek cities actively traded across the Mediterranean basin, economic life primarily occurred within the *oikos*, the private household. The *oikos* was a sphere of structural inequality where the male householder ruled over slaves, women and children. It was also a sphere governed by biological necessity where the requirements of life and shelter were regularly satisfied.[65] The emergence of a distinctively modern economy corresponds to the birth of the nation state. In western Europe, from the Italian Renaissance forward, economic activity gradually moved out of the private household and into the public marketplace. The domestic economy of the modern family became increasingly dependent on the political economy of the national household. This novel dependence was part of a revolutionary transformation that overturned the social and political structures of the West.

At the onset of modernity, agriculture was the primary economic activity, and the landed gentry the dominant economic and political class. By the end of the eighteenth century, trade and finance had replaced agriculture as sources of national wealth, and the political rivalry between bourgeois merchants and bankers and the landed nobility had become intense. In Great Britain, France, Germany and North America, a market economy slowly developed in which land, labor and capital became objects of commercial exchange. During the feudal period, the essence of private property had been the ancestral home and estate of a multigenerational family. The family dwelling was an important source of historical continuity, providing a tangible space of privacy, shelter and intimacy for family members over many generations. These private domestic properties marked the spatial boundary and limit of public authority and law. The private home was a visibly recognized, spatially limited enclosure suffused with common memories and meaning.[66]

The commercialization of private property radically changed its cultural significance. Commercial property is essentially real estate, an objective commodity like any other to be bought and sold for profit. Like other commodities, its monetary value depends on constant fluctuations in supply and demand. Taken together, the gradual emergence of a market economy, popular acceptance of the exchange market as a/the primary public institution, the reconception of all physical objects as potential commodities, constitute a major historical event. During the mid to late eighteenth century, Western Europe embraced a new conception of land and property, a new set of relations between individuals and their families, a new attitude to profit and gain. *Homo mercator*, the capitalist merchant, became the cultural symbol of this emerging commercial mentality.[67]

What was the governing *ethos* of *homo mercator*? Then and now it was an individualist mindset. Human beings enter the commercial marketplace as private individuals intent on advancing their enlightened self interest. Buyers and sellers constantly engage in competitive social relations as each tries to profit at the expense of the other. The deliberate pursuit of individual profit is guided by calculative reason, as merchants and their customers seek to maximize personal gain. *Homo mercator* consistently prizes a negative conception of liberty, the freedom of individuals to buy and sell, to trade and barter, without restrictive interference by political or ecclesiastical authority.[68]

Important cultural backing for the commercial mentality came from its religious and intellectual allies. The Protestant reformers accepted the market economy as a critical part of their struggle with the landed gentry. Supporters of democracy admired the apparent meritocracy of the market, its institutional independence of inherited power and privilege. French liberal thinkers like Montesquieu, Voltaire and Constant openly praised the virtues of "*le doux commerce*," endorsing the commercial mentality in its cultural struggle with the warrior ethic of feudalism. For these economic liberals, the aristocratic *ethos* had been barbaric and warlike, a recurrent source of death, bodily injury and devastated property. The commercial ethic, by contrast, was pacific and conciliatory, softening manners and speech and greatly expanding public and personal wealth.[69]

The most influential defender of homo mercator and the market economy was the Scottish theorist, Adam Smith. In the *Wealth of Nations*, Smith argued that the unregulated commerce of the market place, where producers, merchants and customers freely sought their economic advantage, provided an effective impersonal control over prices and wages, a control that ultimately benefited both commercial participants and the national economy as a whole. It was unwise and unprofitable for any public authority, political or religious, to seek to regulate market transactions. Why? Because there existed "an invisible hand" lawfully guaranteeing that public benefit would flow from the commercial pursuit of private gain. Later liberal theorists generalized Smith's defense of commercial *laissez faire*, converting his economic apology for rational egoism into a comprehensive theory of social and political order. The enlightened pursuit of self-interest soon became a universal moral imperative, displacing the passion for public justice as the basis of a good society.[70]

European capitalism took a decisive turn after the French Revolution. The alliance of scientific discoveries with their technical applications dramatically increased the productive capacity of the national economies. Rapid technological innovation and the extension of financial credit to emerging industrial enterprises also enhanced economic productivity. Wage labor became cheap and abundant as vast numbers of European peasants abandoned the rural economy to seek work in the new urban factories. The rise of the factory system intensified the historic societal shift to urban industrial settings. The disciplined artistry of the Renaissance craftsman (*homo faber*) skillfully producing durable objects for a limited patronage, was steadily replaced by the mass production of urban laborers, creating cheap commodities for an expanding international market.

Industrial capitalism differed in scale and character from its commercial predecessor. Although the profit motive remained dominant, new economic agents and institutions had entered the competitive field. Late nineteenth century capitalists required vast sums of money and credit to purchase the machinery and replicate the innovations of the industrial economy. The constant need for credit magnified the importance of bankers, financiers and private speculators, the indispensable middle men who bankrolled new factories and equipment and invested their capital in larger and riskier economic enterprises. The urban labor force, however, remained largely unskilled. Because many workers had recently left the great landed estates, their new jobs were deliberately simplified to meet the requirements of mass production.

The public image of industrial capitalism was far less benign than Adam Smith's flattering portrait of private individuals freely engaged in commercial exchange. The intense competition to accumulate capital and to maximize profit forced many business owners into bankruptcy. But the greatest harm was suffered by the urban working class who labored long hours under dangerous conditions for subsistence wages. Cheap labor confined to repetitive tasks in crowded and unsafe factories meant poverty and exhaustion for the working family but unprecedented wealth and power for factory owners and their financial supporters. When the glaring inequities created by capitalism brought vehement cries for reform, capitalist owners evoked the liberal ideology of *laissez faire* to oppose governmental intervention on behalf of the workers. In the jaundiced eyes of the bourgeoisie, all forms of private property (economic capital) were sacred; government should never intervene in economic affairs; and the benevolent effects of profit would eventually work to everyone's advantage. The operation of "the invisible hand" guaranteed the success of unfettered capitalism in the long term.[71]

The disciples of the French Revolution, however, were haunted by a despair driven question. What had happened to the original promise of liberty, equality and fraternity for all? The aristocratic defenders of the *ancien regime* had been weakened, the urban bourgeoisie had politically supplanted the landed gentry, the caste structure of feudal society had been destroyed, but the new capitalist inequities were even more intolerable than the old. Under the *ancien regime*, there were traditional ties and obligations joining noble to peasant; there were strong bonds of loyalty and affection between the king and his subjects; there was the reassuring familiarity and mutual support available in rural communities. These sustaining human connections had been destroyed by the impersonal logic of the market, the unlimited pursuit of capital, the wretchedness of the urban working class, and the implacable ideology of rational egoism and *laissez faire*. Understandably, factory workers, miners and industrial laborers began to organize and resist; radical socialist leaders challenged the sacred claims of private property; and democratic reformers struggled to extend the suffrage to workers and peasants and to enlist government support for the poor and oppressed. The bitter many leveled struggle between European labor and capital was now fully engaged.[72]

This very brief synopsis of Europe's economic history helps to contextualize Marx's critique of capitalism. It is important to remember that Marx was a secular European of the mid-nineteenth century, a passionate man who had lived in Germany, the Low Countries, France and Great Britain. A man who had studied Hegelian philosophy, French social theory and British political economy, and who had witnessed directly the misery and oppression of industrial society. A radical intellectual of the European left, Marx was openly allied with the socialist movement and with the revolutionary opposition to bourgeois society. To understand and appreciate his hostility to capitalism, we need to know: what he explicitly opposed; what motivated his intense opposition; the rational core of his criticism; and the alternative socio- economic order he advocated.

Marx's comprehensive critique has three principal targets: industrial capitalism as an economic system, the politics and culture of bourgeois society and the liberal ideology embraced by capitalist owners, bourgeois politicians, and their cultural allies and apologists. Marx was deeply ambivalent about industrial capitalism as an economic system. He accepted capitalism as a necessary phase of human economic development. It had radically enlarged the forces of production and was the greatest source of material progress in the history of the world. But it had clearly outlived its provisional utility and needed to disappear into history. Industrial capitalism had created a pattern of social relations that were profoundly unjust and inhuman. These structural inequities sustained new forms of despotism in Europe; not the tyranny of the *ancien regime* but the despotism of bourgeois society that constantly oppressed its most productive members. The bourgeois oppression of labor was evident in: restricted ownership of capital and the forces of production; the dehumanizing influence of money and wealth; the idolatry of profit; the material and spiritual impoverishment of the working class.[73]

Why had bourgeois societies and European governments callously resisted reform? Marx interpreted the blindness and cruelty of the bourgeoisie through deterministic principles. In the Marxian dialectic, each social class is governed by its perceived self-interest. The privileged classes in every age inevitably seek to preserve and expand their wealth and power. They habitually ignore, deny or feebly justify the social mutilation caused by their economic behavior. Their engrained self-deception is buttressed by explicit ideologies that rationalize social cruelty as the necessary consequence of inviolable economic laws. To undermine the institutions of capitalism, Marx thought it imperative to discredit the ideology legitimating the capitalist order.[74]

Classical liberalism, first proposed in defense of commercial capitalism, had extended its protective umbrella to the industrial societies of nineteenth century Europe. Liberalism was an atomistic ideology with limited relevance to an industrial economy based on economic and social interdependence.[75] Marx began his critique by challenging the liberal myth of individual autonomy. Bourgeois owners of industrial capital were not autonomous economic agents, but favorably situated businessmen heavily dependent for their success on scientific discoveries, technological innovation, accessible credit, cheap labor, and steadily expanding commercial markets. The productive laborers they exploited also depended on forces and relations of production over which they had limited control.[76]

Marx argued that classical liberals were also insensitive to history. Liberal economists believed that the laws governing industrial society were invariant and universal. Concerted attempts to redress the inequities of capitalism were pointless, for economic inequalities inevitably resulted from impersonal laws human beings were unable to change. Marx insisted that liberal theorists with their ignorance of history, had overlooked the dialectical process through which economic laws arise and are eventually destroyed.[77]

He then extended his critique to bourgeois notions of freedom. Liberal theories of freedom consistently espoused negative liberty, the absence or prevention of public interference in private economic activity. Under this banner of liberty, capitalist production, exchange and consumption were evidently free activities, since capital and labor had been left to themselves to do as they pleased. Marx criticized negative liberty as an ideological myth. Both capital and labor were regularly subject to governing forces that largely determined their economic behavior. Capitalists were constrained by the relentless competition for profit in the industrial economy. Their workers faced the even harsher necessity of sustaining their families on subsistence wages in a merciless labor market.[78]

Classical liberals had also predicted the benevolent results of unfettered competition. Autonomous individuals responding energetically to the profit motive would create through their efforts increasing public wealth and a constantly improved standard of living. Marx's prophetic critique of capitalism explicitly rejected the idolatry of profit, the dehumanizing influence of money and wealth, and the imaginary benefits of unlimited market competition. For Marx it was the ruthless competition for profit that drove capitalist owners into bankruptcy and kept industrial laborers in extreme deprivation.[79]

What motivated Marx's systematic study and critique of capitalism? It is difficult to assess any thinker's personal motives; in Marx's case the difficulty is compounded by complexity of character and diversity of formative influences. That said, we can identify several concerns that fueled his relentless critique. Marx was a utopian thinker with extravagant hopes for human liberation and fulfillment. From his perspective, industrial capitalism thwarted the legitimate aspirations of the French Revolution. It subverted traditional values and social institutions; and transformed everything humanly significant into marketable commodities for commercial exchange. It celebrated the lust for profit and smugly accepted working class deprivation as the price of collective wealth. For Marx the utopian secular humanist, capitalism was deeply and irremediably dehumanizing.[80]

Marx was also a prophetic moralist, even though he denied the efficacy of moral causes in history. He sincerely believed that capitalism depended on the unjust exploitation of labor, that it compounded the avoidable scandal of poverty with the pervasive misery of the industrial proletariat. His moral critique of capitalist property relations is a forceful demand for distributive justice in allocating the benefits and burdens of industrial society. His personal hostility to bourgeois society also has a prophetic edge. The complacency and heartlessness of the bourgeoisie are particularly appalling to Marx, the secular prophet and revolutionary champion of the oppressed.[81]

As a philosopher of history, Marx saw bourgeois capitalism as the dominant economic reality of the modern age. It had destroyed the *Ancien Regime*, dramatically enlarged mankind's productive capacity, and transformed the institutional and cultural life of Europe. But as a dynamic economic system it had exhausted its historical energy. Capitalism had ceased to be a progressive force and now functioned as a barrier to economic growth. The cunning of history no power can resist demanded its abolition and replacement.[82]

As a critical economist, Marx was certain that capitalism would destroy itself. Its underlying dynamic, the relentless drive to maximize profit and accumulate capital, would inevitably lead to economic collapse. Through intense competition, the ownership clas would steadily shrink; the proletarian class of wage laborers would continue to expand while remaining impoverished, unable to purchase the stream of commodities they regularly produced. Thus the capitalist economy would eventually implode due to excessive supply and insufficient demand. Simply by adhering to its own laws of development, capitalism was fatally doomed.[83]

In Marx's self-presentation, the scientific historian and critical economist clearly supercede the utopian humanist and secular prophet. Economic determinism and dialectical necessity are repeatedly invoked to convert Marx's moral concerns into ostensibly scientific predictions. This reductive strategy satisfies the explanatory constraints of historical materialism, while enabling Marx to conceal his moral indignation and utopian hopes under an impartial mask. A passionate moral and political critique of capitalism is misleadingly presented as disinterested scientific analysis.[84]

For the sake of argument, let us grant Marx the causal significance he assigns to collective egoism and dialectical laws. Given these assumptions, what are his basic objections to capitalism as an economic system? The chief criticism is that capitalist success depends on the alienation of productive labor and the laboring class. But for Marx productive labor is the supreme expression of human identity, the specific way humans distinguish themselves from the other animals. Labor enables human beings to master nature and increase their control over mankind's historical destiny. Only by liberating labor's productive capacity can the full species potential of humanity be achieved. Creating networks of social cooperation among wage laborers throughout the world is an essential part of this dialectical process. The global solidarity of labor will accelerate the fulfillment of the revolutionary ideals, bringing the *telos* of history to completion.[85]

Alienated labor, capitalist labor, does not promote self-fulfillment but dehumanizing poverty and estrangement. Subsistence wages prevent the laboring class from escaping biological necessity. Industrial patterns of production confine the laboring process to a repetitive cycle of boredom and drudgery. Intense competition for jobs in a precarious labor market makes industrial workers economic rivals rather than fraternal allies. And capitalist patterns of distribution prevent workers from owning and enjoying the objects they have produced. How can such productive activity and collective effort yield so inhuman a result?[86]

The principal cause of alienated labor is the capitalist commitment to maximizing profit. Paradoxically, profit is the sacred idol of capitalism and the avenging angel that will eventually destroy it. But what are the sources of economic profit, and how does Marx explain their contradictory role in a capitalist economy? To answer these questions we shall contrast Marx's labor theory of value with the analysis of prices and wages offered by classical liberalism.[87] For liberal economists, the market price of an object is determined by supply and demand. No exchangeable commodity has an inherent value, a value independent of human needs and desires. What an object costs in a commercial exchange is a function of what other buyers are willing to pay for it. If the supply of a commodity is great and demand is small, prices will decline; conversely, if demand is great and supply is small, prices will predictably rise. Enlightened self-interest leads buyers and sellers

208   *Chapter 4*

to adapt their economic behavior to prevailing market conditions. If free and unfettered exchange can be reliably assumed, this alternating process should lead, over time, to an impersonal equilibrium of prices favorable to the enlightened and patient consumer.

The liberal account of a commodity's market value is inherently relativistic. The price of an exchange object basically depends on how badly other people want it. In challenging liberal economic theory, Marx wanted to assign all human commodities an objective or intrinsic value. As a scientific economist, he wanted the source of an object's measurable value to be mathematically quantifiable. As a critic of capitalism, he wanted his theory of value to explain the coexistence of profit and poverty within a capitalist economy.

Marx's labor theory of value is based on the following premises:[88]

1. The true price of a commodity is its objective value.
2. The objective value of all commodities is ultimately reducible to the amount of labor it takes to produce them.
3. What the individual laborer owns and brings to the capitalist exchange market is his labor power, his personal capacity to produce exchangeable goods.
4. What the individual capitalist owns is a determinate share of the forces of production. This joint ownership gives the capitalist employer decisive control over the jobs the laborer needs to exist.
5. Rival capitalists are engaged in an intense competition to maximize profits, a merciless competition in which only the fittest survive.
6. But how does the capitalist's profit emerge if all genuine value is based upon the activity of labor?
7. Under capitalism, every conceivable object is treated as a commodity to be bought and sold.
8. In the capitalist labor market, the economic value of a worker is determined by the wages he accepts from the capitalist employer for his productive labor and time.
9. The capitalist is driven by the profit motive and by the competitive demands of his rivals to pay the laborer merely subsistence wages, only what the laborer needs to survive while continuing to produce.
10. Thus a critical gap opens between the labor time needed to produce an exchangeable object and the legally contracted time for which the laborer is actually paid. The surplus value the laborer creates is the uncompensated labor that is present in the objects produced.
11. But the finished objects belong to the capitalist owner who then sells them for their true (objective) value and thus realizes a profit.

12. For Marx, the only objective and quantifiable source of profit in capitalist exchanges is the surplus labor value appropriated by the owner for which the laborer is never compensated.

The profit of the capitalist is only achieved at the expense of the laborer. Capitalists grow rich by deliberately keeping their workers poor. But for Marx, this clearly exploitative process is governed by economic imperatives rather than by moral choice. While the biological needs of the laborer force him/her to participate in the unequal exchange, the capitalist is driven to exploit the laborer by the economic demands of the system. To survive economically in a competitive market, he must maximize profits, cut costs, resort to labor-saving machinery, and drive down the wages of his workers. Marx believed that as capitalism evolved, machines would replace human beings as sources of production, the rate of profit would fall, bankruptcies would increase, the working class would become increasingly impoverished and hostile, and the cunning of history would lead to the destruction of capitalism and the idolatry of profit that animated it.[89]

For Marx, no internal reforms can save capitalism from itself. The ownership class is severely constrained by the competition for profit; bourgeois governments will resist economic and social reforms because they function as servants of the dominant class; as workers become destitute under capitalism, their self-interest drives them to oppose the system with radical fervor. Once the economic benefits of capitalism have been achieved, the dialectic of history will require the system's extinction.

To what will the abolition of capitalism lead? Marx believes it will lead to new socialized relations of production. Private ownership of capital will be replaced by collective control of the forces of production.[90] What collective control means concretely (how economic decisions will actually be made and how distributive justice will be reliably guaranteed) is exceedingly vague. In practice, socialism has usually meant state control of the economy. The public officials, planners and managers of the socialist state, acting as the declared representatives of the people, make the critical economic decisions: expropriating private property; controlling wages and prices; determining what should be produced, under what conditions, by whom and for how long. Although Marx seemed to favor some form of economic democracy, where workers would function as planners, producers, distributors and consumers, unlimited state control has actually meant a dangerous concentration of economic and political power. The heartless despotism of the bourgeoisie has typically been replaced by the bureaucratic despotism of state managers and planners, putatively acting on the people's behalf.[91]

Why should the oppression of industrial society be miraculously ended by abolishing private property and repudiating the profit motive? Marx believed he had found the key to resolving the "social question," the scandalous mixture of deprivation and wealth in modern society. Capitalism was an agent of historical progress because it enormously developed the forces of production. But it generated profound alienation and misery due to the exploitative property relations it created. To Marx it seemed evident that collective ownership and control of the economy would preserve the advantages of capitalism while permanently destroying human alienation.[92]

Material abundance cooperatively shared and fraternally distributed would finally eliminate class struggle. A classless society would also mean a stateless society and an end to political oppression and violence. Without economic and political oppression, there would be no human need for false consciousness and ideology. After millennia of hostility and struggle, after centuries of self-interested behavior, after ages of systemic deceit and rationalization, the godlike potential of humanity would finally be realized. If the *telos* of history can only be actualized by destroying capitalism, if the secular hopes of the species depend on a socialist order, then the friends of humanity must rally to the Marxian cause: let the decisive revolution begin.

THE ARENDTIAN CRITIQUE OF MARX

"The moderns look at action, at ethics and politics, from the perspective of a productive knowledge permeated with theory."[93]

Let us return to the Arendtian appraisal of Marx, seeking the sources of their affinity and opposition. Arendt perceived Marx as a distinctively modern thinker, attuned to modern realities and imbued with modern assumptions and prejudices. He embraced secularization, the exclusive commitment to human life on this earth and this world. He rejected philosophical and religious idealism, dismissing the quest for God and eternal life as illusory diversions rooted in oppressive social conditions. Once humanity's secular aspirations were met, all longing for the divine would completely disappear.

Marx also endorsed the modern reversal of the classical ethical hierarchies. He glorified what the ancients had disparaged and criticized what they had openly prized. His polemical critique of the *vita contemplativa* had two related dimensions. He scorned the ideal of disinterested knowledge, the understanding of reality pursued for its own sake, insisting that all human thinking occurred in the service of material interest and need. As biological animals, humans use reason for specifically practical ends. They seek to improve their living conditions, to produce fruits and works in abundance, rather than leaving reality as they have found it. Human thinking revolts against the natural and historical given rather than gratefully accepting its intelligible order and beauty.[94]

Marx combined his objections to the contemplative life with a strong affirmation of the *vita activa*. The limited dignity of theory depended entirely on its subordination to *praxis*. For Marx, humans are essentially active beings who develop their productive capacities and social connections by transforming the sensible world. Modern praxis deliberately changes the natural and historical given, humanizing the sensible world by making it progressively amenable to human desire and need.

Marx emphasized two types of transformative *praxis*: productive labor that humanizes nature by bringing its causal forces under human control, and revolutionary action (strategic violence) which humanizes society by reshaping the web of economic relations within which production occurs. Human labor and violence are glorified, in part, because they transform the order of nature and the structure of social existence. As a romantic expressivist, Marx also celebrated their transformative effect on human agency itself. By radically reshaping the sensible world, human beings recreate their species, in the sense that they dramatically expand their collective power and freedom. This dialectical process of species self-creation is extremely complex. Real human freedom is only enlarged through historical struggle and conflict. The expressive development of the species occurs through severe alienation, as the historical sources of human fulfillment are also the causes of human oppression. There is no way to actualize the *telos* of humanity apart from the dialectic of transformative *praxis*, radical alienation, and the violent overcoming of alienation that culminates in concord and peace.

Marx's commitment to the dialectical process adds complexity to his critical stance. From the terminal perspective of the classless society, the historical forces and relations of production have consistently been unjust. Productive labor has always been exploited; the ruling class has always been oppressive and ideological. But the dialectical movement to actualized freedom requires these alienated forms of production and governance. They belong inescapably to the lawful dynamic of history.

In Marx's anthropology, human history begins with needy biological animals and culminates in a species that is godlike in power. As a committed atheist, Marx repudiates both the Biblical and the Hegelian conceptions of God, crediting the human race with Promethean self-creation. The full realization of the species requires collective autonomy and mastery of nature and society. At the climax of history, nothing remains to resist the unified will and unlimited power of humankind.[95]

The beginning of history is the antithesis of the ideally projected end. The biological animals who first engage in productive labor have minimal power and freedom; for them the dream of Promethean autonomy is inconceivable. They are immersed in the struggle for existence with limited resources at their command. Marx wants to explain naturalistically how starting with so little the human race can achieve so much. His evolutionary naturalism credits the original humans with material needs and limited abilities. The philosophical and political capacities prized by the ancients, capacities that allow for sustained self-transcendence, are deliberately excluded from the Marxian story. The dialectical trick is to show how without disinterested reason (*nous*) and deliberative *logos*, without the classical virtues of intellect and character, and relying solely on transformative *praxis* driven by need, human beings can fulfill their extraordinary secular destiny.

Hannah Arendt was deeply critical of Marx's "political philosophy." In this section we shall focus on three principal targets of her criticism: Marx's reductive anthropology, his deterministic conception of politics, and his ideological philosophy of history. While Arendt welcomed Marx's support for the *vita activa*, she thought he conflated important distinctions within it. She accused Marx of blurring the distinction between labor and work, between productive activity that satisfies biological requirements and productive activity that builds and maintains a stable and durable world.[96] By emphasizing the life process of the species, Marx diminished the worldliness of human beings and overlooked their essential plurality. These two reductions are related, for Arendt, because only in an historically created world and a web of free action and speech can humans actualize their individual uniqueness and become capable of personal distinction.

Moreover, building a common and durable world and freely inserting oneself into the human web are essentially different activities. For Arendt the celebrated Marxian concept of praxis conflates or assimilates human production and action. While the forms of the *vita activa* belong together, since they are all sensible activities that change the phenomenal world, they do so in strikingly different ways. Labor transforms natural resources into objects of human consumption thereby sustaining the metabolism of life. Work transforms natural entities into durable artifacts that serve as the basis of a multigenerational world. Action and speech first establish and then transform the associative connections among human beings. By conflating labor and work, Marx effaced the Arendtian distinction between life and world (the distinction that, for Arendt, marks the true emergence of humanity). For Marx, animals become human when they produce their own means of biological subsistence; for Arendt, they become human when they cooperatively build a world in which successive generations can dwell and act. While the labor of the body and the work of one's hands are both productive activities, they produce different kinds of sensible objects and respond to strikingly different human concerns.[97]

By conflating productive activity with cooperative action, Marx made coercive violence rather than public liberty the historical essence of politics. Both the lawful violence of the ruling class and the emancipatory violence of the revolutionary opposition are modeled on human fabrication. In the fabrication process, natural materials are consistently refashioned to comply with preconceived ideas. The point of making is utilitarian, forcing nature to serve the aims of artisans and their clients. In the artisan's work, nature is accorded no independent dignity; it is treated as a manipulable resource to exploit however humans desire. Arendt repeatedly warned against transferring the logic of fabrication into the conduct of politics. Whenever that transfer occurs, political agents typically see themselves as remaking the future society in the same way engineers construct buildings and bridges. A preferred architectural model determines the planned transformation, and recalcitrant human materials are molded to accord with the architect's will.[98]

This recurrent temptation is magnified when revolutionaries believe they are acting in the name of historical necessity. If there were an historical *telos* to be actualized through revolutionary violence, and that *telos* could be known in advance by the Marxian theorist, then revolutionary agents would become Promethean "makers of history" by remodeling bourgeois society to comply with the utopian plan. Under these highly inflated assumptions, the only way to achieve justice and liberty would be to reject political reform and to embrace infallibly guided strategic violence. The practical result of Marx's anthropological errors are the dangerous dialectical paradoxes in which peace comes through violence, freedom through lawful necessity, and fraternal equality through unscrupulous manipulation.[99]

Arendt acknowledged that Marx was a secular humanist deeply committed to human greatness and liberty. But his political philosophy cleared a path for ideology and terror. Why did Marx's legacy diverge so radically from his humanistic aspirations? Three contributing factors were clearly at work: his reductive anthropology, his violence based conception of politics, his deterministic theory of history. Let us briefly explore Arendt's objections to these core elements in Marx's Promethean humanism.[100]

THE GLORIFICATION OF LABOR AND THE NATURALIZATION OF MAN

Marx incorporated the antipolitical prejudices of modernity into his philosophical anthropology. As an evolutionary naturalist, he conceived of human beings as biological animals engaged in the struggle for existence. His anthropology focused not on individual persons, nor the free historical communities they establish, but on the developing life of the species. In opposing bourgeois individualism, Marx radically socialized human beings. He situated them within economic classes, confining their effective motivation to the dominant material interests of their class. Both the biological naturalism and the class-based analysis have a leveling and reductive effect. Neither perspective allows for a plurality of free persons capable of intellectual and political self-transcendence. The free Arendtian citizen (the singular and irreplaceable who), the complex web of mutual action and speech, and the sheltering world of durable artifacts and dwellings are all conspicuously absent from the Marxian story. In Arendt's terms, the free republican citizen actively devoted to the commonweal has been replaced by a worldless *animal laborans*, politically vulnerable to loneliness, ideology, and the lure of mass movements.[101]

Marx also embraced the imperial assumptions of economics. He asserted the causal primacy of productive labor and the teleological primacy of material abundance and species autonomy. He elevated productive labor to the defining human capacity, the specific difference that raised human animals above the unthinking brutes. Labor was glorified because of its productive fertility, its ability to meet and exceed evolving human needs. It was the original example of transformative *praxis* that began human history and sustained the dialectical movement to species autonomy. Indeed, Marx measured historical progress in terms of labor's fecundity as the developing forces of production increased collective power and mastery, while transforming human need and desire.[102]

Arendt rejected Marx's economic imperialism. She opposed the primacy of economics both causally and teleologically. Nor did she regard the steady expansion of consumable objects as the true measure of historical progress. She denied that the history of freedom followed a discernible path lawfully bound to material abundance and productive fertility. Arendt treated Marx as the most influential advocate of the "social" mentality, the reductive confinement of human existence within the parameters of the life process. Within the narrow horizon of the "social," all sensible realities eventually become objects of species consumption.[103] Arendt is especially critical of Marx's biological naturalism. From the biological perspective, material production and consumption are repetitive processes that follow the cyclical patterns of nature. However, Marx thinks of labor not only biologically but also in romantic expressivist terms. Thus he treats labor not as repetitive and cyclical but as historical and anthropologically creative. In his revisionary narrative, labor is the engine of history. Beyond meeting recurrent and evolving needs, "labor" produces the tools and machines that exponentially magnify the forces of production. As productivity increases, the material burdens of labor diminish, until the laboring class enjoys the activities of leisure traditionally reserved for the ruling elite.[104]

While Arendt's analysis of labor emphasizes its consumable products and repetitive cycles, Marx celebrates labor's transformative effect on the human producers themselves. On his socialized version of expressivist theory, productive laborers actualize their historical potential through a complex dialectical process. Initially they express their creative capacity in some sensible external object (initially objects of consumption, but later objects of capital accumulation). However, they fail to recognize their expanding creativity due to the oppressive social relations they collectively create (in the alienated stage of production, laborers are estranged from their own productive capacities, from their co-producers, and from the objects they jointly produce). At the climax of history, they overcome their alienation through transformative revolutionary violence, the violent *praxis* in which they overthrow capitalism and usher in the classless society. Arendtian labor is the cyclical activity of individual human beings producing and consuming their means of subsistence. Marxian labor is the historical activity of a self-creating species that develops its collective power and freedom by abolishing both natural and social alienation.[105]

Marx's concept of productive labor spans the gamut of the *vita activa*.[106] Initially it produces objects of material consumption; then it produces technical objects of use, like tools and machines; finally it "produces" a harmonious web of socialized relations completely purged of capitalist alienation. Through this increasingly diversified "production," labor supposedly creates the human species itself. To assert that "labor created man" is to claim that human beings have transformed themselves from the humble servants of nature to the proud masters of all they survey. Obviously, no individual person or social community could plausibly make this claim. Marx's thesis is only intelligible if we conceive of the evolving species as a single creative agent actualizing its autonomy on the model of the Hegelian God. But Marx's illusion of total creativity ignores the natural reality that persists through the historical process. Human beings, even the human species if we grant Marx its fictional agency, never create *ex nihilo*. They always depend, to varying degrees, on natural forces that resist complete humanization.[107]

Arendt rejects Marx's socialized humanism because it is too reductive and too grand. It is reductive in its causal reliance on evolutionary naturalism and economic imperialism. It is far too grand in its Promethean aspirations and epistemic illusions. The great weakness of Marx's anthropology is what it excludes from the human condition: free and independent individual thinking, disinterested theoretical insight, the multiple forms of human cognition not driven by need and material interest; interpersonal dialogue and persuasive speech, public spirited cooperative action, the political solidarity of mature citizens; world building craftsmanship, a rectilinear form of production that creates a durable world for the free *praxis* and *lexis* of mortals. The most significant omission is the dignity and worth of the individual person who first appears in the world at birth and finally disappears at death. Arendt's political humanism recognizes the worldly potential and inherent vulnerability of particular persons whose intrinsic importance does not depend on their ephemeral role in a grand historical drama or narrative.[108]

By emphasizing anthropological invariants like personal natality, individual need, common worldliness, human plurality and interdependence, Arendt presents a picture of freedom that avoids the illusion of autonomy. Human freedom requires political security, guaranteed civil liberties and diverse public forums for engaging with one's peers in responsible self-government. Freedom does not depend on collective mastery and sovereignty but on the unpredictable interactions of finite mortals whose individual purposes frequently conflict; it is the uncertain fruit of mutual respect and voluntary cooperation, rather than the inevitable outcome of dialectical necessity and law. The Promethean desire for unlimited power must be clearly demystified. Sovereign power threatens human liberty rather than supporting it.[109] When humans attempt to become gods, they resort to ideology and terror and violate the rights of their peers. While Arendt generally remains silent about the truth claims of Judaism and Christianity, she deeply opposes the Promethean project of replacing the Biblical god with a fictional substitute. The defense of human dignity precludes the biological reduction of the human person and the inflated divinization of the human species.

VIOLENCE AS THE ESSENCE OF POLITICS

> "The practice of violence, like all action, changes the world, but the most probable change is to a more violent world."[110]

Marx's political philosophy, like his philosophical anthropology, is an uneasy blend of enlightenment and romantic prejudices. Like Hobbes, Marx conceives of politics in the categories of modern natural science. The political theories of both men are driven by powerful reductive assumptions: they tend to reduce the sphere of politics to the realm of government and to restrict the actions of government to the legalized use of force or violence. For Hobbes, individual citizens freely surrender their natural rights to the state in exchange for protective security. The socially conscious Marx rejects Hobbes' fictional account of individual consent to the authority of centralized power. For Marx, the origin and purpose of government actually derive from oppressive economic relations. Throughout history, government has been the coercive instrument of the privileged economic class. While governments frequently claim to act for "the common good," their primary function is to protect and defend existing property relations. Because political action and speech are invariably bound to economic interests, public action is authorized violence, and public speech the rhetorical concealment of government's exploitative purpose.[111]

Politics would be a demoralizing enterprise, if this were the whole story. But Marx is a social expressivist as well as a naturalist captivated by economic prejudices. While government officials use legalized violence to defend economic oppression, revolutionary *praxis* is a genuine source of liberation. Emancipatory violence is "the midwife of history," of every old society economically pregnant with its dialectically determined successor. In history's decisive transitions, the laboring class rises to overthrow their economic and political oppressors. These revolutionary eruptions drive history forward without abolishing alienation and misery. In fact, proletarian misery under capitalism visibly undermines the liberal illusion of continuous historical progress.

While earlier social revolutions served the interests of the emerging class, the proletarian revolution will supposedly be decisive and final. The proletariat will act as a universal emancipator, destroying the historical sources of alienation and oppression. The abolition of capitalism will mean the permanent end of economic alienation and class struggle. Without class conflict, there will be no need for the legalized violence of the state. Politics, as we've known it since the slave owning Greeks, will completely disappear.[112]

Marx's utopian dream has prophetic overtones, but he justifies his vision by appeals to historical necessity. Romantic and anarchistic calls for liberating violence tend to be rooted in sentiment and feeling. But Marx despises uncritical sentiment and revolutionary strategies divorced from scientific insight. Gratuitous violence against systemic oppression is futile until the economic contradictions within capitalism precipitate internal collapse. Strategic violence must wait till the classless society appears in the womb of its bourgeois antagonist.[113]

Marx's assessment of violence and politics is deeply ambivalent. The history of government is a record of legalized violence by the ruling class against the economically oppressed. The use of compulsory force by the state is lacking in moral legitimacy. Since Marx reduces traditional politics to the coercive activity of government, he treats political activity as a source of human oppression. Revolutionary violence, by contrast, is historically liberating although its benefits until now have been limited. The liberated class has inevitably become an oppressive power in its own right. Yet these revolutionary episodes remain fundamental, preparing the way for the proletarian revolution and the classless society.

Marx's "science" of history convinced him that the collapse of capitalism was inevitable and that proletarian violence would end human alienation. Given the certainties of Marxian theory and the prospect of the classless society, we can partly understand the tragic path that led Marx's disciples from limited violence to unlimited terror.[114] Marxian ideology guaranteed revolutionary success if the messianic class acted decisively at the climactic moment. From Marx's perspective, the human stakes in the war against

anarchist

capitalism are apocalyptic: the end of world history and the permanent abolition of injustice and violence. To achieve such utopian ends, everything is permitted to the agents of global revolution: not only violence but terror, not only revolutionary struggle but the dictatorship of the communist party. Merciless treatment of the enemy is justified when the radical fulfillment of humanity is at hand. Absolute ends require unlimited means.

Marx's acceptance of revolutionary violence coexists with explicit hostility to practical reason and speech. As Glen Tinder observed, Marxism combines a passion for universal community with an open disdain for communication, the distinctively human way of establishing lasting connections and alliances.[115] Why this systemic distrust of *logos* and argument in the conduct of human affairs? Why this aggressive disdain for persuasion, deliberative dialogue, political debate, the making and keeping of promises as the way to establish communities of justice and freedom? Marx's contempt for the traditional political faculties (nous and logos) is strikingly over-determined; it is rooted in his reductive anthropology, his economic naturalism, his bitter experience of bourgeois ideology, and his cynical analysis of human motivation. If human beings are essentially productive animals, governed by material interests and needs and irrevocably moved by the prejudices of their economic class, then they are incapable of disinterested action and speech. To pretend otherwise is to mask or conceal the true dynamics of political life. Government is inherently oppressive because its real purpose is to protect economic inequities. Public law and authority are tools of class domination rather than instruments of impartial justice. Political argument and debate are vehicles of ideology and false consciousness rather than sources of practical wisdom. The dominant economic class and the government agencies serving its interests are incapable of meaningful reform, because moral norms and imperatives have no causal influence on political behavior. Promises of corrective action are simply ideological devices for pacifying the anger of the oppressed. Normative theories of politics and government conceal the violence of the state and divert revolutionary energies into useless reforms.[116]

Arendt also criticizes the history of government in the West. From her civic humanist perspective, most of what traditionally counts as politics has violated the republican ideal. The problem is not that governments have acted to protect economic interests, but that the equality and liberty of citizens are incompatible with traditional conceptions of rule, whether despotic or benevolent in nature. Not only have rulers narrowly pursued their self-interest, they have regularly prevented their citizens from participating meaningfully in public affairs.[117]

From the Marxist perspective, Arendt is a political idealist supporting a model of republican self-government with no chance of realization. Human beings are simply incapable of the sustained self-transcendence that republican politics requires. Moreover, to promote the republican ideal in a capitalist society is to conceal the dominance of the bourgeoisie and dissipate effective opposition to the *status quo*. From Arendt's civic republican perspective, Marx has denigrated participatory citizenship and discredited the political capacities on which it depends, while endorsing dangerous assumptions about the nature and purpose of political power.

A comprehensive political philosophy requires a realistic understanding of power.[118] The English term 'power,' from its Latin root *potentia* and the French derivative *pouvoir*, (to be able to, to be capable of) is not synonomous with 'force' or 'violence.' In contrast to the strength of individual human beings, power is the fruit of human cooperation, the capacity for worldly change that citizens create when they agree to act in concert. Such agreement is typically achieved through public speech and argument. It normally expresses itself in mutual promises or in provisional or enduring political alliances. Of course, the power potential achieved through cooperation can be exercised for good or ill. Despotic power is regularly used to dominate others, to treat them unjustly, to deny them their rights and liberties. But political power can also be exercised legitimately to promote public peace, security, prosperity, liberty, education, social justice, the deepening of civic and associative union. Because humans are fallible and weak, and because power can be easily abused, the most effective check on abuse is not Marxian violence but federated dispersal, creating independent centers of power to correct and balance each other.[119] The persisting political danger is not the generation of power (there is no genuine politics without power), but concentrated power, despotic power, without effective public constraints on its use.

Violence is also a form of action. It is typically an expression of weakness rather than power, the form of action the weak adopt to accomplish ends they cannot achieve through power. Violence is inherently instrumental, a calculated means to achieve nonviolent ends. Though violence can destroy or cripple power, it cannot create it. When organized power resorts to violence, it should do so as a last resort, an *ultima ratio*, when the persuasive potential of speech and argument has been exhausted. Because discourse and persuasion are essential to genuine politics, violence as such is antipolitical. Its presence in public affairs symbolizes the limits of what can be done through relying on discourse alone.[120]

The legitimate use of violence must always be proportionate. The normative ends that violence serves are protective in nature, securing the public and private realms from grave threats to their integrity and survival. The repeated use or threat of violence is the mark of despotic rule; but despotism represents the abolition of politics and the end of political civility. Violence tends to beget violence, whether its use is legitimate or not. A strategy of violence as a means of changing the world is therefore exceedingly dangerous. This danger is magnified when unlimited violence, what Arendt calls terror, is chosen as the way to achieve utopian ends. Both Stalin and Hitler officially licensed terror, unlimited revolutionary violence, as the authorized way to achieve their ideological aims.[121]

The traditional conflation of action with making is a further reason for confusing power with violence. Fabrication typically entails violence, transforming natural materials in accord with the artisan's preconceived plan. If human beings strive to become "makers and molders of history," then the logic of fabrication justifies violence as part of their historical mission. The same confusion threatens successful revolutionaries who must establish a just society after overthrowing a despotic order. How do they prevent their liberating violence from becoming the basis of the new regime? Arendt insists that liberation from despotism and the constitution of enduring liberty cannot conform to the same pattern of action.[122] The founding of a free and just society depends on mutual promises and covenants, on a shared agreement to live in accordance with law and the protections of liberty, rather than coercively constructing the new community on the fragmented remains of the old. At the root of this difference are contrasting conceptions of political freedom. If founding a new community is modeled on making, on shaping human beings to fit a utopian design, then freedom will be modeled on sovereignty, maintaining unfettered control over the reconstructive process. But if public freedom is rooted in human plurality, on different political opinions and spontaneous practical initiatives, on spirited debate of alternative courses of action, then political engineering yields to the fallible process of achieving limited and fragile agreements together. In civilized societies, violence exists at the margin of politics, never at its center. Though violence will never disappear from human affairs, responsible communities deliberately limit its role in political life.[123]

THE SCIENCE OF HISTORICAL NECESSITY

Marx's rebellion against "the tradition" is clearest when his revisionary claims are compared with Plato's myth of the cave. In Plato's provocative story, philosophers are unable to discover wisdom and truth unless they withdraw from the polis where change is incessant and the power of opinion (*doxa*) prevails. Only under the sky of eternal ideas can lovers of wisdom find what they erotically seek.

Marx forcefully rejected Plato's transcendent metaphysics, exclusively affirming the dignity of the secular realm and the history that unfolded within it. Following Hegel, Marx insisted that secular history was an appropriate object of theoretical study. Only by understanding the causal dynamics within "the cave," could human beings remake the world into a suitable home for their species.

For Arendt, the attribution of dignity to history should have led to the suspension of Platonic biases, fostering an unprejudiced account of political events and experiences and a deeper appreciation of human plurality and freedom. It should also have reconciled thought and action, closing the tragic rift between them that followed on Socrates' death.[124]

Arendt's political thinking had two complementary dimensions: her linguistic phenomenology discloses the intelligible structure of recurrent political phenomena like action, power and speech; her critical genealogy recounts the history of politics as a continuous struggle between freedom and despotism, where the periods of public freedom are few but glorious, and the forms of despotism many and varied. To complement these reflections on politics, Arendt acknowledged two other types of political thinking: practical deliberation, in which citizens debate the best course of future action, and reflective judgment, in which they compare their appraisals about what has already been done, said and suffered in the public realm.

The French and American Revolutions offered a rare opportunity to renew political thought. But Arendt contended that these adventures in liberty foundered, due to a failure of memory in America and European absorption in the philosophy and science of history. European thinkers largely ignored the American Revolution, concentrating their attention on the cataclysmic upheavals in France. Throughout the nineteenth century, conservatives, liberals and Marxists offered opposing accounts of this landmark historical event. Each of them tried to fit the French revolution into a polemical narrative of historical progress or decline. The unhappy result was one-sided reflection on the ultimate purpose of history, and the failure to develop a public philosophy attuned to the realities of the democratic age.[125]

In opposition to Plato, Hegel believed human history was inherently intelligible, that it constituted the dialectical fulfillment of an absolute rational idea.[126] World history, universal history, was a lawful rational process with a determinate beginning and end. This process was intelligible because it concretely expressed the dynamic realization of the divine idea, the idea of absolute spirit. For Hegel, both Platonic and Kantian "ideas of reason" were abstract, incomplete, and therefore lacking in truth. Only when rational ideas had been actualized in history, could they be fully understood and affirmed.[127]

Despite his striking originality, Hegel remained an essentially contemplative thinker. He focussed philosophical inquiry on the dynamic historical process that culminates in the actualization of freedom. By freedom, the immanent telos of history, Hegel meant the absolute autonomy of the Divine Spirit. Unlike the Christian God, Hegel's temporal divinity became fully autonomous only by achieving self-knowledge. The fulfillment of the Divine Spirit, therefore, required the rational cooperation of finite human spirits. Divine self-knowledge depended on the philosophical insights of Hegel who conceptually grasped the meaning of history by understanding its ultimate purpose.

For Hegel, history was meaningful because it was purposive, and because the purpose it achieved fulfilled the divine will. But only in retrospect, when the owl of Minerva had taken flight, could this immanent meaning be grasped and articulated. Until then, humans misunderstood history, believing it had no purpose or mistakenly identifying its telos with the limited aims of particular men and societies. While these provisional aims play a role in the actualization of spirit, they fail to constitute the meaning of history.

Absolute spirit fulfills its intention through conflict and struggle; it deliberately creates external obstacles before overcoming them through its expressive development. The stages of developing spirit incorporate into its cumulative life whatever is essential and enduring in this dialectical process of growth. Individual human beings, particular cultural communities, the evolving history of western philosophy, all play instrumental but indispensable roles in the divine saga. It is human thoughts, human passions, human purposes that drive history forward; yet nearly all human agents fail to comprehend what they are doing. They are like theatrical performers without a script, unaware of the dialectical laws governing their interaction and struggle.

How is the autonomous freedom of absolute spirit intelligibly related to the subjective freedom of finite spirits? In a limited sense, human subjects are free because they act on their immediate desires and strive to achieve their particular aims. But their rational freedom is deficient, since they don't know what they are doing. The significance of their actions is not the meaning they ascribe to them, but their role in fulfilling the divine plan. Only fully autonomous, fully rational spirit is genuinely free.

Arendt argued that Hegel remained bound by traditional philosophical prejudices.[128] The dialectical process culminating in freedom had to be necessary because reason was averse to contingency in its objects of study. Moreover, the particular agents, events and societies constituting history had no intrinsic dignity or importance. They derived their limited instrumental value from their subordinate roles in the drama of absolute spirit. Thus Hegel tragically endorsed two dangerous revolutionary assumptions: that the emergence of freedom is the result of dialectical necessity; that the value of historical particulars depends on their functional role in a pre-scripted teleological drama.[129]

Marx agreed with Hegel that history is a lawful dialectical process necessarily culminating in freedom. He also believed in a privileged historical agent, the evolving human species, that progressively develops through time.

But for the anti-religious Marx, this historical agent was human rather than divine, and for the anti-contemplative Marx the great human contributions to history were practical and not theoretical. *Pace* Hegel, philosophy's true purpose is to change the world not merely to understand its progressive development. In The Republic, Plato created an imaginary city that subordinated the *vita activa* to the demands of philosophical inquiry. In overturning the tradition, Marx created a philosophical blueprint for abolishing capitalism and achieving collective autonomy.

Marx radically naturalizes the substantive content of Hegel's philosophy of history. The underlying historical dynamic is the economic conflict between the forces and relations of production; the critical players in the drama are the socio-economic classes locked in continuous struggle; the critical moments in the dialectic are the periodic social revolutions in which the exploited class overthrows its economic and political oppressor. History's teleological climax will be the fulfillment of the French Revolution through the destruction of capitalism and the emergence of a classless and stateless society. Only then will true human freedom exist; only then will human alienation be fully overcome.[130]

The poverty of philosophy, its failure to abolish human alienation, is clearly revealed in Hegelian thought. The evidence of alienated thinking is pervasive: the conception of philosophy as contemplative reconciliation with the past; the narrative reliance on a fictional divine agent; the spiritualizing of the dialectical process; the failure to acknowledge the determinative power of economic causality. For Marx, Hegel reveals both the power and the limits of speculative thought. Hegel's lasting discovery was that history is lawful and purposive. But Hegel's dialectical narrative relies on spiritual fictions that Marx scornfully rejects. The culmination of history will permanently eliminate the false consolations of religion and philosophy.

To understand Marx's philosophy of history, we must first understand his conception of science. He inherited from the Enlightenment and ultimately from Aristotle, what Bernard Lonergan calls the "classical theory of science": the belief that science consists in true, certain knowledge of causal necessity.[131] In modern physics, the sources of causal necessity were not eternal Aristotelian essences, but universal and invariant laws. These laws were interpreted as mathematical descriptions of the irresistible processes governing the natural universe. All natural objects, all spatio-temporal occurrences, were supposedly subject to their implacable necessity. Marx believed that the historical process was also governed by universal laws, though the laws of history are dialectical unlike the classical laws of physics. While natural laws tend to be cyclical, history follows a rectilinear pattern based on the genesis and perishing of economic classes.

Marx departed from Enlightenment naturalism on another critical point. Modern physics explicitly rejected natural teleology, arguing that the lawful motions of nature lacked meaning and purpose. But both Marx and Hegel wanted to preserve the meaning of history; and both assumed that for history to be meaningful it had to be purposive, that it had to advance towards an ultimate and attainable telos.[132] They attempted to combine the lawful necessity they attributed to science with a traditional notion of practical teleology.[133] To achieve this improbable synthesis, they resorted to an historicized version of Adam Smith's invisible hand. In Hegel's case he appealed to the cunning of absolute reason; in Marx, the desired teleology is guaranteed by the cunning of history. Hegel's absolute spirit, like the providential God of the prophets, employs human passions and purposes to satisfy a divine intention of which human beings are largely unaware. Marx's analogous claim is that the great social classes in history, by pursuing their narrow material interests, create the necessary conditions for radical human autonomy.

What sort of freedom does economic determinism leave to human agents in history, to the class-bound laborers, capitalists, statesmen, philosophers and artists? As in Hegel's dialectic, they enjoy a form of alienated freedom. They act on their narrow intentions and purposes, they consistently pursue the self-interest of their class, they promote the productive capacity of the human species. But alienated freedom is not autonomous agency. Just as alienated labor radically differs from socialized labor, so alienated political violence differs from impartial public administration in a classless society. The same divergence obtains between alienated and autonomous thought. Alienated thought is the opposite of genuine science. Ideologies, as Marx uses the term, serve to justify oppressive economic conditions and the state's reliance on violence to protect them. Genuine science, autonomous thought, discovers history's dialectical laws and proves its validity by successfully directing revolutionary praxis. While liberal ideology justifies the violence of the bourgeois state, Marx's science of history provides strategic directives for the proletariat in constructing a classless, and therefore, autonomous society.[134]

Are all serious thinkers who criticize Marx's philosophy of history ideologues? Are their critical objections inevitably constrained by the biases of their social class? Or are they able to transcend group bias, achieving rational insight into society and history?[135] If Marx can avoid economic determinism in discovering historical truth, why are he and his disciples the only exceptions to the sway of ideology? For if the recognized power of group bias does not preclude disinterested thought, then how can we distinguish ideology from science except on empirical grounds? The issue is not whether economic causes play an important historical role, but whether they play the determinative role Marx assigns to them. To put it bluntly, how does Marx know that class struggle functions in history as gravity functions in nature? What historical fruits and works could confirm this explanatory theory?

Following Michael Polanyi, I want to propose a reading of Marx that differs from his own self construal.[136] Despite his radical critique of capitalism, Marx was an historical optimist convinced that the scandalous contradictions of modernity would finally be overcome. When this decisive transformation occurred, the utopian hopes of the French Revolution would be fulfilled. He was equally convinced that the key to the riddle of history was the continuous conflict between the forces and relations of production. Because this conflict had reached its zenith under capitalism, the climactic moment in the liberation of the species was at hand.

Marx asserted these beliefs not as romantic hopes or speculative theories, but as scientific certainties. He claimed to have discovered an historical science that truthfully explained the human past and infallibly predicted the future. This "science of historical necessity" also satisfied the Baconian demand for uniting theory and practice. Marx's science of history provides practical guidance for the revolutionary praxis that will conclusively achieve his utopian ends.

Marx's polemical strategy is to defend his utopian hopes by grounding them in infallible science. Revolutionary hopes are not mere romantic longings, because lawful and impersonal processes are working inexorably to fulfill them. Marx's theories are true because they explain the contradictions of modernity and provide the only effective strategy for resolving them. Revolutionary violence, though admittedly heartless and cruel, is historically justified because it is the dialectical path to universal freedom and equality. The followers of Marx can be supremely confident because they are cooperating with historical necessity for the benefit of the entire human species.

The most reasonable way to challenge Marx is to question the evidence for his truth claims. But the dogmatic certainty Marx attributes to science tends to make him intolerant in the face of criticism. He does not advance his account as the most reasonable explanation to be amended in the light of recalcitrant evidence. Instead, he advances his theories and predictions as incontrovertible truths. They uniquely explain the conflicts of the past and justify a revolutionary strategy certain to produce the utopian outcomes that will permanently silence his critics.[137] Until then, all rival accounts are dismissed as ideologies; they cannot explain the contradictions of modernity nor provide an infallible strategy for overcoming them.

Chapter 4
MARXISM AS IDEOLOGY: AN ARENDTIAN CRITIQUE

> It was the scientist in Marx, and the ambition to raise his 'science' to the rank of natural science, whose chief category then was still necessity, that tempted him into the reversal of his own categories.[138]

Hannah Arendt explicitly rejects the scientific status of Marxian theory. She views Marx's "science" of historical necessity as a fictional science, an ideology. As she uses the term, an ideology is a reductive explanation of historical complexity that seeks to unify the past through a single explanatory category like race or class.[139] She treats the national Socialist appeal to race and the Marxian appeal to class struggle as perfect examples of ideological thinking. Both ideologies create the illusion that there is a single interpretive key to history and that they possess it exclusively. This Gnostic pretension is then used to justify unlimited violence against whomever history has marked for extinction. The terrible confidence that flows from complying with historical necessity exempts ideological agents from powerful moral prohibitions against murder. The tragic results of ideological politics dominate the modern history of Europe. Hegel's fateful dialectic of historical necessity corrupted the French and Russian Revolutions and poisoned the spirit of the greater revolutionary tradition. But the totalitarian regimes in Nazi Germany and the Soviet Union were the nadir of political history as ideology and terror became the governing principles of criminal states.[140]

Arendt criticizes Marx for degrading the human capacities he originally intended to celebrate. He spurned Hegel's theory of history for a Baconian project of revolutionary praxis allegedly based on infallible truth. In this way, he carried the logic of dialectical theorizing into the realm of free action and speech. This had the terrible effect of making political activity depend on the strategic guidance of "scientific theory."[141] But in Marxism, the directive theory is a powerful ideology that superimposes "the laws of history" on politics and culture. These deterministic laws, when strictly interpreted, reduce human action and thought to mere functions of economic causality. While Marx exempts his own theory and praxis from these unwelcome reductions, he provides no credible warrant for distinguishing Marxian science from Arendtian ideology.

Arendt strongly opposes the Hegelian and Marxist strategies for preserving the dignity of history. While they emphasized world historical process, she believed that history consists of particular events and actions performed by individual persons in the company of their peers. These memorable actions are free and contingent occurrences inherently unpredictable in advance. In fact, genuine action, as opposed to habitual behavior, cannot be subsumed under an explanatory covering law.[142] Though all human actions are motivated by specific intentions, their historical meaning does not depend on achieving the ends they intended. And since free actions elicit the free response of their peers, there is no way to predict or control the full range of their historical effects.

It is a serious error to confuse the meaning of a human action, known only in retrospect by disinterested observers, with the intended purpose of the action or the results to which it may lead.[143] Only if you dogmatically assume a single historical agent whose governing purposes cannot be resisted by mortals, are you tempted to reduce the significance of particular human beings to their functional roles in an inevitable process. But for Arendt, this is precisely what Hegel and Marx uncritically assume. For Hegel, human agents and actions derive their instrumental value by unconsciously contributing to the governing purpose of absolute spirit. For Marx, they derive their functional value from creating the necessary conditions of the classless society. Both thinkers deprive the historical past and present of intrinsic worth; individual persons became disposable tools in the achievement of a preordained future. Since all derivative meaning depends on achieving the absolute end, once the speculative teleology collapses, intrinsic meaning and value disappear from the world.[144]

If Marx's secular hopes are extravagant and his guarantee of success ideological, where does that leave the understanding of history and our collective responsibility for the world?

THE MERITS AND LIMITATIONS OF MARXISM

My purpose in this final section is not to restate Arendt's criticisms of Marx. Though I have benefitted greatly from her commentary, my appraisal of Marx follows a somewhat different tack. We are indebted to Marx and the radical enlightenment that inspired him for their critical diagnosis of economic and political injustice. Although Marx saw himself as a scientific critic of capitalism, it is his prophetic passion for justice that makes his critique so compelling. For Marx, capitalism was a necessary but not a permanent phase of the world historical process. Driven by internal contradictions, capitalism would eventually collapse from within, giving way to a socialist economy and a utopian classless society. Though Marx's apocalyptic predictions failed to materialize, his moral critique of capitalism retains its force. The ruthless struggle to maximize profits, the pursuit of unlimited wealth, the reduction of everything human to commodity status, the brutal character of the factory system, the squalor of working-class neighborhoods, the scandalous concentration of wealth and political power, the degradation of the natural world, the periodic instability of the business cycle, the historical ties to imperialism, are all unjust and dehumanizing. We needn't share Marx's utopian dreams to support his objections to capitalism.

Marx's moral critique of bourgeois society was also legitimate. The nineteenth century bourgeoisie were too often smug and pretentious. Faced with evident economic injustice, they eschewed solidarity with the working class and deliberately used the powers of government to protect their possessions and privileges. They also fostered a shallow optimism about the future of Europe, cloaking the injustices of industrial life under the mask of liberal ideology.

Bourgeois capitalists used the ideology of laissez faire to defend the economic and political order they had created. Justified calls for reform were rebuffed by invoking "the iron laws of economics" and the benevolence of "the invisible hand." The shibboleths of classical liberalism kept European governments from acting on behalf of the working class and the vast majority of capitalists from reforming their economic conduct. Marx correctly emphasized the role of liberal ideology in excusing systemic injustice.

Marx was also properly scandalized by the deepening "social question." The coexistence of deprivation and material abundance was and remains intolerable. The grinding poverty of the working class is not essential to economic progress. New forms of production have created a surplus of exchangeable goods and services that require new patterns of distribution and compensation. They also require an important role for national governments and international authorities to referee the conflicts between capital and labor, to guarantee the basic needs of the people, and to promote the prosperity of the larger society. Concerted bourgeois opposition to political and economic reform led Marx to believe that only revolutionary violence could solve "the social question." Though I agree with Arendt that Marx's justification of violence is a counsel of despair, I reject her assumption that political decisions and actions are economically irrelevant. The creation of a social safety net, the development of a mixed economy, the enactment of reasonable fiscal and monetary policies, the exemption of important public goods from market-based patterns of allocation, these political decisions and policies will not solve the problem of poverty, but they can and do alleviate it.

Scientific inquiry has dramatically increased the fund of human knowledge. Human productive capacity has grown exponentially with modern economic and technical developments. The political institutions created by democracy enable millions of citizens to act cooperatively on behalf of national and global purposes and projects. Our peers increasingly accept collective responsibility for our common world. They share the conviction of Marx and Arendt that the secular realm has a meaning and dignity of its own, that it merits our knowledge, attention and love.

This shared commitment to protecting and preserving the world and to working for justice within it should not be confused with Marx's revolutionary project. Shared responsibility for the world does not require an ideology of historical progress, a definitive solution to the riddle of history or an end to human alienation. Responsible citizenship does not depend on a socialized humanity magically freed from the egoistic, group and general biases that make human existence a morally tangled knot. Authentic hopes for the world are far more sober than Marx's utopian dreams. Human beings acting together responsibly can make our world better in numerous ways: more secure, more peaceful, more free, more just. What they can never do is make the world perfect and sinless. Practical wisdom and historical sobriety confirm the power and the limits of individual and collective activity.

What lasting insights can we draw from Marx's philosophical anthropology? The human being is a causal agent situated in nature, society and history. As natural beings we share biological needs with the animals, though our evolving desires and the ways that we meet them are regularly transformed by the social and historical communities in which we live. Marx treated our social embeddedness as reducible to membership in an economic class. While economic realities are certainly important, they typically lack the causal influence Marx attributed to them. His emphasis on class membership also obscures the range of associations that command our allegiance and effort, religious, political, moral, artistic, etc. Marx claimed that these cultural and political allegiances are essentially determined by economic interests, and in some forms of society that may be true. But as a universal account of human affiliation and commitment, it is deeply implausible and reductive.

We are historical beings, and the various communities to which we belong are saturated with historical effects, both helpful and harmful. Our individual and collective actions occur within complex communities that frame the horizon for our various undertakings and projects. We can never leap out of history, either into a past for which we're nostalgic like the classical *polis*, or into a revolutionary future that is clearly utopian and unreal.[145]

The exercise of freedom, both personal and public, is always partial and finite. We will never become autonomous in either the Kantian or the Marxian sense. But we are responsible for what we do with our lives within a world we did not create and in the company of others, most of whom are strangers. I agree with Arendt that we should explicitly reject the Marxian conflation of freedom with sovereignty. Human progress in the healing and creative arts is always partial and incomplete; and the Marxian ideal of sovereignty is incompatible with human plurality.

The Promethean project Marx passionately espoused needs to be deflated by humility and realism. Because of our natality, we will always be dependent and developing beings, always newcomers in an old world that we share with peers of different ages and backgrounds. We are endowed with an unrestricted desire to know and a need to make sense of all that we experience. The quest for knowledge and the search for meaning will never desert us, but our discoveries are fallible and subject to revision in the light of experience and criticism. Because we share the earth and the world with others, we cannot escape the question of justice, nor the exigent norms of responsible action that the concern for justice imposes. Because we are mortal, our reach exceeds our grasp, and we inevitably die with important hopes unfulfilled. There is enduring wisdom in the ancient trope that we humans exist between the brutes and the gods. Far more than instinctual animals, we are considerably less than the divine. This intermediate ontological status is a discernible constant in our historically variable condition.

There is no science of historical necessity. There is no permanent human solution to the contradictions of earthly life. Our tempered and responsible hopes for the future will have to rest on humbler and far less inflated grounds.

NOTES

1. Arendt, *Between Past and Future* (New York: Penguin, 1968), p. 32.
2. *Ibid.*, p. 17.
3. *Ibid.*, pp.17-40.
4. These hierarchical contrasts are articulated in *Republic* VI and VII where Socrates distinguishes "true philosophers" from both their sophistic rivals and ordinary non-philosophical citizens.
5. For Arendt, Plato's political philosophy originated in a specific historical event, the trial of Socrates and the conflict between the philosopher and the *polis*. She reads the philosopher-king as Plato's revisionary attempt to resolve that conflict in favor of philosophy. *Human Condition*, p. 12, pp. 221-230; *Thinking*, p. 81.
6. Aristotle, *Nicomachean Ethics* I, 5, 1095b,-13-1096a 10.
7. *Karl Marx: Selected Writings*, edited by David McLellan (New York: Oxford University Press, 1977). "The abolition of religion as the illusory happiness of the people is the demand for their real happiness. The demand to give up the illusions of their condition is the demand to give up a condition that requires illusion." p. 69.
8. "If Being and Appearance part company forever, and this—as Marx once remarked—is indeed the basic assumption of all modern science, then there is nothing left to be taken on faith." Arendt, *Human Condition*, p. 270. Arendt later traces this remark to *Das Kapital*, vol. III.
9. "Communism . . . is the definitive resolution of the antagonism between man and nature, and between man and man. . . . It is the solution of the riddle of history and knows itself to be this solution." Marx, *Selected Writings*, p. 89.
10. Arendt, *Between Past and Future*, p. 25.
11. Arendt, *Between Past and Future*, p. 21 and the endnotes on p. 284 where she provides the textual sources in Marx for these concise formulations.
12. See the opening lines of Herodotus' *History*, translated by David Greene (Chicago: U of CP, 1987). Arendt cites this Herodotean passage in *Between Past and Future*, p. 41.
13. See Arendt, *On Revolution*, p. 12, and *Between Past and Future*, p. 23. "The Greeks, living together in a *polis*, conducted their affairs by means of speech, through persuasion (*peitho*), and not by means of violence."
14. Marx, *Selected Writings*, p. 158.

15. Hegel, *Reason in History* (New York: Library of Liberal Arts, 1953.) p. 47. "The insight to which philosophy should lead us is that the actual world is as it ought to be. God governs the world. The actual working of His government, the carrying out of His plan is the history of the world. Philosophy strives to comprehend and articulate this plan."

16. Francis Bacon, *Novum Organon*, (Oxford, 1889) p. 265. See the chapter on "Fruits and Works" in Nicholas Lobkowicz, *Theory and Practice*, (Notre Dame, University of Notre Dame Press, 1967) pp.89-108.

17. *Republic*, 540a. "We shall require them (the philosopher-rulers) to turn upward the vision of their souls and fix their gaze on that which sheds light on all, and when they have thus beheld the good itself, they shall use it as a pattern for the right ordering of the state and the citizens and themselves."

18. Marx, *Selected Writings*, pp. 388-391, Preface to a *Critique of Political Economy*.

19. Marx, *Selected Writings*, pp. 389-390 For the evolution of Marx's concept of ideology, see Paul Ricoeur, *Ideology and Utopia* (New York: Columbia University Press, 1986), chapters 2-6 and Lobkowicz, *Theory*, pp. 261-270.

20. Arendt,*Between Past and Future*, pp. 21-25.

21. Ibid., p. 19.

22. Ibid., pp. 21-25.

23. How does Marx's "socialized humanism," grounded in the primacy of socially productive labor, differ from Arendt's "political humanism" rooted in the human capacity for speech and action? How does "socialized man," the *animal laborans*, differ from Arendt's republican citizen, the *zoon politikon*. These are two of the central questions addressed in this chapter.

24. For Marx as a "romantic expressivist," see Taylor, *Hegel and Modern Society*, (Cambridge: Cambridge University Press, 1979) pp. 140-158.

25. Marx, *Selected Writings*, p. 89 "Communism as completed naturalism is humanism and as completed humanism is naturalism."

26. Marx's numerous references to the French Revolution emphasize the contrast between its universal aspirations and its limited results. The Revolution effectively destroyed the *Ancien Regime*, emancipating the bourgeoisie from the feudal order rather than emancipating humanity as such.

27. Arendt, *Human Condition*, pp. 61-67.

28. See Albert Hirschman, *Rival Views of Market Society*, (Cambridge: Harvard University Press, 1997), pp.105-141.

29. See Edmund Burke, *Reflections on the Revolution in France*, (New York: Library of Liberal Arts, 1955) and Joseph de Maistre, *Considerations on France*, (Montreal: McGill. Queens University, 1974).

30. See Hirschman and "The Doux-Commerce Thesis," pp. 106-109, and Hirschman, *The Passions and the Interests*, (Princeton: Princeton University Press, 1977), Part Two "How Economic Expansion Was Expected to Improve the Political Order," pp. 67-113.

31. Marx, *Selected Writings*, "The Communist Manifesto," pp 221-245.

32. See Arendt, *On Revolution*, pp. 59-66, for Arendt's analysis of the "social question" and its critical role in Marx's thought.

33. For the complex nature of Marx's critique of capitalism, see Jeffrey Reiman, "Moral Philosophy: The Critique of Capitalism and the Problem of Ideology," *The Cambridge Companion to Marx*, (New York: Cambridge University Press, 1991), pp. 143-167.

34. See Nicholas Lash, *A Matter of Hope*, (Notre Dame Press, 1981). Lash carefully explores whether Marx's thought can be read as a secularized doctrine of providence.

35. Marx, *The Portable Karl Marx*, (New York: Penguin, 1985) p. 177.

36. Arendt, *Between Past and Future*. "To think, with Hegel, that truth resides and reveals itself in the time process itself is characteristic of all modern historical consciousness." p. 68. Arendt is at pains to distinguish Hegel's secular time consciousness from the Christian understanding of history in Augustine's *City of God*.

37. Hegel, *Reason in History*, p. 27. "A principle, a law is something implicit, which as such, however true in itself, is not completely real (actual)."

38. See Hegel, *Spirit*, chapter 6 of Hegel's *Phenomenology of Spirit*, (Indianapolis: Hackett, 2001) and chapter 3. "Self Positing Spirit" in Taylor, *Hegel*, (Cambridge: Cambridge University Press, 1975), pp.76-124.

39. See Taylor, *Hegel*, chapter 19, "Philosophy." "The vocation of philosophy from the very beginning is to be the vocation of spirit's self-recognition in everything that is." p. 512.

40. Marx, *Selected Writings*, pp. 63-64; p. 106. "If I know religion as externalized human self-consciousness . . . thus I know that the self-consciousness that is part of my own self is not confirmed in religion, but in the abolition and super-session of religion." See Lash, *Hope*, chapter 13, "The Criticism of Religion."

41. Marx, *Selected Writings*, p. 69.

42. For Marx's account of the history of metaphysical materialism, see *Selected Writings*, pp.149-155.

43. See Richard McKirahan, *Philosophy Before Socrates*, (Indianapolis: Hackett, 1994) pp. 303-343, for the core principles of ancient Greek *Atomism*.

44. Marx, *Selected Writings*, pp.160-161 "The Premises of the Material Method."

45. Marx, *Selected Writings*, "Men begin to distinguish themselves from animals as soon as they begin to produce their means of subsistence." p.160.

46. Ibid.,pp. 389-390.

47. See Isaiah Berlin, *Karl Marx*, (New York: Oxford University Press, 1959); Nicholas Lobkowicz, *Theory and Practice*; Nicholas Lash, *A Matter of Hope*; Taylor, *Hegel and Modern Society*; Raymond Aren, *Main Currents in Sociological Thought; The Cambridge Companion to Marx*.

48. Arendt, *On Revolution*, p. 52.

49. Arendt was especially critical of Marx's "preference for collective subjects like the 'proletariat'; or 'mankind,' which act in accordance with supposed class or species interests." Dana Villa, "The Development of Arendt's Political Thought," p.7, *The Cambridge Companion to Hannah Arendt*, (Cambridge: Cambridge University Press, 2000). Within such collective subjects, the human plurality Arendt repeatedly emphasized is effaced.

50. Marx, *Selected Writings*, "The German Ideology" and "Preface to a Critique of Political Economy."

51. See Taylor, *Hegel and Modern Society*, pp.140-158.

52. This synoptic account follows Marx's schematic outline in "Preface to the Critique of Political Economy." It supplements that outline with insights from a wide range of Marx's writings.

53. *Selected Writings*, p. 389.

54. For the argument that Marx's economic narratives force a qualification of his alleged determinism, see Richard Miller, "Social and Political Theory: Class, State Revolution," pp. 101-105 in *The Cambridge Companion to Marx*.

55. Arendt had grave reservations about this project long before its destructive environmental effects were known. See "Life As The Highest Good" and "The Victory of the Animal Laborans" in *The Human Condition*.

56. See "The Communist Manifesto," *Selected Writings*, pp. 221-247.

57. The modern project of achieving mastery by obeying impersonal law is clearly articulated in Descartes' and Bacon's interpretations of modern science.

58. "We can call it the cunning of reason that the idea makes passions work for it, in such a way that the means by which it posits itself in existence lose thereby and suffer injury." Hegel, *Reason and History*, pp. 31-43. Arendt argues that this influential Hegelian metaphor shaped the European revolutionary tradition with "the obvious and yet paradoxical result that instead of freedom necessity became the chief category of political and revolutionary thought." *On Revolution*, pp. 52-53.

59. For Marx's argument that earlier revolutionary agents did not really know what they were doing, see "The Eighteenth Brumaire of Louis Bonaparte," *Selected Writings*, pp. 300-324.

60. Ibid., pp. 71-73.

61. For Marx, these appear to be constitutive features of full human emancipation.

62. See Michael Polanyi's description of Marxism as "a prophetic idealism spurning all reference to ideals." *Personal Knowledge*, (Chicago: University of Chicago Press, 1967) pp. 227-233.

63. Robert Heilbroner, *The Worldly Philosophers*, (New York: Simon and Schuster, 1986), p. 140.

64. I have drawn on Marx's "Economic Writings 1857-1867" in the McLellan volume for this synoptic portrait of capitalism. I have also benefited from Heilbroner's *The Worldly Philosophers*, particularly chapters 1-6.

65. For Arendt's portrait of the classical household, see *Human Condition* II, "The Public and the Private Realm."

66. Ibid., pp. 61-66.

67. See Heilbroner, "The Economic Revolution," pp. 18-41.

68. See Hirschman, *The Passions and the Interests*, pp.101-113 and Hirschman, *Rival Views of Market Society*, pp.106-109.

69. Montesquieu, *The Spirit of the Laws*, p. 8. "Commerce . . . polishes and softens barbaric ways as we can see everyday." A similar note is struck in Constant's famous essay, "The Liberty of the Ancients Compared with That of the Moderns."

70. See Hirschman, "The Concept of Interest: From Euphemism to Tautology," *Rival Views*, pp. 35-55.

71. For a plausible account of why the "Doux-Commerce Thesis" of commercial capitalism became "the self-destruction thesis" of industrial capitalism, see Hirschman, *Rival Views*, pp. 105-119.

72. See Charles Breunig, *The Age of Revolution and Reaction, 1789-1850*, (New York: Norton, 1977), chapter 4. "The Industrial Revolution and Its Impact on European Society."

73. For Marx, the central paradox of bourgeois capitalism was the coexistence of unprecedented wealth with working class deprivation.

74. Marx's exposition and critique of political economy provides an important connection between the early and later phases of his thought. See "The Holy Family," p.184.

75. See Hirschman, *Rival Views*, and Heilbroner, p. 147.

76. Marx, *Selected Writings*, pp. 345-362.

77. Ibid., pp. 206, 348, 350, 385, 411.

78. Ibid., pp. 223, 232-235.

79. Ibid., "The Rise and Downfall of Capitalism," pp. 362-365, 488-492.

80. Marx took the revolutionary ideal of universal emancipation for granted. He relentlessly criticizes any aspect of modern reality or thought that obstructs or compromises his revolutionary vision.

81. Marx, *Selected Writings*, pp. 222-231. ". . . for exploitation, veiled by religious and political illusions," it has substituted naked shameless, direct, brutal exploitation."

82. Ibid., p. 226, "The weapons with which the bourgeoisie felled feudalism to the ground are now turned against the bourgeoisie itself."

83. Ibid., pp. 362-365, 485-492.

84. See Polanyi, *Personal Knowledge*, "The Magic of Marxism," pp. 227-233.

85. *Selected Writings*, pp. 77-87, 117-122, 365-370.

86. Marx emphasizes the alienation of labor under capitalism in all phases of his intellectual career.

87. *Selected Writings*, pp. 195-197, 248-268, 393-414, 453-470. See Arendt, "The Exchange Market," *Human Condition*, pp. 159-167, and *Past and Future*, pp. 32-35.

88. This account synthesizes multiple passages from Marx's economic writings.

89. "Modern bourgeois society . . . is like the sorcerer, who is no longer able to control the powers of the netherworld which he has called up by his spells." *Selected Writings*, p. 226.

90. See "Private Property and Communism," pp. 87-96, 179-187, 231-238.

91. For Arendt's critique of socialism and communism in practice, see *Crises*, pp. 211-215. "In essence, socialism has simply continued and driven to its extreme, what capitalism began."

92. The rhetorical expression of this thesis is the heart of *The Communist Manifesto.*

93. Lobkowicz, *Theory and Practice*, p. 44.

94. See Arendt, *The Human Condition*, for "The Reversal of Contemplation and Action in the Modern Age." "Contemplation itself became altogether meaningless," p.292; and *Crises*, pp.114-115.

95. All the destructive antagonisms that have darkened human history, between man and nature, man and man, and man and himself, will be transformed into relations of harmony. For Freud's stark critique of the utopian strain in Marx's thought, see *Civilization and Its Discontents*, and the concluding essay "Weltanschauung" in *New Introductory Lectures on Psycho-Analysis*.

96. Arendt, *Human Condition*, pp. 87-109.

97. For the Arendtian distinctions between labor-life, work-world, and action-web of plurality, see sections III, IV and V in *The Human Condition*.

98. See "The Traditional Substitution of Making for Acting," *The Human Condition*, pp. 220-230, and *Between Past and Future*, pp. 77-86. For Arendt, the fateful substitution of making for acting connects Plato, the beginning of western political philosophy, with Marx, its putative end.

99. For the moral appeal of an explicit contempt for moral scruples, see Polanyi, *Personal Knowledge*, pp. 227-237. "The more inordinate our moral aspirations and the more completely amoral our objectivist outlook, the more powerful is a combination in which these contradictory principles mutually reinforce each other."

100. See Margaret Canovan, *Hannah Arendt. A Reinterpretation of Her Political Thought*, "Totalitarian Elements in Marxism," pp. 63-108.

101. For the loneliness of mass society, see *Origins*, pp. 474-479; for the wordlessness of the *animal laborans*, see *Human Condition*, pp. 118-119.

102. The predicted demise of capitalism resulted from its inability to sustain the productive momentum it had originally unleashed.

103. *The Human Condition*, p. 89.

104. "The modern age in general and Karl Marx in particular, overwhelmed, as it were, by the unprecedented actual productivity of western mankind, had an almost irresistible tendency to look upon all labor as work and to speak of the *animal laborans* in terms much more fitting for *homo faber*." *The Human Condition*, p. 87.

105. See Bikhu Parekh, "Hannah Arendt's Critique of Marx." *Hannah Arendt: The Recovery of the Public World*, pp. 67-100.

106. See Parekh, pp. 85-87 and Lobkowicz, p. 419.

107. See Taylor's critique of the Marxist aspiration to species autonomy in *Hegel and Modern Society*, pp. 141-154.

108. See "The Concept of History" in *Past and Future* and *Lectures on Kant's Political Philosophy*. "Man's dignity demands that he be seen (every single one of us) in his particularity and, as such, be seen—but without any comparison and independent of time—as reflecting mankind in general." p. 77.

109. For the critical contrast between freedom as virtuosity and freedom as sovereignty, see *Past and Future*, pp. 163-165. "Under human conditions . . . freedom and sovereignty are so little identical that they cannot even exist simultaneously." p.164.

110. *Crises*, p. 177.

111. "Political power, properly so called, is merely the organized power of one class for oppressing another." *Selected Writings*, p. 238.

112. "In place of the old bourgeois society, with its classes and class antagonisms we shall have an association, in which the free development of each is the condition for the free development of all." *Selected Writings*, p. 238.

113. "No social order ever perishes before all the productive forces for which there is room in it have developed, and new, higher relations of production never appear before the material conditions of their existence have matured in the womb of the old society itself." *Selected Writings*, p. 390.

114. Marx clearly believed that only limited violence would be needed to overthrow capitalism once it had exhausted its economic viability. It is unfair to attribute directly to Marx the limitless terror unleashed in his name. Still, Arendt was leery of the "totalitarian elements in Marxism." See *Crises*, p. 113.

115. Tinder, *Against Fate*. "Fate and Fraternity," pp. 106-113.
116. For Arendt, Marx's glorification of violence was critically paired with his suspicion of *logos* and persuasive speech. See *Between Past and Future*, pp. 22-25 and 76-84.
117. "The hallmark of all such escapes (from politics) is the concept of rule . . . the notion that men can lawfully and politically live together only when some are entitled to command and others forced to obey." *Human Condition*, p. 222.
118. For Arendt's distinctions between violence, power, force and strength, see "On Violence," *Crises*.
119. For Montesquieu's conception of divided power and its role in shaping the American Constitution, see *On Revolution*, pp.149-154.
120. *Crises*, p.176. "Violence, being instrumental by nature, is rational to the extent that it is effective in reaching the end that must justify it."
121. See chapter 13, "Ideology and Terror" in *Origins*.
122. See the critical distinction between liberation and constitution in *On Revolution*, pp. 232-234.
123. See *Past and Future*, pp.136-141.
124. See "History and Politics," pp.75-86, *Past and Future*.
125. See "The Revolutionary Tradition and Its Lost Treasure." *On Revolution*, pp.215-231.
126. When Hegel refers to an idea of reason, he is tacitly invoking the history of western metaphysics. Like the *eide* of Plato's *Republic* or the noumenal ideas of Kant, Hegelian ideas are the intentional objects of philosophical inquiry. They are the unconditioned realities reason seeks in its quest for wisdom. But Hegel believes these ideas are inherently generative, that they produce their embodied expressions in space and time; and that the fullness of such expressions actualizes the idea, achieving its intended truth. True knowledge of the idea requires rationally understanding its fully embodied expression. Thus the rational idea of freedom or spirit actualizes itself in world history, providing philosophy with its proper field of inquiry.
127. "Thus philosophy does not tend to arise when an age is in its prime, in the bloom of youth, but rather when it has already started to grow old." Taylor, *Hegel*. "Philosophy begins with the decline of the world."
128. For Arendt, these were traditional prejudices about the objects of rational knowledge, in particular, the alleged causal necessity that reason demands in genuine science.
129. These assumptions, rooted in the classical theory of science, imposed a procrustean grid on the revolutionary tradition. Practical insights drawn from revolutionary events and experiences were sacrificed to traditional prejudices about historical intelligibility.
130. Marx's classless society, therefore, is a secular analogue to the Christian ideal of the kingdom of God. In both kingdoms, universal harmony is achieved by overcoming the sources and effects of sin and alienation.
131. See Lonergan, *Collection* (Toronto: University of Toronto Press, 1988) pp. 238-240.
132. For Arendt's criticism of the conflation between meaning and purpose (end), see *Between Past and Future*, pp. 78-81.
133. By practical teleology, I mean the *telos* at which a deliberative agent aims in intentional action.
134. Marx seems to distinguish two different kinds of ideology: religious ideology is a form of false consolation that creates fictional satisfactions for unmet human needs. By contrast, liberal economic theory may be an accurate reflection of bourgeois capitalism, but it fails to reveal the contradictions within the capitalist system. Both forms of ideology lack the critical dimension Marxian theory requires. They serve to justify rather than critique alienated forms of economic and political organization.
135. For the distorting role of bias in human inquiry, see Lonergan, *Insight*, pp. 218-242.
136. See Polanyi, *Personal Knowledge*, pp. 218-245.
137. See Arendt's analysis in *Origins* of how historical ideologies use terror to corroborate their factual claims, pp. 460-479.
138. *On Revolution*, p. 65.
139. *Origins*, pp.158-161, 345-351.
140. See "Ideology and Terror," pp. 460-479 in *Origins*.
141. *Between Past and Future*, p. 30.

142. For the distinction between action and predictable behavior, see *The Human Condition*, pp. 40-46.

143. See *The Human Condition*, pp. 184-187; 191-192.

144. "The growing meaningless of the modern world is perhaps nowhere more clearly foreshadowed than in this identification of meaning and end." *Between Past and Future*, p. 78.

145. See Tocqueville, *Democracy in America*, vol. II, p. 352. "Providence has not created mankind entirely independent or entirely free."

Chapter Five

THE DISCONTENTS OF LIBERAL DEMOCRACY
and
THE CONTINUING RELEVANCE OF ARENDTIAN THOUGHT

PART I

"Liberal democracy has many faults, but it is a well established and relatively successful political and social practice. Strong (participatory) democracy may derive from an attractive theoretical tradition (civic republicanism), but it is without a convincing modern embodiment."
Benjamin Barber, *Strong Democracy*[1]

THE CRITICAL APPROPRIATION OF TRADITION

The historical optimism of the radical enlightenment and the utopian hopes of Marx were shattered by the events of the twentieth century. Two world wars, the great depression, the totalitarian regimes in Nazi Germany, the Soviet Union, Maoist China, Pol Pot's Cambodia, and the spectre of nuclear annihilation and irreversible environmental decline have chastened the innocence of liberalism with its naïve confidence in human progress. They have also shown conclusively that the despotic and totalitarian resort to violence and terror as solutions to historical injustice are counsels of despair. Modern secular humanists have wanted to locate the root of the human dilemma in social institutions they could actively reform and in cultural prejudices they could eventually correct. However, candid historical reflection reveals that the sources of human alienation and ideology cannot be eliminated by social engineering. There is no exclusively human solution to the problem of moral evil and death. Human power is always checked by human impotence; human achievement by human failure; human freedom and development by demoralizing captivity and decline. Human existence is, and always has been, a tangled knot of greatness and wretchedness.[2]

This cautionary skepticism about secular ideologies does not imply a leveling moral equivalence among human societies. Although all political communities are imperfect, there are significant differences in their scale of imperfection. The sobering lesson of the twentieth century is that the blatantly utopian social projects often produced the most terrible results: the refusal of civil liberties in the name of freedom; the denial of the rule of law in the name of justice; the expropriation of property in the name of collective harmony; the slaughter of the innocent in the name of permanent peace.[3]

Although the alluring promises of modernity have been extravagant, modern political theory has not been lacking in insight. To take three examples of failed ideologies that still merit our critical attention. Post revolutionary conservative thought provides a needed corrective to historical optimism. While a return to the world of the past is impossible, inordinate attention to an unknowable future is invariably shallow. Memory remains the faculty of human depth. The best way to prepare for the demands of the future is to understand the complexity of the past, which as Faulkner reminds us, is never dead; it is not even past.[4]

Secular modernity beginning with Descartes has wanted to discredit the roman trinity (religion, tradition, and authority) as sources of historical stability and wisdom. But Arendt has argued that the revolutionary tradition needs to forego this cultural arrogance. We need to think together and in tension what the revolutionary ideologues have taught us to oppose: tradition and innovation; authority and liberty; spiritual faith and worldly devotion; historical permanence and political creativity.[5]

The great merit of conservative thinking since the time of Aristophanes, has been its critical stance towards the fashionable arrogance of the "enlightened."

There is considerable diversity within the European liberal tradition. For this reason, it is essential to distinguish between liberalism as an economic and political ideology, devoted to laissez faire and minimal government, and the enduring achievements of the broader liberal tradition: the rule of law and the equality of citizens under the law; legally recognized civil liberties; religious toleration and freedom of worship and conscience; limited constitutional government based on a balance of powers and an independent judiciary; the economic benefits of free enterprise and free commercial exchange; the political importance of voluntary associations within a strong civil society; the ideal of responsible personal freedom or ordered liberty. Political liberalism has rightly been critical of the Jacobin excesses in revolutionary France and the Bolshevik reliance on despotism and terror in the Soviet Union and Eastern Europe.[6]

Nor can conservatives and liberals afford to ignore the challenge of Marxism. "Although the earthly ideal of Socialism-Communism has collapsed, the problems it purported to solve remain: the brazen use of social advantage and the inordinate power of money, which often direct the very course of events. And if the global lesson of the twentieth century does not serve as a healing inoculation, then the vast red whirlwind may repeat itself in entirety."[7] Marx forced western governments and societies to focus their attention on the social question, the scandalous coexistence of wealth and deprivation both within and between nation states. Marx highlighted the systemic abuses of capitalism and unmasked the fictional anthropology used to justify economic liberalism. He rightly emphasized human historicity and sociality and the systemic impact of economic decisions on the cohesiveness of capitalist societies.

Marx's critique of capitalism was weakened by deterministic prejudices; his secular humanism was simultaneously inflated and leveling, and his solution to the riddle of history licensed violence and terror in the service of utopian dreams. The collapse of the Soviet Union and the eclipse of Marxism as a revolutionary doctrine, however, will be a mixed blessing unless the West draws the appropriate lessons from their precipitous rise and decline.[8]

The civic humanism of the republican tradition should not become ideological in its own right. It is essential to distinguish between the meaningful political engagement of citizens and the myth of universal and total participation. In modern societies, political liberty is forced to compete with a multiplicity of goods that are also worthwhile: the personal quest for individual authenticity; the affirmation of ordinary life, which celebrates marriage, the blessings of the family, and a broad range of significant public callings; the aspiration to human benevolence on a global scale; economic prosperity and the attendant reduction of human suffering; the protection of human rights both at home and abroad.[9]

Neither of the most influential modern cultural traditions, neither the Enlightenment nor Romanticism, provides an adequate account of the richness of modern existence. The Enlightenment's anti-political prejudices have tended to dominate the public realm; atomistic utilitarianism, in particular, has reduced the traditional ideal of the common good to a formless aggregate of private satisfactions. Romantic expressivist prejudices, with their emphasis on private happiness, are extremely influential in our personal relationships and in the prevailing conceptions of marriage and the family. When romantic aspirations for autonomy penetrate the political sphere, they tend to coalesce around the demand for unlimited freedom, the direct engagement of all citizens in determining every aspect of their personal and public lives.

Charles Taylor is masterful in deflating the Enlightenment's ontological prejudices and the Romantic counter illusions they tend to provoke, while accepting the important contributions these umbrella traditions have made to creating the modern identity. His defense of moral and cultural pluralism, to a diversity of human goods and to a variety of moral sources, is combined with an explicit critique of totalizing ideologies.

> What should have died along with communism is ideology, the belief that modern societies can be run on a single principle, whether that of the general will (political romanticism) or free market allocation (economic liberalism). Governing a contemporary society is continually recreating a balance between requirements that tend to undercut each other.[10]

For Taylor, these competing institutional requirements include: market allocations in economics; state planning for recurrent public goods like security, education, public health, distributive and criminal justice; adequate collective provision for the social needs of the populace, particularly the young, the elderly, and the disabled; a secure defense of individual rights and personal liberties; credible opportunities for cooperative action by an informed and responsible citizenry.

Taylor insists that contemporary civic republicanism should not seek a return to the classical *polis*. Because of their severe restrictions on citizenship and their dependence on a martial imperial culture, the ancient republics are unsuitable models for existing democratic societies. What should be critically retrieved from the civic humanist tradition is the important good of republican citizenship, of meaningful participation in democratic self-government. While that participation is necessarily partial and selective for most democratic citizens, it is an intrinsic good that must be institutionally and culturally strengthened to offset the democratic individualism Tocqueville properly feared.

Taylor also affirms the civic republican emphasis on patriotism, the shared love of one's country, its institutions and history that unites the citizens of a free society.[11] This is not an uncritical patriotism, but a reflective loyalty to the imperfect institutions and practices that have historically shaped our minds and hearts. Given the religious and moral pluralism of the West, and the domination of our public culture by liberal individualism, critical patriotism has lost none of its relevance. Liberal assurances to the contrary, enlightened self-interest is not the animating spirit of a responsible society. In fact, free societies, far more than their despotic antagonists, require voluntary sacrifice and civic discipline from their citizens, a readiness to put the public good before their private happiness. Civic virtue is particularly needed in periods of public adversity and economic contraction, or when the nation must respond to long-standing injustices and to the complex needs of future generations.[12]

Although public liberty is indispensable, its political significance today is ambiguous. Unless it is complemented by a strong commitment to the common good, by a shared sense of justice and collective responsibility, the spirited exercise of political freedom may heighten existing partisanship and intensify group fragmentation. To prevent this divisive effect, we need to distinguish two opposing models of citizen participation.

The adversarial pressure group model, centered on partisan loyalties, ideological programs and aggressive self interest, treats political activity as the conduct of war by nonviolent means. The power of special interest lobbying, the reliance on negative and distorted advertising, and the conduct of government as an exercise in public relations that this model supports, have made democratic politics in the United States a dismal and dispiriting spectacle.

The prevalence of competitive adversarial politics has weakened an alternative approach to democratic governance, the formation of coalescing majorities around responsible and farsighted policies aimed at critical national and global concerns. The influence of single issue pressure groups has made coalition building increasingly difficult. It has impeded the emergence of a bipartisan, multilateral foreign policy; in domestic affairs, it has prevented the achievement of fiscal justice, comprehensive health care reform, environmental protection, the restoration of American cities, and the creation of a balanced and responsible safety net.

The acute danger of group fragmentation cannot be remedied by public liberty alone. In fact, it will be exacerbated by civic participation modeled on adversarial conflict. The greatest need of modern liberal democracies is to establish and revitalize meaningful centers of civic identity and participation (political parties, voluntary public associations, municipal institutions, regional, national and global movements for economic and environmental justice) committed to the practice of collaborative action for the public good. A newly collaborative and participatory politics would constitute a revival of civic republicanism, for to paraphrase Tocqueville, we need fresh and original political thinking for an interconnected world.[13]

The novelty of our situation does not require us to confront it as orphans deprived of our ancestral inheritance. While our political traditions are flawed, they remain important sources of insight and guidance. Because these traditions are fallible we cannot adopt them uncritically; because they connect us to the past, we shouldn't cavalierly abandon them. Taylor's project of critical retrieval provides a model of the balanced approach we require. Taylor argues for the continuing relevance of two important pre-modern traditions, the civic republican tradition of public liberty and the Aristotelian tradition of the common good. He seeks to articulate what these ancient goods really are and why they remain of enduring political importance. But he also acknowledges skeptical challenges to their validity, as well as the institutional and cultural obstacles they face in regaining acceptance. Taylor's hermeneutics of retrieval is a valuable counter weight to the hermeneutics of suspicion, the dominant interpretive stance in our partisan adversarial culture.[14]

These hermeneutical stances are potentially complementary. Appeals to tradition, authority and custom continue to be used in defense of illegitimate practices and institutions. There is no human principle, however sound, that is not subject to distorted application. But the hermeneutics of suspicion is misguided if it bases its critique of the present on a wholesale emancipation from the past. All significant critique draws on one part of our cultural inheritance to oppose the limitations of another. As Paul Ricoeur ironically reminds us, the revolutionary ideal of liberation from the *Ancien Regime* is actually rooted in the central episodes of the biblical tradition: the exodus of the Jews from Egypt and Jesus' deliverance from death through his resurrection.

I agree with Ricoeur that "nothing is more necessary today than to renounce the arrogance of critique and to carry out with patience and humility the endless work of distancing and renewing our historical substance."[15] This is the interpretive stance I have tried to adopt in assessing Arendt's challenge to "our tradition of political thought." Her critical insights have transformed my reading of classical and modern texts and authors. Although I am permanently in Arendt's debt, I find more continuity and less rupture than she does between the needs of the present and the resources of the tradition. In my judgment, the tradition she criticizes has lost its authority, its power to command our assent and allegiance, but not its practical relevance.

In introducing this book, I compared Arendt's challenge to our political traditions to Nietzsche's genealogy of morals and Heidegger's deconstruction of western metaphysics. All of these authors claim to identify a pre-Platonic period of integrity before politics, morality, and ontology underwent a systemic inversion. In Arendt's case, it is the politics of Periclean Athens that serves as the primary benchmark by which all later political thinking is measured. I say 'primary' because we have identified different strands in Arendt's political thought, the expressivist and the communicative, that place radically different emphases on the heroic quest for worldly immortality.[16] Because of grave reservations about Pericles' model of civic greatness, I have been unwilling to use it as a normative measure in judging the successive political traditions. Both Plato and Aristotle, for example, preserve classical standards of political excellence, *arete*, without subscribing to the injustices of Periclean imperialism. If we are to retrieve civic republicanism in a form appropriate to our time, we must be more critical than Arendt about the limitations of the ancient republics.

THE OLD AND THE NEW

Many of the goods to which we moderns are devoted are deeply traditional: friendship, patriotism, and distributive justice, among others.[17] Many of the obligations we recognize have their sources in the distant past: respect for parents, the education of children, and the duties of citizenship. At the same time, there are distinctively contemporary concerns that would have perplexed our classical ancestors.

Both the Greeks and the Jews placed the primary emphasis on the moral community, the Greek *polis*, or the chosen people of Israel. By contrast, modern ethical consciousness is focused on the individual. Each person is a bearer of rights that must be respected by the state, the various groups in civil society, and other private individuals. In matters of conscience and worship, the integrity of the individual must be honored, and in the private realm of negative liberty each person's right to authentic self-expression must be protected. Given this focus on personal autonomy, it is understandable that the problem of community in its multiple guises has recently come to the fore.[18]

Aristotle, following Greek custom, drew a sharp distinction between merely living and living well. Slaves, manual workers, all those confined to the classical household were unable to lead the good life. Only the male citizens, who escaped the domestic constraints of necessity and utility, enjoyed the leisure and liberty required for virtuous activity. Ordinary life was a necessary means to the good life, not an end in itself. But the "affirmation of ordinary life" is a central part of the modern identity. We place an extremely high value on marriage and the family, on sexual intimacy and personal relationships; and our self-respect depends heavily on having a job, earning a living, supporting a family, making a contribution to national wealth and prosperity.[19]

In evident tension with modern individualism is the steady expansion in the scope of our moral concern. We are embarrassed by western colonialism and imperialism; we insist on sexual and racial equality throughout the world; we monitor the protection of human rights on a universal scale; we are expected to respond to human suffering, wherever it occurs, with disaster relief and financial assistance.

We have a renewed sensitivity to natural and moral ecology. It is no longer acceptable to think, as the early moderns did, of the earth, the air, the water, the sky as meaningless collections of matter for us to manipulate at will. The high price we have paid for reckless economic development and sustained social neglect has forced us to recognize the fragility of the natural systems and cultural communities on which we and future generations depend.

We have also been forced to think of economic life, of capital, production, investment, finance, trade, consumption, labor and profits on a global and intensely competitive scale. The volatility of the global economy, the rapid and unregulated movement of capital, the continuous displacement of labor, have profound implications for international order and peace; their troubling tendency to aggravate existing inequalities raises major questions of distributive justice and international solidarity.[20]

Two contradictory trends appear to be accelerating simultaneously: on the one hand, an unprecedented deference to the "autonomous individual"; on the other, an unprecedented expansion in the scope of our moral concern. The first trend leads to the libertarian emphasis on individual self-reliance, on the absolute right to be left alone to do our own thing. The second trend is based on profound recognition of the depth and complexity of human interdependence. The libertarian trend relies on an atomistic conception of the individual, on the disengaged model of rational subjectivity that emerged with enlightenment science. The ecological trend perceives the individual person as inherently belonging to natural and cultural networks whose internal well being is essential to personal freedom and flourishing. The cultural traditions of Athens and Jerusalem clearly favor an anthropology of "situated subjectivity" and a politics of human interdependence. The modern liberal tradition, with its Kantian and Utilitarian moral pictures, as well as its expressivist and Nietzschean variations, tends to pull in the opposing direction.

The political and cultural stakes are high in this struggle of opposing moral ontologies. If we collectively abandon or cease really to believe in the theistic and philosophical moral sources that originally defined the West, will we be able to sustain the universal benevolence, the global solidarity, the respect for human rights, the devotion to international justice to which we are nominally committed. Ethically speaking, we are, perhaps, already living well beyond our means.[21]

The danger of moral bankruptcy does not mean that we should retreat to the classical *polis* or to the original Christian community in Jerusalem. Nor does it mean that the enduring insights of modernity and post-modernity should be rejected. Despite the contradictions that presently confront us, there is no escaping history, no way of leaping out of the troubled societies to which we belong. But in what spirit should we belong to the tangled knot of the contemporary world?

Neither passive acceptance nor radical refusal seem justified. The civic stance I want to defend is the way of critical belonging. This is the way Socrates belonged to the Athenian *polis*, the way Jesus belonged to the covenant community of Abraham and Moses, the way Augustine belonged to the Roman Empire, the way Tocqueville responded to the emerging democratic age. It is also the way Arendt participated in the American republic that had offered her shelter and citizenship.[22]

What are the cultural responsibilities entailed by such critical belonging? We need to create local, national, and global communities of inquiry, "big enough to be at home in the old and the new, painstaking enough to work out one by one the transitions to be make, strong enough to refuse half measures and insist on complete solutions even though it has to wait."[23] Such critical appropriation is what the great integrative philosophers, Aristotle, Aquinas and Hegel did so effectively. Our task is especially difficult for our uneven cultural inheritance is considerably richer and more complex than theirs. As our dialogue with Arendt has shown, the tradition we inherit includes: the politics and philosophy of ancient Greece; the law and the prophets of traditional Judaism; the trinitarian gospel of Christianity; the imperial appropriation of an originally pacifist faith; the revolutionary dynamism of modern science and technology; the correlative expansion of global capitalism; romantic self-exploration and the politics of the heart; the imperial assumptions of economics; the utopian hopes of Promethean humanism; the gradual emergence of a fragmented global society. This complex western inheritance remains alive whether we like it or not. Our common task as educators is to appraise with wisdom and patience our turbulent history. Critical appraisal and transmission of the past are the primary cultural obligations of a civilized community.

THE DISCONTENTS OF LIBERAL DEMOCRACY

Let us shift our attention from the legacy of history to the concerns of the present and future. While the age of catastrophe that shaped Arendt's thinking is over, so is the golden age of liberal capitalism. As we enter the third millennium, we need once again a "new science of politics," this time for an emerging global society. In critically assessing the contemporary world, three questions shall focus our inquiry: What are the signs of growing discontent with the project of liberal democracy? What are the threats to justice and ordered liberty posed by globalization? What is the true state of American democracy today?[24]

A CRISIS OF LEGITIMACY

A troubling irony has marked international politics since the collapse of the Soviet Union and the end of the Cold War. As global support for democratic institutions and civil liberties has increased, so has growing discontent, especially in the United States, with the state of liberal democracy. The spirited critique of liberal society, liberal political and economic theory, and of liberal democratic culture have come from numerous quarters: from civic republicans like Michael Sandel; communitarian thinkers like Robert Bellah; critics of American capitalism like Noam Chomsky; neo-Nietzscheans inspired by Michel Foucault; critical social theorists like Jurgen Habermas; historically minded Aristotelians like Alasdair MacIntyre; even political conservatives like George Will.

Drawing on these critical sources as well as his own historical analysis, Charles Taylor has argued that modern democratic societies, particularly in the United States, are faced with a growing crisis of legitimacy. Taylor points to disturbing signs that indicate these societies have lost the allegiance and cooperation of their citizens, particularly their younger and poorer members.[25]

To what signs of disaffection is Taylor referring? Very high rates of criminality and imprisonment; widespread drug and alcohol abuse; frequent divorce, irresponsible parenting, the neglect of children and the elderly poor; a serious decline in public education, evidenced by widespread illiteracy, inadequate job skills, and numerous threats to physical security in the schools; a staggering public debt that distorts the government's fiscal policies and aggravates the burdens of future generations; an irresponsible and profit driven fourth estate (the media actively promote a scandal-seeking, celebrity driven politics); the disgrace of contemporary electoral campaigns, dominated by unlimited money, misleading advertising, the influence of organized interest groups and demoralizing levels of voter participation and engagement; the deepening conflict between a global economy based on continuous growth and the seemingly incompatible demands of a sustainable natural and social environment. The unraveling of civil society (weaker families, neighborhoods, churches, and schools) is disturbing in its own right. But the recurrent needs these communities no longer satisfy threaten to create a demand overload on governmental institutions, while public confidence in government is historically low and ideological partisanship unusually high. The accelerating economic and educational inequality between the affluent and the poor, coupled with the flight from responsible citizenship on the part of the rich and powerful, compromise democratic solidarity just when the safety net is fraying or being deliberately shredded by the Republican right.

This broad-based critique of liberal societies, coupled with growing public unease about emerging national and global realities, has made democratic legitimacy and the discontent and alienation of democratic citizens major concerns of contemporary political thought.[26]

THE PROMISE AND PERILS OF GLOBALIZATION

In economic and political affairs, the whole earth has become the principal unit of interaction. Though what we call "globalization" constitutes a new stage in human history, its occurrence is not a sudden and unexpected event. Several powerful currents in modernity have converged to bring it about. These converging forces include: the productive alliance of scientific research and applied technology; the economic and political commitment to constant technological innovation; the electronic and digital revolution that accelerates the transmission of ideas and information; rapid and reliable international transportation that facilitates the movement of people and products; the expansive nature of capitalism which constantly seeks profitable markets for investment and trade across national boundaries; the economic and demographic imbalance between the developed and developing countries which provokes continuous immigration and labor instability.

Globalization means that space and time, national frontiers and deeply entrenched cultural traditions are no longer effective barriers to the movement of human beings, the goods they produce, the institutions they adopt, and the cultural beliefs and values that inform their living together. Globalization also means that the technological and economic dynamism of modernity has outpaced its political inventiveness. While the nation state, the characteristic form of modern government, has not disappeared, its vaunted claims to autonomy and sovereignty have lost credibility. The great majority of nations no longer exercise effective control over their economic destinies. The end of the cold war and the collapse of the socialist trading bloc have completed the formation of a single world economy that stretches from Seoul to Seattle, from Shanghai to Sao Paulo, from Pittsburgh to Pretoria.

Like the industrial capitalism which preceded it, globalization is marked by internal contradictions. The human world has become more interdependent, but some continents and regions have grown increasingly isolated. Global air travel brings tourists and traders across oceans and mountains, but it also transports terrorists and instruments of violence. The internet permits nearly instantaneous communication, but it also spreads divisive rumors and dangerous lies. Many of the rich countries grow richer as poor countries grow poorer, and the scandal of the social question assumes global dimensions. We have a dynamic world economy without a governing political authority, an expanding population that strains human and natural resources, and an innovative technology that threatens the economic security of workers and the obsolescence of its most recent achievements.

In my judgment, we find ourselves in a situation analogous to Tocqueville's nearly two hundred years ago. He believed that the triumph of democracy as a governing principle in human affairs was irreversible. What remained to be determined by human reflection and choice, however, was whether the emerging democratic societies would be despotic or free. By critically distinguishing the sources of democratic despotism from those of ordered liberty, Tocqueville contributed immeasurably to the preservation of human freedom. In the twenty first century, we shall live in a global international order whether we want to or not. What remains to be determined by our reflection and choice, is whether the global society we are creating will be just or oppressive. That is, perhaps, the great unresolved political question of our time.[27]

AMERICAN DEMOCRACY REVISITED

One of the most salient accounts of the present political situation in the United States is offered by William Galston, a fellow at the Brookings Institution and a former advisor to President Clinton.[28] Galston's analysis is sensitive to both the critique of democratic legitimacy and the pervasive effects of globalization. He believes that we stand at a critical turning point in American political theory and practice. The present crisis in legitimacy has partly arisen because a transformative period in American public life has come to an end. This impressive period of political creativity is closely associated with the presidencies of the two Roosevelts, Theodore and Franklin.

The closing decades of the nineteenth century and the opening decades of the twentieth were marked by progressive political thinking in the United States. In the "gilded age" context of unregulated capitalism and the monopoly of economic and political power by industrial interests, critical economic reforms, including antitrust and labor legislation and the graduated income tax, as well as the beginning of national environmental policy were enacted during the administrations of Theodore Roosevelt and Woodrow Wilson. Franklin Roosevelt's New Deal and Lyndon Johnson's Great Society initiatives dramatically expanded these progressive public policies. Most of the environmental and social welfare legislation of the United States (social security, unemployment insurance, aid to dependent children, worker's compensation, Medicare, Medicaid, and the creation of the federal regulatory agencies) derive from this period of political activism and pragmatic social reform.

The progressive tide began to turn, however, in the mid-1960s when passionate divisions about the war in Vietnam destroyed Roosevelt's New Deal coalition, and Lyndon Johnson's commitment to "guns and butter" created inflationary pressures on the American economy. In 1964, the Republican party nominated Barry Goldwater, an outspoken political conservative, for president. Johnson's crushing defeat of Goldwater created political majorities for passing important civil rights legislation, but it also cost the Democrats political control over the solid south. During the next forty years, in a reversal of historic proportions, the Republicans replaced the Democrats as the majority party in the southern United States. This dramatic shift in allegiance played a major role in the GOP's electoral successes in both presidential and congressional campaigns after 1968.

The national movement for civil rights, the demoralizing defeat in Vietnam, the counter-cultural excesses of the sixties and seventies, the weakening of the American labor movement, the economic ascendancy of Germany, Japan and then China, the demographic shift to the sunbelt, and the oil shocks and hyper-inflation of the 1970s effectively converged to end the progressive era. One of Goldwater's ardent supporters, Ronald Reagan, won two presidential terms in the 1980s by appealing to wounded national pride and by escalating the conservative critique of the federal government's legislative and regulatory agenda. Reagan argued, using the glib jargon of modern advertising, that "the federal government is the principal source of our problems, rather than the solution to our unmet needs." Reagan promulgated a new conservative orthodoxy that was disproportionately anti-government and pro-market in its public stance. In principle, he rejected the mixed economy of the New Deal, though in practice, he was unable to check the growth of federal programs. Reagan's neoconservative agenda did move the United States rightward, however, and put the proponents of social and economic justice on the defensive.[29]

The bitter political stalemate in Washington since Reagan's presidency has been between those who want to refine and extend the progressive legacy of the Roosevelt era (the clear majority within the national Democratic party) and those who want to weaken or abolish the core elements of the moderate welfare state (the conservative majority among the Republicans). Yet even among liberal theorists like Galston, there is an active search for a progressive policy agenda that is less bureaucratic, less regulatory, less dependent on massive federal programs, and more open to experimental initiatives by state and local governments and the voluntary associations of civil society. Galston argues that a progressive majority in the twenty first century will need to address three powerful sources of public discontent: economic anxiety, cultural fragmentation (the loss of a cohesive civic community), and the decline of public confidence in our major democratic institutions.[30]

Contemporary economic anxiety in the United States has three related aspects: economic inequality, economic insecurity, the concentration of economic power. At the root of national economic anxiety is an historic transformation in both the global and the American economy. The United States is structurally changing from an industrial mass production economy, based largely on unskilled labor, to a global information economy based on continuous technological innovation, the global movement of capital, knowledge and jobs, and the constant need to upgrade economic skills for a highly competitive labor market. The technological revolution, the competitive challenge of globalization, and heightened sensitivity to the ecological dangers of unregulated growth have created a nest of new problems for progressive policy makers and planners.

Inequality

During the post-war boom (1945-1972), which Eric Hobsbawm has called the golden age of capitalism, the fruits of American prosperity were broadly shared.[31] The rising tide of the mixed economy lifted all boats, as inequalities of wealth and income in the United States measurably diminished. A greatly improved standard of living, based on sustained economic growth, nearly full employment, and rising productivity became widely available to the American middle class.

During the last four decades, however, since the oil shocks of 1973 and the heightened competitiveness of the global market, the incomes of the majority of American citizens stagnated or fell, while dramatic gains in wealth were enjoyed by a very small minority. As America again became a more stratified society, the post war political consensus collapsed, causing a serious decline in civic solidarity. Those at the peak of the economic pyramid prospered as never before, while the middle class, despite the massive entry of women into the labor force, became financially squeezed. With growing political opposition to the welfare state and the radical restructuring of the economy, the poor and unskilled fell further behind. A new underclass emerged in the nation's cities whose economic and social plight was widely regarded as insoluble. The most troubling dynamic was that economic and social inequalities regularly translated into significant disparities in educational achievement. In the global economy these disparities of competence led to restricted economic opportunity, crippling social pathology, and political withdrawal among those citizens most in need of public support. While the condition of the elderly improved, due to effective political organization, the inner city and rural poor clearly lost ground. Even worse, they lost a national political constituency committed to social justice for the least advantaged Americans.[32]

Insecurity

The global information society shatters the traditional expectations of American workers. In the older industrial economy, workers could often expect to have one career and one employer for their whole working life. There were periods of cyclical unemployment corresponding to declines in the business cycle, but the combined efforts of business, government, organized labor and supportive neighbors and family provided the majority of workers with significant economic security.

In the new global economy that security has largely disappeared. Automation results in a permanent loss of manufacturing jobs. Repeated "downsizing," constant mergers and acquisitions, unexpected plant closings, the pressure of international competition, and the absence of employer loyalty have both blue and white collar workers understandably anxious about the future. As the power of organized labor has declined, employers seek regularly to reduce the benefits they guarantee their workers, often resorting to temporary contractual relations without any benefits at all.

Despite the sustained economic growth of the nineties, high levels of economic insecurity threaten individual workers, their families and neighborhoods, and whole regions of the country like the rust belts of the north and midwest. The new international division of labor has meant structural as well as cyclical unemployment and a major shift in the balance of power between capital and labor. This imbalance is further magnified under republican governments ideologically committed to market fundamentalism and financially dependent on corporate wealth.[33]

Power

The third source of anxiety is concentrated and unchecked economic power. Because of globalization, individual nations and governments have lost a substantial measure of control over their economic destinies. Multi-national corporations often operate beyond the effective reach of regulatory power. But the deeper sources of change include the diffusion of technological innovation, the unregulated flow of capital and investment, and a competitive global market in labor, information, goods, and services. These momentous changes have weakened existing political authority while allowing concentrated economic power to grow unchecked.[34]

We find ourselves in a political situation analogous to that of the late nineteenth century. Responding to the leadership of progressive reformers, national governments then began to assert their authority over the unregulated power of the trusts. Government ceased to be the protective ally of the powerful and became a voice for the weak and disadvantaged. This shift of political priorities was later consolidated under the New Deal and the Great Society. The collapse of the New Deal coalition, however, meant the end of the progressive era. What are the prospects for a new progressive coalition geared to the realities of our time? The creation of a progressive agenda today faces formidable obstacles. At a time when governments are distrusted and 'politics' is a dirty word, we need to articulate transnational norms of conduct and to strengthen global institutions capable of asserting democratic authority over existing concentrations of economic power. Despite the assurances of neo-liberal ideologues, competitive market forces, even when they operate fairly, are unreliable guarantors of economic and political justice.

As public demonstrations against the IMF, the World Bank, Wall Street and the WTO indicate, there is growing recognition of this urgent international need, but a noticeable lack of agreement about what these binding norms and institutions should be like, and to whom they should be politically accountable. Public protests, while dramatic and newsworthy, are of limited practical value. They highlight the problems in the global economy: the need for workers' rights and equitable labor standards, the scandal of national and global inequality, the serious dangers to the world environment, and the dissolving of responsible bonds both within and between nations. But they cannot provide wise and effective solutions to the serious dilemmas they publicize. That is an international political responsibility that clearly depends on an informed north-south dialogue and on significant reform of the global institutions that have become the lightning rods of economic unrest.

These three sources of economic anxiety are interdependent. Inequalities of wealth, power, and political influence are mutually reinforcing. Powerful interest groups use money, lobbyists, and organizational resources to influence government officials who then shape public policies and rules that disproportionately advantage the already well off. The benefits and burdens of national life are unfairly distributed. Recognizing these systemic inequities but uncertain how to correct them, the majority of citizens become disaffected and withdraw from the political struggle. Pervasive alienation from "politics as usual" prevents the majority from concerted action on their own behalf. In this way a vicious cycle emerges perpetuating systemic injustice and deepening democratic discontent.[35]

The Decline of Civil Society

A second important source of democratic disquiet is the decline in America's civil society.[36] The term "civil society" refers to the broad range of voluntary institutions and public associations that mediate between individual citizens and governmental agencies and the competitive marketplace. A healthy democratic culture requires an effective civil society because representative government on a national scale is typically remote and bureaucratic, and economic markets are mercilessly driven by the imperative of maximizing profit. Since the major players in the global market are even more remote and less accountable than government officials, the political contributions of civil society are especially important today.

Tocqueville credited civil society, which he called "independent secondary powers" with three major contributions to democratic liberty.[37] They check concentrations of political and economic power; they help to secure and extend individual rights; they provide public forums for civic education, where ordinary citizens learn the arts of cooperative action and the expression of political dissent. As independent centers of democratic power, they serve to counteract the hegemonic tendencies of both government and the market.

Important examples include: strong and influential families, neighborhood associations, synagogues, mosques and churches, schools and universities, a free and responsible press, political parties, labor unions, charitable foundations, a complex array of voluntary associations, religious, moral, intellectual, cultural, and economic. These intermediate associations play an indispensable role in creating an informed and engaged democratic citizenry. Their participatory *ethos* checks the democratic tendency to narrow self-interest and the democratic passion for material prosperity and comfort. They provide critical arenas of social trust and collective action where citizens learn to accommodate differences of interest, opinion, and judgment. It is within civil society that ordinary men and women become responsible citizens, that they learn to know, love, and act for the common world.

Not only do these "grammar schools of liberty" cultivate the arts and virtues of citizenship, drawing individuals out of their private homes and into the public realm, but they also create common sites for pursuing important goods that are neither political nor economic in nature: familial love, mutual friendship, disinterested knowledge, the performance and enjoyment of the arts, religious worship, the free exchange of ideas and opinions on every subject of human concern.

Galston agrees with Robert Putnam and Charles Taylor that American civil society, the principal source of American civic education, is showing serious signs of decline: families are weaker and the marital bond more fragile; neighborhoods are less cohesive and therefore less secure; schools provide deeply unequal educations; the university's moral and civic authority has eroded; the public media have become superficial and profit driven; labor unions, churches, political parties, traditional civic associations are rapidly declining in membership and influence. What Tocqueville called the vice of "democratic individualism" is becoming widespread. "Private life in democratic times is so busy, so excited, so filled with wishes and work that hardly any energy or leisure remains to each individual for public life."[38]

As the institutions of civil society weaken, democratic citizens feel isolated from and indifferent to the national community. The focus of their attention turns inward. They live within the important but narrow circle of self, family, and friends; they mistakenly think and act as though their individual destinies were disconnected from their fellow citizens and the rest of humankind. Isolated individuals lacking a clear sense of worldly realities and power are easily manipulated by propaganda and public relations. When their interest is drawn to politics, it is personal scandal, collective scapegoating or orchestrated resentment that normally captures their attention and concern.

Why has the cohesiveness of civil society declined in the last thirty years? Political conservatives blame the federal government for usurping the social service functions of families, neighborhoods, churches, and private charities. Liberals and progressives argue that severe economic inequities are incompatible with active civic participation. Communitarians believe that a rights based individualism has eroded the American spirit of civic responsibility and national solidarity. Robert Putnam in his excellent study of American communal decline, *Bowling Alone*, identifies four principal reasons for civic disengagement: the pressures of time and money, particularly in families where both parents work; individual mobility and suburban sprawl; the power of television and the electronic media (television privatizes individual leisure and promotes a demoralizing image of the citizen as private consumer); the generational shift from the "long civic generation" (1920-2000) that fought World War II to their disaffected children and grandchildren who have steadily eroded America's "social capital." Of particular note is the striking emergence in the United States of "identity politics" where the citizen's primary allegiance is not to the national political community but to one's race, gender, or ethnic group, or to the single public issue or concern that the individual feels strongly about.[39]

There is a measure of truth in these partial explanations, for the weakening of America's civil society is heavily over determined. What requires closer scrutiny, however, is the important correlation between this decline in civic engagement and the rise in political alienation.

The Erosion of Political Authority

In the civic republican vision, politics, the symbol of the commonweal, enjoyed directive authority over economics, the symbol of self-interested activity. Today, American politics is heavily dominated by economic interests and market oriented models. The conduct of government increasingly resembles commercial activity, as bargaining, public relations, and partisan advocacy

DISCONTENTS AND CONTINUING RELEVANCE 255

become pervasive. Individual citizens, voluntary associations and elected officials regularly conceive of political activity as a way to advance their private concerns. Periodic references to the common good or the general welfare become largely ceremonial and vacuous. The principles and precepts of republican democracy become disconnected from existing political practice.

In this dispiriting atmosphere, the wealthiest and best organized economic interests become the dominant influence on government. Economic power readily translates into political power. Public officials become heavily dependent on wealthy individuals, business corporations, labor unions, and political action committees to defray the rising costs of their electoral campaigns. Lobbyists, the professional advocates for well-organized interest groups, have become the pivotal intermediaries in American politics, devising electoral strategies and shaping public policy and legislation. Concentrated corporate wealth and special interests of every kind employ lobbyists, lawyers, public relations and media experts, even hired intellectuals and ideological think tanks to advance their political agenda. There is no shortage of public activity, but it is almost entirely self-interested.[40]

The loss of governmental independence and impartiality has steadily eroded the substance of our democratic faith. The majority of Americans now believe that the people are governed by their elected representatives for the benefit of an influential minority. While professional lobbyists actively promote the economic interests of their clients, partisan pleading is not restricted to business and labor. The gun lobby, the religious right, and various pressure groups on the political left have political influence wholly disproportionate to their electoral strength. The growing conviction that the government serves the interests of the powerful and well-organized has had a demoralizing effect on American democracy. It has gravely weakened public confidence in government, generated contempt for public officials and institutions, and significantly reduced the political engagement of ordinary citizens.

The signs of political alienation are everywhere: declining levels of voter participation; reduced attention to and knowledge of world affairs; the political indifference and disaffection of the young; the reluctance of serious citizens to enter public life; the restriction of political debate to the formulaic chatter of journalists and entertainers; the pernicious influence of the sensationalist media in shaping political perceptions and judgments; the absence of honest public discussion about taxes, regulations and government services; the deepening mood of political impotence and despair.

Public cynicism about politics and pervasive distrust of government are harmful to American democracy. They strengthen democratic individualism, lessen civic participation, increase the influence of the wealthy and powerful, and diminish the prospects for significant economic and political reform. Two centuries after its creation the great American experiment in democratic self-government is in serious trouble.

TOWARD A NEW PROGRESSIVE AGENDA

The most powerful forces at work today are anti-political. Their dominance of the public realm helps explain the erosion of political authority and the sad state of civic engagement and education. If government is invariably the servant of economic power, as Marx asserted, it would be foolish to rely on its commitment to significant reform. The historical record provides substantial, but not unqualified, support for Marx's pessimism. As Robert Putnam reminds us, the original progressive movement actually emerged during the Gilded Age when the discontents of American democracy were equally troubling. At that time, the nation confronted the concentration of economic and political power that defined industrial capitalism. The goal of progressive reform was to break that corrupting alliance and to correct the inequities it had created. At stake in the progressive challenge to monopoly power was the appropriate relation between economics and politics. Was industrial capitalism to dominate American democracy, or was a reformed and strengthened democracy to regulate and restrain American capitalism?[41]

I believe that globalization has created a comparable challenge for democracy today. We are experiencing new sources of inequality, insecurity, and monopoly power while governments are either allied with global capital or fragmented and ineffective in resisting its hegemony. The time is ripe for new progressive initiatives at both the theoretical and practical level. A revitalized progressive movement must understand and accept the historic lessons of the twentieth century. We don't need to revive the discredited ideologies of Marxism and liberalism. Neither the socialist reliance on the centralized state nor liberal idolatry of the market can adequately address the complex challenges of our time. But the critique of discredited ideologies is never enough; to be effective and credible, today's progressive movement must develop a theoretical framework and a policy agenda attuned to the realities of the global society. Three concerns seem particularly urgent: the political challenge of globalization, a newly articulated federalism, and the recreation of civic community.

The integration of the global economy and the competitiveness of the global market require democratic theorists to rethink the relationship between economic and political power. Many of the political institutions shaped by modernity have been subverted by global capitalism. Most national governments can no longer control the economic health of their countries.

In a repeat of the gilded age, democratic politics has lost its effective authority over economics. If we are to create appropriate political institutions for the global economy, we will need new forms of democratic authority, new structures of international law, and new patterns of transnational cooperation capable of regulating global commerce without stifling its wealth creating potential. We will need to develop an international analogue to the mixed economy that emerged during the progressive era. The mixed economy combines free enterprise and commerce with state regulation and oversight, while making collective provision for public goods and social needs. As Charles Taylor argued, mixed economies seek to create a balance between economic and political requirements that tend to undercut each other. Mobilizing international support for such experiments and securing democratic acceptance of new institutions will be exceedingly difficult in an era when the competence and integrity of government are rejected at both ends of the ideological spectrum.[42]

A Global Federalism

The federalist principle supports multiple centers of political power. In a global society, these centers of power should begin at the local level and extend outwards to the county, the state, and the nation, culminating in international centers of authority. To avoid conflicting jurisdictions, a credible federalism must respect the principle of subsidiarity. Public responsibilities should be assigned to the lowest level of authority capable of meeting their practical demands. The evident attractions of local control do not obviate the need for a strong and independent state and for carefully designed global institutions. But what is the proper balance between local, state, national, and international authorities and between the obligations of government and the contributions of civil society? To answer these questions wisely, we need contemporary thinkers with the realism and insight of the early American federalists.[43] Political decentralization has the advantage of localizing power and accountability and creating opportunities for independent civic initiatives. Municipal institutions remain the strength of free nations, as Tocqueville insisted. They bring self-government near the people and teach ordinary citizens the political arts of deliberation, compromise and constructive dissent. There remains, however, a continuing need for federal power to conduct foreign policy, to defend legitimate national interests, to oversee the economy, to protect the environment, to preserve civil rights, to remedy regional injustices, to support the weak and the vulnerable, and to provide an effective counterweight to transnational forces that local communities lack the power to resist or restrain.

A new federalism faces challenges from several different directions. It must create international institutions with sufficient authority to regulate the global economy. It must effectively respond to the decline of civil society and the epidemic of political alienation. It must allow individual citizens and political communities to think and act locally and globally. The merits of local participation must be combined with effective representation in a political context where that strategic balance has clearly been lost.[44]

For democratic theorists, the questions confronting global federalism are much clearer than the answers. They can turn for guidance though not for reliable models to the history of American federalism, to the creation of the United Nations and the World Bank, and to the formation of the European Union. But the flawed performance of these very institutions has brought us to the present impasse. We need to understand the reasons for their uneven achievement, and to base realistic proposals for reform on those critical insights.

What are the inescapable questions confronting a new federalist project: How should global political institutions be connected to national governments? How should international officials be selected, and to whom will they be reliably accountable? How can we prevent international governing bodies from becoming bureaucratic and increasingly ineffective? Institutional remoteness and rigidity are endemic flaws within representative institutions; the larger the institution the greater these dangers become. At the national level, can the federal government effectively satisfy the growing demands upon its limited resources? And what are the appropriate obligations of national governments in a global society? Has the centralization of federal power during the New Deal and the Cold War weakened the effectiveness of state and local governments and diminished the importance of civil society? What balance of federal, state, and local power best satisfies existing political needs while encouraging civic participation and consent? What are the limits of law, litigation and regulatory oversight as sources of sustainable justice? The sanctions of law should be complemented with a renewed emphasis on personal and collective responsibility. Without significant cultural changes in the beliefs and convictions of the people, structural reforms will have limited effect.

Sobriety and realism are also required. At every level of engagement, politics is an uncertain enterprise. There are deeply important goods at stake in politics, peace, justice, liberty, security, and enhanced community, but the risk of failure and demoralization is always high.

E PLURIBUS UNUM: THE CHALLENGE OF CONTEMPORARY PLURALISM

Revised immigration laws and shifting demographic patterns have transformed the American electorate during the last forty years. The dramatic increase in immigrants from Latin America, the Pacific Rim, Southeast Asia and the Middle East has created a more complex ethnic and racial consciousness. The sharp divisions between black and white have been blurred by intermarriage, and by a body politic composed of Nicaraguans, Koreans, Vietnamese, Iranians, and Filipinos, to name just a few of the new Americans. As the racial and ethnic composition of the United States has diversified, new sources of political identity and loyalty have emerged based on gender, religion, and sexual orientation. We can no longer speak, as Tocqueville did, of the Anglo Americans unified by their common religious and moral convictions. Between Tocqueville's era and our own new realities have intervened, irreversibly changing the political culture of the United States: industrialization, urbanization, secularization, and globalization. Most Americans today are no longer farmers, and they no longer live in small towns and villages. While the great majority still believe in God, the biblically-based moral community that reassured Tocqueville in the 1830's has steadily declined. Tocqueville looked to Christianity and patriotism as unifying forces within American democracy. But the religious, moral and ethnic pluralism of America today undermines his sense of a unified national community rooted in common religious and cultural traditions.[45]

Earlier patterns of immigration transformed America in the late nineteenth century as well. Irish Catholics from the north, Italians from the south, Jews from the ghettos of central and eastern Europe flooded American cities and challenged the hegemony of the Protestant majority. Those fierce tensions were eventually resolved by time, education, intermarriage, shared military service, and working class solidarity. A new civil religion and a new internationalist patriotism emerged from World War II, as the great American melting pot blended its ethnically diverse citizens together (African Americans remained the scandalous exception to this integrative pattern). The liberation movements of the sixties and seventies, demanding civil rights for everyone, equal treatment of women, full respect for every ethnic and cultural group, and the public acceptance of gays and lesbians, have shattered the melting pot imagery, as competing groups of citizens strongly insist not on their commonality as Americans, but on their distinct moral and cultural identities.

The American political project has been historically committed to *e pluribus unum*. Out of many peoples, traditions, languages and cultures, to create a unified national community. The traditional sources of community were linguistic, institutional and cultural. We Americans shared allegiance to a common language, to representative democracy and the bill of rights, and to the cultural convictions of our puritan and republican ancestors. But the flawed record of representative democracy and the cultural diversity of contemporary America have eroded these earlier allegiances. The commonality defining us as Americans today is primarily commercial in nature. We are individual producers, merchants, and consumers, who meet, when we do meet, in places of commerce and entertainment (malls and stadiums). We are rarely cooperative citizens united in the work of collective self-government. For most Americans, the government is they not we, for we are independent individuals, defined by narrower identities and deeply committed to our private or group centered business.

What should be, what can be, the substance of a unifying democratic faith in a pluralistic democracy? Sober liberals, like Galston, believe that our civic aspirations should be modest, that we should accept a narrow conception of citizenship. Expecting too much from contemporary citizens, already alienated from politics and devoted to other allegiances, will only be divisive and disappointing. We should limit the civic obligations of our citizens to the bare essentials: obeying the law, supporting our families, paying our fair share of public expenses, refraining from violence and coercive activity. Within this narrow frame of civic requirements, we should leave maximal space for personal, moral, religious, and cultural diversity.[46]

Civic republicans, like Michael Sandel, Charles Taylor and Benjamin Barber, believe that a much stronger conception of citizenship is necessary. Mobilizing coalitions of citizens to contend with economic anxiety, distributive justice, the power of special interests, and the demands of a global economy will require moral and civic energies that are presently in short supply. Sandel argues against cautious liberals, like Galston and Rawls, that progressive economic, political and environmental policies presuppose an ethic of solidarity and reciprocal obligation that classical liberalism does little to cultivate.[47]

All these important debates, about the political challenges of globalization, about the appropriate distribution of public and private responsibilities, and about the shared obligations of citizenship are intelligibly connected. They belong to a national and global conversation that crosses all boundaries, a conversation among citizens struggling to articulate a democratic public philosophy adequate to the dynamic realities and urgent demands of our time.

Let us explore the relevance of Arendt's political humanism to this critical public dialogue. What are the merits and limitations of her civic republicanism for the world as we know it today?

PART II

> Republican politics is concerned with enabling interdependent citizens to deliberate on and realize the common goods of an historically evolving community, at least as much as promoting individual interests or protecting individual rights. Emphasizing responsibility for common goods sets republicanism apart from libertarian theories centered on individual rights. Emphasizing that these common goods are politically realized sets republicanism apart from neutralist liberal theories which exclude substantive questions of values and the good life from politics. Finally, emphasizing the political construction of the political community distinguishes republicans from those communitarians who see politics as expressing the pre-political shared values of a community.
> I. Honohan, *Civic Republicanism*[48]

What can Hannah Arendt's political humanism contribute to a public philosophy attuned to the realities of the global society? Arendt brought to her study of politics a deep historical consciousness. She had reflected carefully on both ancient and modern political phenomena, and on the canonical texts of the western tradition. She was a critical reader of these texts, provocatively interpreting them through the lens of her civic republican convictions. The political tradition she espoused had been effectively silenced in the nineteenth century by the economic debate between classical liberals and socialists, and by the twentieth century struggle against Nazi and Soviet totalitarianism. Arendt herself embraced civic republicanism as the most credible political alternative to the totalitarian threat. Although critical of liberalism on historical and philosophical grounds, she accepted important elements of liberal democracy, especially its commitment to civil liberties, limited government and the rule of law. Yet she criticized bourgeois liberalism for its role in corrupting European politics, and she believed the liberal tradition incapable of reversing the political alienation of our time.

Neither a liberal nor a socialist herself, Arendt was an independent political thinker who emphasized the anti-political character of modern life. To substantiate her appraisal of modernity, she developed a political genealogy and a linguistic phenomenology that required us to rethink our assumptions about government and citizenship. Both aspects of her work emphasized important public goods constantly threatened with extinction. Together with fellow civic republicans like Taylor and Sandel, Arendt made the concepts of political liberty, civic virtue and public happiness essential to her understanding of citizenship. Equipped with these normative conceptual resources, she directly challenged the reductive anthropologies that had reduced human beings to a racially inferior biological species or to calculating economic animals. These ideological reductions had been used to justify political despotism, European imperialism, and totalitarian terror. They had also contributed to the political alienation of democratic citizens in contemporary liberal societies. A more authentic understanding of human existence will require a richer and deeper conception of citizenship.[49]

Ancient philosophers and medieval theologians had subordinated politics to the contemplation of eternal truth. In modernity, political action and speech had been placed in the service of economic concerns. This has meant making the *zoon politikon*, the republican citizen, the servant or agent of *homo mercator* and the animal laborans. It also meant turning statesmen and public officials into the instruments of organized interest groups, and granting capitalism priority over democratic politics.

A credible public philosophy will need to rethink the connection between political and economic institutions and practices. Arendt's contribution to this critical re-assessment is important but limited. Drawing on classical insights, she insisted on the normative primacy of politics over economics, of genuinely liberal activities over those motivated by necessity or utility. But she failed to acknowledge the economic basis of secure human liberty, as well as the material requirements of independent citizenship in a democratic age.[50]

Classical republican citizenship had been deep but narrowly available. The exercise of political liberty had been limited to male property owners and household masters. In representative democracies, citizenship has been significantly broadened, but the extension of suffrage has coincided with a decline in civic engagement and a contraction of public responsibility. Can civic republicanism combine inclusive citizenship with meaningful public liberty; can it strengthen our civic obligations without threatening the individual rights modern citizens are unwilling to surrender? The traditional strength of liberalism is its commitment to individual liberties; the traditional strength of civic republicanism is its commitment to responsible self-government. Arendt carefully distinguished public liberty from secure civil rights, but her passionate argument for a republican alternative to liberalism would benefit from showing the dependence of civil liberties on the exercise of political freedom. The public philosophy we require must combine the insights of both the liberal and republican traditions.[51]

This critical synthesis must also extend to the reconception of government. Arendt consistently opposed the conflation of political activity with rule. Acting in concert with one's civic peers did not entail governing them, even with their consent. Her paradigm examples of action and speech are drawn from the revolutionary activities of liberation and constitution, and not from the normal exercise of governmental power. In fact, she faulted the American constitution for failing to establish public forums for citizenship at the level of the ward or the township. Arendt correctly distinguished the political activity of democratic citizens from the conduct of government, and the deliberative formation of policy and law from public administration. But limiting the scope of government and insisting on public accountability are not enough. The proper allocation of governmental power, starting at the local level and advancing to global political institutions, is a critical task for the new federalist project.

The strengthening of intermediary powers between individual citizens and their government is a basic Tocquevillian principle. Though a vibrant civil society is essential to democratic liberty, it is no substitute for governmental power and law. Reconceiving government in accord with federal principles and renewing the vitality of civil society must be done in a way that recognizes the importance of these different forms of power. Civil society connects citizens to their government and renders government more accountable to the people. It promotes important public goods, intellectual, religious, artistic, cultural and economic, that government cannot directly provide. But there is no credible substitute for government's role in securing personal and public liberty, conducting foreign and defense policy, guaranteeing criminal and distributive justice, monitoring and regulating corporate power, promoting conditions favorable to economic prosperity, overseeing education, and providing the necessary safety net for children, the elderly, the poor, and the disabled.[52]

Public power, whether exercised by government or civil society, is designed to promote and preserve public goods and to prevent or correct public harms. Arendt placed great emphasis on knowing, loving and assuming responsibility for the common world into which we are born. She apparently believed that accepting common goods as the *telos* of politics would mean treating political activity as an instrumental means to an extra-political end. In criticizing her appraisal of Aristotle, I argued that purposive action can be useful and noble simultaneously. We can acknowledge that political actions and discourse are intrinsic goods without denying that they are directed towards achieving common ends. In fact, public deliberation and debate, activities Arendt explicitly commended, are discursive operations designed to discover and advance the commonweal. *Pace* Arendt, the common world is not a rival of the common good; rather it serves as the public horizon and deliberative framework for a plurality of citizens seeking collective agreement about communal well being.

Restoring the common good to its legitimate place within civic republicanism should help to correct a separation Arendt often lamented. She claimed that after the death of Socrates, serious thinkers and responsible citizens had followed diverging paths, creating a demoralizing rift between thought and action.[53] Classical philosophers turned away from human affairs and towards the sky of eternal ideas, their modern counterparts towards the Cartesian ego and the Galilean cosmos. Deliberative reasoning in politics, the sort of reasoning that yields practical opinions and judgments, had been narrowly confined to calculating means to ends. Such calculative reasoning explicitly served the individual or group interests of the agent(s) who practiced it. But narrowly defined economic reasoning effectively excludes the "enlarged mentality" of Arendtian citizenship.

It is often difficult to determine what Arendtian citizens reason practically about. But when the common good is conceived as a practical heuristic notion, rather than an antecedently specified telos of action, then the shared discovery and actualization of public goods become the purpose and measure of free political activity. The responsible judgments and decisions of citizens, sharing "enlarged mentalities" and the objective horizon of a common world, provide a way to recover the practical wisdom so highly regarded by classical republican thinkers. However, practical wisdom at the level of our time is not the singular possession of an individual *phronimos*, but the collective achievement of democratic citizens exercising their political liberty together.[54]

Is there a way to proceed from contemporary liberal democracies to Arendt's vibrant republics of liberty? Or is her commitment to federated political communities (the council system) and engaged and disinterested citizens a utopian dream? Can we reasonably hope to reach Arendt's free republic from where we are now?

THE CRITIQUE OF LIBERALISM

Long before the recent debates about liberal democracy, Arendt criticized the anti-political prejudices of the European liberal tradition. While her critique of liberalism had several overlapping dimensions, it did not prevent her from recognizing valuable aspects of modern liberal societies.

By weakening the bonds of political community within the nation state and encouraging the limitless pursuit of wealth and power, bourgeois liberalism promoted social unrest and class instability. The deep social antagonisms fostered by capitalism prevented the creation of a shared political culture within the nations of Europe. And the imperial strategy combining military power with extravagant profit offered dangerous models for the racist domination of "inferior" peoples. The scandalous history of imperialism provides the intelligible link between the "progressive" century of the liberal bourgeoisie and the demoralizing century of Lenin, Hitler, Stalin and Mao Tse-tung.[55]

While England, France and the United States did not adopt imperial models of governance, they were not immune to the dangers of liberal ideology. The enduring merit of liberal societies is their commitment to civil liberties, limited constitutional government, an energetic civil society, an independent judiciary and the rule of law. These institutional strengths, however, have historically been compromised by racism, greed, and patriarchy; and they receive minimal theoretical support from liberalism's philosophical convictions. Liberal theory has favored an atomistic political ontology, an instrumental view of political cooperation and a utilitarian account of the public good. These political prejudices are typically grounded in a reductive anthropology that narrows human motivation to an exclusive concern for self-interest and self-preservation.

The clearest way to contrast Arendt's republican vision with that of liberalism is to compare their conceptions of liberty, virtue and happiness. While liberalism emphasizes negative liberty, encourages the pursuit of private happiness and celebrates prudential self-interest, Arendt hoped to retrieve a set of political goods that first flourished in classical antiquity. These republican goods of political liberty, civic virtue, and public happiness inspired the American Revolution, but eventually became its forgotten treasure.[56]

At the heart of this cultural contrast are opposing conceptions of the public realm. For civic republicans, the public realm is a space of freedom and dignity where citizens can achieve self-transcendence. They can transcend their individual fears, interests and prejudices to deliberate, decide and act in concert, benefitting not only their contemporaries but their ancestors and descendants as well. They can embrace the world they inherited at birth and enjoy the public happiness of acting cooperatively rather than competitively with their peers.

Classical liberalism typically treats the public realm as a space of commercial exchange where individuals and groups pursue their self-interest. On this market based model of politics, either government is required to leave commerce alone or its power is recruited on behalf of private investment and capital. This privatized conception of government fosters a fiercely partisan politics dominated by organized interests, professional lobbyists and financially compromised public officials. While the advertising strategies of consumer capitalism have corrupted the democratic electoral process, the domination of government by partisan interests heightens contempt for political activity and trivializes the reality of citizenship.[57]

The political alienation of ordinary citizens is profoundly demoralizing. It benefits the powerful and well connected, while subverting serious efforts at institutional reform. It discourages conscientious citizens from seeking elective office and populates the seats of power with the wealthy and self seeking. Massive civic alienation, however self defeating its effects, is not an unreasonable response to our anti-political politics, a deeply corrupt enterprise that cynically exploits public spirit for the sake of partisan ends. Political liberalism, Arendt believes, is a source not a remedy for the discontents of liberal democracy.

PUBLIC LIBERTY

From Arendt's republican perspective, the constitutional phase of the American Revolution was an ambiguous success. The new constitution contained many elements of which she approved; a lawfully ordered structure of federated power; multiple centers of governmental action and responsibility; the secure protection of individual liberties and rights. But by neglecting to incorporate the colonial townships, the source of the revolutionary spirit, into the federal system of power, the constitution left ordinary citizens without a public space of liberty in which to speak and act. The American Revolution gave independence to the people, but failed to provide them with public forums where they could regularly exercise and enjoy it. The constitution granted them the right to electoral representation in government, but failed to create local republics for their civic education and political apprenticeship. For the vast majority of Americans, the revolutionary spirit of public liberty, of sustained engagement in responsible self-government, withered away until it was largely forgotten.[58]

Profound conceptual confusions attended this loss of civic vitality. Liberal political theory and the liberal emphasis on private happiness distorted the understanding of American history. Public liberty, the right of citizens to participate actively in political affairs, became confused with the civil liberties that preserve our security and individual rights. Public happiness, the active collaboration of citizens in discovering and achieving the common good, was reduced to the utilitarian formula of the aggregative happiness of the greatest number of private individuals. And public spirit, the creation through active debate and responsible argument of a judicious conception of the public good, was degraded into the despotism of public opinion as measured by the polling techniques of the consumer society. The constitutional failure to secure an elementary space of liberty for ordinary citizens was compounded by a theoretical and narrative failure to explain to the new Americans what the deeper purpose of the revolution had been. The "American dream" was gradually transformed from the republican promise of liberty and justice for all, to the bourgeois fantasy of a land of milk and honey, of unfettered private enterprise, where everyone could potentially strike it rich.[59]

No matter how we conceive of the public-private distinction, whether we think of it as a demarcation of spatially different realms, as Arendt did, or as contrasting orientations within the intentional outlook of the same person, the public signifies what is common, *koinon*, while the private signifies what is properly one's own, *idion*. The public stance of the informed citizen has both cognitive and practical dimensions. Cognitively, it refers to what is visible or audible to every attentive observer, either directly through the senses or through a reliable communicative medium. Public objects, agents and events can become the shared focus of civic discussion and appraisal. They can be carefully described, objectively understood and impartially evaluated. A common world of sensible particulars provides an inter-subjective horizon for the speech and action of dedicated citizens. From the practical perspective, ordinary citizens treat as public what they mutually care about and accept responsibility for, namely public benefits and harms that they have the power to create, protect, preserve, prevent, remedy and, when necessary, suffer together. These public or common goods and evils can be economic, social, political, cultural or religious. Shared concern for these goods and shared responsibility for their promotion and protection create the bonds of true civic community.[60]

Human liberty, whether public or private, is situated in nature and history. At birth, human beings enter an old world and a complex web of interpersonal relationships. The common world they share is situated on the earth and partly dependent on nature for its continued existence. The newcomers rely for their nurture and education on concerned adults willing to share the complex legacy of the past. The interdependent freedom of old and young is existentially conditioned by natality, mortality, plurality, worldliness and life. Human liberty is always constrained by objective realities to which it must thoughtfully respond. The interweaving of personal freedom with the natural and historical world and with the free actions and aims of other persons precludes the conflation of liberty with sovereignty or arbitrary choice. Genuine freedom is clearly distinct from license, the mythical fantasy of doing what we please without regard for the consequences.

Human liberty has negative and positive dimensions. The essence of negative liberty is freedom from natural necessity, human coercion, arbitrary power, and the exercise of terror in every form. The essence of positive liberty is effective agency, the authentic and responsible direction of personal and public life.[61] The ancient concept of liberty clearly recognized these complementary dimensions, though it failed to acknowledge and secure individual rights. The modern concept of freedom has emphasized negative liberty, a guaranteed zone of non-interference, and tended to view positive liberty with distrust and suspicion. Advocates of negative liberty are haunted by the memory of despotic and totalitarian governments ostensibly acting on behalf of utopian ends.[62]

Alexis de Tocqueville, Arendt's most trusted political mentor, articulated one of the richest modern accounts of liberty. Love of liberty and hatred of despotism were the animating passions of Tocqueville's life. We should pay close attention to his nuanced analysis for it combines both ancient and modern conceptions of freedom.

Tocqueville's concept of negative liberty coincides with personal security. He argued that no one is genuinely free whose person, life and property are not legally protected against illegitimate power, whether that of the state, organized social groups, unruly mobs or lawless individuals. In a free society, the basic rights of all citizens are reliably secured by law and custom.[63]

Tocqueville's account of positive liberty has two related aspects, personal and political. Personal liberty is the freedom to think, to speak, to write, to express one's opinions and convictions in public; it includes freedom of worship and conscience, the right to choose one's spouse and vocation, freedom of economic initiative and the right to acquire, inherit and dispose of private property. These many personal freedoms give human beings real but limited control over their individual lives.

Tocqueville's account of political liberty corresponds closely to the ancient understanding of freedom. Political liberty requires abundant opportunities for citizens to share in the conduct of public affairs. It means the freedom to engage directly through participation and indirectly through elected representation in political life: to deliberate, to evaluate, to decide, to act in concert with others in determining public policy and law. Public liberty is supported by township government, by freedom of assembly and association, the right to petition for redress of grievances, the regular accountability of elected officials, the freedom and independence of the press, the right of public dissent and criticism. Tocqueville repeatedly emphasized the importance of public liberty for a viable democracy: "The only effective remedy for the evils of democratic equality is political or public liberty."[64] He cautioned that political liberty is easily lost and frequently neglected in democratic cultures. Aristocratic in origin and spirit, and in permanent conflict with the democratic passions for wealth and material comfort, public liberty requires an extended apprenticeship in "grammar schools of liberty." The rights of citizenship do not guarantee political freedom, an acquired capacity that only develops through considerable experience in exchanging informed opinions and debating contested judgments with others. Through conversing with our peers, we enlarge our minds to understand their opinions and judgments, and we enlarge our hearts to appreciate their hopes and fears. These political arts and virtues only flourish in a responsible community that deliberately promotes the education of its citizens through discussion and collective action.[65]

Aristotle stressed an important principle about mastering and enjoying the arts. "Those things we need to learn before we can do them, we learn by doing them." We learn to read and write, for example, by first reading and writing awkwardly; we only begin to enjoy reading and writing when we're able to do them well. Aristotle's practical maxim directly applies to the arts and virtues of citizenship. Public liberty only becomes public happiness when citizens begin to enjoy their engagement in public affairs.[66] In modern liberal democracies, the vast majority of citizens deliberately avoid the public realm and view with suspicion "the politicians" who enter it. The dominant ideology of market capitalism promotes a narrow attachment to private interests, and most citizens tolerate a demoralizing public life if their individual rights and interests are protected.

As democratic citizenship has become more inclusive, it has also become less significant. The majority of citizens prize the ideal of freedom, which they identify with negative liberty and minimal government. Those who demand a more active government typically view it as a means for correcting injustice or promoting their special interest or cause. The adversarial model of freedom receives insidious support from the culture of "democratic individualism." "Individualism is a mature and calm feeling, which disposes each member of the community to sever himself from the mass of his fellows and to draw apart with his family and friends, so that after he has thus formed a little circle of humans, he willingly leaves society at large to itself. Selfishness originates in blind instinct; individualism proceeds from erroneous judgment, more than from depraved feelings."[67]

What are the errors of judgment that sustain democratic individualism? The first is an illusion about human independence. From birth until death, we are interdependent beings constantly requiring the cooperation and assistance of others. We could neither conceive nor attain our personal goals without the institutional and cultural resources that the political community sustains and protects. Even the individual rights that we cherish are precarious; genuinely secure civil liberties are protected by the citizens, laws and customs of a just society. In all three of its relevant dimensions, personal security, individual rights and public liberty, freedom can only be realized in a vibrant political community. Positive laws may be unjust, governments are often oppressive, and political engagement is frequently demoralizing, but without the protection of just laws, responsible governments and a culture of tolerance and mutual respect, communal life would be despotic rather than free.

Secure civil rights require corresponding civic obligations; inequalities of power can only be checked by countervailing centers of power that depend on sustained cooperation. In human affairs, the real alternative to collaborative power is impotence. When citizens withdraw from public life, when they cease to cooperate with their peers, they become politically impotent. As democratic citizens, we pay a heavy price for our political passivity. The global conjunction of economic and political power is inherently dangerous. It threatens the economic security of citizens, endangers their personal liberties and makes political participation seem increasingly futile. These threats to our freedom can only be corrected through cooperative action and concerted resistance. We need political remedies for our democratic discontents.

PARTICIPATION AND REPRESENTATION

> Representative politics as currently practiced minimizes most citizens' active contribution to decision-making and meaningful participation.
> I. Honohan, *Civic Republicanism*[68]

Can significant political participation be achieved in contemporary democratic societies? Even if public liberty is recognized as an intrinsic good and an essential part of democratic reform, has it become irreversibly marginalized in a global political culture? Is civic republicanism a credible political alternative to liberal democracy?

The recorded history of public liberty began in the city states of ancient Greece. The Greek *poleis* were small self-governing communities, warlike in orientation and unified by a common political culture. They restricted citizenship to property-owning males whose economic independence often depended on owning slaves. They made high demands on the time, energy and loyalty of their citizens whose public responsibilities substantially exceeded their civil rights. In these ancient republics citizenship was deep but exclusive. To paraphrase Hegel, freedom belonged only to the few.

The European nation states that arose in the sixteenth and seventeenth centuries were radically different from the classical republics admired by Hegel and Arendt. Both the extent of their territory and the size of their populations dwarfed the scale of the Greek poleis. They chose centralized monarchy as their primary form of government and actively suppressed provincial centers of political power. While not abandoning war as a means of territorial expansion, they also relied heavily on commerce and colonies as sources of national wealth.

The American constitution in the eighteenth century introduced a new form of representative government. In the *Federalist Papers*, Madison argued that representative democracy could combine republican liberty with a diverse population inhabiting a nation of continental dimensions.[69] In practice, the new federal democracy curtailed the political participation of citizens, largely directing their energies to economic pursuits. With westward expansion and the death of the revolutionary leadership, the colonial townships diminished in importance and a partisan politics based on competing regional interests began to dominate the national scene.

Public liberty, with its emphasis on economic independence and disinterested virtue, became ideologically suspect. Nineteenth century Americans largely shifted their focus from public to private life, from political participation to the passionate quest for economic success. A new cultural consensus emerged on the value of ordinary life, of marriage and the family and the importance of personal and public prosperity. The majority of Americans lacked the time, the energy and the inclination to devote themselves to public affairs. They were starting new businesses, emigrating westward, and restlessly conquering a continent. They remained grateful to the American revolution for its tangible benefits, individual liberty, social mobility and the right to pursue private happiness. For them, politics typically meant government, and they associated government with the despotic monarchy they had recently cast off.[70]

Two centuries after its founding, the United States has become a global power whose military, cultural, and economic influence extends to all corners of the earth. Some civic concerns remain of great local interest: education, property taxes, public services and neighborhood planning, for example. But these concerns are eclipsed by national and global problems that affect local communities while radically exceeding their remedial power and influence. Problems like nuclear proliferation, global warming, international terrorism and the power and influence of trans-national corporations.

The civic republican agenda in a global society must directly address these historical realities. There is no retrieving the ancient republics of Greece and Rome nor the fledgling American democracy of the early nineteenth century. We must continue to learn from these political experiments, while recognizing their limited application to present circumstances. To paraphrase Tocqueville, we need a new republican politics for a genuinely global society. What can Tocqueville and Arendt contribute to the public philosophy we urgently need?

The key to their continuing relevance is their shared commitment to republican federalism, to the vertical federation of political power. They both insist that public power and accountability should originate at the local level and be gradually incorporated into higher levels of political authority. What institutional and cultural practices support the exercise of federated liberty?[71]

Active, independent and responsive local governments. "Municipal institutions constitute the strength of free nations. Town meetings are to liberty what primary schools are to science. They bring liberty within the people's reach and teach them how to use and enjoy it."[72] Participation in local government continues to provide an important entry into politics and a valuable apprenticeship in public liberty.

A federal constitution that establishes numerous centers of power and delegates responsibility to the lowest effective governmental level. The Catholic principle of political subsidiarity emphasizes the benefits of local experience and insight and the dangers of centralized administration. Subsidiarity can be blended with federated power at the local, state, regional, national and international levels of authority. When national governments are unable to address global problems and concerns, then international institutions must be authorized to act in their stead.[73]

When political representation is necessary, elected representatives must be directly accountable to their constituents on a regular basis. Democratic accountability means far more than making electoral promises, providing useful services to citizens and reporting the results of congressional activity. It requires delegated representatives to engage their constituents in substantive dialogue, taking account of their opinions and judgments, taking seriously their critical dissent.

Federalism favors a division of power at every level of governmental authority. An independent and impartial judiciary with the right of judicial review is essential to check the despotic tendencies of the legislative and executive branch. Even when centralized authority is necessary, the administration of public policy should be as decentralized as possible. Democratic citizens are easily demoralized by remote, impersonal, paternalistic bureaucracies. There should be an effective and immediate local response to public emergencies, even when the policy directives and funding originate at the national level.[74]

Political activity is not identical with the actions of government. As important as the duties of government are, free societies need an energetic civil society composed of voluntary associations committed to promoting and protecting public goods. For most citizens, who will never be government officials, voluntary associations provide important public forums for refining political opinions, initiating public actions and expressing political dissent and opposition.

Freedom of religion requires an effective separation of church and state. The state should refrain from shaping or enforcing the theological and moral doctrines of the churches. The churches, in turn, acknowledge the legitimate authority of the state and preserve the right to criticize public policies they consider unjust. The institutional separation of church and state does not mean excluding religious concerns from the public realm. Religious citizens, motivated by the practical convictions of their faith, have an inherent concern for justice and for protecting the weak and vulnerable. Public spirited religious communities that comfort the afflicted and challenge the comfortable, play an important role in a democratic civil society.[75]

The most important source of democratic liberty is a free, self-disciplined and civically responsible fourth estate. The major purpose of a free press is to inform and enlighten the people, to show them what is really happening in public life, to provide the background they need for responsibly judging elected officials, political parties and movements and concrete public policies. With a few notable exceptions, the communications media today have been driven by partisan ideology and the zeal for profit into crass sensationalism, trivial entertainment and superficial political analysis and commentary.

Finally, institutional and cultural support for public liberty needs to be balanced by a detailed bill of rights that law and custom are prepared to enforce, particularly during periods of war and national emergency.[76]

Arendt's primary contribution to the federalism debate was her explicit support for the council system, a form of republican governance combining broad civic participation with multiple levels of accountable representation. In defending conciliar models of government, she sharply contrasted two ways of structuring political democracy.

The traditional European party system, which she connected with the triumph of bourgeois liberalism, encourages the political pursuit of economic advantage. Party politics is essentially adversarial in nature, pitting one interest group against another. Intense partisan rivalry effectively undermines most cooperative ventures and weakens the bonds of national solidarity. For Arendt, the party system transfers the spirit and methods of competitive capitalism into the heart of democratic politics.[77]

The council system actively encourages public liberty and citizen participation, while seeking to avoid divisive partisanship. Conciliar government, as Arendt reminds us, developed historically during Europe's political revolutions when the inherited structures of public authority had collapsed. The Paris commune of 1870, the short-lived soviets during the initial phase of the Bolshevik Revolution, the wartime resistance movements in Nazi occupied France, the Hungarian workers councils in 1956, provided emergency spaces for public action and speech when traditional governments had been swept away. Arendt insists that the spirit of these spontaneously created councils was remarkably non-partisan. Ordinary citizens, normally excluded from the corridors of power, freely entered these self-created assemblies with the well-being of the whole community in mind. Within the liberating solidarity of the councils, they cooperated freely with their civic peers, rejecting the partisan for and against of party politics.[78]

In conciliar forms of government, as Arendt describes them, what matters is not the economic interest you represent, nor the passion with which you oppose countervailing interests. The political focus is on the direct accountability of citizens to one another in their mutual deliberation and debate. Participating citizens are judged on the basis of properly political criteria: courage, independence, integrity, impartiality, a commitment to justice, and a respect for the opinions and liberties of others. Those who display these political virtues are commonly trusted, their opinions taken seriously, and their practical judgments respected even when they diverge from the emerging consensus.

Within conciliar government, political power is generated from below through the cooperation of citizens in their local communities. Elementary republics or wards provide forums of participation for everyone who chooses to enter them. The active participants at higher levels of power are delegated representatives chosen by their peers at the next lower level of participation. In principle, the chosen representatives are selected on the basis of shared political engagement and the reliable display of the relevant virtues. Because they have gained the confidence of their conciliar peers, representatives are trusted to act knowledgably and responsibly at the next level of governing authority.

The council system supported by Arendt clearly combines political participation with representation. Every citizen has a real opportunity to participate, and representatives are chosen based on their independence and integrity. In Arendt's genealogy of political liberty, the tragic irony of the French and Russian Revolutions is clearly acknowledged. When real institutions of public freedom (the councils and soviets) spontaneously arose in the course of liberating the people, they were ruthlessly crushed by the Jacobins and the Bolsheviks to preserve despotic control over the revolutionary process.[79]

Although different versions of the council system have emerged, none has survived long enough to allay serious misgivings about their practical viability and effectiveness. Arendt's spirited defense of conciliar politics, while provocative and striking, is highly schematic. Her forceful critique of the European party system is reasonably clear. What remains unclear is the relation of conciliar politics to existing constitutional governments. Is the council system intended as a realistic alternative to constitutional federalism based, for example, on the American model; or is it intended to implement federalist principles when established forms of constitutional authority have been publicly rejected? Arendt believed that the American Revolution originated in the colonial townships, but the Constitution failed to recognize their legitimate role in the new structure of federated power. But what if the townships had been legally authorized by the federal constitution? What would have been the scope of their authority in relation to state and federal power? And how would active participation at the township level relate to delegated representation at higher levels of government? In a representative democracy, public officials are chosen on the basis of contested elections in which all citizens, active and inactive, are eligible to vote. The protracted, painful and often bloody movement towards universal suffrage lies at the center of American political history. But conciliar democracy, as Arendt describes it, would bypass normal elections and restrict those choosing higher level representatives to a self-selected minority of citizens. Surely, traditional American resistance to the authority of government would intensify if the "consent of the governed" were truncated in this radical way.[80]

Is conciliar politics incompatible with popular elections on a regional or national scale? Is it incompatible with establishing legitimate authority through accepted forms of popular consent? The great strength of conciliar politics is its stress on political participation and public accountability. It seems an admirable way to organize local politics, many associations in civil society, and periodic movements for political and social reform. Its great liability is its "aristocratic" method of selecting political representatives and its wholesale rejection of electoral politics and universal suffrage. Despite Arendt's critical arguments, it is difficult to imagine contemporary citizens freely adopting the council system as an alternative to representative democracy.

THE PRIMACY OF POLITICS OVER ECONOMICS

Arendt did not develop her own economic theory. She was openly critical of both commercial and industrial capitalism, but no less critical of Marxism and European socialism. She defended private property, the citizen's need for a privately owned place in the world, but carefully distinguished tangible property from intangible wealth. She viewed wealth as insubstantial and fluid, lacking in worldly durability and incapable of protecting personal privacy.[81] She believed capitalism and socialism had equally contributed to the world alienation of modernity. Both originated in the expropriation of private property; both tended to foster a worldless and alienating culture that transformed every sensible object into an instrument of use, material consumption or profit.

She passionately opposed the anthropological assumptions underlying modern economic theories. Her political humanism was expressly designed to resist the ideological imperialism of *homo faber*, *homo mercator* and the *animal laborans*. She struggled to protect the public realm from the economic ethos, which she labeled the ascent of "the social." The triumph of the social meant that properly private concerns had achieved a monopoly on public attention and discourse. In liberal democracies, the competitive culture of capitalism had corrupted the spirit of democratic citizens, who increasingly viewed political activity through the prism of economic metaphors.

When Arendt did address economic matters, her approach was pragmatic and flexible. She favored experimenting with several economic strategies and models, and was hostile to the dominance of a single institutional paradigm. She particularly distrusted the intrusion of ideology into economic activity, a pattern she attributed to European imperialism and the Soviet collectivization of agriculture. She believed that economic questions were technical in nature and could reasonably be settled by technical experts and competent administrators.[82]

While Arendt distrusted classical liberalism, she did not support the welfare state. Welfare based politics, she believed, had largely reduced governmental activity to satisfying private needs and desires, blurring essential distinctions between public policy and public administration, and between practical and technical rationality. Political questions, for Arendt, exceeded the competence of economic experts and bureaucrats, for demonstrated excellence in action and speech differs markedly from technical mastery or administrative skill.[83]

Her desire to separate politics from economics, as the ancient republics had separated the *polis* from the *oikos*, creates several intractable problems. Classical Greek and Roman politics depended heavily on a slave economy, as the ancients based political engagement on a structure of economic injustice. In modern democracies, where slavery has been abolished and nearly all citizens work for a living, and where government is directly involved in monetary, fiscal and regulatory policy, this segregative strategy is no longer viable. Though politics and economics should be conceptually distinguished, they are presently inseparable in practice. There are numerous areas where political decisions directly impact economic reality: the regulation of markets and workplaces; the enforcement of contracts; the lawful protection of consumers and the natural and historical environment; insuring the soundness of currency; establishing budget priorities; promoting and sustaining economic prosperity; guaranteeing a safety net for all citizens; struggling for distributive justice.[84]

Throughout history, individual citizens could engage in public affairs with an "enlarged mentality" only if their economic needs had already been met. Determining the substance of those needs under present conditions, and determining how and by whom they should regularly be satisfied are political questions directly related to economic reality. Arendt had limited experience of global capitalism, but she would have deeply distrusted it. She believed that technology could be politically helpful if it liberated citizens from the burden of necessity and the recurrent demands of onerous labor. But she denied that the material prosperity and technological power of the West had created a culture of public freedom. She did not reject technological development nor the expansion of global commerce as such, but she did reject the ideological assumption that global economic processes are beyond human direction and control. While there is an autonomic character to all economic activity, concerted action and speech can interrupt economic processes, subjecting them to public appraisal and systemic reform.[85]

If political institutions are to regulate economic behavior impartially, they must remain independent of economic power. An acute danger of global capitalism is that transnational corporations will either evade political authority or cynically purchase its protective influence and support. While Arendt might support political oversight of the global economy, she would have cautioned against technical bureaucrats largely sheltered from public accountability.

In economic affairs, it is much clearer what Arendt was against than what she was for. She rarely addressed questions of economic justice and security, nor what economic policies promote republican liberty in a modern economy. She clearly asserted the normative primacy of politics over economics, of action and speech over fabrication and labor, of political self-transcendence over calculated self-interest, but she failed to acknowledge the deep interdependence of economics and politics within modern democracies. She showed convincingly how capitalist economics could corrupt republican politics, but never explained how economic activity might support a public culture of freedom and dignity.[86]

THE SOCIAL QUESTION REVISITED: DISTRIBUTIVE JUSTICE AND POLITICAL EQUALITY

> "Just as socialism is no remedy for capitalism, capitalism cannot be a remedy or an alternative for socialism."[87]

Why did Arendt seek to segregate economics from politics? Why did she believe that action and speech were irrelevant to resolving the "social question," the scandalous coexistence of modern affluence and poverty? Why did she minimize the political importance of economic concerns in her vision of human existence?

Even sympathetic critics of Arendt are uneasy about the economic aspects of her anthropology. One can share her opposition to the primacy of economics and to the pernicious political influence of capitalism and socialism, without endorsing her sharp distinction between social and political concerns. Let us carefully explore the sources of that distinction before assessing its merits and limitations.

Arendt wanted to protect the integrity of the public realm as a space for freedom and excellence, for individual distinction and self-expression. Only in public forums, she believed, could human beings achieve lasting greatness by enacting memorable deeds and speaking memorable words. Only in the company of civic peers, liberated from reductive concerns with necessity and utility, could they could rise above parochial self-interest, creating an "enlarged mentality" and a genuinely public spirit. A sound public realm was essential if human beings were to become disinterested citizens and achieve self-transcendence.

But the public realm is easily corrupted by alien concerns.[88] Without a republican political culture, the common world becomes neglected like an unweeded garden, or trivialized like a house of worship surrendered to commerce. By insisting on a sharp public-private distinction, Arendt sought to teach her peers to enter this civic space with the appropriate spirit and outlook. As people of faith reverently enter a church or a temple to worship, so citizens should impartially engage in civic affairs, joining with their peers in the care and protection of the world.

In the modern age, the "rise of the social" threatens to corrupt the space of freedom and personal distinction. Arendt's use of 'the social' has multiple senses, but it essentially signifies the intrusion of private interests and homogenizing forces into a worldly space where they don't belong. These interests and forces turn the world of memorable action and speech into a realm of predictable behavior and partisan rhetoric. By converting the domain intended for greatness into a sphere of uniform mediocrity, the "triumph of the social" deprives human beings of occasions for worldly remembrance.[89]

Arendt shares with Kant a deep attachment to the ideal of regional autonomy. As Kant sought to protect moral autonomy by segregating practical reason from natural desires and passions, so Arendt hoped to segregate republican politics from the cultural prejudices of Platonic philosophy, Christian theology, Galilean physics, and Darwinian inspired economics and social science. Like Kant, Arendt was leery of admitting the concerns, norms and reasoning patterns of very different activities into the pure realm of public action and speech. Despite their laudable intentions, however, neither Kantian nor Arendtian segregation really seems feasible.

Kant attempted to segregate phenomena and noumena ontologically because he believed that Newtonian nature was a realm of causal necessity. Since moral activity requires volitional freedom, and rational freedom and natural necessity are incompatible, he located autonomous moral choice beyond the reach of natural law. A similar reasoning pattern shapes Arendt's insistence on strict political autonomy. She deeply distrusted capitalism and socialism, the dominant economic ideologies of the last two centuries. She believed they both were anti-political in nature and imperialist in their historical ambitions. Capitalism advocated the hegemony of unregulated commerce, socialism that of the omnicompetent state. Both distrusted politics and independent governmental authority and employed political power to serve economic objectives. Both confused economic growth with genuine historical progress, and productive abundance with the expansion of human liberty. Despite their mutual hostility, both embraced, though for different reasons, the imperial assumptions of economics.

But what about social democracies that protect civil liberties while promoting economic equality, or the liberal welfare state committed to creating a safety net for the poor and the powerless? Arendt's objections to these political hybrids were less severe than her critique of bourgeois capitalism and Marxian socialism. She admired all forms of government that observed the rule of law, protected civil liberties and broadly distributed political power. But she did not believe that these mixed regimes actually promoted genuine citizenship or enhanced political liberty.

From Arendt's perspective, both democratic socialism and welfare liberalism accepted the teleological primacy of economics over politics. Both are committed to unlimited economic growth that threatens the natural universe and the stabilizing structures of the world. Both tend to centralize political power, conflating governmental activity with public administration. Both tend to support a claim driven politics where competing interest groups make endless demands on the limited resources of government. Both offer their citizens minimal opportunities for political engagement, sacrificing public liberty for the promise of economic security and private happiness. While these hybrid political forms avoid the ideological extremes of capitalism and socialism, they fail to restore the dignity of politics and the norms of disinterested citizenship.[90]

Why do economic activities and goals corrupt the essence of politics as Arendt conceives it? She insists that economic concerns tend to be homogenizing or divisive. When economic interests are shared by a class or group, they promote uniformity of opinion and political behavior. When economic interests divide opposing classes, they intensify partisanship and erode civic solidarity. Moreover, economic questions are properly settled by technical analysis or administrative skill. They are not, she argues, appropriate matters for political deliberation and debate. Action and speech cannot create objects of use or consumption. They contribute little, therefore, to resolving the dilemmas of poverty and material inequality. When political and economic power are combined in the state, the outcome is usually despotic. The stipulated goal of this dangerous alliance is often to accelerate economic growth, growth that threatens the stability and permanence of our common world. Finally, the defining mentalities of the different economic agents, *homo faber*, *homo mercator* and the *animal laborans* undermine the republican spirit of Arendtian citizens. The artisan's skilled fabrication is governed by the spirit of utility; the commercial mentality of buyers and sellers is governed by the passion for profit; the productive labor of the unskilled worker is subject to cycles of natural necessity. These powerful cultural outlooks threaten the integrity of the public realm, compromising the independence of the citizens who enter it.

Arendt's position on the social question is a confusing mixture of insights and oversights. She was certainly right to oppose the subversion of politics by economic activities and concerns. In capitalist societies, self-interest is rampant and constantly threatens to privatize the public realm. The scandalous contradictions of capitalism made the socialist alternative initially appealing. But the history of revolutionary attempts to overthrow capitalism and establish a socialist utopia is dismal and sobering. Mixed economies that guarantee civil liberties and political rights while addressing the needs of the poor and the powerless are far less objectionable than their ideological rivals. Yet centralized power tends to limit political participation, while unregulated growth threatens the stability of the natural and human environment. Economic models and metaphors invariably distort the understanding and appraisal of political agents and institutions. Responsibly governing free and independent citizens is very different from managing a business, amassing a private fortune, or trading in speculative markets. These forceful and familiar Arendtian criticisms are instructive and practically relevant.

What are Arendt's most significant oversights? As Hanna Pitkin reminds us in criticizing Arendt, politics and economics have always been interdependent.[91] Their symbiotic relationship is especially pronounced in a global society, and will not diminish in importance simply because of the dangers it creates. The critical variable is the question of teleological priority. Will economic policies contribute to political well-being as civic republicans desire, or will political actions and energies be regularly subordinated to economic ends? Economic transactions have inevitable political consequences; there is an inescapable political dimension to economic planning and practice. To ignore these realities in the hope of promoting political autonomy, leaves the public realm under the effective control of economic interests, and protects transnational corporations from critical regulation and oversight.[92]

The goal of a credible republican strategy is to recover important goods lost or neglected in the modern age. These goods include: meaningful citizenship, significant political participation, and a deep cultural commitment to public liberty, civic virtue and public happiness. Because none of these goods is presently secure, conceptually or practically, the difficult work of critical retrieval is necessary: to clarify what these goods really are; to identify the forces that threaten them; and to specify the institutional and cultural arrangements that promote their achievement and flourishing.[93]

To be genuinely committed to a specific good we must also be committed to its enabling conditions. But what conditions are required for meaningful political participation in contemporary democracy? Like their ancient counterparts, modern citizens need to be free from natural necessity and human coercion. Concretely, this requires economic independence and a fair measure of economic security. Although public liberty does not require economic equality, scandalous levels of inequality threaten civic solidarity and cooperation. Though private property rights are clearly important, they are never absolute. Just economic policies support progressive rates of taxation that generate sufficient public revenues without stifling economic initiative and technological innovation. The political equality civic republicans support requires distributive justice in education, housing, health care and family income. Working citizens need sufficient economic independence and adequate levels of political education to participate responsibly in public life.

When public policies are designed to promote political as well as economic goods, there is a clear role for government in the economic sector. All citizens benefit from just laws and regulations that enforce contracts, prevent fraud, check the formation of monopolies, and protect the natural and historical environment. And there are many public goods that the market economy is not designed to promote or protect: personal and economic security, sound public education, affordable housing and health care, publicly financed museums, parks, theatres and wilderness. The entire country benefits from the communal solidarity strengthened by social justice. Both luxury and poverty are politically corrupting and profoundly divisive. Fiscal and monetary policies, while attuned to the realities of global competition, should have a strong social justice dimension. In striking the mean between economic and political considerations, partisan ideologies should give way to the self-correcting process of experimental trial and error.[94] The same caution applies to counter-cyclical macro-economic policies intended to correct reversals in the business cycle. Fiscal policies that favor the powerful and privileged, and mounting levels of public debt that threaten the security of future generations are clearly inconsistent with a just democracy. In critically assessing policy proposals, citizens should examine their probable effects on the economy, the polity, and the global society as a whole.[95]

Pace Arendt, I support a republican version of the mixed economy that combines market allocations in economics with state planning for recurrent public goods and collective provision for enduring human needs. A historically minded republicanism strengthens the social welfare versions of the mixed economy by providing a distinctively political justification for distributive justice and regulatory oversight. Without economic independence and security and effective constraints on economic power and privilege, the Arendtian synthesis of political equality and liberty will never be achieved.[96]

THE RENEWAL OF CIVIL SOCIETY

Nearly all of Arendt's references to 'society' are negative. The "rise of the social," on her account, corrupted the public and the private realms by failing to respect their autonomous dignity and character. The public space of distinction and excellence is compromised whenever biological necessity, economic self-interest, rule governed conformity or partisan behavior are granted legitimacy within it. The private space needed for personal growth and familial intimacy is also endangered whenever the harsh light of public attention is focused upon them. Although Arendt often refers to the 'social' as a uniform danger, the historical societies she criticizes are importantly different in character.

Chapter 5

... society of eighteenth century France, the provincial nobility ... their public obligations for the courtly intrigue and hypocrisy of ... the class society of nineteenth century Europe, bourgeois in... ...nd financial speculators used the power and credit of the nation... ...ent to protect their economic interests. From Arendt's perspective, bourgeois society was philistine to its core, subverting the independence of the state while treating the cultural treasures of the past as private sources of public esteem. Rootless individuals vulnerable to ideological and political manipulation composed the mass societies of Europe that emerged after World War I. And citizens in contemporary consumer societies are preoccupied with economic prosperity, material comfort and the allure of private happiness.

Although the rise of society regularly threatens political institutions and conduct, the specific threat varies in different historical settings. The jaded aristocrats at Versailles indirectly contributed to the concentration and abuse of monarchical power. The bourgeois ethos in England, France and Germany supported imperial adventures in Asia and Africa. The mass society created by total war and global depression cleared a path for popularly supported totalitarian movements and governments. The consumer culture in modern democracies fosters political alienation among their citizens while deepening suspicion of public officials and governments.

In each case, the "social" thrusts alien passions and concerns into the public realm of action and speech. The hunger for social and cultural acceptance threatens personal integrity and critical thought and dissent. Homogenizing economic interests either stifle diverse opinions or foster vacuous policy debates in which the adversarial positions are known in advance. Focussing on private happiness leads to withdrawal from the world and indifference to civic obligations. And society's intrusion into private concerns threatens familial integrity and the human need for solitude and intimacy.

Given Arendt's repeated opposition to "the social," would she have been an unqualified critic of civil society? The answer to this question is complicated. If civil society refers to nongovernmental associations or political movements created to promote genuinely public goods or to prevent public harms, she would have welcomed and encouraged their emergence. But if civil society refers to organized pressure groups created to lobby the government on behalf of private and sectarian interests, she would have been their implacable foe. Like Tocqueville, Arendt saw the need for voluntary associations to mediate the distance between the remoteness of government and the isolation of individual citizens. For most citizens, these voluntary forums of political education and action serve as the focus of their civic loyalty. Arendt never conflated the public realm with the province of the state, nor public action and speech with governmental activity. In supporting the council system, she emphasized the need for local forums of liberty rather than the coordination of governmental authority. In the end, she never explained how civil society and federated government should be effectively integrated.

She carefully distinguished between voluntary associations for advancing private interests and popular movements based on shared political opinions and principles.[97] For Arendt, organized interest groups corrupted the public realm by using political power for essentially private ends. But citizens' movements to secure civil rights, to oppose unjust wars, to preserve the natural and historical environment, as well as numerous associations for the promotion of knowledge and the preservation of culture, are genuine expressions of public liberty. Although Arendt's sharp distinction between private interests and public principles is not always clear in civil society, it is important to distinguish the reasons why citizens unite. Associations based on mutual interest or need are typically united by economic objectives or essentially sectarian concerns. But in voluntary associations to oppose injustice, to secure unprotected rights, to shed light on official misconduct, to preserve the treasures of the world for future generations the unifying concern is not protecting one's own (*idion*), but acting in concert for the commonweal. These "associations of opinion" are schools of civic virtue where citizens learn to deliberate, decide, remember and judge in the company of strangers and friends. Most democratic citizens acquire their political education in these forums of discussion and action.

When the energy of the state is primarily devoted to business and commerce, government power is exercised despotically, important public goods are neglected or threatened, and the political equality of citizens consistently compromised, the associations of civil society can create visible centers of resistance and collaborative movements for political reform. When democratic politics becomes anti-political, as it has today, we require intermediary powers between the bureaucratic state and the merciless marketplace, to resist despotism, counter democratic individualism and teach citizens to think and act for the common good.[98]

THE COMMON WORLD AND THE COMMON GOOD

Why does Arendt rarely use or endorse the traditional language of the common good?[99] She seems to fear that both classical and Christian thinkers were guilty of political instrumentalism, reducing public action and speech to mere technical means to extra-political ends. For Arendt, as a critical disciple of Kant, human freedom and action are deprived of dignity when treated as instrumental goods. While Arendt endorses civic virtue, the secular self-transcendence of public spirited citizens, she keeps a deliberate distance from the teleology of the common good. Her detachment flows from several sources: practical scepticism about knowledge of the human essence and *telos*; her uncritical embrace of the Periclean politics of greatness and glory; her strict separation of normative political criteria from moral precepts and principles. Drawing on these complex convictions, she dispenses with the telos of the common good, replacing it with her humanistic concern for the common world.[100]

This important rejection leaves Arendt's account of politics incomplete. The common world is not a substitute for the common good, but the communal horizon within which public goods can be discovered and enacted. Let us briefly explore why these normative political concepts are complementary rather than antithetical.

For Arendt, a republican political culture helps to create disinterested citizens, informed adults who've come to know, love and accept responsibility for the world. This humanly created world is the common background of their interpersonal discourse and action. Each person has a unique perspective on the durable objects and structures that stabilize the world, and on the memorable events that give its history drama and meaning. This plurality of perspectives is politically expressed in the personal opinions citizens exchange in the public realm. These individual opinions are not static and unalterable thoughts. As they learn to appreciate the outlook of their peers, citizens refine and revise their own conceptions of the world. They gradually achieve "an enlarged mentality"; their initial opinions and judgments are deepened and altered through this reciprocal and continuous dialogue.

But why do adult citizens enter the public realm? What draws them together and keeps them responsibly connected? Arendt tends to emphasize their quest for personal distinction and historical remembrance.[101] But that is a small part of the larger political enterprise. Citizens chiefly assemble to fulfill their collective responsibility for the world. They seek to honor the contributions of their ancestors, collaborate fruitfully with their peers, and fulfill their obligations to posterity. The principal forms of public discourse are communal deliberation and historical remembrance. In shared deliberation, citizens seek to discover what ought to be done here and now; in shared remembrance they strive to reach a just appraisal of the achievements or failures of their peers and predecessors. As the common world provides the objective horizon for their civic interaction, so the common good provides its legitimate *telos*.

Pace Arendt, there are distinctively common goods for which citizens are collectively responsible: security, liberty, justice, economic prosperity, public education, civic solidarity, the protection of the natural and historical environment. The achievement and protection of these critical goods also requires an enlarged mentality, a deepening knowledge of the world and its history, the consistent transcendence of individual and group bias in evaluative decisions and judgments.

Irreducibly public goods are highly variable in their concrete realization. It is only through shared discussion and argument that citizens discover what security, justice, liberty and prosperity, for example, actually require in the thicket of historical existence. The common good, then, is not a fixed and determinate *telos*, always and everywhere the same. Rather, it is a practical heuristic concept that specifies what political deliberation is attempting to discover and concerted action is attempting to achieve.[102]

Bernard Lonergan's distinction between originating and terminal goods is relevant here. Terminal goods are the purposive ends at which practical activity aims. Originating goods make the discovery and achievement of terminal goods possible. They include our native human capacities, both cognitive and practical, the discursive arts and virtues we acquire through our political apprenticeship, and the intentional speech and action we share with our civic peers. Both sets of goods are intrinsically valuable and internally related. Originating goods, then, are not disposable means to an externally defined end. In a republican polity, the common good cannot be determined apart from the way it is collectively discovered, reasonably affirmed and jointly enacted. Even when the specific aims of collective action are not achieved, the originating goods of public liberty retain their worth. It is good to interact freely with our peers, to determine together our common purposes, to create a unified political community, to exercise collective responsibility for the world and its future.[103]

I agree with Arendt that public liberty is an intrinsic and important good. But Arendtian freedom has an ambiguous political significance today. Unless it is complemented by the norms and virtues of the common good tradition, a tradition based on a shared commitment to justice and collective responsibility, its spirited exercise may actually heighten our political divisions and paralysis.

Contemporary defenders of the common good rarely make the effort to articulate its relevance for liberal democratic societies embedded within a global economy. Unlike the classical *polis* of Aristotle, or the medieval kingdoms of Aquinas, modern democracies are characterized by universal suffrage, guaranteed civil liberties, representative government, free market economies, and a highly diverse civil society. To restore the credibility of the common good today, its defenders must establish its importance for dynamic societies of this type. They must also respond persuasively to the philosophical criticisms and cultural suspicions that have made this teleological concept appear quaint or utopian. What concrete steps are needed to restore the common good to its central place in practical inquiry?[104]

Articulation: we need to clarify what the common good is and is not. It is a second order heuristic concept that specifies the goal of deliberative inquiry. When citizens deliberate intelligently, evaluate reasonably and decide responsibly in concrete historical situations, they are attempting to discover the terminal goods they are jointly committed to actualizing. While these public goods are objective in nature, they are also situation-specific. They embody the objective relativity that Aristotle attributed to the judgments of practical wisdom.[105]

The common good, then, is not "already out there now" waiting to be discovered through the infallible intuitions of private individuals, cultural groups or charismatic leaders. It cannot be known and affirmed apart from collective inquiry and debate; it cannot be actualized without respecting the rights and legitimate concerns of everyone affected by its enactment.

Responding to critics: Critical objections to the notion of the common good are broadly based. Numerous critics sceptically question whether there are public goods that can be clearly distinguished from the preferences of individuals, the partisan objectives of social groups, the interests and security of the national community. And if such goods exist, who knows what they are, and who has the authority to promote them without abridging the rights of individuals and the legitimate concerns of dissenting minorities?[106]

Although there is weight to this sceptical challenge, the basic idea that the critics reject is in one sense clear and indispensable. The common good is what responsible citizens and public officials are seeking to discover through practical deliberation and argument. In its general outlines, it is broadly known in advance, but in its essential concreteness, especially as it bears on public policy, law, and regulatory oversight, it remains to be discovered through informed and responsible debate.

The parameters of the common good are clearly articulated in the preamble to the United States Constitution: "to form a more perfect union, to establish justice, to insure domestic tranquility, to provide for the common defense, to promote the general welfare, and to secure the blessings of liberty for ourselves and our posterity." It is one thing to articulate the goals of a common enterprise, quite another to specify the relevant policies and actions advancing those goals here and now. The task of practical wisdom and the purpose of political deliberation is to determine concretely what national unity, justice, security, prosperity, and liberty actually require in the thicket and turmoil of a constantly changing world.

Appraisal: An historically minded conception of the common good must be flexible, objective and critical. It must be flexible with respect to the size and nature of the relevant community, the different ways in which collective decisions are reached, and the changing circumstances to which they apply. It must also be objective. When particular communities arrive at reasonable judgments and responsible decisions through deliberative dialogue and debate, the results of their efforts are genuinely good. Authentic political activity is both an originating and a terminal value. It is intrinsically good in itself, and it tends to actualize the common goods at which it deliberately aims.[107]

A realistic conception of the common good must also be critical. It must be sensitive to human fallibility and all forms of distorting bias. The egoistic bias of individuals, the group bias of organized interests, the general bias of an uncritical or suspicious culture, all threaten the discovery and enactment of the common good. Even with bias provisionally in check, the unpredictability of human action remains in force. Laws that initially seemed wise, public policies that once appeared sound, collective decisions judged to be responsible, often produce unintended and unwelcome consequences. Each community's search for the common good is a fallible self-correcting process of learning from well intentioned mistakes and noteworthy achievements.

The price of loss: What political price do we pay for rejecting or ignoring the common good as the goal of public deliberation and action? We lose a critical norm for distinguishing legitimate from despotic power.[108] Legitimate authorities seek the comprehensive and enduring good of the historical communities to which they are accountable; despots seek their private advantage or the narrow interests of their group or class. We also indirectly accept the political validity of egoistic and group bias by treating public activity as a legitimate way to achieve private interests and purposes. When the public good is invoked today, it is usually interpreted in utilitarian terms. But classical utility, despite its repeated invocation, remains an incoherent concept, for the common good should never be confused with the aggregative sum of private satisfactions and pleasures.[109]

The several practical obstacles confronting the common good tend to be interdependent. They include anthropological prejudices about human motivation, philosophical scepticism about the objectivity of evaluative judgments, cultural suspicion of hidden agendas and ideologies, the political alienation of ordinary citizens and the contested legitimacy of modern democracies. Sceptical mistrust of this vital normative concept presently covers the political spectrum.

On what intellectual resources can we draw in this work of critical retrieval? Bernard Lonergan's epistemic realism is an invaluable resource, as are David Hollenbach's, *The Common Good in Christian Ethics* and John Courtney Murray's, *We Hold These Truths*. Civic republican theorists like Charles Taylor and Michael Sandel have also made important and original contributions to the new public philosophy we require. Communitarian critics like Robert Bellah, Amitai Etzioni and Philip Selznick have emphasized the civic alienation that a liberal political culture tends to create. Finally, Iseult Honohan's study of *Civic Republicanism* shows the practical benefits of uniting the classical ideals of public liberty and civic virtue with a pluralistic and deliberative understanding of the common good.

The revitalization of political philosophy that began with John Rawls' *Theory of Justice* has made this an especially fertile period for articulating the political teleology we require. In the adversarial culture of American democracy, the critical retrieval of the common good has become a matter of practical urgency.

HEALING THE RIFT BETWEEN THOUGHT AND ACTION: THE IMPORTANCE OF PRACTICAL WISDOM

When Hegel and Marx directed theoretical attention to history, they compromised their efforts by searching for invariant dialectical laws. They made lawful necessity rather than freedom the basic interpretive category of historical research. Under their influence, political thinking became rigidly ideological, and political action was reduced to the ruthless implementation of an infallible utopian vision. Ideological thinking reinforced the traditional tendency to confuse action with making, confining political activity to the faithful execution of a pre-existing model or formula.[110]

Arendt's political thinking focused on the common world of sensible appearances and on the free agents, actions and events that occur within it. She taught her readers and students to approach the public world impartially, *sine ira et studio*. In her linguistic phenomenology, she articulated the internal structure of the *vita activa,* clarifying the important differences among labor, work and action. In her historical narratives, she recounted the triumphs and tragedies of mortal men and communities, memorialising the republics of liberty as well as the totalitarian death camps. Her insightful account of political thinking was, I believe, incomplete. She clearly understood political remembrance and story telling and the communities of memory they help to create. She was less clear about political deliberation, the communal effort to discover and articulate common goods and the best ways to enact them concretely. I trace these oversights about deliberative inquiry to her consistent scepticism about political teleology. Since deliberative thinking is inherently purposive, and Arendt believed that a teleological politics is modeled on *poiesis* not *praxis*, her account of the intelligible connection between thought and action remains obscure.[111]

Although practical wisdom is the supreme political virtue, Arendt is surprisingly silent about it.[112] This silence reveals a serious lacuna in her political philosophy, for practical wisdom provides the best way to re-connect thought and action in a genuinely republican politics. When the common good is conceived as a second order heuristic notion, it clearly lacks specificity. Normative appeals on its behalf, offered in isolation, leave conscientious citizens and statesmen groping in the dark. Although wise and effective action needs to be guided by deliberative thinking, it is important to distinguish the various levels of inquiry that culminate in responsible decisions and choices. In the practical inquiry of an individual or a community, factual knowledge of the world needs to be integrated with evaluative knowledge of the normative principles and precepts that govern responsible choice. Only through the dynamic integration of factual and evaluative knowledge can we concretely determine what ought to be done and avoided here and now.[113]

At the different levels of collective responsibility, policy making and planning invariably depend on numerous sources of insight: the norms and principles of public ethics, the institutional analysis and cultural criticism of the human sciences, the depth dimension of historical research, disinterested dialogue and debate among citizens and their political leaders, and our common sense knowledge of the factual circumstances in which human action really occurs. Egoistic, group and general bias can distort human reflection and decision making at each of these interconnected levels. Discerning the presence of bias and critiquing the persuasive ideologies with which bias disguises and justifies itself are essential to understanding and resolving practical conflict. Because the operation of bias is nearly inevitable and the resort to justifying ideologies recurrent, practical inquiry must be a fallible, self-correcting, constantly revisable, cooperative blending of thought and action.

Practical inquiry culminates in concerted action when historically situated citizens carry out the public decisions that emerge from their shared deliberation. There is no substitute in politics for informed and responsible men and women on the scene to enact the plans and to execute the policies that have been jointly agreed upon. As Bernard Lonergan constantly emphasized, the human good is always concrete. It is in the lived concreteness of the home, the classroom, the shop floor, the court house, the neighborhood, the subway, the pollution site, the housing project, the welfare agency, the obsolete manufacturing plant, the emergency room, the prison, the homeless shelter, the supermarket, the public park, the thriving or abandoned commercial center that human good and evil are directly experienced and made real. In relatively primitive and stable societies, the gap to be mediated between common sense knowledge and effective group action is generally narrow. In our highly specialized and dynamic global society, that epistemic gap has become steadily broader and deeper.[114]

Practical reflection operates like a scissors with an upper and lower blade. The upper blade is relatively invariant and universal; it exhibits a notable continuity though the long course of human history and practice. The lower blade, by contrast, is highly variable and particular; it undergoes significant institutional and cultural variation with emerging differences in time and place. The upper blade articulates the moral horizon or background framework within which practical reflection occurs. The lower blade concentrates on the concrete social and political situations that human conduct will ultimately affect.[115]

The weakness of the upper blade taken in isolation is its lack of required specificity. It can tell us what is unwise and unjust in the way we live as individual persons and historically organized communities. However, it is characteristically unable to identify appropriate and effective remedies to correct what is wrong, or to recommend insightful policies and plans to promote what is right and good. The weakness of the lower blade taken in isolation is its lack of principled normativity. Proponents of the lower blade tend to take the factual status quo for granted and, in the name of supposedly hard-headed realism, characteristically reduce normative standards of conduct to the level of existing practice.

The upper and lower blades of practical reflection concretely intersect in the formation and execution of public policy. It is in shaping policy that normative principles and precepts are directly applied to the factual universe. It is in enacting policy, in initiating and engaging in cooperative action, that practical inquiry fulfills its legitimate purpose of promoting the human good and remedying the effects of human folly and sin. The indispensable virtue required for effective policy making and planning is practical wisdom. It is practical wisdom that unites the moral vision and normative precepts of the upper blade with the concrete realism and required flexibility of the lower blade. It is practical wisdom that correctly determines the right thing to do, the best thing to do, here and now.[116]

But who are the practically wise? In everyday life, they are the friends whose counsel we seek when we are confronted with important and difficult personal decisions. In public affairs, they are the counselors whom conscientious statesmen consult in the course of governing the political community. In both the personal and public sphere, they are the adults whose practical advice and guidance we trust, when the chips are down. In traditional societies that were far more stable than our own and more self-sufficient in meeting the needs of their members, the lower blade of practical inquiry remained relatively constant, and practical wisdom could be ascribed to the wise men and women, the respected elders of the community, who knew from the funded experience of cooperative life the right thing to do. But in contemporary global societies, where the lower blade is in constant flux, and where human knowledge and practice are linked in a mutually transforming symbiosis, practical wisdom is much harder to achieve. Practical wisdom in a dynamic global society will require interdisciplinary collaborative teams deliberately organized to integrate the upper and lower blades of political reflection in a self-correcting process of learning and doing.

As there is no substitute for the reliable common sense of men and women on the scene who depend on their own practical insights for the implementation of law and policy, there is also no substitute for the concrete feedback they provide to policy makers and planners on the success or failure of their enacted decisions. Paralleling an empirical canon of operations in the natural sciences that regularly connects theory and practice, there is a moral canon of operations in human affairs providing constantly new data and evidence on the uneven and unexpected results of cooperative action. This essential feedback procedure keeps theologians and philosophers, cultural analysts and critics, policy makers and planners in regular contact and dialogue with actively engaged citizens and local communities. Reciprocal dialogue and feedback lessen the dangers of academic remoteness and unbridled idealism, on the theoretical side, while checking the familiar tendency to egoistic, group and general bias among hard-headed practical "realists."[117]

We live in an age of epistemic specialization and differentiation. We presently have within the global and national community highly specialized experts in the many different fields of theory and practice. What we conspicuously lack are operating centers of integration and coordination to bring the different levels and kinds of human knowledge jointly to bear on the most important contemporary problems. What we urgently need are new centers of public liberty at the various levels of political and collective responsibility to remedy that glaring deficiency.

In these centers of practical reflection, informed and responsible citizens would engage in a serious dialogue about our cultural beliefs and values, and about the justice and wisdom of our economic and political policies. Such critical public inquiry would be eminently practical; it would be directed to what we are doing and how we are living, and the changing character of our relations with other countries and the natural universe. But it would be profoundly practical, drawing on the entire range of cultural resources we have inherited. The depth dimension, so noticeably lacking in contemporary public argument, would come from theology, philosophy, history, economic and political theory, critical social and cultural analysis, the study of international relations, works of art and literature. This public moral and political conversation directed towards the critical appraisal and reform of contemporary life, would be open to all who accept responsibility for the world, and who are prepared to enlist their specialized knowledge, their practical competence, and their civic energy in the service of the commonweal.

While contemporary public debate is narrowly focused and driven by the shifting winds of opinion research, the sustained political and moral conversation we need is genuinely comprehensive and committed to taking the long view. To sustain such conversations, we need a new type of public institution, centers of liberty operating independently of government, but profoundly devoted to political purposes. These centers would draw upon the diverse cultural resources presently existing in civil society, on the churches, the universities, the private research foundations, the humanitarian aid groups, and the broad range of voluntary associations and political movements in every region of the world. Their explicit purpose would be to integrate the upper and lower blades of inquiry in the service of justice and international solidarity, to bring disinterested thought and responsible action together, not only in the minds of individual citizens but in the historical communities they've created to fulfill their obligations to posterity.[118]

IS THERE A WAY TO GET THERE FROM HERE?

There is no escaping human history. We cannot leap out of the global economy, the welfare state or the pluralism of modern democracy. Yet we should never succumb to the illusion of historical inevitability. We are surely not powerless before the economic, political and cultural forces that have shaped our lives and our world.

Although Arendt was highly critical of modernity, she accepted it as the starting point for genuine thinking and action. The first imperative of thought is to face the challenge of reality, to acknowledge the world as it is and has been. But free thinking is critical as well as realistic, discerning in the complexity of the world not only sources of alienation and discontent, but undeveloped possibilities and alternative paths of reflection and action.

The revelatory power of Hannah Arendt's public discourse, her memorable narratives, her phenomenological insights, her unsparing critical judgments have taught us to look at the history of politics in a new way. She has taught us to see that most of what passes for political activity today is actually anti-political; she has helped us understand how our massive retreat from collective responsibility paralyzes democratic action and governance.

She has also revealed the inherent dignity of the public realm and of the activities that transpire within it. She convincingly affirmed the intrinsic worth of undervalued political realities: action, speech, phenomenal appearance, opinion, judgment, common sense, power, citizenship, and civic solidarity. Through her passionate writing and teaching, she strengthened our love of the world, drawing us out of our shelters of solitude and privacy into the world's service and partial redemption. She did not provide explicit directions leading from our world to her idealized republic of liberty, but she did articulate the republican norms of public happiness, public virtue and public freedom to inspire our quest for a more responsible and authentic common life.

Inspired by her example, I want to suggest some additional ways to restore legitimacy to American democracy. The deepest reforms we require are intellectual and cultural. At every level of our society, Americans need to reexamine the ways we think, speak and feel about citizenship and government. We have created a political culture that emphasizes individual rights and neglects public responsibilities, that celebrates the pursuit of self-interest and casts suspicion on the great civic virtues, that highlights individual misconduct and glosses over systemic injustice, and that cultivates sceptical distrust of the discovery and attainment of the common good.[119]

In the civic republican tradition, politics, the symbol of the commonweal, enjoys directive authority over economics, the historical symbol of self-interested activity. But democratic politics, today, is heavily dominated by economic interests and free market practices. Nearly everyone involved, their inflated rhetoric aside, conceives of political activity as a way of advancing limited private and group concerns. As long as this capitalist mentality prevails and excludes other ways of conceiving political life, a sustained cultural critique of American democracy will be difficult to mount. If the pursuit of self-interest is the operative political norm, then lobbyists, their corporate clients, public officials, journalists and citizens are fully justified in pursuing their private advantage, without concern for the needs of the vulnerable and their fiduciary obligations to posterity.

Credible political reform must be guided by the imperative of justice.[120] Public confidence in democratic governments rests on the belief that the needs and concerns of all citizens are accorded equal weight, that the concrete requirements of political equality are actually met. Citizens must also be convinced that economic and political power are fairly distributed and reasonably balanced, and that public officials remain independent of the organized interests they are intended to regulate.

Justice also requires an equitable distribution of the benefits and burdens of human cooperation. The regulative principle in a modern democracy is civic equality, equality under the law, equality of opportunity, and equal treatment in the many sectors of institutional life. But democratic equality is in practice complex. Where no distinction is made among the claims of individual citizens, the appropriate form of equality is arithmetic; for example, equality of individual rights and liberties and equality of political representation (one person—one vote). But in those domains where relevant differences of merit exist among citizens, the appropriate form of equality is geometric or proportional. In distributing public benefits, such as honors, offices, and income, those who contribute more to the collective good are entitled to receive more in return. But the benefits they receive should be proportional to their contribution. The same principle applies to the sharing of public burdens such as taxation or military service. Those citizens better able to bear the burden should carry the heavier load. Everyone should contribute in accordance with their ability and resources; no one should carry a disproportionate share, but to whom much is given much will be expected in return.[121]

In a modern democracy political solidarity depends on the achievement of economic and social justice. There should be an equitable distribution of wealth, income, opportunity, and economic security, with guarantees of a decent minimum for all. Scandalous inequality in the distribution of public goods and obligations is both politically and socially unwise. Politically, it erodes public trust in the legitimacy of both government and business; socially, it creates dangerous cycles of poverty, alienation and crime. The radical inequality of wealth and income in the United States, and the warranted fear that economic inequality translates directly into massive political inequality, raise legitimate alarms about the justice and integrity of our collective life.[122]

These justice-based concerns are relevant to all citizens; to public officials, lobbyists, scholars, thinkers and critics, to the nation as a whole. Restoring soundness to our democracy and strengthening our political union is a shared responsibility.[123] Correcting failures in democratic justice will require individual, institutional, and cultural change. Individuals will need to think and act like responsible citizens rather than petitioning consumers. Structural inequities in our political and economic institutions will need to be remedied through democratic processes (to paraphrase Madison, we are seeking republican remedies for democratic ills), and the usurpation of our civic culture by the capitalist values of self-interest and unbridled competition will need to be resisted by a renewed commitment to civic virtues and the common good. The great challenges to the American democratic experiment differ from generation to generation. We are not called today to create a new constitution, to end slavery, to overcome economic depression, or to resist the totalitarian menace of Nazism and Stalinism. The grave challenge we face is to create economic justice, political solidarity and civic participation in a global society marked by scandalous inequities and new forms of ideology and terror. The courage and wisdom of Hannah Arendt are invaluable resources in meeting this daunting challenge. We continue to remain in her debt.

NOTES

1. Benjamin Barker, *Strong Democracy* (Berkeley: University of California Press, 1989).
2. The image of the tangled knot is drawn from Pascal's *Penseés*. For the reasons behind the moral and political impotence that checks human progress and structures the surd of concrete existence, see Bernard Lonergan's *Insight*, pp. 627-633 and 687-693.
3. See Glenn Tinder, *Against Fate* (Notre Dame: University of Notre Dame Press, 1981).
4. Arendt, *Between Past and Future*, p. 10.
5. Arendt, *On Revolution*, pp. 223-224.

6. Constant and Tocqueville exemplify the liberal critique of the Jacobins, Isaiah Berlin and Raymond Aron the liberal critique of the Bolsheviks.

7. Alexander Solzhenitsyn in *New York Times*, November 28, 1993, cited in Eric Hobsbawm's *The Age of Extremes* (New York: Vintage, 1996) p. 558.

8. The decline of Marxism has created disarray within the political left and given a new impetus to economic liberalism. The moral limitations of capitalism are only enhanced, however, within an intensely competitive global economy.

9. See Charles Taylor, *Sources of the Self*, for a sympathetic account of contemporary moral pluralism. Unlike Berlin, Taylor wants to combine moral pluralism with a distinctively positive account of liberty.

10. Taylor, *Ethics of Authenticity*, p. 110.

11. See Taylor, *Philosophical Arguments* (Cambridge: Harvard University Press, 1995) pp. 187-188. Taylor is developing a line of thought articulated by Tocqueville in *Democracy in America*.

12. Taylor, *Philosophical Arguments*, pp. 193-197.

13. Charles Taylor, Michael Sandel, Nicholas Boyle, David Hollenbach and Robert Bellah are good examples of this cooperative intellectual effort.

14. See Michael McCarthy, "The Critical Appropriation of Tradition," *Soundings*, vol. 82, p. 3-4, 1999.

15. Paul Ricoeur, *Hermeneutics and the Human Sciences* (Cambridge: Cambridge University Press, 1981).

16. Maurizio Passerin D'Entrèves, *The Political Philosophy of Hannah Arendt* (London: Routledge, 1994) pp. 64-100.

17. See McCarthy, "The Critical Appropriation of Tradition," pp. 495-497.

18. Charles Taylor has clarified ontological differences within the tradition of liberal individualism, while aligning himself with the holistic individualism of von Humboldt. Holistic individualists "represent a trend of thought that is fully aware of the ontological (social) embedding of human agents but, at the same time, prizes liberty and individual differences very highly." See Taylor, *Philosophical Arguments*, pp.181-186.

19. Taylor's "affirmation of ordinary life" stands in tension with the Periclean strain of Arendt's civic humanism. For Arendt, the concerns of ordinary life should be restricted to the private realm and denied public attention and significance.

20. Amartya Sen, Thomas Friedman, George Soros, Nicholas Boyle, Benjamin Barber, Robert Heilbroner and Joseph Stiglitz are just some of the contemporary thinkers debating the social justice implications of the global economy.

21. "The question which arises from all this is whether we are not living beyond our moral means in continuing allegiance to our standards of justice and benevolence. Do we have enough ways of seeing good which are still credible to us, which are powerful enough to sustain these standards?" (Taylor, *Sources of the Self*, p.517).

22. For a fuller account of the concept of critical belonging, see McCarthy, "The Critical Appropriation of Tradition."

23. Bernard Lonergan, *Collection* (Toronto: University of Toronto Press, 1988) pp. 266-267.

24. In this highly synoptic account of the discontents of liberal democracy, I have drawn on the work of Michael Sandel, Charles Taylor, William Galston, Benjamin Barber, Iseult Honohan, Robert Putnam, among many others.

25. See Taylor, "Legitimation Crisis?" in *Philosophical Papers*, vol. II (Cambridge: Cambridge University Press, 1985) pp. 248-288.

26. See the broad range of essays in *Debating Democracy's Discontent* (Oxford: Oxford University Press, 1988).

27. See Alexis de Tocqueville, *Democracy in America*, author's preface to the twelfth edition.

28. See William Galston, "Political Economy and the Politics of Virtue: U.S. Public Philosophy at Century's End," *Debating Democracy's Discontent* (Oxford, Oxford University Press, 1988).

29. For the diminished commitment of the democratic party to economic and social justice, see Thomas Edsall, *The New Politics of Inequality* (New York: Norton, 1984).

30. Galston, *Debating Democracy's Discontent*, pp. 63-69.

31. See Hobsbawm, *The Age of Extremes*, "The Golden Years," pp. 257-286.

32. Edsall's analysis of the political trends of the 1980s is partly echoed in Thomas Frank's work, *What's The Matter With Kansas?* (New York: Metropolitan Books, 2004).

33. See Paul Krugman, *The Great Unraveling* (New York: Norton, 2003).

34. See Soros' *On Globalization* and Boyle's *Who Are We Now?*

35. When alienated citizens withdraw from the public realm, they create a vacuum of power favorable to despots and demagogues.

36. See Robert Putnam's *Bowling Alone* (New York: Simon & Schuster, 2000).

37. Tocqueville, *Democracy in America*, vol. I, "Political Associations in the United States," and vol. II, Book II, chapter V.

38. For Tocqueville's analysis of the nature and consequences of democratic individualism, see *Democracy in America*, vol. II, Book II, chapters 2-8.

39. Putnam, *Bowling Alone*, pp. 276-284.

40. See The *Ethics of Lobbying: Organized Interests, Political Power and the Common Good* (Washington, D.C: Georgetown University Press, 2002), and the numerous publications of the Center for Public Integrity.

41. For the complex relationship between democracy and capitalism, see Robert Dahl, *On Democracy* (New Haven: Yale University Press, 1998), pp.166-179, and Albert Hirschman, *Rival Views of Market Society* (Cambridge: Harvard University Press, 1992).

42. See Taylor, *Ethics of Authenticity*, "Against Fragmentation," pp.109-121.

43. In the *Federalist Papers*, Madison argues for the clear advantages of representative democracy on a continental scale. In *On Revolution*, Arendt insisted that the principle of political federation was not consistently applied at the level of the ward and the township. For her later reflections on the federal principle, see *Crises of the Republic*, pp. 229-233.

44. See Arendt, *On Revolution*, "The Revolutionary Tradition and Its Lost Treasure."

45. "All the sects of the United States are comprised within the great unity of Christianity, and Christian morality is everywhere the same." Tocqueville, *Democracy*, vol. 1, 314.

46. Galston, *Debating*, p. 85.

47. Michael Sandel, *Democracy's Discontent* (Cambridge: Harvard University Press, 1996) pp. 317-350, and *Liberalism and the Limits of Justice*, second edition (Cambridge: Cambridge University Press, 1998) pp. 66-104.

48. Iseult Honohan, *Civic Republicanism* (London: Routledge, 2002) p. 1.

49. A philosophical anthropology centered on republican citizenship provides an alternative to both inflated and reductive conceptions of the human being. It checks the inflated conception of humans as autonomous sovereign masters as well as their ideological reduction to expendable economic animals.

50. See Honohan, *Civic Republicanism*, p. 129, pp. 191-192; and Sandel, *Democracy's Discontent* for an extended treatment of the political economy of citizenship.

51. One of Taylor's great strengths is his ability to show that particular strands in the liberal tradition complement civic republican principles. See "Liberal Politics and the Public Sphere," *Philosophical Arguments*, chap. 3.

52. See Michael Walzer, "The Civil Society Argument" in Chantal Mouuffe's *Dimensions of Radical Democracy* (London: Verso, 1992) pp. 89-107.

53. "The hostility between philosophy and politics, barely covered up by a philosophy of politics, has been the curse of western statecraft as well as of the western tradition of philosophy ever since the men of action and the men of thought parted company—that is ever since Socrates' death." *On Revolution*, p. 319.

54. For the internal connection between common goods and public virtues, see Honohan, pp. 147-179; and Taylor, *Philosophical Arguments*, pp. 136-145, 186-203.

55. See the extended argument in chapter 1, The City in Ruins.

56. *On Revolution*, pp. 221-223.

57. See *The Ethics of Lobbying*, pp. 57-69; and Taylor, "Against Fragmentation," *Ethics of Authenticity*, pp. 109-121; and *Philosophical Arguments*, pp. 257-288.

58. *On Revolution*, "The Revolutionary Tradition and Its Lost Treasure."
59. Ibid. p.139.
60. For the important notion of collective responsibility see Lonergan, *Third Collection*, pp. 169-183; Honohan, pp. 170-174.
61. For the distinction between essential and effective freedom, see Lonergan, *Insight*, pp. 619-633.
62. Isaiah Berlin, "Two Concepts of Liberty."
63. Tocqueville, *Democracy in America*, vol. I, pp. 253-258; vol. II, pp. 344-346.
64. Tocqueville, *Democracy in America*, vol. II, p. 113.
65. Tocqueville emphasizes these apprenticeships in liberty. "Nothing is more fertile in prodigies than the art of being free; but there is nothing more arduous than the apprenticeship of liberty." *Democracy in America*, vol. I, p. 256.
66. Arendt rightly contrasts the pursuit of "private happiness" with the experience of "public happiness," but doesn't adequately connect that republican experience with a formative apprenticeship in liberty. *On Revolution*, pp. 126-140.
67. Tocqueville, *Democracy in America*, vol. II, p. 104.
68. Honohan, *Civic Republicanism*, p. 215.
69. Madison, *Federalist X*.
70. See Gordon Wood's analysis of the shift in American civic culture from republicanism to democracy in *The Radicalism of the American Revolution* (New York: Vintage, 1993).
71. For Arendt's reflections on federalism, see *On Revolution*, pp. 245-280; and *Crises of the Republic*, pp. 229-233. For Tocqueville's analysis of American federalism, see chapters V-IX, *Democracy in America*, vol. I.
72. *Democracy in America*, vol. I, p. 63. For Arendt's examples (town meetings and jury duty) of citizen participation today, see *Hannah Arendt: The Recovery of the Public World*, edited by Melvin Hill (New York: St. Martin's Press, 1979) p. 317.
73. See Boyle, *Who Are We Now?* pp. 47-51.
74. For Tocqueville's useful distinction between centralized power and administration, see *Democracy in America*, vol. I, pp. 89-101; and *Democracy in America*, vol. II, pp. 337-339.
75. The role of religion in public life is inherently ambiguous. In the nineteen sixties, religiously motivated concerns for equality drew many citizens into the struggle for civil rights and economic justice. As the political energies of the religious left waned, evangelical Christians became a dominant influence within the increasingly conservative Republican party.
76. Though civil rights and public liberty are distinct, both are required in a genuinely free political community.
77. Arendt, *On Revolution*, pp. 247-277; and *Origins*, pp. 250-266.
78. For the impressive spirit of solidarity within the councils, see *Between Past and Future*, pp. 3-9; *On Revolution*, pp. 247-275; *Crises of the Republic*, pp. 229-233.
79. *On Revolution*, pp. 243-248.
80. "To be sure, such an 'aristocratic' form of government would spell the end of general suffrage as we understand it today; for only those who have demonstrated that they care for more than their private happiness and are concerned about the state of the world would have the right to be heard in the conduct of the business of the republic." *On Revolution*, p. 279.
81. *The Human Condition*, pp. 61-67, p. 253.
82. *Crises of the Republic*, pp. 211-222; *On Revolution*, pp. 65-66.
83. *Hannah Arendt: The Recovery of the Public World*, pp. 317-320.
84. For the political economy of citizenship, see Sandel, *Democracy's Discontent*, Part II. For a thoughtful response to Sandel, see Galston, *Debating Democracy's Discontent*, pp. 63-85.
85. For the difficulty of achieving political freedom in the face of market pressures and ideology, see Boyle, *Who Are We Now?*, pp. 31-33, 86-87, 165-168.
86. "Arendt's views on the relationship between politics and economics are much misunderstood but also very obscure." Hanna Pitkin, *The Attack of the Blob*, (Chicago: University of Chicago Press, 1998), pp. 11-12, 179-180, p. 239; pp. 322-323.
87. "In essence, socialism has simply continued and driven to its extreme, what capitalism began. Why should it be the remedy?" *Crises of the Republic*, p. 215.

88. "Precisely because republics required civic virtue and disinterestedness among their citizens, they were very fragile polities, extremely liable to corruption." Wood, *Radicalism*, pp.104-105.

89. Hanna Pitkin carefully distinguishes the different strands within Arendt's problematic concept of the social. *The Attack of the Blob*, pp.10-18. Seyla Benhabib and Margaret Canovan also distinguish different senses of the 'social' in Arendtian thought. For a slightly different emphasis, see Peter Baehr's Introductory essay in *The Portable Hannah Arendt*.

90. "What protects freedom is the division between governmental and economic power." *Crises of the Republic*, p. 213.

91. Pitkin, *The Attack of the Blob*, "Rethinking the Social."

92. One unintended consequence of sharply segregating the political and the economic is that it fortifies the ideology and practical dominance of economic liberalism.

93. See Charles Taylor "The Inarticulate Debate," *Ethics of Authenticity*, pp. 13-23; and *Sources of the Self*, "The Ethics of Inarticulacy."

94. The model is Aristotle's treatment of the concrete mean in the *Nicomachean Ethics*. Aristotle suggests that one way to find the mean is to slightly reverse our habitual predilections. For us, this would require giving priority to political over economic considerations, of subordinating efficiency to equity.

95. In section H, I argue for a revised conception of practical wisdom suited to the responsibilities of a global society.

96. For the internal connection between republican equality and economic independence, see Wood, *Radicalism*, pp. 232-243.

97. Arendt, *Crises of the Republic*, pp. 94-102; and *On Revolution*, pp. 226-229.

98. See Christopher Lasch, *The Revolt of the Elites*, and *The Betrayal of Democracy* (New York: Norton, 1995); and Putnam's *Bowling Alone*.

99. Although the normative concept of the common good was first articulated by Aristotle, it has been kept alive in the modern period by Catholic social thinkers like Jacques Maritain and John Courtney Murray. For the central role of the common good in Christian social ethics, see David Hollenbach, *The Common Good and Christian Ethics* (Cambridge: Cambridge University Press, 2002).

100. Arendt, *The Human Condition*, pp. 35-55; *On Revolution*, p. 221.

101. *The Human Condition*, pp. 17-21, p. 197, p. 232; *On Revolution*, pp. 118-121.

102. For the central role of heuristic concepts in mathematics, physics and common sense reasoning, see Bernard Lonergan, *Insight*, pp. 36-37, p. 63, pp. 217-244, pp. 683-684.

103. For Lonergan's distinction between originating and terminal values, see *Method in Theology*, pp. 51-53. For the relevance of this distinction to the common good, see McCarthy, "Liberty, History and the Common Good," *Journal of the Lonergan Workshop*, vol.12, 1996.

104. See McCarthy, "Liberty, History and the Common Good" and "The Critical Appropriation of Tradition"; and Hollenbach, *The Common Good,* "Recovering the Commonweal."

105. Aristotle, *Nicomachean Ethics*, pp.1140a 29-1140b 30 and 1141b 10-1143a 15.

106. For the political risks of promoting the common good, see Sandel, *Democracy's Discontent*, pp. 317-324. On the contemporary need for a shared public philosophy, see Murray, *We Hold These Truths*, pp. 79-123.

107. "In the world mediated by meaning and motivated by value, objectivity is simply the consequence of authentic subjectivity, of genuine attention, genuine intelligence, genuine reasonableness, genuine responsibility. Mathematics, science, philosophy, ethics, theology differ in many manners, but they have the common feature that their objectivity is the fruit of attentiveness, intelligence, reasonableness and responsibility." Lonergan, *Collection*, p. 265.

108. Aristotle, *Politics*, p. 1279a 20-1279b 10 "The true forms of government, therefore, are those in which the one, the few, or the many, govern with a view to the common interest, but governments which rule with a view to the private interest . . . are perversions."

109. For a trenchant critique of the classical notion of utility, see Alasdair MacIntyre, *After Virtue* (Notre Dame: University of Notre Dame Press, 1981) pp. 60-63, and Bruce Douglas, "The Common Good and the Public Interest," *Political Theory*, XIII (1), February 1980.

110. Arendt, *On Revolution*, p. 319. "The hostility between philosophy and politics, barely covered up by a philosophy of politics, has been the curse of western state-craft as well as of the western tradition of philosophy ever since the men of action and the men of thought parted company—that is, ever since Socrates' death." See Frederick Dolan, "Arendt on Philosophy and Politics," *The Cambridge Companion to Hannah Arendt*, pp. 261-276.

111. Arendt, *Between Past and Future*, p.30.

112. Though Arendt never denies that practical judgments occur prior to action, judgments for which the agent is morally responsible, she focuses her attention on retrospective judgments that appraise what has already been done. Her model of judging tends to be that of a jury deciding the guilt or innocence of a defendant, or of the Israeli judges condemning Eichmann to death. See "The Crisis in Culture," *Between Past and Future, the Postscript to Eichmann in Jerusalem and Lectures on Kant's Political Philosophy*.

113. For a noteworthy counter-example, see *Between Past and Future*, p. 221.

114. For the tripartite structure of teleological reasoning, see Alasdair MacIntyre, *After Virtue*, pp. 50-59; and Bernard Lonergan, *Second Collection*, pp.189-190.

115. For the importance and limitations of common sense in practical inquiry see Lonergan's *Method in Theology*. The general bias of common sense tends to concentrate "on short term benefits and to overlook long term costs," *Method in Theology*, p. 53; and *Insight*, pp. 218-242.

116. For the complex interplay of human nature and human historicity in practical inquiry, see Lonergan, *Third Collection*, pp. 169-183.

117. For a thoughtful synthesis of Aristotelian *phronesis* and Thomistic *prudentia*, see Josef Pieper's *Prudence* (New York: Pantheon Books, 1959).

118. I am attempting to connect the political strengths of Athenian democracy with the prophetic concern for the "widow and the orphan."

119. For the interdependence of personal and historical responsibility, see Lonergan "Natural Right and Historical Mindedness," *Third Collection*, pp.169-183.

120. Both cultural and institutional reforms are needed to restore a genuinely democratic politics. In contrast to Marx, I believe that the governing beliefs and aspirations of a community provide the constitutive ground of its collective institutions and practices.

121. The primacy of justice as a political imperative provides a unifying theme in pre-modern political thought. It is central to Plato's and Aristotle's political theories, to the prophetic tradition in Judaism and Christianity, and to the political theologies of Augustine and Aquinas. Important contemporary treatments include John Rawls' *Theory of Justice*, Michael Walzer's *Spheres of Justice* and Michael Sandel's *Liberalism and the Limits of Justice*, among others.

122. See Aristotle's influential account of justice in Book V, *Nicomachean Ethics*; and "Justice as a Virtue: Changing Conceptions" in MacIntyre's *After Virtue*. For a critical retrieval of the classical theory of justice, see MacIntyre's *Whose Justice? Which Rationality?* (Notre Dame: University of Notre Dame Press, 1988).

123. Political concerns about justice are relevant to every level of politics, from local concerns about equitable taxation to global concerns about the profound inequalities generated by trans-national capitalism.

Selected Bibliography

Basic Works by Hannah Arendt

Between Past and Future. New York: Viking Press, 1968.
Crises of the Republic. New York: Harcourt Brace Jovanovich, 1972.
Eichmann in Jerusalem: A Report on the Banality of Evil. New York: Viking Press, 1963.
The Human Condition. Chicago: University of Chicago Press, 1958.
Lectures on Kant's Political Philosophy. Chicago: University of Chicago Press, 1982.
The Life of the Mind, Volume 1, Thinking. New York: Harcourt Brace Jovanovich, 1978.
The Life of the Mind, Volume 2, Willing. New York: Harcourt Brace Jovanovich, 1978.
Love and Saint Augustine. Chicago: University of Chicago Press, 1996.
Men in Dark Times. New York: Harcourt Brace Jovanovich, 1983.
On Revolution. New York: Viking Press, 1963.
The Origins of Totalitarianism. New York: Meridian Books, 1958.

Selected Works about Hannah Arendt

Baehr, Peter. *The Portable Hannah Arendt.* New York: Penguin Books, 2003.
Benhabib, Seyla. *The Reluctant Modernism of Hannah Arendt.* Thousand Oaks: Sage Books, 1996.
Canovan, Margaret. *Hannah Arendt: A Reinterpretation of her Political Thought.* Cambridge: Cambridge University Press, 1992.
Feldman, Ron. *The Jew as Pariah: Jewish Identity and Politics in the Modern Age.* New York: Grove Press, 1978.
Hill, Melvyn. *Hannah Arendt: The Recovery of the Public World.* New York: St Martin Press, 1979.
Hinchman, Lewis P. and Sandra K. *Hannah Arendt: Critical Essays.* Albany: SUNY Press, 1994.
Kateb, George. *Hannah Arendt: Politics, Conscience and Evil.* Totowa, New Jersey: Rowman and Allenheld, 1983.
Kristeva, Julia. *Hannah Arendt.* New York: Columbia University Press, 2001.
Passerin D' Entreves, Maurizio. *The Political Philosophy of Hannah Arendt.* London: Routledge, 1994.
Pitkin, Hannah F. *The Attack of the Blob.* Chicago: University of Chicago Press, 1998.
Robinson, Jacob. *And the Crooked Shall Be Made Straight.* New York: Macmillan, 1965.
Villa, Dana. *Arendt and Heidegger: The Fate of the Political.* Princeton: Princeton University Press, 1995.

Villa, Dana. *The Cambridge Companion to Hannah Arendt*. New York: Cambridge University Press, 2000.
Young-Bruehl, Elisabeth. *Hannah Arendt: For Love of the World*. New Haven: Yale University Press, 1982.
Young- Bruehl, Elisabeth. *Why Arendt Matters*. New Haven: Yale University Press, 2006.

Other Works Cited or Discussed

Allen, Anita and Regan, Milton editors. *Debating Democracy's Discontent*. New York: Oxford University Press, 1998.
Aquinas. *Basic Writings of Thomas Aquinas, Vols 1 and 2*. Ed. Anton Pegis. New York: Random House, 1945.
Aristotle. *The Basic Works of Aristotle*. Ed. Richard Mc Keon. New York: Random House, 1941.
Aron, Raymond. *Main Currents in Sociological Thought. Vol 1*. New York: Basic Books, 1965.
Augustine. *The City of God*. New York: Modern Library, 1950.
Bacon, Francis. *Novum Organon*. New York: Oxford University Press, 2004.
Barber, Benjamin. *Strong Democracy: Participatory Politics in a New Age*. Berkeley: University of California Press, 1984.
Bellah, Robert et al. *Habits of the Heart: Individualism and Commitment in American Life*. Berkeley: University of California Press, 1985.
Benhabib, Seyla. *The Rights of Others: Aliens, Residents and Citizens*. New York: Cambridge University Press, 2004.
Berkeley, George. *Principles of Human Knowledge/ Three Dialogues*. New York: Penguin, 1988.
Berlin, Isaiah. *Four Essays on Liberty*. New York: Oxford University Press, 1969.
Berlin, Isaiah. *Karl Marx*. New York: Oxford University Press, 1959.
Boyle, Nicholas. *Who Are We Now?* Notre Dame: University of Notre Dame Press, 1998.
Breunig, Charles. *Age of Revolution and Reaction, 1789-1850*. New York: Norton, 1977.
Burke, Edmund. *Reflections on the Revolution in France*. New York: Library of Liberal Arts, 1955.
Dahl, Robert. *Democracy and its Critics*. New Haven: Yale University Press, 1989.
Dahl, Robert. *On Democracy*. New Haven: Yale University Press, 1998.
Darwin, Charles. *The Origin of Species*. New York: Dutton, 1928.
Descartes, Rene. *The Philosophical Works of Descartes, Vols 1 and 2. New York:* Cambridge University Press, 1972.
Dummett, Michael. *Frege: Philosophy of Language*. New York: Harper and Row, 1973.
Dunne, John. *A Search for God in Time and Memory*. New York: Macmillan, 1969.
Dunne, John. *The Way of all the Earth*. Notre Dame: University of Notre Dame Press, 1978.
Edsall, Thomas. *The New Politics of Inequality*. New York: Norton, 1984.
Federalist Papers, Ed. Ian Shapiro. New Haven: Yale University Press, 2009.
Freud, Sigmund. *Great Books of the Western World, Vol 54*. Chicago: Encyclopedia Brittanica, 1952.
Galilei, Galileo. *Dialogue Concerning the Two Chief World Systems-Ptolemaic and Copernican*. Berkeley: University of California Press, 1953.
Hegel, GWF. *Phenomenology of Mind*, trans. J.B. Bailie. London: Allen and Unwin, 1964.
Hegel. *Reason in History*. Indianapolis: Library of Liberal Arts, 1953.
Heidegger, Martin. *Being and Time*, trans Macquarrie and Robinson. New York: Harper and Row, 1962.
Heilbroner, Robert. *The Worldly Philosophers*. New York: Simon and Schuster, 1986.
Herodotus. *The Histories*, trans Robin Waterfield. New York: Oxford University Press, 2008.
Hirschman, Albert. *The Passions and the Interests*. Princeton: Princeton University Press, 1977.
Hirschman, Albert. *Rival Views of Market Society*. Cambridge: Harvard University Press, 1997.
Hobbes, Thomas. *Leviathan*. London: Norton, 1997.
Hobsbawm, Eric. *The Age of Extremes*. New York: Vintage, 1996.

Hollenbach, David. *The Common Good and Christian Ethics*. New York: Cambridge University Press, 2002.
Homer. *The Odyssey*, trans Robert Fitzgerald. Garden City:Doubleday, 1961.
Honohan, Iseult. *Civic Republicanism*. London: Routledge, 2002.
Husserl, Edmund. *The Crisis of the European Sciences and Transcendental Phenomenology*, trans. David Carr. Evanston: Northwestern University Press, 1970.
Husserl. *Phenomenology and the Crisis of Philosophy*, trans Quentin Lauer. New York: Harper and Row, 1965.
Jaeger, Werner. *Paideia, Vols 1-3*, trans Gilbert Highet. New York: Oxford University Press, 1939.
Kant, Immanuel. *Critique of Judgment*, trans. J.H. Bernard. New York: Hafner Publishing, 1951.
Kant. *Critique of Practical Reason*. New York: Bobbs Merrill, 1956.
Kant. *Critique of Pure Reason*. New York: St Martin's Press, 1961.
Kant. *Groundwork of the Metaphysics of Morals*, trans. H. J. Paton. New York: Harper Torchbooks, 1964.
Kohn, Hans. *Political Ideologies of the Twentieth Century*. New York: Harper Row, 1966.
Krugman, Paul. *The Great Unraveling*. New York: Norton, 2003.
Lasch, Christopher. *Revolt of the Elites: And the Betrayal of Democracy*. New York: Norton, 1995.
Lash, Nicholas. *A Matter of Hope*. Notre Dame: University of Notre Dame Press, 1981.
Lobkowicz, Nicholas. *Theory and Practice: History of a Concept from Aristotle to Marx*. Notre Dame: University of Notre Dame Press, 1967.
Lonergan, Bernard. *Collection, Collected Works of Lonergan, Vol 4*. Toronto: University of Toronto Press, 1988.
Lonergan. *Insight: A Study in Human Understanding*. New York: Harper and Row, 1978.
Lonergan. *Method in Theology*. New York: Herder and Herder, 1972.
Lonergan. *A Second Collection*. Philadelphia: The Westminster Press, 1974.
Lonergan. *A Third Collection*. New York: Paulist Press, 1985.
MacIntyre, Alasdair. *After Virtue*. Notre Dame: University of Notre Dame Press, 1981.
MacIntyre. *Whose Justice? Which Rationality?* Notre Dame: University of Notre Dame Press, 1988.
Machiavelli, Niccolo. The Prince and the Discourses. New York: Modern Library, 1950.
Marx, Karl. *Karl Marx: Selected Writings*, Ed. David Mc Lellan. New York: Oxford University Press, 1977.
Marx. The Cambridge Companion to Marx. New York: Cambridge University Press, 1991.
Marx. *The Portable Karl Marx*. New York: Penguin, 1983.
Mc Kirahan, Richard. *Philosophy Before Socrates*. Indianapolis: Hackett, 1994.
Montequieu, Charles. *The Spirit of Laws*. Cambridge: Cambridge University Press, 1989.
Murray, John Courtney. *We Hold These Truths*. New York: Sheed and Ward, 1960.
Nietzsche, Friedrich. *The Genealogy of Morals: a Polemic*. New York; Russell and Russell, 1964.
Pascal, Blaise. *Pensees*. New York: Penguin Books.
Pico della Mirandola, Giovanni. *On the Dignity of Man*, trans Charles Wallis. Indianapolis, Bobbs Merrill, 1965.
Pieper, Josef. *Faith, Hope and Love*. Ignatius, 1997.
Pieper. *Prudence*. New York: Pantheon Books, 1959.
Pieper. *The Four Cardinal Virtues*. Notre Dame: University of Notre Dame Press, 1966.
Plato: The Collected Dialogues, Ed Hamilton and Cairns. Princeton: Bollingen Series. Princeton University Press, 1996.
Polanyi, Michael. *Personal Knowledge*. Chicago: University of Chicago Press, 1958.
Putnam, Robert. *Bowling Alone*. New York: Simon and Schuster, 2000.
Rawls, John. *A Theory of Justice*. Cambridge; Harvard University Press, 1971.
Ricoeur, Paul. *Ideology and Utopia*. New York: Columbia University Press, 1986.
Ricoeur. *Time and Narrative*. Chicago: University of Chicago Press, 1984.

Rorty, Richard. *Philosophy and the Mirror of Nature*. Princeton: Princeton University Press, 1979.
Rousseau, Jean Jacques. *Emile: an Education*. New York: Basic Books, 1979.
Rousseau. *The First and Second Discourses*. Ed. Roger Masters. New York: St Martin's Press, 1964.
Rousseau. *The Social Contract and other Later Political Writings*. New York: Cambridge University Press, 1997.
Sandel, Michael. *Democracy's Discontent*. Cambridge: Harvard University Press, 1996.
Sandel. *Liberalism and the Theory of Justice*. Cambridge: Cambridge University Press, 1995.
Sandel. *Public Philosophy: An Essay on Morality in Politics*. Cambridge: Harvard University Press, 2005.
Smith, Adam. *Wealth of Nations*. Oxford: Clarendon Press, 1976.
Soros, George. *On Globalization*. New York: Public Affairs, 2002.
Spinoza, Baruch. *The Ethics and Selected Letters*. Indianapolis: Hackett, 1982.
Strawson, Peter. *Individuals*. London: Methuen, 1959.
Taylor, Charles. *A Secular Age*. Cambridge: Harvard University Press, 2007.
Taylor. *The Ethics of Authenticity*. Cambridge: Harvard University Press, 1991.
Taylor. *Hegel*. New York: Cambridge University Press, 1975.
Taylor. *Hegel in Modern Society*. New York: Cambridge University Press, 1979.
Taylor. *Philosophical Arguments*. Cambridge: Harvard University Press, 1995.
Taylor. *Philosophical Papers, Vols 1 and 2*. Cambridge: Cambridge University Press, 1992.
Taylor. *Sources of the Self*. Cambridge: Harvard University Press, 1989.
Thucydides. *History of the Peloponnesian War*. Indianapolis: Hackett.
Tinder, Glen. *Against Fate*. Notre Dame: University of Notre Dame Press, 1981.
Tocqueville, Alexis de. *Democracy in America, Volumes 1 and 2*. New York: Vintage Books, 1961.
Tocqueville. *Souvenirs d'Alexis de Tocqueville*. Paris: Gallimard, 1942.
Tocqueville. *The Old Regime and the French Revolution*. Chicago: University of Chicago Press, 2001.
Walzer, Michael. *Spheres of Justice: A Defense of Pluralism and Equality*. New York: Basic Books, 1983.
Weber, Max. *The Essential Weber*, Ed Sam Whimster. New York: Oxford University Press, 1958.
Whitfield, J. H., *Machiavelli*. Oxford: Oxford University Press, 1947.
Wittgenstein, Ludwig. *On Certainty*. New York: Harper and Row, 1972.
Wittgenstein. *Philosophical Investigations*. New York: Macmillan, 1965.
Wittgenstein, *Tractatus Logico Philosophicus*. New York: Humanities Press, 1963.
Wood, Gordon. *The Radicalism of the American Revolution*. New York : Vintage, 1993.

Index

Aquinas, Thomas: critical appropriation, 245; *vita contemplativa* 95, 183
Arendt, Hannah: alienation, earth, 88; alienation, political, 252, 255; alienation, world, 48, 61n60, 61n70, 61n75, 81, 82, 94; action, atelic, 145, 151; action, instrumentalized, 143; action, irreversibility of, 175n84; action, limitations of, 139; action, substitutes for, 139–140; *animal laborans* 94, 234n104; appearance, 65; Archimedean point, 88; *arête* 98; Aristotle, appraisal of, 263; Aristotle, dependence on, 134; Aristotle, insights of, 136; Aristotle, limitations of, 139, 154, 167; Aristotle, virtue in, 160; arts, performing, 145; associations, of memory, 8; associations, of opinion, 283; associations, voluntary, 283; Augustine, dissertation on, 32; authority, in education, 155; authority, epistemic, 152; authority, loss of, 242; authority, models of, 153; autonomy, political, 145, 278, 280; banausic spirit, 96, 105n38; *bios politicos* 36, 78; Blücher, Heinrich, 33; bourgeoisie, 42; capitalism, 275, 277, 297n87; citizenship, 40; civility, 73; civil society, 282; common good, 283, 284; common sense, 93–94; common world, 77, 263, 284; consent, 274; constitution, 12, 22n14, 220, 235n122; council system, 10, 264, 273, 273, 274, 283; craftsmanship, 98, 142; crisis, of humanism, viii; crisis, political, vii–viii, 21, 34, 37, 38; death camps, 10; debts to Heidegger, 7, 22n6; decline, European, 33; decline, nation-state, 38; deliberation, 288; democracy, impotence of, 44; democracy, social, 278; domination, 28; despotism, 28, 133, 173n42; economics, and politics, 276, 277; economics, primacy of, 279; education, 67; Eichmann, 22n16; ends, and means, 144, 150; enlarged mentality, 15, 276, 277, 284; equality, civic, 152; equality, political, 281; evil, 31; excellence, political, 276; excellence, quest for, 275; spaces of, 277; fabrication, 98; federalism, 296n43; finitude, 84; freedom, 103, 185; goodness, anti-political, 105n37; goodness, and greatness, 174n46; Heidegger, debt to, 7, 22n6; *homo faber*, 234n104; *homo faber*, ambiguity of, 100; *homo faber*, triumph of, 96; homelessness, 44, 48; humanism, 118, 186; humanism, political, 3, 34, 36, 118, 186, 231n23, 275; *humanitas* 7, 15; ideology, 38; ideology, critique of, 7; ideology, function of, 226; ideology, and terror, 9, 28, 29, 220, 226;

305

individualism, 35; instrumentalism, 99; interiority, 69; judging, 14; judging, aesthetic and political, 16; judging, criteria of, 15; judging, dependence on thinking, 22n19; judging, objectivity of, 15; Kant, Immanuel, 18, 145, 146; *lexis* 36, 72; liberalism, bourgeois, 20, 261; liberalism, critique of, 264; liberation, 12, 22n14, 220, 235n122; liberty, 11, 12; liberty, communities of, 10; liberty, negative and positive, 11; liberty, political, 281; liberty, public, 4; liberty, republic of, 164; life, as highest good, 103; life, and world, 65; loneliness, 46; love, of the world, 67, 72, 74; Luxemburg, Rosa, debt to, 60n54; Marx, Karl, humanism of, 215; Marx, limitations of, 210, 212; mass society, 38, 45, 46; memory, 67, 104n18, 172n4; mentalities, 98; mentor to, 19; modernity, 82, 119; modernity, appraisal of, 261; modernity, prejudices of, 213; monism, teleological, 127; myth of the cave, 53, 173n40; narrative, genealogical, 180; natality, 4, 66; nationalism, 42; nation state, collapse of, 45; necessity, economic, 103; necessity, historical, 13; need to think, 47, 111; *oikos* 68; opinion, 125; pariah, 32; participation, 273–274, 280, 297n72; particulars, 226; party system, 41, 46, 273; permanence, 49, 85; persuasion, 153; persuasion and violence, 230n13; phenomenology, 59n25; philosopher kings, 173n42; philosophy, 122, 124; *phronesis* 23n29; Plato, objections to, 135, 141; Plurality, 30, 220; *polis* 152; classical 11, 68; *polis*, *telos* of, 121; political liberty, 274, 281, 285; political *telos* 284, 288; political thinking, 221; political violence, 175n98–176n99; politics, anti-humanist, 218; politics, antipolitical, 292; politics, communicative, 242; politics, corruption of, 279; politics, debate in, 128; politics, dignity of, 126; politics, and economics, 102, 276, 277; politics, epiphanic, 142, 147; politics, escape from, 140, 142; politics, expressive, 242; politics, instrumentalized, 143; politics, perplexities of, 124; pre-Socratic, 144; politics, separation from, 145; politics, supremacy of, 126, 262; power, despotic, 280; power, philosophy of, 219; power, of tradition, 186; pre-political relationships, 152; pragmatism, 172n8; *praxis* 36, 72; privacy, 74; public liberty, cause of, 5; public liberty, defense of, 4; public realm, 68, 71, 73, 78; reconciliation, 38; republicanism, 265; republic, of liberty; revelation, 76; revolution, American, 13; revolution, French, 120; revolution, Scientific, 88; rights, 31; rightless, 30; Romantic prejudices, 35; Roman Trinity, 39, 49–50, 114–115, 172n9; rule, 56; rule, despotic, 152; rule, primacy of, 11, 231n17; rule, royal, 152; secularization, 80; self-transcendence, 120; self-transcendence, political, 79, 218; self-transcendence, secular, 241; social, triumph of, 278, 281; socialism, 275, 277, 297n87; social question, 110n143, 277, 279; society, classless, 185; society, consumer's, 103; sovereignty, 98–99, 216, 234n109; stateless, 33; storytelling, 8; suffrage, universal, 274; taste, 17, 23n29; *techne* 98, 154; terror, 27, 28, 29, 30, 220; thinking, against tradition, 115; thinking, political, 221, 288; thinking, without banisters, 57, 64, 104n6, 179; thought, 57; Thucydides, 134; townships, 274; tradition, anti-political, 179; tradition, break in, 64; tradition, critique of, 55; tradition, end of, 180; tradition, failure of, 5; tradition, overcoming, 111; tradition, power of, 186; tradition, revolutionary, 12; *union sacre* 40; violence, as pre-political, 182; violence, *ultima ratio* 219; virtuosity, 163, 234n109; *vita active* 173n43, 211, 212; *vita contemplativea* 95, 96; war, the great, 120; waste economy, 86; wealth, 85–86; welfare state, 275, 278; willing, 14; wisdom, practical, 288; work, 100–101; world, 65; world, love

of, 67; worldliness, 65, 69
Aristotle: ancient city, 26; *arête*, forms of, 137; *arête*, hierarchies of, 137; *arête*, school of,3.133; banausic mentality, 147; *bios politikos* 55, 168; *bios theoretikos* 148, 166, 168; causal matrix, 136; causes, formal and final, 136; civic republican, viii; coercion, 158; contemplative life, 94; critical appropriation, 245; democracy, appraisal of, 162; *eidos* 28, 105n31, 196; *energeia* 149, 176n120; *ergon* 59n34; *eudaimonia* 2n146 3.102 3.108 3.145 3.151; excellence, 169, 170; hierarchies of 127; hierarchies, political, 242; freedom, lives of, 147; friendship, 139, 175n79; functional complements, 135, 137, 171; good, common, 242, 263; good, human, 146; good, internal, 148; good, noble, 176n116; good, useful, 176n116; honor, life of, 165; inequality, 156; inquiry, practical, 135; inquiry, theoretical, 135; insight, practical, 135; justice, 165; *kinesis* 149, 176n120; learning by doing, 268; leisure, 168, 176n112; limitations of, 56; living well, 102, 243; medieval recovery of, 115; middle class, 161; mixed regime, 160; opinion, 137; persuasion, limits of, 164; philosophical, citizenship, 170; philosophical, life, 2; philosophical, wisdom, 168; philosophy, practical, 134; *phronesis* 18, 150, 157, 162; *phronimos* 163; physics, 86; Plato, 56, 134, 154; pluralism, hierarchical, 146, 149, 166, 171; *poiesis* 56, 139, 141, 149; *politeia* 138, 155, 158, 159, 298n108; political science, 167; power, sources of, 158; practical wisdom, 286, 290; *praxis* 56, 139, 141, 148, 149; psychology, 156; public happiness, 268; realism, 161; reason, architectonic, 163; reason, deliberative, 163; reason, practical, 18; rule, constitutional, 138, 155, 157, 164; rule, forms of, 155; rule, household, 138; rule, legitimacy of, 156; science, theory of, 171, 175n74, 223; statesman, responsibility of, 136, 158; teleology, 19; *telos* 28, 105n31, 196; *techne* 150; theory, supremacy of, 135; theology, 169; theology, philosophical, 171, 180; violence, 158; virtue, moral, 157; theme of, 160; voluptuous life, 165; weaknesses of, 171; wholeness, 169, 170; wonder, 25; *zoonpolitikon* 60n36

Augustine: City of God, 26; critical belonging, 245; critique of Rome, 118; dissertation on, 32; independent thinker, 6; memory, 14, 34; political thought, 173n22; two loves, 106n67

Bacon, Francis: dismissal of tradition, 172n12; fruits and works, 96, 184; influence on Marx, 194; interpretation of science, 232n57; prediction and control, 114; union of theory and practice, 225

Barber, Benjamin: global economy, 295n20; republican thinker, 260; strong democracy, 237

Benhabib, Seyla: just membership, 58n13

Berkeley, George: "*esseestpercipi*" 90

Canovan, Margaret, 58n6, 58n7
Cato, 16
Cicero, 169
Constant, Benjamin: *ledoux commerce* 188, 202, 233n69; liberal critique, 295n6

Darwin, Charles: similarities with Marx, 195; triumph of the social, 278

Della Mirandola, Pico: limits of autonomy, 2; modern humanism, 1

Descartes, Rene: absolute standpoint, 90; Cartesian ego, 263; common sense, 92; dream world, 87; epistemic uniformity, 91; Roman Trinity, 90, 238; Suspicion, 89, 186

Dinesen, Isak, 59n21
Dunne, John, 104n19

Faulkner, William, 238
Feuerbach, Ludwig: idea of God, 192; influence on Marx, 192

Freud, Sigmund: master of suspicion, 115; utopian critique, 234n95

Galilei, Galileo: absolute knowledge, 90; being and appearance, 87; causal explanation, 101; common sense, 92; modern cosmos, 263; telescope, 86, 107n91; universal physics, 86
Galston, William: civil society, 253; economic anxiety, 250; minimal citizenship, 260; policy agenda, 249–250; progressive era, 248–249; turning point, 248

Hegel, GWF.: classical polis, 270; contemplation, 183; cunning of reason, 199; dialectic, 184, 190–191, 222; freedom, 222, 270; ideas of reason, 221, 235n126; influence on Marx, 190; Marx's critique of, 186, 195, 221; phenomenology of spirit, 40; philosophy of history, 119, 190, 221, 222, 224, 288; reconciliation with reality, 60n42; spirit, 191; theology of, 191, 195, 196, 222, 231n15; vocation of philosophy, 232n39
Heidegger, Martin, 22n6; Arendt's debt to, 7, 22n6; classical polis, 11; Dasein, 104n11; forgetfulness of being, 116; metaphysics, 5, 62n93, 242; ontological difference, 172n14; truth, 109n120
Herodotus, 15, 182
Hobbes, Thomas: dismissal of tradition, 172n12; reductive assumptions, 216
Hobsbawm, Eric : age of catastrophe, vii; golden age of capitalism, 250
Homer: deeds and words, 177n174; impartiality of, 15; Odyssey, 130; poetic immortality, 121; teacher of Hellas, 122; warrior ethos, 117, 122, 144
Honohan, Iseult: civic republicanism, 261, 270, 287; public virtues, 296n54
Husserl, Edmund, 115

Jefferson, Thomas, 7
Jesus of Nazareth, 68, 78, 118; admonitions of, 189; critical belonging, 245; good news, 79; kingdom of God, 235n130; redemption, 106n65; truth and poetry, 112

Kant, Immanuel, 1; aesthetic appraisal, 18; autonomy, 2, 229; Copernican Revolution, 96; critique of judgment, 14; dignity and utility, 100; happiness, 145; ideas of reason, 221; independent thinker, 6; instrumental goods, 283; kingdom of ends, 102; model of judgment, 17; moral autonomy, 145, 278; moral criteria, 16; morality of intention, 99; *phenomena and noumena* 278; sensible appearance, 115; taste, 146

Lonergan, Bernard: authentic subjectivity, 298n107; canon of operations, 291; classical theory of science, 223; collective responsibility, 297n60; common sense, 108n109; concreteness of the good, 289; critical appropriation, 245; deliberative reason, 286; distorting bias, 235n135; effective freedom, 297n61; epistemic realism, 287; forms of bias, 287, 289, 291; general bias, 108n110, 137, 299n115; learning, 287; originating and terminal goods, 285, 287, 298n103; practical reflection, 289–290; public liberty, 291; public policy, 290

Machiavelli, Niccolo: civic humanism, 10, 64, 119; crisis of humanism, 34; need for force, 143; political imperatives, 106n70; republican vision, 12; reversal of Augustine, 119; revolutionary tradition, 3; Roman culture, 80, 173n23; secularization, 80; united Italy, 26; *virtu* 11
MacIntyre. Alasdair: critique of Aristotle, 178n179; critique of Pericles, 129; critique of utility, 298n109; internal goods, 176n115; living tradition, 114
Madison, James: representative democracy, 270, 296n43
Marx, Karl: action and speech, 216; distrust of, 218; *animallaborans* 36, 119, 214; alienation, 215; anthropology,

philosophical, 194, 229; anthropology, revisionary, 182, 196; autonomy, ideal of, 195; autonomy, limits of, 229; Bacon, Francis, debt to, 184; being and appearance, separation of, 107n92, 230n8; capitalism, contradictions of, 196; capitalism, critique of, 200, 204, 206; capitalism, destruction of, 209; capitalism, fate of, 206; capitalism, industrial, 203; capitalism, inequities of, 204; causes, 207; classical hierarchies, 181; classless society, 185, 190, 210, 235n130; class struggle, 183, 189, 193; consciousness, revolutionary, 198; contemplation, distrust of, 181; contradictions in, 185, 189; cunning of history, 206; Darwin, 195; determinism, economic, 197, 199, 214; determinism, and freedom, 224; dialectics, 173n20; disdain for communication, 218; ends, absolute, 218; expressivism, 217; factory system, 203; Feuerbach, 192; freedom, alienated, 224; freedom, autonomous, 224; freedom, and determinism, 224; French revolution, aspirations of, 188; French revolution, completion of, 197; government, critique of, 218; Hegel, critique of, 222; Hegel, dissent from, 183, 184, 186, 192; Hegel, indebted to, 190; Hegel, parallels with, 195; Hegel, reversals of, 117, 119; history, climax of, 200; history, end of, 218, 225; history, masters of, 199; history, philosophy of, 180, 194; history, riddle of, 230n9; history, science of, 217; humanism, 186, 215; humanism, atheistic, 192; humanism, limitations of, 210, 212; humanism, naturalized, 187, 231n23; humanism, socialized, 186, 194, 231n23; idealism, prophetic, 233n62; ideology, bourgeois, 193; ideology, capitalist, 205; ideology, critique of, 198; ideology, forms of, 235n134; ideology, function of, 185; ideology, and science, 224, 226; labor, 182, 193, 195, 204, 212, 214; labor, alienated, 207; labor, created man, 182, 197, 211, 215; labor, productive, 215; labor, theories of, 214; laissez faire, 188; laissez faire ideology of, 203; laws, economic, 228; laws, natural and historical, 223; *ledoux commerce* 188; liberalism, biases of, 195; liberalism, classical, 205; liberalism, opposition to, 35; liberalism, prejudices of, 35; liberation, 196, 233n80; liberty, 205; magic of Marxism, 233n84; masters of suspicion, 115; making history, 184; materialism, dialectical, 193, 194, 197; mentality, commercial, 202; modernity, 181; naturalism, 192; necessity, 225; opium of the people, 192; paradoxes, 213; philosophy, poverty of, 223; philosophy, purpose of, 199, 223; politics, abolition of, 217; politics, antihumanist, 218; poverty, 189, 208; power, concentration of, 209; *praxis* 215; *praxis*, inflated, 212; *praxis*, transformative, 211, 212, 215; production, forces of, 184, 193, 195; production, relations of, 184, 193, 195, 209; profit, 207–208; profit, capitalist, 209; profit, proletariat, 217; Promethean humanism, 182, 212–213, 229; property, 201; prophetic moralist, 190, 206; providence, secularized, 231n34; reading of, 225; religion, abolition of, 230n7, 232n40; Romantic strains in, 187; secularization, 181; socialism, 233n91; social question, 189, 184; supply and demand, 207; terror, 217; tradition, end of, 180; tradition, ensnared by, 186; tradition, power of, 186; tradition, rebellion against, 217; tradition, reversal of, 179; utopia, 200; utopia, hopes for, 206, 237; value, labor theory of, 207, 208–209; value, surplus, 208; *vita active* 211; violence, as midwife, 182, 198; violence, emancipatory, 217; violence, glorification of, 235n116; violence, political, 216; violence, proportionate, 219; violence, revolutionary, 143, 183; violence, strategic, 217

Montequieu, Charles: despotism, 58n8; ledoux commerce, 202, 232n59; political taxonomy, 9; political thinking, 7; republican government, 20

Nietzsche, Friedrich: classical polis, 11; genealogy of morals, 5, 116, 242; greatness, 16; suspicion, 115; warrior ethic, 116

Pascal, Blaise: tangled knot, 238; unity and multiplicity, 84, 294n2
Paul, Saint: apocalyptic expectations of, 78, 118; Christian withdrawal, 180; community of faith, 106n70
Pericles: Athenian democracy, 11, 61n77, 121; Athens, splendor of, 28; death of, 173n35; divine life, 121; funeral oration, 11, 48, 121; imperial quest, 118, 129, 243; political greatness, 123, 242, 284; political thinker, viii; school of virtue, 129, 167; warrior ethic, 144
Pitkin, Hanna: aspects of the social, 298n89; critique of Arendt, 280; politics and economics, 280
Plato : *arête* 109n129; being and seeming, 129; city of greed, 129; city in speech, 174n51, 223; common sense, 131; contemplation, 117, 172n19, 183; conversion, ontological, 128; conversation, philosophical, 131; democracy, 129; dialogues, political, 58n3; dialogues, Socratic, 122; *doxa* 125; *episteme* 125; excellence, political, 242; goods, 176n116; hierarchies, 180; Homer, reversal of, 130; immortality, 123; imperialism, 170; intelligible forms, 125, 128; intelligent forms, as prototypes, 141; intelligent forms, separate from things; justice, 129; *logos* 123, 124; Marx, 179; moral psychology, 156; myth of the cave, 53, 117, 130, 131, 172n18, 220; *nous* 123, 124; orders, hierarchical, 124; Peloponnesian War, 122; Pericles, 122; philosophy, 128; philosophical life, 2; philosophical loyalty, 54; philosophical ruler, 55, 132, 173n42, 230n5, 231n17; Platonic tradition, 118; *polis*, as prison, 26; *polis*, and philosophy, 131; political philosophy, criticism of, 53, 128; political philosophy, legacy, 133; political philosophy, origins of, 39, 55; political typology, 40, 153; republic, eternal, 26; rule, non-despotic, 153, 154; silence, 129; Socrates, death of, 127, 153; sophists, 123; speech, 129; soul, 171; *techne* 109n124; truth, and poetry, 112; truth, as revelation, 95
Polanyi, Michael: magic of Marxism, 233n84; Marx's prophetic idealism, 233n84; moral appeal of immorality, 234n99; personal knowledge, 108n107; reading of Marx, 225
Putnam, Robert: *Bowling Alone*, 254; civic disengagement, 254; civil society, 253; progressive movement, 256; social capital, 254
Pythagoras: contemplative prejudices, 167; festival of life, 83

Rawls, John: political liberalism, 260; theories of justice, 288
Ricoeur, Paul: critique, 242; hermeneutics of retrieval, 115, 242; ideology, 231n19; liberation, 242; memory and narrative, 9

Sandel, Michael: civic republicanism, viii, 260, 261; liberal democracy, 246; public philosophy, 287
Smith, Adam, 199–200, 202, 203; commercial exchange, 203; invisible hand, 224, 228; wealth of nations, 202
Socrates: accusers of, 174n52; *arête* 123, 129, 174n55; critical belonging, 244; death of, 122, 123, 127, 153, 173n34, 221, 263, 296n53; dialectic, 129; fate of, 124, 132; the Good, 174n65; impiety of, 127; *kosmos and polis* 26; love of wisdom, 118; morality, 58n15; origin of philosophy, 25; Socratic thinking, 6, 14; truth and poetry, 112

Taylor, Charles: adversarial politics, 241; civic participation, 240; civic republicanism, 240, 260, 261; civic virtue, 240; civil society, 253; coalitions, 241; crisis of legitimacy, 246; group fragmentation, 241; hermeneutics of retrieval, 241–242,

280; holistic individualism, 295n18; ideological monism, 240; mixed economy, 257, 281; modern prejudices, 239; ordinary life, 243, 295n19; patriotism, 240; pluralism, 240, 295n9; public philosophy, 287

Tinder, Glen: disdain for communication, 218

Tocqueville, Alexis de, 1; *Ancien Regime* 26; apprenticeships in liberty, 297n65; centers of power, 253; critical belonging, 245; democracy, triumph of, 248; democratic greatness, 23n32; democratic individualism, 19–20, 240, 254, 269; democratic liberty, 253; equality and liberty, 105n43, 268; grammar schools of liberty, 253; liberty and despotism, 19–20, 248; mentor to Arendt, 19; new science of politics, 245; participation and representation, 268; past and future, 9, 37; personal and public liberty, 268; political liberty, 268; political thinker, 7; power and administration, 297n74; Providence, 236n145; security, 268; secondary powers, 253; townships, 20, 257; voluntary associations, 272, 282

Virgil, 49

Weber, Max, 110n135

Wittgenstein, Ludwig: the world, 65; forms of life, 109n114

Wood, Gordon: civic republicanism, 297n70, 298n88, 298n96

Printed in Great Britain
by Amazon